RELIGION IN ESSENCE
AND MANIFESTATION

G. VAN DER LEEUW

RELIGION
IN ESSENCE AND MANIFESTATION

VOLUME TWO

Translated by J. E. Turner with Appendices to the Torchbook edition incorporating the additions of the second German edition by Hans H. Penner

GLOUCESTER, MASS.

PETER SMITH

1967

RELIGION IN ESSENCE AND MANIFESTATION. Appendixes copyright © 1963 by Hans H. Penner. Printed in the United States of America.

The German original, *Phanomenologie der Religion,* was published in Tübingen in 1933. The first English edition was published in 1938 as one volume by Allen & Unwin, Ltd., London, and is here reprinted by arrangement.

First HARPER TORCHBOOK edition published 1963 by Harper & Row, Publishers, Incorporated, New York and Evanston.

Reprinted, 1967 by Permission of
GEORGE ALLEN & UNWIN, Ltd., London

CONTENTS: *Volume II*

PART THREE: *OBJECT AND SUBJECT*
IN THEIR RECIPROCAL OPERATION

A. OUTWARD ACTION

B. INWARD ACTION

PART FOUR: *THE WORLD*

PART FIVE: *FORMS*

A. RELIGIONS

B. FOUNDERS

EPILEGOMENA

PART THREE

OBJECT AND SUBJECT IN THEIR
RECIPROCAL OPERATION

A. OUTWARD ACTION

CHAPTER 48

CONDUCT AND CELEBRATION

1. ONCE again I wish to recall the initial principle laid down at the outset: the Subject of religion is, in the sense of religion itself, the Object, and its Object the Subject. Even now, when it has become a question of the reciprocal relationship between Subject and Object, the expressions are to be understood only in their figurative meaning. Nor must the designation of the actions performed by the subject, as either "external" or "internal", be taken to imply any essential distinction; for Chantepie has already stressed the point that any "external" activity can always be understood as "internal". Still further, when the relationship between man and Power is to be dealt with, it is in the first instance not at all a matter of subjectivity or inwardness. It is principally and primarily a question of the way and the means which either Power, or man, must employ if they are to influence each other. In other terms, it is an affair of what we have hitherto learned to know, but only quite superficially, as "the world above" or "the conjoint world", and which I shall henceforth call simply "world".

Thus whether in seeking, or fleeing from, any relation to Power, or again in possessing it, man still exists in the world. But that means not only that he is fixed in the world like a coin in my pocket: it implies still further that he participates in the world and is seriously concerned with it; and Heidegger has clearly and acutely interpreted this being-in-the-world as "care". Man, that is to say, does not simply accept the world in which he lives: he also feels apprehensive about it; or expressed in religious terms, this means that the world *appears alien or strange* to him and alarms him. For even choice has its own power, and in fact an unfamiliar and troublous power. Man therefore, thus placed in the world, does not immediately and straightway find himself at home therein: he experiences a foreignness that can all too readily deepen into dread or even into despair. He does not resignedly assent to the world given to him, but again and again says to it: "No!" This saying "No!" is indeed the very basis of his humanity; it proves that he has spirit: "Spirit is life which itself cutteth into life."[1] In life, then, man sees far more than givenness: he perceives possibility also. But this possibility demands his activity; his sense of foreignness must therefore expand into *conduct* and his conduct, still further, into *celebration*: his behaviour, in other words, must accord with the Powerful which reveals itself to him. How he behaves, even how he sits or stands or lies down, is thus no matter of indifference, and only in sleep does he ever sink back into the choiceless affirmation of the maternal womb. But in his waking hours he must always be prepared; his "care" must never cease: he must be ever on the alert; and as has been previously observed, the word *religio* itself indicates this alertness.[2] Therefore in order to dominate life for oneself, to seize upon the possibilities concealed within it, man must force it into a fixed course of activity. This can result from the fear equally of Power and of impotence; but in any case fear resounds in care. A child from a pietist household, for instance, keenly enjoyed pushing a barrow about, but reproached itself bitterly because this was sinful pleasure. Then it pacified its conscience by thinking that the infant Jesus lay in the barrow, so that he was pushing the Lord for His pleasure.[3] Thus from the game a rite has arisen: that is, conduct out of the unconstrained game. For a game bound by rules is, as such, always a rite, conduct, dominance; and the rite gained control over life, and drew power therefrom, long before thought could do so: "man was a ritualist before he could speak".[4] The rite also discovered the way of worship far in anticipation of thought. Like the child, then, man pushes his barrow, but his sense of alienation causes him to apply some fixed standard to his activities, so that dread may be silenced and he may feel at home therein. Then he places his god in it: and now he pushes Power itself! But he can also pause, and kneel before the god in the cart of his life.

2. Thus it is no indifferent matter how man conducts himself. His behaviour must in all respects duly respond to the goal which is power; and to that end he sets his own powerfulness as prominently as possible in the foreground. Ritual nakedness for example, the *ritus paganus*, is just such behaviour: the potency of one's own body is to ward off evil

---

[1] Nietzsche, *Thus Spake Zarathustra*, 122 (Foulis Ed.); *cf*. Chap. 23, and P. Tillich, *Die religiöse Lage der Gegenwart*, 34; also Scheler, *Stellung des Menschen*, 46.
[2] *cf*. Chap. 4.
[3] H. R. G. Günther, *Jung-Stilling*, 1928, 165; *cf*. Marett, *Faith, Hope and Charity*, 12.
[4] Chesterton, *Heretics*, 97.

powers and awaken fruitful ones.[1] Or, again, man gives his body the
appropriate pose: holding it rigid, braced up, alert, attentive and prepared, in *Standing*: allowing everything to go and abandoning himself
in the abasement of *Prostration*: bowing down all that is in himself,
and expressing his impotence by *Kneeling*: raising his hands so that
his "soul stream may flow freely": folding them and placing them, as
though bound, within God's hands.[2] He casts down his glance, or raises
it to heaven: turns away his face, or even hides his head, as if his
powerfulness were ashamed of itself, in direct contrast to the *ritus
paganus*. The frontier between such conduct and celebration, however,
cannot be exactly delineated, although in celebration proper there is
more of premeditated action, of undertaking something, or of changing
or securing it. But conduct too has precisely the same purpose: Anna
Schieber's Grandfather Hollermann, the old shepherd whose cult consists in jumping thrice over his staff, is certainly already celebrating.
Some instant or other, some fragment of life, some sort of potency,
must be arrested, repeated and celebrated; for if that were not done
man would have no correct relationship to Power. I may, for example,
simply run out of the house, but I may also leave it every day at the
same time, walking deliberately. The first act is a deed; the second is
a celebration, a rite: it solidifies the flux of life and gives it support.[3]
Man therefore should not remain simply within the given and in dread:
he should make some gesture, "do something about it". But the basis of
his gesture is always the yearning for the Wholly Other:

> Now I know that you must become like a little child:
> All dread is only a beginning;
> But the Earth is without end,
> And fear is but the gesture
> The meaning of which is yearning.[4]

[1] K. Weinhold, *Zur Geschichte des heidnischen Ritus* (*Abh. d. preuss. Akad. d. Wiss.*,
phil.-hist. Kl., 1896). It is practised to increase fertility and destroy weeds (Bertholet,
Lesebuch, 4, 7), in processions and other pageants (rain-maidens, Lady Godiva at
Coventry, plough processions, *etc.*), for averting evil influences (in Brandenburg, when
the cow kicks while being milked, the milkmaid must sit on the stool with bare
posterior; then the animal will be quiet); also to confirm an oath, in prophecy (Saul,
Cassandra) *etc.*; *cf.* further, R. Thurnwald, *Reallexikon der Vorgeschichte*, Art. *Zauber*.
[2] Guardini, *Von heiligen Zeichen*, 13 ff.
[3] Nothing whatever can occur without rites. In Australia, when rain falls without
the rites having been observed, friendly spirits are supposed to have caused it (Lévy-
Bruhl, *How Natives Think*, 251); *cf.* Marett, *Faith, Hope and Charity*, 18: "Born in
the mud like the other beasts, man alone refuses to be a stick-in-the-mud. . . . So he
dances through his life as if he would dance until he drops, finding out, however, on
trial that he can develop as it were a second wind by dancing to a measure."
[4] Rainer Maria Rilke, *Die frühen Gedichte*.

3. Finally, whoever conducts himself in accord with the sacred, whoever celebrates the holy, acts as an officiant: he not only carries out something, but he accomplishes what must be executed, τὰ δρώμενα. He, as it were, adopts some specific posture: he wields the sacred: he repeats the acts of Power. Every cult, then, is repetition.

R. GUARDINI, *Von heiligen Zeichen*, 1929.

L. LÉVY-BRUHL, *Primitives and the Supernatural*.

H. USENER, *Heilige Handlung* (*Kleine Schriften*, IV, 1913).

R. WILL, *Le culte*, 1925–1929.

CHAPTER 49

PURIFICATION

1. NOT without profound reason does the housewife's "Spring cleaning" still retain a tinge of ritual. For the ultimate motive of purification is no more liberation from actual dirt in the sense of modern hygiene, but release from evil and the induction of good. Occasionally life's power dwindles: it grows paler and loses its freshness; and all this must be prevented by a periodical turning over a new page in the book of life, so that it begins anew. The accumulated impotence, which is really an evil power, must be removed; and thus the Roman vestal temple, a state shrine, was annually purified. The purification period, nonetheless, was calamitous; so the dirt was either carefully deposited in a *locus certus* or thrown into the Tiber. Then the *dies nefasti*, when it was unlawful to transact any secular business, ended, and in the calendar this memorandum was attached to the fifteenth of June: QStDF: "lawful when the dirt has been cleared away"—*quando stercus delatum fas.*[1]

This custom characterizes all ideas about purification: a new beginning is made, power thrust out and fresh potency drawn in. Thus the correct relationship to Power, which in the course of a long year has suffered loss, is once again established; as soon as the dirt has been removed the proper relation again predominates: it is *fas.* The ground of this, and of countless similar rites, is of course the simple carrying on of ordinary life, of washing and cleaning. Yet they have quite another purport than the morning routine in one's home; and with children, and seamen washing down the decks, something of the primeval feeling of life is still retained. Children often observe a certain washing rite, and it is frequently a matter of complete indifference to them whether they become really clean; while sailors, and Dutch housewives too, burnish and polish in quite a ritual manner even when there is no dirt at all to be found! In religious phraseology, then, "dirt" includes far more than mere filth. "Dirt" means all the hindrances and annoyances that prevent the perpetuation and renewal of life, so that

---

[1] Ovid, *Fasti*, VI, 713; Fowler, *Roman Festivals*, 145; L. Deubner, *AR.* 16, 1913, 134 *f*. In Greece it was customary to throw away the dirty water, with which anyone had washed, behind one with averted gaze; Aeschylus, *Choephoroe*, 98 *f*.

some celebration must set the arrested current in motion again. The means employed, however, need not "cleanse" in our modern sense, provided only it is powerful; and thus the ancient Persians used the urine of oxen as we do some sort of disinfectant.[1] This had its ground in the animal's sacredness and not in the purifying efficacy of the means.

Purification, again, has a dual purpose: to impart benevolent, and avert wicked, power. The most widespread means of purifying is water;[2] but water not only cleans: it has a power of its own which it communicates. It is "living water". In ancient Egypt there were innumerable purifications; and the most frequent designation of the priest was in fact Wab, that is, "the pure one". In the grave figures the priest or the deity himself pours water from a vessel in a curve over the dead person, and the same process occurs in the case of the king. But in certain delineations the stream of water is replaced by an arched series of little ankh, the hieroglyphic symbols for life; thus a purification in unison with, and for the purpose of, life is carried out.

An excellent example of the periodic purification of the community is also afforded by the ancient Roman custom of lustration, especially the lustrum; lustrum condere, it was said, which really was to bury a lustrum. By analogy with many popular customs elsewhere, this means that the dirt of some particular period was buried, so that a new period might be begun. Lustrum would then be the equivalent of *lōstrum, *laustrum, that is, water for washing.[3] After it has served as purifying water, however, the dangerous cleansing liquid must be removed. The positive, too, outweighs the negative: the carmen of the lustrum was intended to move the gods "to make the condition of the Roman people better and greater".[4] At the commencement of the new year also (originally on March 1) a general cleansing was undertaken in Rome; and the entire last month of the year was named after the cleaning utensils, the februa.[5]

I shall now place side by side two examples of what was understood by "dirt". In Central Celebes, in the first place, when a case of incest has made a village unclean, a buffalo, a pig and a cock are slaughtered by a man standing in the water of the river; and in the water, which has been mixed with the blood of the animals sacrificed, both the

[1] Lehmann, Zarathustra, 233.   [2] Chap. 6.
[3] Deubner, Lustrum, 127 ff. Usener, Kleine Shriften, IV, 117 f. Similarly the carnival, fair, year and the Greek charila are buried in popular customs.
[4] Valerius Max. IV, 1, 10.   [5] Fowler, Roman Festivals, 6.

guilty parties and the other inhabitants of the village must bathe, "in order in this way to rid themselves of the dirt of the incest".[1] The "dirt" is therefore neither moral nor purely physical, but both and something more. The second instance occurs in the Old Testament: "When he has finished the expiatory rites for the sacred place and the Trysting tent and the altar, Aaron shall bring forward the living goat; laying both hands upon its head, he shall confess over it all the iniquities of the Israelites and all their sinful transgressions, laying them on the head of the goat and sending it away to the desert in charge of a man who is held in readiness; the goat shall bear away their iniquities into solitude, and shall be set free in the desert."[2] The "iniquities" are therefore the dirt which the "scapegoat" takes with it into the wilderness after the priest has laid them on its head;[3] the "spiritual" or "moral" and the concretely dirty are conceived as wholly one.

Besides incense, which was already familiar to the ancient Egyptians, the "holy water" that purifies the faithful at the door of God's house, but with which animals are also sprinkled and in which bread is dipped so that the cattle may eat it,[4] is the means of purification most frequently employed in our own times.

2. In the religious life, then, any celebration that not only removes dirt, but also makes new life possible, must be of the greatest importance. It brings about, as it were, a new birth; and it would in fact be better to omit "as it were". For in ancient Egypt the idea prevailed that purification was "an imparting of the divine life of the water, a means of resurrection";[5] and of the dead man it was said that he "purifies himself on the day of his birth", that is of his resurrection.[6] He carried out this self-cleansing in the "primeval water", which existed at the commencement of all being, and whose reproduction was to be found in a pool near the temple.[7] Thus the life of the dead person was, as it were, immersed in the act of creation: it was born anew, the water of purification being regarded as the seed of the god Atmu, who effected the rebirth. Thereby the celebration of purification became so

[1] Kruyt, *Measa*, II, 79.   [2] *Lev.* xvi. 20 *ff.* (Moffat).
[3] *cf.* I. Benzinger, *Hebräische Archäologie*², 1907, 380.
[4] Heiler, *Katholizismus*, 170. A poor woman burns incense daily for her husband buried in a silver mine; a year later he is found alive and well: the incense perfume has preserved him: P. Zaunert, *Rheinlandsagen*, II, 1924, 22 *ff.*
[5] Kristensen, *Livet*, 101.   [6] *Totenbuch* (Naville), *Kap.* 17, 20.
[7] *cf.* A. de Buck, *De egyptische voorstellingen betreffende den Oerheuvel*, 1922. A. Blackman, "Egyptian foretaste of baptismal regeneration" (*Theology*, 1, 1920). H. P. Blok, *Acta orientalia*, VIII, 3, 208 *f.*

important that it touched life in its profoundest depth: it resulted in
rebirth, re-creation.

Christian baptism, again, is not merely a purifying from dirt and sin,
not merely an induction of sacred power, but is the "washing of regeneration",[1] a birth "of water and of the Spirit",[2] the type of which is
the waters of the flood.[3] Thus baptism washes away sins, and is closely
connected with the expulsion of the devil (exorcism); it originates in
man a new power. Nevertheless its real essence lies in rebirth: the
baptized has become a new man. As in the case of the baptism in
Jordan, it effects "adoption", υἱοθεσία. Here too there is the same
parallelism, between the water of creation and of baptism, as we have
already found in ancient Egypt. In Roman Catholic ritual the prayer
benedictio fontis reads: "O God, whose Spirit in the very beginning of
the world moved over the waters, that even then the nature of water
might receive the virtue of sanctification: O God, who by water didst
wash away the crimes of the guilty world, and by the overflowing of the
deluge didst give a figure of regeneration, that one and the same element
might in a mystery be the end of vice and the origin of virtue."[4] This
again means a warding off of evil, and induction of good, included in
the one *regeneratio*; and the great baptismal passage in the *Epistle to
the Romans* (Chap. VI) connects this ancient idea with justification
from sin: "for once dead, a man is absolved from the claims of sin".[5]
To be in the water means to be dead, to be buried. Here therefore the
profoundest life-feeling and the most powerful creaturely feeling appear
together. Immersion in water is regression to the primal ground, either
(cosmically) of Chaos or (individually) of the maternal womb. But over
the primeval waters hovers the vivifying spirit of God, which creates
an entire life anew, καινὴ κτίσις. Here then we are already in the heart
of the realm of the sacrament.

Of course it is not only water that possesses purifying power. In the
mysteries of Attis and Mithra there was a baptism of blood, *tauro-*

---

[1] *Titus* iii. 5.   [2] *John* iii. 5.

[3] 1 *Peter* iii. 20 f. cf. W. Heitmüller, *Im Namen Jesu*, 1903, 278 ff. H. Usener, *Das
Weihnachtsfest²*, 1911. Dieterich, *Mithrasliturgie*, 139 f. L. Duchesne, *Les origines du
culte chrétien⁴*, 1908, 299 ff.

[4] *Deus, cujus spiritus super aquas, inter ipsa mundi primordia ferebatur: ut jam tunc
virtutem sanctificationis, aquarum natura conciperet. Deus, qui nocentis mundi crimna per
aquas abluens, regenerationis speciem in ipsa diluvii effusione signasti: ut unius ejusdemque
elementi mysterio, et finis esset vitiis, et origo virtutibus. Taufe und Firmung, nach dem
römischen Missale, Rituale und Pontificale*, edited by Ildefons Herwegen (*Kleine Texte*,
144), 1920, 22; cf. further *Rom.* vi, *Gal.* iii. 26 f., *Col.* ii. 12.

[5] Moffat.

bolium; the blood of Christ too is pre-eminently the means of purification, and this in no merely figurative sense. Fire also, as was previously observed,[1] has great purifying power, while baptism by fire finds a place in primitive puberty rites;[2] in Bohemia house and stables are "smoked out" at the feast of St. Lucia,[3] while "blood and fire" is still to-day the effective summing up of the great means of purification, as coined by the Salvation Army. Sacred oil, as the *materia* of the sacrament of confirmation, originally intimately connected with Christian baptism, is also a "seal" and sign by which the faithful can be recognized, like the military brand in the Mithras mysteries.[4] It renders the Christian capable of active participation in the sacrifice of the church, makes him "worthy" in the official sense, and grants him *dignitas regalis et sacerdotalis*. Further, extreme unction purifies the entire body of the dying and endows him with new power; the old administration formula runs: *accipe sanitatem corporis et remissionem omnium peccatorum*— "receive bodily health and the remission of all thy sins".[5]

Purification, however, has not always the character of washing or cleansing. Very frequently the person to be purified is beaten; and here also we find not only apotropaic power intended to avert evil, but likewise that which imparts salvation. Women especially were beaten, usually with a green twig ("beating with the rod of life"); also cows' udders, and the *muliebria*, *etc*. The thongs of goat hide, again, with which the Roman bands of naked youths, the *Luperci*, struck the women, were called "Juno's mantle", *amiculum Junonis*, a reference to increased fertility.[6]

3. Belief in the potency of celebration, however, disappears not only under the influence of scepticism, but also owing to reduction to the subjective inner life of the soul. The classical expression of scepticism is provided by Ovid's familiar lines: "Fond fools alack! to fancy murder's gruesome stain by river water could be washed away";[7] while we find this reduction to the inner life wherever prophetic or moral

---

[1] Chap. 6.   [2] Chap. 22.

[3] Reinsberg-Düringsfeld, *Das festliche Jahr*, 434.

[4] Heitmüller, *Im Namen Jesu*, 312 f. Thom. Michels, *Die Akklamation in der Taufliturgie* (*Jahrb. für Liturgiewiss*. VIII, 1928), 83 ff.

[5] Thus in imperative form; now replaced by a deprecatory formula; Jos. Braun, *Liturgisches Handlexikon*[2], 1924, 241.

[6] Fowler, *Roman Festivals*, 319 ff. Crawley, *The Mystic Rose*, I, 312 f. Reinsberg-Düringsfeld, *Festliche Jahr*, 176. Mannhardt, *op. cit.*, 251 ff.

[7] *Fasti*, II, 45 (Frazer).

intensity of feeling opposes the constraint of celebration, although the keenest and deepest antagonism must be sought in the Old Testament prophets and in the New Testament.[1] But a closely similar note resounds in other "great religions" also. *Buddha*, for example: "Man is not purified by water, however much he may bathe; he is pure, he is a brahmin, in whom truth and virtue reside."[2] The Law of *Manu* likewise: "The mouth of the girl and the hand of the worker are always clean."[3] Different again the Greek *Theano* who, in reply to the question as to how long is required for a woman to become clean after intercourse with a man, answered: "After her own at once, after another, never."[4]

Despite all rationalism and moralism, however, and all such religious subjectivity also, the necessity for purification still maintains its exceedingly important place in human life, alike in the physical and the psychical sense. For recent psychological and psychiatric studies have shown to what a high degree in life's crisis, where it is reluctantly brought to its very frontiers, this need for cleansing governs man and his conduct, in neurotic states even coercively. The "washing compulsion" was of course familiar to Shakespeare: the incredibly realistic scene in which Lady Macbeth, walking in her sleep, descends the stairs incessantly washing her hands is the tragic but splendid monument to this necessity for purification:[5]

> Yet here's a spot.
> Out, damned spot! out, I say!—
> What, will these hands ne'er be clean?
> Here's the smell of the blood still: all the perfumes of Arabia
>   will not sweeten this little hand.

But in spite of this tragic element, the hopeless celebration becomes again and again the joyful consciousness of being purified. And when purification is a sacrament celebration itself is no longer the principal factor, but the Power that is operative within it, the grace of God. Then the water becomes wine, or indeed blood: the futile washing a rebirth. Nowhere is this more beautifully expressed than in Luther's *Epiphany Hymn*:

---

[1] Especially in the striking passage: *Mark* vii. 14 *ff*.
[2] Bertholet, *op. cit.*,[1] 263.   [3] Lehmann, *Zarathustra*, II, 205.
[4] Zielinski, *The Religion of Ancient Greece*, 126; *cf*. further the lines previously cited from Euripides, *Herakles*, 1230 *ff*. p. 51 *ante*.
[5] *Macbeth*, V, 1.

For us He would provide a bath
Wherein to cleanse from sin,
And drown the bitterness of death
In His own blood and wounds,
And so create new life.

The eye itself sees but the water
As man pours water forth.
But faith in the spirit understands
The power of Jesus Christ's blood.

Here the bathing water and human celebration are indissolubly united with Christ's Power and the act of God.

CHAPTER 50

SACRIFICE

1. THE terms "soul" and "sacrifice" must be included among those presenting the greatest variety of meaning in the whole history of religion; and in both cases we may doubt the advisability of estimating such utterly different phenomena, as are comprised under these words, as being diverse instances of that single self-revelation which will be further discussed in the *Epilegomena*. With respect to these two ideas, nevertheless, and as indeed I hope that I have already shown with regard to the soul, the phenomena prove to constitute a fundamental unity. Usually, however, a distinction is made between the sacrificial gift or the sacrifice of homage, and the sacramental meal; in the latter case it is either the god himself who is consumed, or he is looked upon as a table companion who receives his due share. But even with this classification of the phenomena, justice has not been accorded to all the instances. For in many sacrificial ceremonies it is extremely difficult to point to the presence of the "god" at all.[1] In these circumstances, therefore, it would be quite impossible to maintain that old principle of explanation of sacrifice, the rule of *do-ut-des*[2]—"I give that thou mayest give"—which had in fact been formulated in classical times: "Bribes, believe me, buy both gods and men; Jupiter himself is appeased by the offering of gifts";[3] while the brahminic ritual expresses it equally clearly: "here is the butter; where are thy gifts?"[4] In his famous work, *The Religion of the Semites*, however, Robertson Smith has shown that besides this idea of *do-ut-des* there was at least one other that was quite different and yet was the basis of sacrifice—the idea of a communal meal at which the god is either a participant, or else is identical with the sacrifice, that is with the food consumed.[5]

---

[1] *cf.* an enumeration of the forms of sacrifice in Pfleiderer's *Philosophy of Religion*, IV, 186 *ff*.　　　　　　　　　　　　[2] G. van der Leeuw, *Do-ut-des-Formel, passim*.

[3] Ovid, *Ars amatoria*, III, 653 (Mozley); *cf.* further Alviella, *Idée de Dieu*, 89, where the ancient Hindu formula is quoted: "Give thou to me, I shall give to thee; bring thou to me and I shall bring to thee"; also Jevons, *Introduction*, 69 *ff*. Grimm, *Schenken und Geben, Kl. Schriften*, II, 174 and Note.

[4] *RGG*². Article *Opfer* I.

[5] *cf.* further Reinach who, being the sound evolutionist he is, places the latter type, as the more enigmatical, at the beginning, and sacrificial gifts, as quite clearly comprehensible, at the close of the development.

It appears therefore that we must have interpreted the "gift", which is thus supposed to be the basis of sacrifice, in far too European and modern a sense; we have allowed ourselves to be led away by Ovid, and forgotten what "to give" actually means.[1] "To give" is believed to be "more blessed than to receive";[2] but for this maxim the *do-ut-des* theory leaves no scope whatever. It presupposes quite a different view of giving, or rather a wholly contrasted interpretation of "I give . . . ." For it is incontestable that this kind of argument is, very frequently, the actual ground of sacrifice. But *dare* does not mean merely to dispose of some arbitrary object with a quite indefinite intention; the word *dare* means, rather, to place oneself in relation to, and then to participate in, a second person by means of an object, which however is not actually an "object" at all, but a part of one's own self. "To give," then, is to convey something of oneself to the strange being, so that a firm bond may be forged. Mauss refers, together with other writers, to Emerson's fine essay, *Gifts*, with respect to this "primitive" view of giving: "The only gift is a portion of thyself. Thou must bleed for me. Therefore the poet brings his poem; the shepherd, his lamb; the farmer, corn; the miner, a gem." . . . "The gift, to be true, must be the flowing of the giver unto me, correspondent to my flowing unto him." In fact, giving demands a gift, not however in the sense of any commercial rationalism, but because the gift allows a stream to flow, which from the moment of giving runs uninterruptedly from donor to recipient and from receiver to giver: "the recipient is in the power of the giver."[3] "As a rule, certainly, the receiver of the present appears to gain and the donor to lose, but secretly the gift demands a gift in return. Whoever receives gifts unites himself to the one who bestows them: the accepted gift can bind."[4] We ourselves, in fact, continue to recognize this power whenever we give an employee his "earnest", and that presents maintain friendship we know quite as well as the East African natives who said to Livingstone: "Thou claimest to be our friend; but how are we to know that, so long as thou hast not given us any of thy food and hast not tasted ours? Give us an ox; we will give thee in return everything thou mayest demand, and then we shall be bound to each other by genuine affection."[5] With many primitive peoples, again, refusal to bestow or receive a gift amounts to a de-

---

[1] Grönbech in Chantepie, *op. cit.*, II, 581; Laum, *Heiliges Geld*, 32; Grimm, *loc. cit.*
[2] *Acts* xx. 35.   [3] Grönbech, *loc. cit.*, III, 3.
[4] Grimm, *loc. cit.*, 174.
[5] Cited by R. Kreglinger, *Grondbeginselen der godsdienstwetenschap*, 68; *cf.* further Grönbech, III, 112.

claration of war: it means that community is declined;[1] for the gift is powerful; it has binding force: it has *mana*. Gifts therefore can destroy the recipient; but they can also assist him, and in any event they forge an indissoluble bond. Thus the Maori speak of the *hau* (spirit) of the gift: I give what I have received from thee to a third person, and from him I receive a return gift. This I must now give to thee since it is actually thy gift; the *hau* of thy gift persists in it.[2] "The object received is not a dead thing. Even when it has been handed over by the giver it always retains something pertaining to him." To offer somebody something, then, is to offer someone a part of oneself; similarly, to accept a thing from another person is to receive some portion of his spiritual being, of his soul;[3] and under these circumstances the reciprocal nature of giving is quite obvious. The *Havamal* expresses all this most forcibly: "Friends should cheer each other with presents of weapons and raiment. . . . Those who repay with gifts, and those who respond in the same way, remain friends longest, provided that there is time for matters to turn out well. If you wish to know when you have a friend whom you can trust absolutely, and if you desire to be treated well by him, you must blend your own sentiments with his, interchange gifts with him, and often travel to visit him." In all this there is doubtless an element of calculation: here is the butter, where are the gifts? But there is also involved a just apprehension of friendship; and thirdly, there is something more: a mystic power attached to the gift which establishes *communio*.[4] Or to express this in Lévy-Bruhl's terms: giver and receiver participate in the gift and therefore in each other. Here, too, economic life has its roots; on the Trobriand Islands in Melanesia, for example, the dignified trade in *kula* is distinguished from the ordinary business in *gimwali*; in the first it is not so much a matter of exchange as of the distribution of gifts.[5] The Indian tribes of North-west America, again, practice the "potlatch" system, consisting in two tribes or chiefs engaging in a competition of prodigality; whoever is the richer gives the most and even destroys his own possessions if necessary. All this, however, in order that he himself may prosper,[6] since in this manner he shows that he has power; and we have already observed that the primitive king also demonstrated his power by giving presents. But here, as always, the "power" is just as secular (to use

---

[1] Mauss, *Essai sur le don, forme archaïque de l'échange, Année Sociologique*, N.S. 1, 1925, 51.

[2] Mauss, *ibid.*, 45 *f.*   [3] *ibid.*, 47 *ff.*

[4] Chap. 32.   [5] Mauss, *ibid.*, 64 *ff.*   [6] *ibid.*, 93 *ff.*

our paltry expression) as it is "sacred", the "potlatch" system being simultaneously religious and economic, social and legal;[1] and a wealthy Maori has *mana*, which is at the same time credit, influence and power. Thus "to buy" is a magical action; and according to Mauss the three obligations of the "potlatch" system are to give, to receive and to give in return;[2] the one always has the other as a condition. For whoever buys receives something of the owner's being together with his purchase, and that would be dangerous if an exchange gift did not follow: buying must therefore always be accompanied by a return gift;[3] for objects sold are never completely detached from their possessor.[4]

Under such conditions we can hardly be astonished at *money* also having a sacramental origin; and the oldest Greek measure of value was the ox, the sacred sacrificial animal, the money being the tribute that must be paid to the deity. Thus the sacrificial meal, in the course of which the meat was equally divided, was the "germ of public financial administration". Later, coin appeared instead of the sacrifice;[5] but that the coin was money, that is valid, was also due to its originating in the sphere of sacrifice and bringing with it its powerfulness, or as we should say, its credit.[6] Here we meet with the same relationship as was discerned in the case of retaliation (punishment) and revenge:[7] a stream is released, one motion always setting the other free; therefore just as the evil deed must be balanced by revenge or punishment, so must the gift be "requited" by a gift in return or, in modern terms, be paid for.[8]

Sacrifice, then, and in the first place as the sacrificial gift, has now taken its place within a very much wider connotation. It is no longer a mere matter of bartering with gods corresponding to that carried on with men, and no longer homage to the god such as is offered to princes: it is an opening of a blessed source of gifts. We both give and receive, and it is quite impossible to say who is actually donor and who recipient. For both participate in the powerfulness of

---

[1] Mauss, *op. cit.*, 99.   [2] *ibid.*, 100.

[3] F. D. E. van Ossenbruggen, *Tydschrift van het Ned. Aardr. Genootschap.* 2. *Reeks,* 47, 1930, 221 *ff. cf.* J. C. van Eerde, *ibid.*, 230 *ff.* These considerations place such a custom as bride purchase in an entirely new light; *cf.* H. Th. Fischer, *Der magische Charakter des Brautpreises (Weltkreis,* 1932, 3, 3).

[4] Mauss, *ibid.*, 87.

[5] Is Laum correct in suggesting that the *obol* is really the *obelos*—that is, the roasting-spit? *op. cit.*, 106 *ff.*

[6] Laum.   [7] Chap. 23.

[8] *cf.* A. Olrik, *Ragnarök,* 1922, 460, and the typical Old Norse expression for "revenge", *uphaevelse,* that is, "setting the slain up again".

what is being presented, and hence it is neither the giver nor the receiver, even though he be a god or a divine being, who occupies the focal point of the action. The pivot of the sacrificial act, its power centre, is always the gift itself: it must be given, that is to say, be set in motion. As a rule it is given to another person who may be one's neighbour, or may be some god; but it may also be divided among the members of the community. It may, again, be "given" without any "addressee" at all. For the principal feature is not that someone or other should receive something, but that the stream of life should continue to flow. From this point of view, therefore, not only are gift and communion sacrifices not antitheses but, still further, the sacrifice is transplanted into the very midst of life. It is no *opus supererogatorium*, but the working of the power of life itself. And thus instead of the rationalistic *do-ut-des*, we must say: *do ut possis dare*—"I give in order that thou mayest be able to give": I give thee power that thou mayest have power, and that life may not stagnate because of any lack of potency.

2. "I discern a reference to such a reciprocal effect as this in the Roman sacrificial formula 'Hail to thee'; *e.g.* '*Iuppiter dapalis*, hail to thee by the offering of thy feast: hail to thee by the wine placed before thee'.[1] Probably this can have no other meaning than: 'Hail to thee! with these sacrificial gifts, which I now offer to thee; be strong through these my gifts.' Such an invocation in a fixed formula, in *verbis certis*, however, was never a merely arbitrary form of speech. For the view certainly prevailed at one time that the gods could be rendered capable of bestowing power only by the constant nourishing of their own strength. . . . The Roman, for example, sacrificed to the hearth, to Vesta, by throwing small gifts into the fire, while he was at the same time wholly dependent on this hearth fire, and worshipped it as the essence of the divine fullness of life."[2] Thus the relationship of dependence between god and man, which appears to us to be perfectly obvious, need by no means be actually present; or rather: the dependence certainly subsisted, but it was reciprocal, and may be compared to the status of the Catholic priest in popular piety: "no creature other than he has the 'power' to create God Himself in transubstantiation,

---

[1] Cato, *Agri cultura*, 132; *mactus* originally means "increased, strengthened", then "honoured"; *cf.* R. Wünsch, *Rhein. Mus.* 69, 1913, 127 *ff.*; a similar expansion of meaning to that of the concepts *augeo*, *auctoritas*.

[2] G. van der Leeuw, *Do-ut-des-Formel*, 244 *f.*

to call Him down from His heavenly throne to the altar by his word of consecration".[1]

If however man gives in order that he may also receive, nevertheless he externalizes part of himself in the gift. Here again I believe that I can deepen a certain rationalistic viewpoint, so as to be able to set it in its correct connection with life: that namely of so-called vicarious sacrifice. Usually it is maintained that vicarious sacrifice is a *pis aller*, just as the substitute formerly was in military service: no one ever sacrifices himself willingly, and therefore one sacrifices one's children, and later a slave or prisoner, finally an animal, and if that be too costly, a cake in animal form. In fact, we know how human sacrifice was actually replaced by that of animals, for example in the story of Isaac,[2] and also that the sacrificial cake very often retained the form of the animal whose place it had taken.[3] We recall again that the Toradja native, if he tells a lie while travelling by water, quickly pulls a hair from his head and throws it into the stream with the words: "I am guilty, I give this instead of myself."[4] But all this is not merely some acute business deal transacted with the powers. He who "gives", who sacrifices, *always* gives something of himself with it: whether it be his child which he is giving as a building sacrifice, or his hair that he is tendering as an atonement, or his grain offered as first-fruits, it is always a portion of himself.[5] He who makes a sacrifice sacrifices his property, that is, himself.[6] Just as he chooses, therefore, he can replace a part of himself, of his possessions, by something else, since all that he has has a part in him, and participates reciprocally. Certainly this substitution of something different for the gift can arise purely from a desire for comfort or from greed. But it may also be actuated by humanitarian motives; and it may even conduce to indifference so far as the value of the sacrifice is concerned: "the sacrifice of a fowl has the same value in the eyes of the god as the sacrifice of an ox", say the South African Baronga.[7] And from this attitude the path leads on to the standpoint of the prophet demanding obedience and not sacrifice.

But here yet another highly important idea is born: the sacrifice takes the place of the person offering it. With him it is essentially

---

[1] Heiler, *Katholizismus*, 181.

[2] A parallel from Samoa may be found in *Tales from old Fiji* (L. Fison), 1907, 41.

[3] Cakes shaped like stags were offered to Artemis Elaphebolos; Nilsson, *Griech. Feste*, 224; cf. 202; Samter, *Religion der Griechen*, 47.

[4] Kruyt, *Animisme*, 32 f.   [5] cf. Will, *Le culte*, I, 111.

[6] Chap. 33.   [7] Will, *ibid.*, I, 101.

connected; the sacrificer gives himself in and with his offering, and in this surrender the offering assists him. Thus a different light is cast upon the sacrifice of women, slaves *etc.*, who follow their masters to death. The Hindu burning of widows is universally familiar, while in Nubia slaves and prisoners were slain to accompany the dead man;[1] and the primary purpose of all this was not that the retainers should serve their master in the world beyond. That they must already do, since by their own death and rebirth they facilitated their lord's decease and rebirth. Here then it was a matter of suffering and dying together, whence new life arose. For the broad stream of life, the eternal flux of power, is assured by the greatest possible "expenditure"; and since sacrificer and sacrifice participate in each other, giver and gift can interchange their rôles. The idea of the vicarious sacrifice of Christ should therefore be interpreted from this viewpoint, not in the light of some juristic theory: the sacrifice demanded from man being accomplished by Him Who is simultaneously sacrificer and sacrifice, *sacerdos et hostia.*

3. Still further, sacrifice preserves the cycle of power. The stream of gifts (that is, of power), not only assures community between man and man, between man and god, but can also be conducted through all kinds of difficulties and can avert these by absorbing them within the community. Thus the *building sacrifice* removes the risks of construction: taking possession of the piece of ground, and the expulsion of the foreign demonic power residing in the soil, are rendered harmless by the *communio* of the sacrifice; only in this way can the house become a piece of property. The atoning sacrifice, again, removes the sin impeding the stream of life; life's power is set in motion in favour of the person offering the sacrifice. "In this respect it is somewhat indifferent whether this vital power resides in a god and, by means of the sacred food replete with the strength of life, is compelled to circulate by the maker of the sacrifice, or whether it subsists within the sacrifice itself and is consumed as food at first hand by the sacrificer. Originally the food, on which life depended, was probably eaten in the religious sense, that is, in accordance with later ideas, sacramentally.[2] . . . Then the primitive fare, venerated of old (milk and honey,

---

[1] *cf.* G. A. Reisner, *Zeitschrift für ägypt. Sprache und Altertumskunde,* 52, 1915, 34 *ff.*; A. Wiedemann, *AR.* 21, 1922, 467.

[2] "Every meal places man in connection with life's creative forces and with the eternal life of Deity"; Kristensen, *Livet,* 44.

the Roman *mola salsa, etc.*[1]) became the food of the gods or of their realm. But it might also be regarded as itself divine; and then the meal became a sacrifice".[2]

Pre-eminently does the sacramental meal, brought into prominence by Robertson Smith, now become comprehensible. Some sacred substance, an animal or other kind of nourishment, is divided among the members of a community and consumed by them: thus it becomes the sacred that subsists in common,[3] producing a strengthening of the community's power and binding its members more firmly to each other. The custom of dividing an animal into pieces, thereby effecting unity, is familiar in Saul's conduct during the siege of the town of Jabesh;[4] and perhaps this implied a sacrifice also. The significance of the sacrificial meal, however, becomes quite clear to us in the case of the Ainu, the primitive inhabitants of Japan.[5] The Ainu celebrate a bear feast; a very young bear is captured, suckled and carefully reared by a woman, pampered and spoilt for several years and finally killed; in the slaying the whole community participates, at least symbolically; it is then sincerely mourned, and consumed ceremonially in a communal meal. It is the animal of the community; and this follows from the fact that it can be a sacrificial animal only if it has grown up in the tribe, so that a wild bear would be useless for the purpose; it is as it were the child of the woman who brought it up, and who laments it.[6] A vestige of a similar communal meal occurred in Latin antiquity; the Latin League celebrated the *feriae latinae* on the Alban Mount: there the delegates from the Latin towns ate together a white steer: each town received its share, the ceremonial being called *carnem petere.*[7] And again, in a different way, the so-called *epulum Jovis* celebrated at the Ides of September, in which three gods took part;[8] thus in this instance the sacrifice and the god were not identical, the deity being numbered among the guests. But by both methods alike community among the participants was effected or strengthened;[9] and only from

---

[1] Heiler, *Prayer*, 66. Wide, in *Handbuch der klassischen Altertumswissenschaft*[4], II, 4, 1931, 74.
[2] G. van der Leeuw, *Do-ut-des-Formel*, 251 f.   [3] Chap. 32.
[4] 1 *Sam.* xi. 7; *cf. Judges* xix; Schwally, *Der heilige Krieg*, 53.
[5] Haas, *Bilderatlas*, No. 8.
[6] *cf.* further Frazer, *Golden Bough*, VIII (*Spirits of the Corn*, II), 101 *ff.*
[7] Warde Fowler, *The Religious Experience of the Roman People*, 172. Wissowa, *Religion und Kultus der Römer*, 124 *ff.* During the festival the *pax deorum* was maintained—a general tabu.
[8] Fowler, *Roman Festivals*, 218 *f.*
[9] Thomsen, *Der Trug des Prometheus, AR.* 12, 1909, 464.

the point of view of such community can we comprehend the laments over the sacrifice, and the prayers for forgiveness, met with among so many peoples. This becomes most obvious when totemistic connections with the sacrificial animal predominate. Thus the Zuni of Arizona mourn for the turtle which has been sacrificed: "Ah! my poor dear lost child or parent, my sister or brother to have been! Who knows which? Maybe my own great-grandfather or mother."[1] The sacrifice belongs to the community, indeed *is* the community, constitutes and strengthens it. The community is being sacrificed, "given up", in order to be sustained. And in this sense too only what has been lost can be gained.[2]

4. "This view of sacrifice has been developed in the most magnificent and logical manner in India. There the sacrifice (the ancient Vedic sacrifice of the horse) became a process which was executed with automatic precision: 'Events are apprehended just as they were in the most primitive type of prehistoric ideas of the Universe, as resting on the play of those forces which rule the Universe, and whose mode of operation, remotely comparable to the order of Nature which constitutes the modern concept of the world, the knower is able to calculate and to direct just as he will. But this knower is man himself.'[3] Here sacrifice has become a world process in the literal sense, and man understands how to dominate it. The centre of life's power lies in himself; he is the transitional point of the potencies that move the Universe. Here, then, gods are just as superfluous as they were in the primitive stage."[4]

Actually the sacrifice, as such, is always a sacrament. But where it is expressly called so, that is in Christianity, the concept of the stream of gifts has fused in a marvellous way with the concept of a personal God, and of a Saviour Who is not only the sacrifice, not only the

---

[1] Frazer, *Spirits of the Corn*, II, 175 ff. (*Golden Bough*, VIII).

[2] It may be said that the stream of powerfulness evoked by the sacrifice vivifies all the participants therein, whether men or gods. It may, however, also be expressed thus:—that this stream flows from the god, or again from some one participant, to man or to another member, through the sacrifice. The altar then becomes the point of transition—the theory of Hubert and Mauss (*Mélanges d'Histoire des Religions*). But the sacrifice is far more than such a transitional point; it is itself sacredness, power-stuff; *cf.* the Greek rule οὐκ ἐκφορά—nothing may remain over of the sacred food—a regulation very frequently encountered in sacrificial practice; *cf.* Thomsen, *Der Trug des Prometheus*, *AR.* 12, 1909, 466 ff.

[3] Oldenberg, *Lehre der Upanishaden*, 16 f.

[4] G. van der Leeuw, *Do-ut-des-Formel*, 252.

priest, but also a historic personage. Here the danger certainly threatens
that owing to the repetition inherent in all cult, the historic-concrete
and uniquely given element in the Saviour's sacrifice would be transformed repeatedly into that autocratic automatism which we have just
discerned in India. It is true that the bloodless reiteration of the bloody
sacrifice of Golgotha, as this is prescribed according to the decisions
of the Council of Trent,[1] need repeal neither the unique sacrificial
deed of Christ nor the making of the thank-offering on the church's
part, which is possible only in the concrete situation. Nevertheless a
soupçon of the idea of the luxuriantly flowing stream of grace—but
without God's act of volition and also without the church's gratitude
—once again makes itself constantly perceptible here: Power is striving
with Will and Form. If however the struggle just referred to is not
carried on one-sidedly, and in favour of a pure dynamism or a mere
symbolism, but persists as a living tension, then the Christian Eucharist
implies, indeed, an intensification of the mystic and primitive idea of
do-ut-des. For I cannot perceive any contradiction, such as Luther did,[2]
in the fact that the same entity is simultaneously received and offered.
On the contrary, it is precisely the essence of all sacrifice that it should
be at the same time an offering and a receiving. The centurion, whose
words occur in the mass before communion, says that he is not worthy
that the Lord should enter under his roof; nonetheless at the same
moment he does enter under the Lord's roof; "I am not worthy that
thou shouldest come under my roof", and "Then will I go unto
the altar of God",[3] are *one* celebration and *one* act of God. This
in fact found expression in the ancient Christian liturgy when, in
the anamnesis, the people appear offering thanks to the Lord with the
words "What is His own from what is His own";[4] and it has been
most beautifully interpreted in Paul Gerhardt's *Christmas Hymn*:

> Here stand I at Thy manger,
> O little Jesus, my very life.
> I come to bring and give to Thee
> What Thou hast given to me.

[1] Will, *Le culte*, I, 96 *f.*

[2] *Of the Babylonian Captivity of the Church:* the contradiction "that the mass should
be a sacrifice, because we receive the promise, but give the sacrifice. But one and the
same object can neither be simultaneously received and offered, nor simultaneously
given and received, by the same person."

[3] *Matt.* viii. 8; *Ps.* xliii. 4.

[4] τά σὰ ἐκτῶν σῶν σοὶ προσφέροντες κατὰ πάντα καὶ διὰ πάντα. H. Lietzmann,
Messe und Herrenmahl, 1926, 51.

ALFRED BERTHOLET, *Der Sinn des kultischen Opfers* (Abh. preuz. Akad. d. Wiss., 1942, Phil. Hist. Kl. 2).

J. GRIMM, *Schenken und Geben* (*Kl. Schriften*, II, 1865, 173 ff.).

H. HUBERT and M. MAUSS, *Mélanges d'Histoire des Religions*, 1909.

B. LAUM, *Heiliges Geld*, 1924.

G. VAN DER LEEUW, *Die Do-ut-des-Formel in der Opfertheorie* (*AR.* 20, 1920–21, 241 ff.).

A. LODS, *Examen de quelques hypothèses modernes sur les origines du sacrifice* (*Revue d'histoire et de littérature rel.*, 1921, 483 ff.).

A. LOISY, *Essai historique sur le sacrifice*, 1920.

B. MALINOWSKI, *Argonauts of The Western Pacific*, 1932.

M. MAUSS, *Essai sur le don, forme archaïque de l'échange.* (*Année Sociologique*, N.S. I, 1925.)

S. REINACH, *Cultes, Mythes et Religions*, I, 1905.

W. ROBERTSON SMITH. *The Religion of the Semites*[3], 1927

ADA THOMSEN, *Der Trug des Prometheus* (*AR.* 12, 1909, 460 ff.).

CHAPTER 51

SACRAMENTALS

1. ACCORDING to the doctrine of the Roman Catholic Church, those celebrations which endow a person or thing with a sacred character, or sacredness, are sacramentals. These are especially considered to be: consecration, blessing and exorcism;[1] and I shall discuss these celebrations more fully in dealing with sacred words. But at this stage, and before treating of sacraments, I must introduce this concept because it shows in a most impressive way that sacred action always tends towards the sacramental. For life, that is to say, a fixed number of sacraments is quite insufficient; certainly the idea of the sacrament as such is frequently restricted to some degree, both theoretically and often practically also; nevertheless its essence persists in celebration effecting superior powerfulness, activating a power. The Roman church to-day still recognizes very many sacramentals, while in the Middle Ages they accompanied almost the whole of life; and thus it becomes clearly enunciated that life cannot be "carried on", in the actual sense of the word, without powers being brought into action; existence, once again, is "care", which on its part leads to celebration; and this, finally, has no significance unless something essential to life is modified by it.

We may also express this state of affairs as follows: life consists not in man controlling things just as he himself pleases, but in his mobilizing the powerfulness of what appear as things. Actually, in other words, there are no "things": there are only conduits and containers, which under given conditions can retain power within themselves. Thus the "things", with which man comes into contact, are either receptacles which he must fill with power or wheels that he must set in motion; this then involves some magical deed, so that man appears to a certain extent as a creator, if not of the things then at least of the powers which endow them with life. Or alternatively: "things" are "creatures", *creaturae*. In yet other terms: they are connected with God directly and immediately, and God can at any moment breathe into them new life and grant them fresh potency; He makes instruments of His Power out of "things", He creates and

[1] Braun, *Liturgisches Handlexikon*, 304 *f.*

renews them. Thus a deed, a word, a person can at any moment become "powerful", either because of the fullness of power that is in man and that forces power into them, or because of the fullness of Power in God the Creator. In the first case man utters an incantation, in the second a prayer; but in both instances we speak of sacramentals.

2. As we have already been in the position to observe, *eating and drinking* are genuine sacramentals; and our drinking customs, or the fixed observances of the students' drinking bout, are all vestiges of a time when every occasion of communal drinking was actually a celebration—a celebration or, in other words, a consolidation, renewal and recreation of the common powerfulness. In Nordic sagas, for example, drinking is by no means a matter of mere thirst or desire; they drank in fixed succession, so that the stream of *Minne* should not be interrupted,[1] while the term *Minne* is better translated as *salus* than as *amor*. The magic drink again, also a sacramental!, is (as Grönbech remarks) actually nothing but any drink whatever which binds the drinker fast to the house or the circle that has given him the beverage; every drink "bewitches", renders the past forgotten and creates new-love.[2] Exactly so as regards food: the communal meal too is binding; and when Jarl Torfin, unrecognized, breaks off a scrap of King Magnus's bread and eats it, he escapes by this celebration a death which otherwise would have been inevitable.[3] Thus every communal meal is not merely a sacrifice but a sacrament also and, while it is not officially characterized as such, a sacramental. The consecration of food on Easter morning takes account of these conditions even to-day: baskets filled with eggs, bread, salt, ham and little lambs made of sugar, are brought to church to be blessed; and in order that the blessing may actually penetrate the viands the baskets are opened, like the wine-bottles on Midsummer's Day.[4] Yet a step farther and we obtain the sacrament in its original form: people bring their gifts to church and lay them on the altar, where they then become the elements of the sacred sustenance. Of this there are examples of many kinds, quite apart from Christianity. On the island of Buru in the Moluccas, for instance, each clan holds a communal rice meal, to which each member contributes some fresh rice, and this is called "eating the soul of the rice".[5] In ancient Rome, again, at the *ludi saeculares*

---

[1] Grönbech, *op. cit.*, IV, 32.   [2] *ibid.*, III, 125 *ff.*
[3] *ibid.*, III, 117 *f.*   [4] Heiler, *Katholizismus*, 170 *f.*
[5] Frazer, *The Golden Bough*, VIII (*Spirits of the Corn*, II), 54.

suffimenta and *fruges* were brought to the quindecimvirs, and after they had been lustrated were again distributed to the people;[1] this is a vivid reminder of the *oblationes* of the Christian Eucharist.

3. From the inexhaustible wealth of sacramentals I shall cite two further important examples. First of all, *alms.* "Alms obliterates sin as water extinguishes fire", says Islamite tradition,[2] and the sanctification of life, the daily enhancing of the power of existence, is expressed as *zakat*: "every articulation of man's body is obliged to bestow alms daily; if the sun rises over him while he mediates between two other persons, then that is a bestowal of alms; if he assists somebody with his (own) animal by allowing him to ride on it or load it with his wares, that is one also; the kind word is another; in every step that he makes in ceremonial obeisance there lies an alms; likewise if he removes a barrier out of the road."[3] From this starting-point, indeed, are spun the threads of religious ethics, but also the fabric of the automatism of power. When a priest sends out an appeal to women, themselves in childbed, for assistance for needy mothers, in which he expresses the hope that "your gift of money may assist your complete recovery and the auspicious growth of your dear child", this is a sacramental in an almost entirely magical sense; and contrasted with this, the words: "Inasmuch as ye have done it unto one of the least of these my brethren, ye have done it unto me",[4] provide the direct connection between sacramental action and the thank-offering brought to the saviour.

A further extreme example of the sacramental is the *Ordeal.* This consists in some simplification of the conditions of life by the immediate introduction of power; in celebration one's own power is at once replaced by that of a different type. We feel as it were convinced that all our acts are futile, and then we transpose our own behaviour *in toto* into association with the activity of the powers. Actually this sacramental is a sacrament like none other, for man's effectiveness is here restricted to merely setting in motion, while everything else with no exception is performed by power. An African husband and wife, for example, lose their child by death: it is clear that one of them must be guilty of causing its death by magic. Together they drink the poisoned potion, *mwamfi*, and say: "Here is our child, dead; perhaps it is we, his parents, who have bewitched him? If it be so, *mwamfi*,

---

[1] cf. A. Piganiol, *Recherches sur les Jeux romains*, 1923, 92 ff.
[2] Bertholet, *op. cit.*, 16, 22.   [3] *ibid.*, 21.   [4] *Matt.* xxv. 40.

then remain in our bodies; but if it be not our fault, do not stay in us, *mwamfi*, but leave our bodies."[1] Thus all their conduct, even guilt or innocence, is brought within the province of celebration. Power not only takes the place of the judge, but replaces even the utterance of conscience; it knows better than the persons actually concerned whether they are guilty or not.

[1] Lévy-Bruhl, *Primitives and the Supernatural*, 180.

FRITZ BAMMEL, *Das heilige Mahl im Glauben der Volker*, 1950.
G. VAN DER LEEUW, *Sacramentstheologie*, 1949.
R. R. MARETT, *Sacraments of Simple Folk*, 1933.

CHAPTER 52

THE SACRAMENT

1. THE word *sacrament* should not be interpreted merely according to its Latin meaning; the Greek expression *mysterion* has to some extent coloured the Roman significance. Thus not only *devotio*, the consecration of the Roman soldier when taking the oath to the colours, but also the entire range of the extraordinarily numinous Greek term, from fulfilled prophecy to the mysterious presence of the *numen*, came to be included in it;[1] "all the richness of the significance of *mysterion* has been transposed to *sacramentum*".[2] If therefore we disregard etymology altogether and enquire what a sacrament implies for religion, then if we do not wish to class all sacramentals with sacraments (which, incidentally, is quite easy to do), we discover a unitary and constant phenomenon by observing two main features: (*1*) the sacrament is the sublimation of some one of the simplest and most elementary of life's functions: washing, eating and drinking, sex intercourse, gestures, speaking; and it is their sublimation because in the sacrament this vital activity is disclosed from its profoundest bases upwards to where it touches the divine. Thus life itself, in its whole extent, is as it were brought into the presence of Power. But (*2*) in those celebrations which I shall henceforth exclusively term sacraments, this Power now becomes bound up with the action, under the form of the saviour.[3] Consequently the sacrament is on the one hand what is quite near, and on the other wholly different and remote: in one respect *fascinans*, in the other *tremendum*,[4] but always *mysterium*. The presupposition of all these ideas, however, is that Power resides within life, and this whether it has developed, or has been created, within it: "if Nature has been rendered impotent, then the sacrament is arbitrary and has no power".[5] On the other hand the sacrament is never the natural process itself, since either magically creating man, or the creative God, must "characterize" Nature.

A. One elementary function of life, thus "characterized", is purifi-

---

[1] *cf.* Anrich, *Mysterienwesen*, 144. H. von Soden, *Zeitschrift f. d. Neut. Wiss.*, 12, 1911, 188 *ff*. O. Casel, *Jahrb. f. Liturgiewiss.* 8, 1928, 226 *ff*. May, *Droit romain*, 228 *f.*
[2] Casel, *ibid.*, 232.　　　　　　　　　　　　　　　　　[3] Chap. 12.
[4] Heiler, *Katholizismus*, 532.　　　　　　[5] Tillich, *Religiöse Verwirklichung*, 167.

cation, which has already been discussed in detail in Chapter 49; there it was explained specifically how purifying became a sacrament. In the *baptismal* act, again, man's status is rendered completely free alike from his own opinion, feeling or approval; the "water" becomes the Power of the blood of Christ. For this reason the blood bath of martyrdom also ranks as a second baptism;[1] through his testimony, the witness by blood participates in the purifying deed of Christ; and I have previously referred to *confirmation* and *extreme unction*.

B. The sacred meal, again, becomes a sacrament in virtue of its connection with the "Lord", the Saviour-God; we find therefore the first *sacramental meals* in the saviour-religions, the so-called mystery religions. "Chaeremon invites thee to dine at the table of the Lord Sarapis in the Sarapeion, to-morrow, the fifteenth, at the ninth hour", reads a very characteristic summons from the circle of Sarapis-Isis initiates.[2] In the Attis mysteries, similarly, the initiate could relate about a sacred meal which he took from the consecrated musical instruments of the cult, and by which alone he appears to have become initiated: "I have eaten out of the drum, I have drunk from the cymbal, I have become an initiate of Attis": ἐκ τυμπάνου βέβρωκα, ἐκ κυμβάλου πέπωκα, γέγονα μύστης Ἀττεως[3]; and the convert and apologist of Christianity, Firmicus Maternus, did not omit to indicate expressly the parallels with the sacred food of his own religion. In the Eleusinian mysteries, likewise, a sacred drink, the *kykeon*, was consumed, which is referred to in a celebrated mystic formula.[4] Finally we find the ancient Persian meal of bread and water, mixed with the juice of the sacred *haoma* plant, retained in the Mithras mysteries, the *haoma* however being replaced by wine, and a pictorial representation from Konjica in Dalmatia[5] brings before our eyes the meal of Mithras. It was reserved for initiates of one particular rank; probably the designation of this grade, μετέχοντες, means nothing else than that these initiates were allowed to "participate" in the sacred meal. Tertullian, again, draws the parallel: "Mithras celebrates the sacrifice of bread".[6] In all these sacraments, then, the bond between celebration and saviour is certainly present, even though it is not transparent. Only the nocturnal Dionysian orgies, in which the god was eaten in the form of some animal, represent a genuine theophagy: the sacred food was

---

[1] Chap. 29.   [2] Haas, *Bilderatlas*, 9/11, Fig. 16.
[3] Firmicus Maternus, *De errore profanarum religionum*, 18, 1.
[4] Clement of Alexandria, *Protr.* 18.   [5] Haas, *op. cit.*, 15, Fig. 46.
[6] F. Cumont, *Die Mysterien des Mithra*[3], 1923, 145 *ff.*

expressly interpreted as the saviour-god, and so the participant became "filled with the god". From this to the Christian sacrament there is, of course, an enormous interval, since in the latter the link between celebration and Saviour becomes apprehended in a quite peculiar and historic way: the Saviour at Whose table persons meet together for the meal, Whose body they eat and Whose blood they drink, is the Lord, with Whom they have so often sat at table during His earthly life.

Thus in the Christian sacrament very different elements are connected in one living unity; and we may here follow the fine outline made by Brilioth,[1] who for his part relies to some extent on Lietzmann. (*1*) There is the actual *Eucharist*, that is the thank-offering as this originated from the Jewish meal; the blessing of the chalice, the breaking of the bread, are performed by the "Lord" Who is present in the *pneuma* and Who will come soon to feed His people; and in the liturgy *maran atha* is understood equally as in the present and the future.[2] (*2*) This meal is a *communio*, as of old; all those participating in it are united among themselves, but here through the bond in Christ: the union with the brethren is at the same time that with the Lord; and the sacramental of the *osculum pacis*, which occurs at this stage, expresses this union. (*3*) But into this celebration there now enters the remembrance of the Lord, the *anamnesis*; and with this the Eucharist leaves the group of sacramentals, that is of sacred repasts, absolutely, and becomes in the fullest sense a sacrament. Historically, this means that the brotherly meal, the *agape*, is separated from the Eucharist to which it was originally the prelude. But the *anamnesis* places in the foreground not only the glory of God in general, not only the *pneuma* of the Lord, but the historic deed of the Saviour, finally, in the mass in the words of the Institution (*Qui pridie*).[3] (*4*) The *anamnesis*, again, leads to the Eucharistic *sacrifice*. The sacrifice of Christ on Golgotha is the sole actual sacrifice: but it is continued in the dual sacrifice of the sacrament, which consists equally in the repetition of the Lord's sacrifice and of the community's thank-offering, which without His sacrifice would be impossible; from His own, that is, the church sacrifices what is His own. But the idea of sacrifice thus gives to *communio* its profoundest meaning, and conversely, the community is the deed of God *in Christo*; this act of God

---

[1] *Eucharistic Faith and Practice*, 276 ff.

[2] Lietzmann, *Messe und Herrenmahl*, 237.

[3] Even in Nietzsche's Parody the *anamnesis* and the eschatological reference persist: "at this (repast) there was nothing else spoken of but the higher man". *Thus Spake Zarathustra*, "The Supper", p. 350 (Foulis Edition).

is therefore no external event, but a participation of the Head in the members and, through the Head, of the members in one another. (5) All these elements of the Christian sacrament attain their highest completion, which is at the same moment their presupposition, in the *mystery* of the Eucharist. This is the sacred presence of the Lord which, in all the elements—the repast, *communio*, *anamnesis* and sacrifice—really gives the celebration the character of a new creation, of a creative deed of God, and compels man to his knees before the mystery of the Incarnation. Christ is present as priest, as sacrifice, and as the church which is His body. "I am the bread of life"; "I am the true vine": this mystical language gives expression to the Eucharistic experience equally as did the amazement of the disciples at Emmaus, who recognized the Lord on His breaking bread, and thus, it may be (according to Lietzmann's acute interpretation), took the first step from the Jewish meal to the Lord's supper—the historical recollection of the *Qui pridie* and equally the boundless praise of "Let us give thanks", εὐχαριστήσωμεν. The sacred food is simultaneously remembrance, sacrifice and the Saviour's presence:

> O thou Memorial of our Lord's own dying,
> O Bread that living art and vivifying,
> Make ever thou my soul on thee to live,
> Ever a taste of heavenly sweetness give.[1]

In this connection, therefore, transubstantiation must be considered as a theoretically grounded reversion to the most primitive aspects in the sacrament. The genuinely primitive sacramental required no transformation whatever: for it, the food in itself was already sacred. In the ancient Christian sacrament, however, this was not the case, but the *epiclesis*[2] was intended to invoke the Lord's spirit into the food. But to-day, in the mass, the consecration, the whispered formula of the Institution, effects a transformation of the elements.[3] In this way power-stuff, changed *ad hoc*, was substituted for the real presence of the Saviour in the Eucharist, equally in the elements and in the sacrificing community, equally in the past (the redemptive

---

[1]   O memoriale   Praesta meae menti
        Mortis Domini,   De te vivere
        Panis vivus, vitam   Et te illi semper
        Praestans homini: Dulce sapere.

Thomas Aquinas, *Rhythmus ad Sanctam Eucharistiam, Adoro te devote.*
   [2] Chap. 62.   [3] cf. Heiler, *Katholizismus*, 224 ff.

history), in the future (*maran atha*), and at the present moment; and in this manner the bond with the historic Lord is relaxed.[1] On the other hand, as against Protestant spiritualizing it must be maintained that the sacrament, in accord with its essential nature, concerns the whole man and descends from a realm which does not differentiate at all between physical and psychical effects. The *pneuma* of the Lord, therefore, produces neither "thinghood" nor "spirituality", but gives new life to "creatures".[2] Nothing that has been created "can blend with the divine. And yet there is another union besides that of mere knowing and loving—the union of subsisting life."[3]

C. The third type of sacramental community is marriage. In the Eleusinian mysteries the "holy marriage", ἱερὸς γάμος, and the birth of the child that succeeded to this, were signs of salvation: "Is not the gloomy descent there, and the solemn meeting between the hierophant and the priestess, he alone and she alone? Are not the lamps extinguished? and does not the vast and countless assembly of the people believe that what they two accomplish in the darkness means their salvation?"[4] And when the torches were lit once more the saviour's birth was solemnly announced to the people.[5] Thus sexual union was "characterized" as the medium of union with divine Power; and since this Power had the form of a saviour we must speak here too of a "sacrament"; it is indeed well known that this celebration was actually apprehended as such, particularly in mysticism and in monastic rites:[6] Christ Himself, for instance, presented the betrothal ring to St. Catherine of Siena. In other respects, however, this sacrament has acquired no adequate form in the Christian church. Among heretics, again, matters were sometimes different: the Valentinians, for example, celebrated salvation by erecting a bridal chamber and subjecting candidates for initiation to a rite which they called spiritual—"pneumatized"—marriage, πνευματικὸς γάμος.[7] Moreover, so far as this sacrament is concerned, a remarkable transposition has

---

[1] *cf.* Heiler, *Katholischer und evangelischer Gottesdienst*[2], 1925, 18.

[2] Chap. 45. The entire famous passage, 1 *Cor.* x, xi, referring to communion with demons in the sacrificial meal and to that with Christ in the Lord's supper, is full of this idea; the physical is most clearly expressed in xi. 29 *f.* Whoever unworthily makes an *agape* out of the Eucharist in order to indulge himself, and thus "fails to distinguish the Lord's body", eats and drinks to his own condemnation, and may indeed die of it.

[3] Guardini, *Von heiligen Zeichen*, 53.

[4] Asterius, *Encom. mart.* 194, Combe; *cf.* Farnell, *Cults of the Greek States*, III, 356.   [5] Hippolytus, *Philosophoumena*, 164.

[6] Chap. 22.   [7] Anrich, *Mysterienwesen*, 77.

been effected in the Christian church; for marriage, as unique among
sacraments, is not celebration of a power external to the ceremony
itself, that is to say of the Saviour's Power, but became exalted to
the rank of sacrament by the potency of the ceremony as such. In
other words, marriage in itself is a sacrament, and the wedded
pair themselves bestow it on one another; thus the profound basis
of the elementary function of life has been declared as in and
of itself sacred, and the union that is entered into is, in its essence,
supernatural.

D. Sacramental *action*, and E, the sacramental *word*, will be discussed in Chapters 53 and 58.

2. It is possible, again, to confer remoteness on the sacrament by
converting it into *myth*; and then neither life's own immediate sacredness, nor that bestowed by the saviour upon life in celebration, is
evident forthwith, but the longed for powerfulness is perceived in the
distance extending from "here" to "there". Thus, as has previously
been observed, the sacred food of the sacrificial repast became the
"food of the gods"—nectar and ambrosia; and the *soma* rite brought
a systematized mythology to maturity. But the saviour-meal also can
be removed into the far distance. In the words of the *Institution* in
the Eucharist, in fact, there is an allusion to the Messianic repast
which the Lord will hold hereafter with His people;[1] and this meal
with the Messiah is to be discerned elsewhere too in Jewish ideas.[2]
On the other hand, the repast in the Mithras mysteries was a continuation of the mythical last supper in which the god took part on
earth.[3] In the legend of the Holy Grail, however, the Christian sacrament became rendered wholly mythical. The Grail, originally probably
a wishing-bowl such as appears frequently in fairy tales,[4] together
with the spear that had pierced the Saviour's side and which allowed
—the Eucharistic—blood and water to flow, became a receptacle of
salus, a communion vessel, and can be understood only in the light of
cult experience, in accord with Burdach's acute exposition.

---

[1] *Matt.* xxvi. 29.
[2] Hölscher, *Geschichte der israelitischen und jüdischen Religion; cf.* Index, *Mahlzeit,
eschatologisch.*
[3] Cumont, *Mysterien des Mithra,* 124, 146.
[4] *cf.* E. Wechssler, *Die Sage vom heiligen Gral in ihrer Entwicklung bis auf Richard
Wagners Parsifal,* 1898. Hertz, *Parzival.* F. R. Schröder, *Die Parzivalfrage,* 1928. K.
Burdach, *Vorspiel,* I, 1, 1925, 161 *ff.* G. Dumézil, *Le Festin d'Immortalité,* 1924, 179.
W. Stärk, *Über den Ursprung der Grallegende,* 1903.

3. From all this it follows that the sacrament may have a threefold significance.[1] It can be (*1*) a *celebration that produces activity:* the action itself brings something into being, causes the sacred power to bestir itself. (*2*) The sacrament is a *celebration which is itself activity:* in the action the Universe gets into motion, to-day as always. Everything is a sacrament, or can at least become one: the world is the living garment of God. This is the concept of the sacrament in romantic mysticism. (*3*) The sacrament may be a *celebration that is grounded in activity,* wherein a Will (of God, or of the Saviour) executes the act of creation or new creation: the sacrament is then creation and bestowal of power in one. In all three types alike, however, Nature is no inanimate object, no thing, but living Power,[2] while this powerfulness breaks forth into salvation in some miraculous way. But the bond with the historical Saviour can be forged only by the third type of significance; and therefore only this third type is a sacrament in its full sense.

But the second, mystic-romantic type requires some further consideration. In certain respects it is a regress, by way of an extensive *détour*, to the most primitive viewpoints. For as in the Dionysiac orgies milk, honey and wine issued from the earth,[3] so according to this mode of apprehending life, Nature presents sacramental power immediately and without any "characterization" at all: once again, therefore, the sacrament becomes a sacramental. No new creation whatever is necessary: without more ado Nature herself is divine food to him who knows how to perceive her in her divinity: God is always on earth, and need not first of all descend. Departing from the Christian sacrament, this idea leads to the regressive transformation of what has been "characterized" into ordinary matter of fact: the sacramental food becomes merely the daily nourishment. From the time he became an anchorite Nicholas Bulgaris, for instance, ate no food except the Eucharist; and this is related about other saints also.[4] Certainly there still persists here the limitation of what has not been characterized. But this may become an expansion of the characterized, such as occurred in Romanticism; Schleiermacher's "Christmas Thoughts" seeks Mary in every mother, while his Ferdinand passes "almost immediately from conversation" to the sacred act of

---

[1] G. van der Leeuw, *Strukturpsychologie und Theologie.*
[2] Tillich. [3] Euripides, *Bacchae,* 142 *ff.*
[4] Jos. von Görres, *Mystik, Magie und Dämonie,* edited by J. Bernhart, 1927, 76 (= Görres, *Die christliche Mystik,* I[2], 1879, 372 *ff.*).

baptism.[1] Many romantics, too, dreamed that they would like to write a Bible themselves; and this universally sacramental piety found its finest expression in Novalis:

> Few know the secret of love;
> Few feel unsatiated, and have eternal thirst.
> To earthly sense the divine meaning of communion
> Is but an enigma;
> But whoso has, some time,
> Drawn the life breath from passionate and beloved lips,
> And whose heart has been molten
> By the sacred glow in quivering waves,
> Whose eye has been opened
> That he can plumb
> The immeasurable depths of heaven,
> He shall eat of His body
> And drink of His blood,
> To all eternity.

Here again, just as in the primitive world, the body's own specific potency is the ground of the sacrament:

> Who has fathomed the exalted meaning of the earthly body?
> Who can say that he understands the blood?

The saviour, too, is the life of the world itself:

> From plant and stone, from sea and light,
> His childlike countenance shines forth.
> In all things His childlike action,
> His warm love, will never rest;
> He nestles eternally close to every breast,
> Unconscious of Himself.
> To us God, to Himself a child,
> He loves us all most tenderly;
> He becomes our food and our drink,
> And faithfulness is the gratitude that He loves most.[2]

Y. BRILIOTH, *Eucharistic Faith and Practice*, 1930.
O. CASEL, *Die Liturgie als Mysterienfeier* [3-5], 1923.
A. DIETERICH, *Eine Mithrasliturgie*[2], 1910.
L. DUCHESNE, *Origines du culte chrétien*[4], 1908.
H. LIETZMANN, *Messe und Herrenmahl*, 1926.
P. TILLICH, *Religiöse Verwirklichung*[2], 1930.

[1] F. Schleiermacher, *Die Weihnachtsfeier*.   [2] *Geistliche Lieder*, 13, 11.

CHAPTER 53

SERVICE

1. IN the sacramental and in the sacrament sacred action is a service, a *ministerium* or an *officium*. For in the cult the actual agent is not man nor the human community, but sacred Power, whether this is merely the sacred common element or a sacred will. In worship, therefore, "to do", "to act", is always sacramental. Something different and something more is done than what is actually performed: things are manipulated to which man himself is not superior; he stands *within* a sacred activity and not above this. He does not govern, that is to say, but serves.[1] In many languages, indeed, "to do" has the subsidiary meaning of: culturally to do, to sacrifice, to perform magic.[2] A *dromenon*, then, always depends on some deed that is superior to man: it is always "re-done" or "pre-done",[3] and in *this* sense cult action is "representative" action: not however in Schleiermacher's sense, when by this expression he implied the symbolic representation of the content of faith,[4] but with the much more profound significance of representing the original sacred action. *It is done*: or, *God acts*; but in both cases man can only *repeat*, "follow", or "represent". In worship, therefore, activity is always "official", representative.

Thus the priest acts and speaks "in the name of Jesus": the actual speaker, the sole actor, is God. Similarly in countless dances, sacred games *etc.* of primitive peoples it is the gods, demons and spirits who act and speak; the priests or other "stage managers" are merely representatives of the sacred power.[5] Only thus can we understand why costume and mask are indispensable in cult activities; the Reformation itself made new priestly costumes out of Luther's scholarly robes. And whoever has ministered in customary garb, even though it may have been only the simple gown of a Protestant clergyman, knows that clothes make the man, or rather abstract the man so that only the *minister*, the *servant*, remains. This, however, holds good to a much greater extent of the *mask*: it converts the man who is acting

[1] *cf.* Usener, *Heilige Handlung*, 423 *f.*
[2] Ancient Egyptian *ir*, Lat. *facere*, Ital. *fattura*, Greek, *dromena*.
[3] Harrison, *Themis*, 43.
[4] *cf.* G. Mensching, *Die liturgische Bewegung in der evangelischen Kirche*, 1925, 26.
[5] Preuss, *Geistige Kultur*, 81.

in the cult into the *representative*,[1] and in the masked dances of many primitive peoples the dancers *re-present*, in the literal sense, demons or gods, and also the event that is being enacted; in other terms, they present the former afresh, and the latter they present anew; they *are* spirits or demons and the occurrence actually *takes place* once again.[2] If the derivation of the word *persona* from the Etruscan φersu be correct, this too implies the same state of affairs: the masks are then the dead, or the gods of the dead, and the name of the departed became that of the mask.[3]

An ancient Egyptian *Text* describes the deceased, that is, in fact, the priest of the dead, as thus addressing the god: "He who speaks should speak what is, and should not speak what is not; the god abhors the lying word. If I greet (?) thee, then do not say that it is I. For I am thy son, I am thine heir."[4] The dead person thus approaches the god officially, in accord with his quality; it is not he who speaks, but his "mask". Similarly in Christian worship, it is not the priest who acts but the church, and this also merely as the Body of Christ.

2. The sacred act is therefore service. But in service man is active: the body receives a rhythmic swing; whoever is celebrating, dances. "All over the world, in the magico-religious stage, primitive man dances where we should pray or praise", as Miss J. E. Harrison has pointed out.[5] Thus the *dance* is not merely an esthetic pursuit existing side by side with other more practical activities. It is the service of the god, and generates power: the rhythm of movement has a compelling force; and this still holds good for us too in the case of erotic dancing. For the dance is the aphrodisiac *par excellence*, of the coarsest as well as of the finest type. But it is not restricted to the power of love alone; and to primitive man it was simultaneously work and pleasure, sport and cult. In the dance life is ordered to some powerful rhythm and reverts to its potent primeval motion, and thus it is possible to attain to all manner of things "by dancing", from one's daily bread to heavenly bliss. There are love-, war- and hunting-dances, which

---

[1] *cf.* Chap. 25 *ff.*

[2] Lévy-Bruhl, *Primitives and the Supernatural*, 123 *f.*; *cf.* G. van der Leeuw, *Pia fraus, Mensch en Maatschappy*, 8, 1932.

[3] F. Altheim, *AR.* 27, 1929, 48 *ff.* An analogous case is *larva*, meaning both ghost and mask.

[4] *Pyramidentexte* (Sethe), 1160.   [5] *Epilegomena*, 12.

represent *in actu* the desired event, the love union, success in war and hunting. But there are also dances which, according to our standards, are of purely economic type; among the Mexican Indians, for example, dancing is equivalent to working. When the harvest is being brought in, someone remains at home and dances all day long so that it may be successful; he sets the power of life in motion. The festival season of the Cagaba Indians, again, is called the "time of work" and consists of a very strenuous dance lasting several days.[1] This economic dance however is no mere matter of business; it is rather a cult, since the sacred power of life is "celebrated" and set in motion.[2] The dance then is originally of the nature of a cult, so that whenever it is performed for pure pleasure the elements of the cult have been suppressed. "Spiritual" good can also be obtained by dancing: in the mysteries the dance was one of the principal means of expression,[3] while the miserable Indian tribes of Central Brazil have repeatedly attempted to reach the coast in their perpetual wanderings, and to become so light through the most strenuous dancing and fasting that they might reach heaven direct from the dance.[4] Indeed even in Christianity the celestial motion itself has been regarded as a dance, and earthly bliss as its imitation: "what can be more blessed than on earth to imitate the dance of the angels?"[5]

But movement in celebration has a dual character. In the first place power is concentrated, restricted, established and elevated by the rhythmic arrangement, and in the second superfluous power is released, cast away in recurrent movement. Powerfulness is either attained by dancing, or else superfluous power is danced away. The second type of motion occurs in the ecstatic dance, or rather in the dance so far as it is ecstatic (and it is almost always so to a certain extent). The dancing Dionysus, satyrs and maenads of Grecian vase paintings provide an excellent ideal picture of this ecstatic dance, which is moreover native to very many peoples. Dancing and mystical losing of self, dancing and ecstatic reeling, are so closely connected that the dance may even become the symbol of mystic unity with God; as Jalaluddin Rumi

---

[1] Preuss, *Geistige Kultur*, 82 *ff. Tod und Unsterblichkeit*, 33.

[2] *cf.* G. van der Leeuw, *In dem Himmel ist ein Tanz. Über die religiöse Bedeutung des Tanzes und des Festzuges, passim;* Lévy-Bruhl, *Primitives and the Supernatural*, 114 *f.*; Oesterley, *The Sacred Dance*, 2.

[3] Lucian, *De saltatione.*   [4] Preuss, *Tod und Unsterblichkeit*, 5.

[5] St. Basilius, *Epist.* ii, *ad Greg. cf.* P. Verheyden, *De Maagdendans (Handel. van den Mechelschen Kring van Oudheidkunde, Letteren en Kunst,* 27, 1922); G. van der Leeuw, *op. cit., passim.*

says: "He who knows the power of the dance dwells in God, for he knows that love slays."[1]

Movement and counter-movement, again, together constitute the *dramatic character* of service. All cult is drama: power is amassed and also repelled. Or in the language of the religion of Will: God comes to man, while man approaches God. The sacred game (*sacer ludus*) represents the process of this encounter, the approach to, and avoidance of, each other; it is found in the celebrations of all peoples, either in the form of actual performances of events as in mask-dances and sacred mystery plays, or in symbolic form as in the liturgy. The classical example of both types is provided in the Eleusinian mysteries, in which the sacred process was represented now in the purely dramatic form of the flower gathering (*anthology*), the carrying off (*harpage*) of Persephone and the wanderings (*plane*) of Demeter, and again in the symbolic dramatic form of the ear of corn mown in silence. The Christian church, however, relegated the dramatic performance type to the merely semi-ecclesiastical medieval "mysteries", while in its own worship the symbolic-sacramental form predominates exclusively.

Participation in dramatic service, still further, was obviously never a mere spectatorship nor listening, since the entire community actually or virtually took part and participated in celebration. This is most clearly demonstrated in the so-called *mock battles*, such as were customary for example in ancient Egypt in the Osiris cult, between the god's adherents and those of his antagonist Set, but which were also common in Greece and Rome and are still to be found to some extent in popular customs to-day.[2] The element of representation *in actu*, of repetition, is excellently interpreted by Piganiol in his account of the purpose of the games as "the renewal of the dead, of the gods, of the living and of the whole world";[3] and "the first introduction of games was intended as a religious expiation", as Livy says.[4] The combat in the games is always a symbol of the staking of life, the contest between life and death.[5] The two opponents (or the two parties forming the *catervae*) acted the game of the powers and its ultimate decision.[6]

---

[1] G. van der Leeuw, *op. cit.*, 50 and *passim*.

[2] For Egypt *cf.* Sethe, *Dramatische Texte;* Greece and Rome, A. Piganiol, *Recherches sur les Jeux romains*, 1923; Kristensen, *Livet*, 221; *Spelen, passim*; Usener, *Heilige Handlung*, 435.

[3] *op. cit.*, 149.   [4] VII, 3.   [5] Kristensen, *op. cit.*

[6] Usener, *Heilige Handlung*; on popular customs, *etc.*, *cf.* I. von Reinsberg-Düringsfeld, *Das festliche Jahr*, 60. E. K. Chambers, *The Mediaeval Stage*, I, 149 *ff.*

Finally, the *procession* is an elementary dance and fulfils the purpose of mobilizing the cult community, that is the sacred common element, the activating of power; and every procession is as it were a sacramental procession, so far as it sets something sacred in motion and extends its powerfulness over a certain region. Thus the blessing enclosed within the Holy of Holies is spread "over village and town, over field and plain"[1] by the blessed sacrament procession, as this is employed by the Roman Catholic Church. But the procession is not necessarily linked to the sacrament,[2] since some other powerful object can be carried around also: in many popular customs it is a naked girl (*ritus paganus*), while in Methana in Greece the husbandman led a menstruating woman round his orchard.[3] Fundamentally, then, the procession is a circuit, whether it wanders about through the village or the town, or makes an actual circle around an object, a field or a house *etc.* It restricts and concentrates power, and on the other hand can avert malicious powers. The ancient Roman farmer's procession round his field boundaries, the *ambarvalia*, aimed at ensuring fertility[4], and in Suabia reading the Gospel at the four corners of the village green at Whitsuntide was regarded as a "weather blessing".[5] But making the circuit may also have threatening significance: power is fixed within a circle in order to destroy, and at the seventh circuit Jericho fell to this charm.

3. From sacred action, the service of power, there developed on the one hand the *liturgy*, and on the other the *drama*; the latter pertains, however, to the Phenomenology of Art.[6] The liturgy is never completely verbal, but remains always dramatic action; and the most ancient Egyptian liturgies we possess already exhibited the character of dialogue and were solemnized dramatically;[7] in the Christian church, also, for a long time no sharp boundary could be drawn between dramatic and liturgical action. Christmas- and Easter-plays, again, developed from the liturgy, and the dialogue form of the Easter trope, *quem quaeritis?*, is still wholly liturgical, while the Easter sepulchre and the *praesepe* with the custom of "rocking the crib of the holy

---

[1] Heiler, *Katholizismus*, 177.   [2] Chap. 52.
[3] Nilsson, *History of Greek Religion*, 87 *f.*
[4] Macrobius, *Sat.* iii, 5, 7; *pro frugibus facere.*
[5] Reinsberg-Düringsfeld, *Das festliche Jahr*, 189.
[6] On the genealogy of the drama *cf.* H. Reich, *Der Mimus*, 1903. G. van der Leeuw, *Wegen en Grenzen, over de verhouding van religie en kunst*, 1932.
[7] Erman, *Denkmal memphitischer Theologie.* Sethe, *Dramatische Texte.*

child" are vestiges of drama in the liturgy; similarly the *elevatio crucis*, which retains the character of a dramatic mysteries celebration.[1]

In course of time, however, the liturgy has shown the tendency to restrict itself more and more to the sacramental word, the sacrament and the sacramental. In its festival calendar the church annually experiences the entire *vita Domini*, the story of salvation; but it does not really act this. It contents itself with a repetition in the potency of the word, the sacraments and the sacramental. For all liturgies, however, the idea of *repetition* remains the standard. Power is served by being actualized; it is represented by being brought into the present. All service, then, is a perpetual *da capo*. Power is either conjured up by man, or it renews itself; or else the Will, in whose guise Power became recognized, creatively makes all things new.

W. B. KRISTENSEN, *Over de godsdienstige beteekenis van enkele oude wedstryden en spelen* (*Theologisch Tydschrift*, N. R. 2 (44), 1910).

G. VAN DER LEEUW, *In dem Himmel ist ein Tanz. Über die religiöse Bedeutung des Tanzes und des Festzuges*, 1931.

W. O. E. OESTERLEY, *The Sacred Dance*, 1923.

[1] Chambers, *Mediaeval Stage*, II, 20 *ff.*, 42 *ff.* H. Brinkmann, *Xenia Bonnensia, Festschrift*, 1929, 109 *ff.*

CHAPTER 54

DIVINATION

1. "AN enquirer", observes Thurnwald, "turns to higher powers through the medium of the *oracle* with the intention of receiving instructions for his own conduct, or for the actions of others, in the form of signs";[1] and the question concerns, first of all, the *locus* of power, the *situation*. The person in doubt as to which course to pursue attempts to discover what the situation is; divination, therefore, yields prophecy with regard to the future only in a subordinate sense. For the enquirer wants to know not what will happen, but that what he himself desires will occur.[2] Thus the signs he perceives and interprets are simultaneously the causes of the event and signs that a power is somewhere operative. Bushmen, for instance, remain dissatisfied with an unfavourable answer from the dice oracle, and so they continue to question the dice till they tell them what they wish to hear;[3] very young children do exactly the same if they do not gain the desired result in a game. And this means that it is not a matter of any mere abstract foreknowledge of some indifferent future, but rather an investigation of the site of the power, pursued until the favourable place and the right time have been discovered. Power, celebrated in the cult, is in divination explored or conjectured.

This investigation into the nature of the situation, which at one time has a calm and almost scientific character and at another a more ecstatic form,[4] cannot of course interrogate the whole Universe. It must therefore select a section, or as it were a ground plan of this; and this it does in an apparently arbitrary, but actually strictly methodical, manner. The task of Chinese wind- and water-sages (*feng-shui*), for example, is to ensure "the harmony of human life with Nature"; they must discover the correct days and other conditions for all important actions (selection of days), and for this task a specific "office for obedient conformity with heaven" is responsible. Building a house, tilling the fields, choosing the site for a grave, *etc.*, must also

---

[1] *Orakel, Lexikon der Vorgeschichte.*   [2] Lévy-Bruhl, *Primitive Mentality,* 141.
[3] Lévy-Bruhl, *Quelques remarques sur la divination dans les sociétés primitives,* 85.
[4] Plato had already drawn this distinction; *Phaedrus,* 244; "Oionistic" and "Mantic".

be brought into precise accord with time, place and the "situation" in general. The whole destiny of someone, it may be the child born in some house, depends on the faithful fulfilment of the conditions,[1] and the knowledge these diviners possess has a very comprehensive basis. Less universal was the knowledge amassed by the Roman *augurs*. The *augur* was an "increaser", one who renders prosperous (*cf. augustus*); he was first of all *auspex*, one who observed the flight of birds; subsequently he interpreted other celestial signs also. State action could be executed only *auspicato*; to be able to interpret the indications a section must be made from existent reality, and this was done by a locality being set free and so declared (*locus liberatus et effatus*): "by the use of fixed and settled words it was detached from its environment and delimited from this" (*fando exempta*). This place, a quadrangle, was designated *templum*, and was thus in the most literal sense a "section" of the given reality in and with respect to which the "situation" was to be investigated.[2] The old formula for the king's augury, again, proves expressly that it was an affair of *fas*.[3]

Thus divination is far more than any mere satisfaction of curiosity or assurance of success. For it was impossible to take any step in life at all without knowing about the "situation", and also whether powers, and which specific powers, would be set in motion by the intended action. Many primitive people, indeed, do absolutely nothing without divination; thus the Dyaks: "When on a campaign, all the movements made by these same Dyaks depend upon omens. They cannot advance nor retreat, not attack nor change their position, until the auguries are known. I have known a chief who lived in a hut for six weeks, partly waiting for the twittering of birds to be in a proper direction, and partly detained by his followers. . . . The white man who commands the forces is supposed to have an express bird and lucky charm to guide him always; and to these the Dyaks trust considerably. 'You are our bird; we follow you,' as they say."[4] The correspondence between reality and the section made from reality, for example the starry heavens, the flight of birds or animals' entrails, is (to repeat) apparently purely arbitrary; yet it is derived from the universal idea that all things without exception are connected with each other, and

---

[1] J. Witte gives a good description in *Die ostasiatischen Kulturreligionen*, 62. *cf.* C. Clemen, *Die nichtchristlichen Kulturreligionen*, I, 1921, 44 *ff.* H. Hackmann, *Chineesche Wysgeeren*, I, 1930, 75.

[2] Wissowa, *Religion und Kultus der Römer*, 523 *ff.*   [3] Livy, I, 18, 7.

[4] Lévy-Bruhl, *How Natives Think*, 291, after Brooke.

that everything participates in everything else: the potency of one may therefore be found in the other. There is in fact no "other" in any actual sense, just as "there is no such thing as chance".[1] The entrails form a kind of microcosm, even where there are no cosmological ideas of the type of the so-called "ancient Oriental *Weltanschauung*". Thus on the Island of Talaut in the Dutch East Indies poultry and pigs are sacrificed before an *accouchement*, so that the signs may be read from the animals' entrails; if these are propitious the people rejoice, while if they are unfavourable a fresh sacrifice is made to induce the spirits to change their minds—that is to realize the "situation" better.[2] It is well known how the inspection of the liver became a sort of science in Babylon;[3] nor need I refer again to astrology, the nature of which has already been indicated.[4]

As regards divination by means of *words*, however, some further remarks are necessary. An old Tonga soothsayer in South Africa compared his own section of reality directly with the Bible; it was a systematic collection of bones, each of which had its special significance: a sheep's bone was a chief, that of a goat a subject *etc.* "You Christians believe in a Bible" said he; "our bible is better than yours: it is the bones of the oracle";[5] here, then, a system of things is opposed to one of words. Thus the word itself becomes powerful as soon as the thing has become merely a thing—in other terms, has had its power abstracted from it.[6] Special potency is ascribed to the written word; the arbitrary opening of the Bible, and the oracular interpretation of the text thus found, are well known, while in a similar way Virgil was opened in the Middle Ages (*sortes virgilianae*).[7]

But when the oracular word is of the ecstatic type it receives another kind of powerfulness. The Pythia, for example, belonged to the category of "enthusiasts";[8] originally she prophesied on the day of the god's epiphany (Apollo), and the fumes arising from the fissure in the ground, over which her tripod stood, threw her into ecstasy.[9] Other sections from reality, from which the situation could be dis-

---

[1] Lévy-Bruhl, *Primitives and the Supernatural*, 57.

[2] H. J. Stokking, *Mededeelingen vanwege het Ned. Zendelinggenootschap*, 63, 224.

[3] Jastrow, *Religion Babyloniens und Assyriens*, II, 213 *ff.*

[4] Chap. 7.   [5] Thurnwald, *loc. cit.*   [6] Chap. 3.

[7] J. Burckhardt, *Die Kultur der Renaissance in Italien*, II[12], 1919, 197. Two suspected persons resolve to fly because they have opened the *Aeneid* at III, 44:—"Ah! fly, fly the ruthless land"; *cf.* the detailed description in Rabelais, *Pantagruel*, III, 10, who remarks, however, that "I do not wish always to conclude that this fate is universally infallible, so that you may not be deceived on this point".

[8] Chap. 29.   [9] G. van der Leeuw, *Goden en Menschen*, 94 *ff.*

covered, were dreams (for example, in antiquity the dream-oracle of Trophonios[1]) and the lot.

2. So far as the word is employed in oracles, still further, it is an unintelligible expression; and whenever it was imparted in a state of rapture, as in ecstatic mantic, this was quite natural. But although the Virgilian or Biblical word, used oracularly, has in itself a comprehensible meaning, this too leads to no intelligible context; it merely ascertains the situation. No matter what method of enquiry has been utilized, then, the oracle furnishes actual intructions only through *interpretation.* The Pythia herself might rave, but her exegetes, the *hosioi* or "theologians", were sane enough:[2] or "the Sybil, with raving lips uttering things solemn, unadorned, and unembellished . . . because of the god in her":[3] nevertheless the Sybilline books played a quite rational rôle in the history of the religion of antiquity. The famous oracle of Amon too, which was revealed to Alexander in the Great Oasis, had a religious-political character; the god, who greeted the Macedonian as his own son, thereby acted as he had already done so frequently at dynastic changes in Egypt: he carried out a wholly reasonable, but at the same time religiously based, political system.[4] It can thus be understood that the oracle has had, in many cases, great cult significance, whether in the religious, the political or the ethical sphere; and in this respect the oracle is typical of the relationship between revelation and cult life.[5] Thus the Hebraic *torah* developed from oracles, the "interrogation of Jahveh", while the significance of the Delphic oracle for Greek culture can scarcely be over-estimated. Ancient lawgivers, too, invoked the oracle's sanction for their work;[6] the religious tendencies of the different eras, among others the cult of Dionysus and the worship of heroes, subsisted under the protection of Delphi;[7] no colonies were founded without questioning the oracle, which indeed almost fulfilled the functions of an emigration bureau;[8] and slaves might use the sanctuary of Apollo as a bank where they

---

[1] *cf.* the detailed description in Samter's *Religion der Griechen,* 40 *f.*

[2] Plutarch, *On the Cessation of the Oracles,* 15. Nilsson, *History of Greek Religion,* 191.

[3] Heracleitus, *Fr.* 92 (Diels). (Burnet.)

[4] G. Maspero, *Comment Alexandre devint Dieu en Egypte* (*Annuaire de l'École prat. des hautes Études,* 1897). Ed. Meyer, *Gottesstaat, Militärherrschaft und Ständewesen in Ägypten* (*Sitz. ber. der preuss. Akad. der Wiss., phil.-hist. Kl.,* 1928, 28).

[5] Chap. 85.   [6] Farnell, *Cults,* IV, 198 *f.*

[7] *ibid.,* 202 *ff.* According to Farnell, Delphi is a parallel to the Curia, which canonizes saints.   [8] *ibid.,* 200 *ff.*

could deposit their savings until they had amassed enough to purchase their liberty.[1]

On the other hand, rationalization of the investigation into the situation brought with it the danger that the inadequacy of the methods and practice might betray itself quite unmistakably. Thus Sophocles retains only Delphi and rejects the other oracles;[2] while "in the Second Punic War Marcellus was carried about in a litter with the blinds drawn in order to prevent the possibility of his seeing anything of ill omen":[3] a remarkable fusion of observance and brutal scepticism. But as is so often the case, together with scepticism subjectivation and moralization expanded: for as naïve belief declines, ethical convictions arise. In any case, the philosophers of the fourth century ascribed the same disposition to the Delphic oracle as is expressed in the parable of the widow's mite: it preferred the Arcadian's simple cereal gifts to the pompous piety of the Asiatic.[4] The story related by Herodotus about Glaucus is also famous: Glaucus had misappropriated some property confided to his charge, and desired to know from the oracle whether he should bring it into his indisputable possession by an oath. The Pythia allowed him to see that she knew all about the matter; so he regretted his question, but the Pythia replied "that it was as bad to have tempted the god as it would have been to have done the deed".[5]

[1] Farnell, *Cults*, IV, 178 f. [2] Nilsson, *History of Greek Religion*, 274.
[3] W. R. Halliday, *Lectures on the History of Roman Religion*, 145.
[4] Farnell, *Cults*, IV, 210; *cf.* R. Herzog, *Das delphische Orakel als ethischer Preisrichter*, in E. Horneffer, *Der junge Platon*, I, 1922, 149 ff.
[5] Herodotus, VI, 86 (Rawlinson); van der Leeuw, *Goden en Menschen*, 106.

CHAPTER 55

SACRED TIME

1. CELEBRATION is carried on in *time*. We moderns, of course, read time from the clock. But this is time that has already become spatialized, a "spurious concept, due to the trespassing of the idea of space upon the field of pure consciousness".[1] The spatiality of time, further, brings with it homogeneity; we count the hours and seconds —regard them, that is to say, as equivalent things. But they are neither things, nor perfectly alike: this they become only in space.[2] Homogeneous time thus measured in hours, days and years, therefore, is only a symbol of real time, of "duration":[3] but in duration itself every moment has its own unique value. On the dial the minutes all look alike; but in duration each possesses its own significance, exactly as in a melody each note has a distinct value.[4] Similarly we describe a circle as a straight line with infinitely many angles; but actually it is a curve, that is each point overflows into the adjacent point; there are no angles whatever, and no one has as yet solved the squaring of the circle.[5]

A time is therefore always some definite time, at first the given, and then the best time, the time of the due situation, *kairos*, the time of grace. For this reason we deal here with "sacred time". The year of the primitive community, for example, is by no means a year like that on an office calendar. It has value: it is a "year of salvation" that brings with it life. Similarly the ancient Greek *horai* (seasons) and *eniautos* (year) appear to ourselves as rather abstract entities; but to the Greeks "their virtue, their very being, was in the flowers and fruits they always carry in their hands".[6] Thus the year brings fruit and is indissolubly linked with the saviour.[7] But in the year, again, each season has some specific value. Spring brings salvation, while Winter withdraws it: Spring is the god's epiphany, Summer his sojourn or *epidemia*, and Winter his departure, *apodemia*; and within the seasons,

---

[1] Bergson, *Time and Free Will*, 98.
[2] Nietzsche, *Human, All Too Human*, 33, 34 (Foulis Edition).
[3] Bergson, *ibid.*, 90, 91, 115.   [4] *ibid.*, 98 *ff.*
[5] *cf.* K. Heim, *Glaubensgewissheit*[2], 81, 70.   [6] Harrison, *Themis*, 185.
[7] Chap. 11, 12.

too, days and hours have individual significance: they are either
favourable or unfavourable.

This specific value of times, still further, distinguishes duration
from dreamless sleep. Certainly the mythical consciousness[1] tends to
allow time "to stand still"; this means however not that the clock
stands still, but that every "when" has become a matter of sheer
indifference. It is in this timelessness that *fairy tales* subsist: in an
eternal present, or "in those days", or "once upon a time". In the
sleeping beauty's castle all movement has ceased; the cook stands
quite still with his hand raised to give the pantry boy a cuff on the
ear, but he will strike only when the charm has been broken.[2] This
cessation of duration acquires the religious designation of *eternity*:[3]
Beatrice sees God

> where all time and place
> Are present.[4]

But while celebration certainly has this background of eternity, it
is itself a part of the time movement; it is at the same moment, however, the deed of man, who stands stationary in the midst of time
because he finds the "situation", and who therefore does not simply
surrender to duration but firmly plants his feet, and for one moment
concentrates both himself and time. He who is celebrating, so to say,
controls time; he attempts to dominate it. For here also he cannot
simply accept the given: he is first startled and then becomes alarmed;
"temporality reveals itself as the significance of actual care".[5] Duration,
then, is the great stream flowing relentlessly on: but man, encountering
Power, must halt. He then makes a section, a *tempus*; and he celebrates
a "sacred time", a festival. In this manner he shows that he declines
the given as such, and seeks possibility.[6]

But in so doing, periodicity is assigned to time; duration unfolds
and rolls on from section to section, and at the halting places Power
manifests itself. They are the beginning and the end, and this in fact
in the Greek pre-Socratic sense of the word ἀρχή, half beginning and
half being.[7] All time passes in periods. A grey mannikin implores a
woman in childbed to go with him, but she cannot; the mannikin

---

[1] Chap. 82.
[2] Chap. 60; *cf.* G. van der Leeuw, *Tyd en Eeuwigheid (Onze Eeuw,* 1922).
[3] Chap. 87.
[4] Dante, *Paradiso,* XXIX, 12 (Cary): *dove s'appunta ogni ubi ed ogni quando.*
[5] Heidegger, *op. cit.,* 326.
[6] For the cultural "distinction" of incisions in Time *cf.* Cassirer, *Philosophie der Symbolischen Formen,* II, 138.   [7] *cf.* Cassirer, *op. cit.,* 4.

departs weeping: "now I must travel on for another hundred years until I find another suitable person".[1] The *motif* of the battle that renews itself nightly is also very well known, among other sources from the saga of Hilde and Gudrun:[2] "mythical eternities are periodic";[3] even eschatology, with its millennial reigns and other periods, cannot escape this.[4] But the *tempus*, the section within the course of time, is never the figure upon the clock: it indicates the critical point which, marked out by celebration, clearly reveals the potency of duration.

2. Thus arose the calendar: not, however, the calendar hanging in an office, but the festival and holiday calendar; not the "civil", but the ecclesiastical year; not the time measurer, but the significance of salvation appearing in time; and "a calendar expresses the rhythm of the collective activities (read: of powerfulness) while at the same time its function is to assure their regularity".[5] Thus the ancient Roman calendar was proclaimed by the *pontifices* at the new moons (*kalendae*), and then by the *rex sacrorum* upon the first quarter, the *nones*; by this method it was possible to keep informed about the "days on which it was lawful, or unlawful, to transact secular business", *dies fasti* and *nefasti*.[6] The calendar, then, indicates clearly which instants of time have value and possess power[7]; each period, each instant, has specific individuality and its own potency.[8] This powerfulness, however, does not persist of its own accord; it must be assisted by celebrations; and thus we can understand what at first sight appears very strange to us in primitive modes of thought:—that time, whose continuance we regard as inexorable and self-evident, does not persist "of itself". It has power, and to this power something must happen: it is not "accepted"; and the calendar interferes, naturally at those situations where power reveals itself. Thus among the ancient Mexicans affairs were arranged according to the renewal of the fires: "the Aztecs spoke of periods of fifty-two years, on whose expiration all the fires were extinguished and kindled anew by boring—the bundles of years"; and on the occasion of a great migration the Mexicans

---

[1] Tobler, *Epiphanie der Seele*, 65.

[2] *cf*. Fr. Panzer, *Hilde-Gudrun*, 1901, 328 *f*., with parallel cases.

[3] Hubert-Mauss, *op. cit.*, 196.   [4] Chap. 87.

[5] Durkheim, *The Elementary Forms of the Religious Life*, 11.

[6] Halliday, *History of Roman Religion*, 43. The Chinese use the paper calendar, or some of its leaves, as amulets, pills of calendar paper being rolled, for use against fever. Clemen, *Die nichtchristl. Rel.*, I, 44.   [7] *cf*. Hubert-Mauss, *op. cit.*, 226 *f*.

[8] Only thus can the personification of periods and seasons be understood: *Horai, Year, Fair, etc.*; *cf*. Hubert-Mauss, *op. cit.*, 200. W. Liungman, *Actes Ve Congrès*, 108 *ff*.

bored fires "in order to express figuratively in this way that their years in Chapultepec had been linked with the past years, for they had been unable to bore fires anew since they had been surrounded by their enemies".[1] Elsewhere, for example in ancient Rome, the calendar commenced with the agricultural season; in Rome, also, the sacred fire was renewed on March 1.[2] The part played by the rising of the stars, again, and above all by that of the moon, is sufficiently well known, the moon's phases being paralleled by feminine periods, so that the celestial potency accords with that of the earth; and "many astronomical-cosmic periods entered into consciousness first of all as the symbolic expression of the corresponding human periods".[3]

The advent of salvation, however, is pre-eminently the *tempus*. The Christian ecclesiastical year is as it were a repetition of the divine life; it is time filled with value, commencing with Advent. But it not merely signifies salvation: it renews it also; liturgical time, moreover, is always the same, filled with salvation. It is, so to say, a "succession of eternities".[4] The day is the symbol of the week, this of the year, and the year of the world-period; the same salvation occurs in each temporal unit, the Babylonian new year festival being the "annual repetition of the unique, primal and universal new year celebration".[5] In the hourly watches of the Egyptian Osiris mysteries, again, the god's life, suffering and death were represented anew each hour; but their totality simultaneously presented the passion of the god.[6] Similarly, at Michaelmas, the Nordic peasant observes each hour of the day from six in the morning till six in the evening, the weather of each hour indicating that of each of the coming months.[7]

H. BERGSON, *Time and Free Will.*

E. CASSIRER, *Philosophie der symbolischen Formen*, II, *Das mythische Denken*, 1925 (Eng. tr., *The Philosophy of Symbolic Forms*, Vol. II, 1955).

JANE E. HARRISON, *Themis*, 1912.

E. PRZYBYLLOK, *Unser Kalender in Vergangenheit und Zukunft* (*Morgenland*, 22), 1930.

P. SAINTYVES, *Les notions de temps et d'éternité dans la magie et la religion* (*RHR.* 79, 1919.)

---

[1] W. Krickeberg, *Märchen der Azteken und Inkaperuaner*, 1928, 351, 100.

[2] Fowler, *Roman Festivals*, 5; Ovid, *Fasti*, III, 137 *ff.*

[3] Th. W. Danzel, *Kultur und Religion des primitiven Menschen*, 1924, 40 *f.*

[4] Hubert-Mauss, *op. cit.*, 206.

[5] H. Zimmern, *Das babylonische Neujahrsfest*, 1926, 9.

[6] H. Junker, *Die Stundenwachen in den Osirismysterien* (*Denkschr. der kais. Akademie in Wien*, LIV, 1910).   [7] Reinsberg-Düringsfeld, *Das festl. Jahr*, 331 *f.*

CHAPTER 56

FESTIVALS

1. THE festival is the *tempus par excellence*, "selected" from the entirety of duration as particularly potent. In itself any time whatever may be chosen to be a festival period, since every one has its own value and specific powerfulness; and in this sense Guardini very finely observes[1] that "every hour of the day has its own note. But there are three that confront us with unusually clear features: morning, evening, and between the two the mid-day hour; and these are all sacred." Morning is a beginning: "the secret of birth renews itself every morning". The mystery of evening, again, is death, while mid-day is the moment, the pure present: "thou standest still, and all time is swallowed up. Eternity contemplates thee. In all the hours eternity speaks, but it is the intimate neighbour of mid-day. There time waits and discloses itself." Day-time and night-time, therefore, have different values; the Romans executed all public duties only between sunrise and sunset, while the Greeks sacrificed both by day and night; but the nightly sacrifice was offered to those powers that walk at night, the sinister and mystic gods, the νυκτιπόλοι.[2] Time may be selected also from the mythical past: some actual event may then be linked with a time which once proved itself potent in the most remote of bygone eras; thus the Egyptian sacred *Texts* often refer to "that day" on which some mythical happening or other occurred.[3] The powerfulness of this mythical "day" extends to the present; thus the Lord's resurrection is renewed each Easter day, then every Sunday and ultimately every morning.

The fixation of the time to be selected is therefore a most important affair, connected in many religions with divination as the choice of days.[4] The selected time is either dangerous or beneficent, *nefastus* or *fastus*; and sacred time is *tremenda*, or *fascinans*, or both. The Sabbath was a day of tabu on which work was forbidden, but it was also a day

---

[1] *Von heiligen Zeichen*, 78 ff.

[2] M. P. Nilsson, *Die Entstehung und religiöse Bedeutung des griechischen Kalenders* (*Lunds Universitets Aarsskrift*, N. F., Avd. 1, 14, 21), 1918, 17 ff.

[3] One of many examples:—the dead should protect the god "as the Father Nun protected those four goddesses *on the day*, when they defended the throne" (an obscure myth); *Pyramidentexte* (Sethe), 606.   [4] Chap. 54.

of recreation and rest; and post-exilic observance, while intensifying
the severity of the ban on labour, also enhanced the sweetness of
repose, as is clear from the fine tradition that on the Sabbath even
the damned in hell enjoy a respite from their torments.[1] Christmas
again, originally not itself a festival but a festival period, and subsequently the Twelve Nights, are symbolical of what the year will
bring. It is a sinister time during which spooks rove about, but it is
also the beautiful period in which the light increases: *crescit lux*![2] The
Greek *anthesteria* too was a festival of blossoming, but was likewise a
kind of All Souls; spirits were abroad and the days were μιαραί:—
polluted, contagious, perilous.[3]

In its own proper nature the calendar, then, is a festal calendar,
designating Sundays and holidays. This it was already in the most
ancient days in Egypt, when a whole series of festivals was indicated
on the Palermo Stone;[4] this it was, too, in Greece and Rome.[5] But
our own farmers' calendar is also a festival calendar which "selects"
the sacred time, for sowing and threshing, for work and holiday.[6]
Among primitives choice of days extends still further into details;
"it is not enough to have favourable omens; it is essential that the
month, day, and hour on which an enterprise is begun shall be
auspicious or 'record' days. We know that the primitive mind does
not 'sense' the successive moments of time as homogeneous. Certain
periods of the day or night, of the moon's phases, of the year, and so
on, are able to exert a favourable or a malignant influence." Similarly
for the Dyaks "every day has five 'times', which are fixed for the first
day (Sunday) only, and for the others there must be recourse to
divination".[7] In its own way the Christian cult also places definite
times of night and day in relationship to Power, and as it were distributes the event of salvation over *horae canonicae* and over the days of
the week. Thus the Lord's day is that of resurrection: Friday of pre-

---

[1] Bin Gorion, *Der Born Judas*, VI, 294. When the Eskimo "were told by their first
missionaries that they must abstain from all work on the Lord's Day . . . they were
amazed, but now they felt that they had obtained an explanation of many misfortunes,
the cause of which they had never been able to discover" (Lévy-Bruhl, *Primitives and
the Supernatural*, 50). They had simply not "selected" the appropriate time!

[2] A. Meyer, *Das Weihnachtsfest*, 1913. H. Usener, *Das Weihnachtsfest*, 1², 1911.

[3] Farnell, *Cults*, V, 216 *ff.*; "the tabooed days".

[4] Breasted, *Ancient Records*, 1, 90 *ff.*

[5] Fowler, *Roman Festivals*. Ovid, *Fasti*. M. P. Nilsson, *Griechische Feste*, 1906; *id.
Kalender*.

[6] Nilsson, *Volkstümliche Feste*; Reinsberg-Düringsfeld, *Festl. Jahr; cf.* further
examples: Reinsberg-Düringsfeld, *Calendrier belge*, 1861 *f.* Heuvel, *Oud-achterhoeksch
Boerleven*.   [7] Lévy-Bruhl, *Primitives and the Supernatural*, 48, 49.

paration on which we should fast *etc.* The cock announces day and
new life: Christ banishes sleep and ancient guilt:

> The bird that heraldeth the day
> Foretells the sunbeam drawing nigh.
> Now Christ arouseth us that lay
> Torpid, to life beneath His eye.
>
> Come, break the spell of sluggish night.
> Sunder, O Christ, her iron chain!
> Come, showering down Thy healing light,
> And purge our nature's ancient stain.[1]

2. Holidays and festivals fall within a *festal cycle*; but this is no
affair of merely secondary importance, since it is in their nature to
continue, to carry onward.[2] They represent the critical points: not the
point only, however, but the celebration also that carries us beyond
the difficult stage. Festivals therefore are not merely recreational; on
the contrary, primitive peoples regard them as affairs of duty and of
useful work, since without them the powerfulness of life would be
brought into stagnation. To the South American Uitoto the purpose
of the festival is more important than the festal joy; "we dance only
because of the sacred words", they say; "we do not dance without
a reason";[3] and in the ideas of country folk with regard to
the fair this opinion still predominates; "it is the pastor's duty to
warn us against the fair", says a Gelderland farmer of the Netherlands,
"just as much as it is our duty to attend it".[4] The Christian calendar
again, which no longer produces natural "fruits", is intended to arouse
grace in the hearts of the faithful and nourish spiritual life.[5]

---

[1] *Hymnus matutinus:* Aurelius Prudentius Clemens.

> *Ales diei nuntius*
> *Lucem proprinquam praecinit;*
> *Nos excitator mentium*
> *Iam Christus ad vitam vocat.*
> *Tu Christe, somnum discute;*
> *Tu rumpe noctis vincula,*
> *Tu solve peccatum vetus,*
> *Novumque lumen ingere.*

[2] Thus it runs in the *Oxyr. Hymn to Isis*, that she institutes Isaea everywhere, and:
πασιν τὰ νόμιμα καὶ ἐνιαν τὸντέλιον παρέδωκας, *cf.* N. Turchi, *Fontes historiae mysteriorum*, 1930. B. van Groningen, *De papyro oxyrhinchita* 1380, 1921, 56.

[3] K. Th. Preuss, *Religion und Mythologie der Uitoto*, I, 1921, 123.

[4] Heuvel, *ibid.*, 322.   [5] Saintyves, *Notions de temps*, 94.

In the cycle, then, the festival becomes as it were a microcosm of the whole of time; for the Jews the new year was the period of judgment and the apportioning of fate, while the end of the year was the day of Jahveh. Each new year is therefore a turning-point of destiny, and each year an abbreviated world-history;[1] while in the Christian calendar every day is a *feria*,[2] and thus the idea of the festival becomes extended without any limit; as sacred, Time is as it were rendered eternal at every instant. Thus there arises the desire to superimpose longer periods on the festal cycle, and such "great years" make the notch after the lengthier eras. The ancient Egyptian feast of Sed has already been referred to in connection with the figure of the king,[3] and in Greece there were ennaeteric and trieteric periods, the festivals occurring every nine, and every three, years respectively, and in Israel a "sabbatical year" every fifty years; in Mexico, similarly, a fifty-two year period, while the Roman *lustrum* has been discussed previously, to which should now be added the *saeculum*, probably originally the time for sowing, subsequently the generation, and ultimately the age. But this "age" was "begun" at definite times; man did not simply wait for it, but brought it about and commenced a new era; originally, the old *saeculum* was buried (*saeculum condere*). Here also man selects the time and refuses simply to accept duration.[4] Particularly after a period of struggle and exhaustion is the necessity of making a fresh start experienced;[5] of this Augustus gave a magnificent example when, in the year 17, he inaugurated a new era by a secular festival: "Pheobus, and Diana mistress of the woods, ye that are the shining beauty of the sky, ye that are ever adorable and adored, grant the blessings we pray for at a hallowed season."[6]

3. Finally, festivals acquire a wholly different significance as soon as the power arrested in and by them becomes one that announces itself historically. One of the most important dates in the history of religion, therefore, was the transposition of the Israelite Nature festivals into *commemorationes* of historical dates, which were simultaneously manifestations of power and deeds of God, so that when the ancient moon and Spring festival of the *Passah*, which was connected with

---

[1] P. Volz, *Das Neujahrsfest Jahves*, 1912, 15 *ff.*
[2] H. A. Köstlin, *Geschichte des christlichen Gottesdienstes*, 1887, 43, 108.
[3] Chap. 13.
[4] Fowler, *The Religious Experience of the Roman People*, 440 *f.* E. Norden, *Aeneis, Buch VI*², 1916, 324. On the "great year" *cf* Chantepie, *op. cit.*, 1¹, 120 *f.*
[5] Thus in the year of peril, 249.   [6] Horace, *Carmen saeculare.*

tabus, was transformed into the festival of God's redemptive deed in the exodus from Egypt, something completely new was inaugurated. The notch in time is then no longer repeatable at will; duration is no longer entirely swallowed up in the festal cycle: God Himself makes the notch once for all: He arrests time and transforms the mere given into a promise.

O. von Reinsberg-Düringsfeld, *Das festliche Jahr*², 1898.
Karl Kerenyi, "Vom Wesens des Festes" (*Paideuma*, I, 1938, 59 *ff.*).
M. P. Nilsson, *Die volkstümlichen Feste des Jahres*, 1914.

CHAPTER 57

SACRED SPACE

1. WHAT is true of time is equally true of space. It is no homogeneous mass, nor a sum of innumerable spatial parts; but just as duration subsists in relation to time, so does *extensity* (*étendue*) to space.[1] Even to the animal, indeed, a locality is not some arbitrary point in space, but a resting-place in universal extensity, a "position" which it recognizes and towards which it directs itself. Parts of space, therefore, like instants of time, have their specific and independent value.[2] They are "positions"; but they become "positions" by being "selected" from the vast extensity of the world. A part of space, then, is not a "part" at all but a place, and the place becomes a "position" when man occupies it and stands on it. He has thus recognized the power of the locality, he seeks it or avoids it, attempts to strengthen or enfeeble it; but in any case he selects the place as a "position". Some *locus* becomes set free and declared so:—*liberatus et effatus*;[3] power resides within it. Thus a sanctuary in Minahassa in Celebes, consisting of sacred stones, under which planks have been buried that are supposed to represent the birds' notes heard at the foundation of the village, together with some captured human heads, is called "the salvation and strength of the village".[4]

Sacred space may also be defined as that locality that becomes a position by the effects of power repeating themselves there, or being repeated by man. It is the place of worship, independently of whether the position is only a house, or a temple, since domestic life too is a celebration constantly repeated in the regulated cycle of work, meals, washing *etc.* Thus we can understand why man clings with such obstinate tenacity to the positions he has once adopted; and a sacred position remains holy even when it has been long neglected. In the course of excavating pre-historic settlements in Drente, in the Netherlands, it was discovered that sites for cremation had been placed in the hollows of the wooden posts of still more ancient shrines. The consciousness of the sacred character of the locality that has once been chosen is, therefore, always retained.[5] And this also is the reason

---

[1] *Time and Free Will*, 97.   [2] Cassirer, *op. cit.*, II, 112 *ff.*
[3] Chap. 54.   [4] Adriani, *Animistisch Heidendom*, 33 *f.*
[5] *cf.* A. E. van Giffen, *Drentsche Volksalmanak*, 50, 1932, 61 *ff.*

why, during its expansion, Christianity has sought its sacred places preferably in localities adopted by the older cults.[1]

2. The place thus selected, because it has shown itself to be sacred, is at first merely a position: man adds nothing at all to Nature; the mysterious situation of a locality, its awe-inspiring character, suffice. It is the place of dread awe, which deeply impresses man: *religio dira loci*:

> Its dread awe made quake
> E'en then the fearful rustics; ay, e'en then
> They shuddered at the forest and the rock.[2]

In fact it is principally forests and caverns, rocks and mountains, that have been chosen as holy.[3] The Roman *lucus* was a grove in which cult activities were carried on: "Under the Aventine there lay a grove black with the shade of holm-oaks; at sight of it you could say 'There is a *numen* here'."[4] Even to-day we remain conscious that the gloomy forest has a numinous character, although to a great extent we have destroyed primitive man's dread of the seat of the powers by our romantic twilight moods. Nevertheless the sacred grove arouses its shiver of fear as well as of ecstasy: "If ever you have come upon a grove (*lucus*) that is full of ancient trees, which have grown to an unusual height, shutting out a view of the sky by a veil of pleached and intertwining branches, then the loftiness of the forest, the seclusion of the spot, and your marvel at the thick unbroken shade in the midst of the open spaces, will prove to you the presence of deity (*fidem tibi numinis faciet*). Or if a cave, made by the deep crumbling of the rocks, holds up a mountain on its arch, a place not built with hands but hollowed out into such spaciousness by natural causes, your soul will be deeply moved by an inkling, a presage, of the divine; (*animum tuum quadam religionis suspicione percutiet*). We worship the sources of mighty rivers; we erect altars at places where great streams burst suddenly from hidden sources; we adore springs of hot water as divine, and consecrate certain pools because of their dark waters or their immeasurable depth."[5] But such a direct experience of the

---

[1] Chambers, *Mediaeval Stage*, I, 95 *f*.; *cf*. Chap. 17 also.
[2] Virgil, *Aeneid*, VIII, 349 *f*. (Rhoades).
[3] Chap. 5; *cf*. among others S. Wide, *Lakonische Kulte*, 1893, 40 *f*. O. Kern, *Die Religion der Griechen*, I, 1926, 77.
[4] Ovid, *Fasti*, III, 295 *f*. (Modified from Frazer).
[5] Seneca, *Epistle* XLI, 3 (Gummere).

presence of the power, and subsequently of the deity, in a locality—an experience which has gained its finest poetic expression in Plato's *Phaedrus*—is possible only in a world which man has not yet reduced to an inanimate thing and deprived of all its power.

Thus the natural shrine is probably the oldest known to man. But side by side with this there soon appeared artificial sanctuaries; for power, man erects a dwelling. But frequently what has been built and what has simply been given, the erection and the grove, remain associated together; and until a late period a sacred grove with a holy tree and spring were found in Uppsala, together with a temple and three statues.[1] In the architecture of places of worship, too, there is much that still reminds us of the wood or the holy mountain: pillars derived from trees or plants: the tower form of the Babylonian *zikkurat*.[2] But the sacredness of the place, that is its character of "selectivity", continues unchanged. In infinite space a "sanctuary" arises; and it is no marvel that this "sanctuary" is such in the sense of a "refuge" also. This in fact applies to even the most primitive shrines; Australian *churinga*,[3] for example, are kept in a small cavern (*arknanaua*) in some lonely spot; the place may not be entered by the uninitiated and the admission of women and children is prohibited under pain of death. The environment of the sanctuary is also inviolable, all strife being forbidden there, while from such a place no wounded animal is ever taken away, and one that has sought refuge there is pursued no farther; even plants growing in the vicinity remain untouched.[4] This idea of refuge is widespread, and has obtained its poetic form in Wagner's *Parsifal*: the precinct of the castle of the Holy Grail is a sanctuary: "Thou couldest murder, here in holy forest, where quiet peace did thee enfold?" asks Gurnemanz of the simple fellow who has slain the swan.[5]

3. House and temple, still further, are essentially one: both can stand firm only in virtue of the power residing within them. The house is an organic unity, whose essence is some definite power, just

---

[1] Ax. Olrik, *Nordisches Geistesleben*[2], 1925, 34.

[2] Th. Dombart, *Der babylonische Turm*, 1930.   [3] Chap. 3.

[4] Söderblom, *Gottesglaube*, 34 *ff*. B. Spencer and F. Gillen, *The Native Tribes of Central Australia*, 133 *ff*. J. Wanninger, *Das Heilige in der Religion der Australier*, 1927, 42 *ff*. Strehlow-Leonhardi, *Die Aranda- und Loritjastämme*, II, 1908, 78. In South Boni (Indonesia), in earlier days, the desert limestone mountain chain Lamontjong was a place of refuge for even the gravest offences such as incest *etc. cf.* J. P. Kleiweg de Zwaan, *Het Asylrecht by overspel in den Indischen Archipel* (*Tydschr. Ned. Aardr. Gen.*, 2. R., 48, 1931, 37 *ff*.).   [5] *Parsifal*, Act I.

as much as is the temple or church. But it is probably difficult for us, semi-americanized as we already are, living in flats and having what we need brought into the house, to form any idea of its unitary power as this is still experienced to some degree in isolated farmhouses, and which not very long ago was an unquestioned reality. For the house with its own fire, which must produce its own means of life, manufacture its own clothing, hew its own wood and have its own well, is a world in itself.[1] And we who purchase the objects we require when we want them, and buy furniture in this or that style, perhaps know only very little about the community of essence between all the parts of the house and its inhabitants, of that participation which fits each member of the domestic group into the same structure, whether it is a so-called "thing", an animal or a human being. In an Irish fairy tale a woman "enchants" every object in her household to prevent the entrance of evil spirits so that the key, the tongs, the axe, *etc.*, cannot move and therefore cannot open the way for the spirits; over the water in the foot-bath alone she has no power, because it does not belong to the household; and for this reason she pours it away before closing the door.[2]

But within the house, again, the power is distributed over the various parts, each of which has its own sacredness. Of this the Roman house is typical; but a similar state of affairs occurs all over the world. First of all the door is there to separate the space inside the house from the power existing outside, the door that protects and constitutes the transition from the secular to the consecrated enclosure; and in Rome the entrance became Janus, the god who was invoked first during prayer.[3] The *threshold* too was the sacred boundary possessing its own special power, and in Palestine to-day a mother may neither chastise nor suckle her child on the threshold; a child who has been punished there may become seriously ill, so that on the threshold one must neither sit nor work *etc.*[4] In Indonesia the main post of the house is regarded as most holy and is erected with sacrifice and ceremony. For the house shelters power: there are the "gods", "gods of the treasure-house within";[5] at the door,[6] or inside the house, are the domestic deities. Once again the classical example is provided by the

---

[1] For a not so distant past it is very finely described in Selma Lagerlöf's novels.

[2] Käte Müller-Lisowski, *Irische Volksmärchen*, No. 30: *Der Berg der lichten Frauen.*

[3] Ovid, *Fasti*, I. Cicero, *De Natura Deorum*, II, 67.

[4] Canaan, *Dämonenglaube im Lande der Bibel*, 37; further examples in E. Samter, *Familienfeste der Griechen und Römer*, 1901.

[5] Aeschylus, *Choëphoroe*, 800 (Murray).   [6] Sophocles, *Electra*, 1373 *ff.*

Roman *penates*, the gods of the *penus* or larder. No unclean person might touch the *penus*; its management was one of the duties of the —pure—children of the household.[1] In a different sense from what he intended, therefore, the malicious Christian apologist of later days was correct when he regarded the *penates* as the gods of those people "who think that life is nothing but licence to feed and to drink".[2] The possibility of eating and drinking is experienced precisely as a divine possibility, and its position estimated as holy. This is also the basis of the sacredness of that most important spot of all in the house, the hearth:[3] it is its central point, the totality of its power. An old Gelderland farmer's son thus relates an incident of his childhood: "When the pot had been taken off the fire, we often set the hook swinging; 'you mustn't do that', said our John, 'or our dear Lord will get a headache'. To us this seemed profane. But we did not know that, since ancient times, the hook has been the sacred position in the house, around which the bride was led and which was seized to take possession of the house."[4] The hook is a sanctuary also: a new labourer has water poured over him, and so he slips into the house by the side door and lays hold of the hook, and then he must no longer be teased.[5] Even to-day the common people have preserved some of the correct feeling that the power of the house accumulates in the kitchen, on the hearth: the "best parlour" usually remains empty! The round Roman temple of Vesta, again, was nothing more than the old round house or tent which had the fire-place in the middle, and models of these pre-historic dwellings have been found in the *Forum Romanum*, as urns for the ashes of the dead.[6]

The house, however, need not be the family dwelling-place: it may also serve as the residence for the whole tribe, as was the case quite recently in Scandinavia,[7] or it may be the power-position of an entire section of the tribe, like the men's houses.[8] But whatever it may be, and in whatever form the sacredness of the place may be "common", its holiness gives it prominence as against the surrounding entirety of space. Hence also the relationship between the sacred place and the whole Universe: the shrine is a centre of power, a world in itself. For the dedication of the Israelitish temple, as for the consecration

---

[1] Fowler, *Religious Experience*, 73 ff; *Roman Festivals*, 213 f., 150, Note 1. Cicero, *De Natura Deorum*, II, 68.

[2] Firmicus Maternus, *De errore profanarum religionum*, 14: *nihil aliud putant esse vitam, nisi viscendi et potandi licentiam.*

[3] Chap. 6. [4] Heuvel, *op. cit.*, 16 f. [5] *ibid.*, 152.
[6] Halliday, *Roman Religion*, 25. [7] Olrik, *op. cit.*, 17. [8] Chap. 33, 34.

of a Christian church, the chanting of *Psalm XXIV* is prescribed; and it has a truly cosmic character. At the dedication of a Babylonian temple, similarly, creation hymns were sung, while in the Egyptian *pr duat*, the "House of the Morning", the rebirth of the sun was cele- brated every day. Actually, indeed, the sanctuary exists not in this world at all, since it has been "selected";[1] and this cosmic significance of the sacred places was still haunting the mind of the bailiff in Eastern Holland when he feared that the swinging of the hook would give the dear Lord a headache.

House and temple, therefore, are one: both are the "House of God". Hearth and altar are also one, the temple-altar being the table and the fire-place of the gods.[2] As soon, however, as the locality is no longer simply provided "by Nature" as the "position", but must first be designated by man, the need of discovering the proper place becomes very evident. In other words, before building is begun it must be quite definitely ascertained whether the place selected is suitable for the "position". This really means that we *cannot* make shrines and *cannot* select their "positions", but can never do more than merely "find" them; and the art of discovering them is called *Orientation*. "The supernatural space, the sacred, is ordered. It is founded upon mystery".[3] The term "orientation" is derived from the custom of building in the direction from West to East, towards the sun; the altar end of the church should indicate the position where the sun rose when the church was founded.[4] Temple building was regulated by other heavenly bodies also: for example, in Egypt according to the rising, or so-called birth, of Sirius.[5]

But if the house becomes a mere place of residence, and the temple an oratory or meeting-place, then the "positions" gradually lose their cosmic-sacred character. They become merely places to stay in and talk, and it is no longer believed that anything really happens there; the extreme stage of this development is constituted by the buildings devoted to preaching of some Protestant communities. This change, certainly, is by no means linked to any one definite stage of the process: when Judaism and Christianity had already converted

[1] A. J. Wensinck, "The Semitic New Year"; *Acta Orientalia*, I, 181. A. M. Black- man, "The House of the Morning", *Jour. Egyptian Archeology*, 5, 1918.
[2] The altar is also a grave (even to-day every Roman Catholic altar has an altar- reliquary); originally, the dead remained in the house, or were buried by the hearth.
[3] Guardini, *Von heiligen Zeichen*, 72.
[4] H. Nissen, *Orientation*, I, 7 (1906–1907).
[5] *ibid.*, I, 36.

their synagogue and basilica into a place of prayer the Christian church arose as a sacred position and a House of God.

4. Not house and temple alone, however, but the *settlement* in general, the village, the town, is a "selected", sacred position; man forms his settlement and thus converts the discovered possibility into new powerfulness. His settlement then stands out from the surrounding extent of space: his tilled land from the uncultivated forest and desolate heath; and the enclosures he thus lays out play the part of the house door, separating the secure sphere of the human dwelling from the "uncanny" realm of demonic powers.[1] The old feeling for the sacredness of the cultivated area, the settlement, is very finely depicted in the legend of the giant's playthings: at her father's command, the giant's daughter returns the husbandman whom, with his oxen and plough, she had packed into her apron, to his own locality, since if the peasant in the valley does not work the giant in the mountains has nothing to eat! For the settlement is always a conquest, a selection.[2] Originally the *lares*, the Roman household gods associated with the *penates*, were probably the powers of the forest clearing, and subsequently the dominant powers in the house built within the cleared ground.[3] Agriculture and the foundation of cities, in fact, went on hand in hand, and in Rome the practice of marking out the line of the walls with the plough, *moenia signare aratro*, was not forgotten.[4] Thus the *pomoerium*, the town's "spiritual frontier", was a furrow, and at its founding, wherever it was intended to erect a gate, the plough was lifted and a tract left unhallowed.[5] Within this *sulcus primigenius*, then, lay the town; but its founding likewise was no chance affair: the "situation" had to be thoroughly investigated, and for this the art of *limitation* was employed which originated from the most primitive, yet at the same time most important, method of orientation man possesses—that is the distinction between right and left.[6] Then the *decumanus*, the main East to West road, was oriented by sunrise, intersected by the North-South road or *cardo*, and thus the ground plan of the town was determined. These *limites*

[1] Grönbech, *op. cit.*, II, 10; *cf.* Wilamowitz-Möllendorff, *Griech. Trag.* II, 224 *f.* Hence Ares remained on the Areopagus in Athens, and Mars *extra pomoerium* in Rome.   [2] Cassirer, *op. cit.*, II, 120 *ff.*
[3] Only thus can the dual character of the *lares*, as gods of the field and of the house, be understood; *cf.* Halliday, *Roman Religion*, 28 *f.* E. Samter, *Der Ursprung des Larenkults*, *AR*. 10, 1907.   [4] Ovid, *Fasti*, IV, 819, 825.
[5] Deubner, in Chantepie, *op. cit.*, II, 428. Halliday, *ibid.*, 65. I. B. Carter, *The Religion of Numa*, 33 *ff.*   [6] Chap. 23. Cassirer, *op. cit.*, II, 119.

stood in immediate relation to the world-order, the town being in this way divided into four, as the world was too;[1] and thus each settlement constituted a world in itself, a sacred whole.[2] The sanctity of boundary stones and their immovability (in Rome *termini*, in Babylon *kudurru*) are universally known, and persisted indeed until quite recent times; in Egypt a boundary stone was set as firm "as the heavens" and based on the whole Universe.[3] Even the earth, therefore, is neither everywhere nor in itself "well founded and enduring"; first of all it is necessary to have made sure of the "situation" and to have selected the suitable place for the "position".

The various legends about the origins of cities are derived from precisely the same necessity. Animals were allowed to roam freely until they lay down in some place or other *etc.*: an origin was thus demanded in what is indubitably powerful. For it was no affair of establishing a mere place of sojourn, but of the foundation of a position where power resided. The god dwelt in the town just as he did in the temple, and whenever they wished to conquer a city the Romans attempted to "evoke" him by adjuration. The god might also forsake the city: this he does in the beautiful Jewish legend of the Jerusalem Gate of Compassion. In leaving the town, the divine majesty strode through this gate, and through it will hereafter return.[4] Jerusalem is, in fact, the city in which the idea of the sacred place appears as it were in its typical form; it was regarded as the world's central point. "In Jerusalem all the winds in the world blow. Before it executes its mission, every wind comes into the holy city to make obeisance here before the Lord".[5] And when the new world rises before the eyes of the faithful, once more it is the vision of the holy city, the new Jerusalem. On the completion of the final conditions, however, the distinction between city and temple again disappears, and in the new world the primitive sacred place is once more present: for in the new Jerusalem no temple whatever is required, because the Lord Himself is its temple.[6]

5. In the holy place, still further, power exists: there its effects become perceptible. What once occurred is repeated at the sacred

---

[1] The oldest ground-plan of the Egyptian city, also, shows this form: ⊕

[2] Nissen, *op. cit.*, I, 79 *ff.*, 90 *ff.* Usener, *Götternamen*, 190 *ff.*

[3] Grave at Beni Hassan; A. Erman, *Ägyptische Chrestomathie*, 1909, 113; *cf.* E. Samter, *Die Entwicklung des Terminuskults*, *AR.* 16, 1913.

[4] Bin Gorion, *Born Judas*, V, 282.

[5] *ibid.*   [6] *Rev.* xxi.

spot: at the altar, for example, Christ's death is reiterated.[1] In the Egyptian temple, similarly, the foundation of the world was renewed at a place erected for that very purpose, the "primeval hill" on which the sun for the first time appeared in the ancient days;[2] and the Babylonian temple tower was an image or model of the world.[3] It is not to be wondered at, therefore, that from time immemorial men have undertaken pilgrimages to places recognized as holy, where the Power of the Universe renewed itself daily, and where the heart of the world could be approached. In a certain sense, indeed, every entry into the temple, every appearance in church, is a *pilgrimage*. But it is places of superior sacredness that attract the faithful to themselves in the literal sense, and in primitive custom the psychology of pilgrimage becomes clear. Thus the sanctuary of Minahassa, previously referred to as "the salvation and strength of the village", is also named "the callers", because the stones forming it call back the villagers from foreign regions, or in other words arouse home-sickness in their breasts.[4] Primitive man's longing for house and home, for his native country or town, is ultimately therefore the yearning for salvation, for the consciousness of powerfulness, bestowed by one's own selected place. Of one's home it is true that

There are the vigorous roots of thy strength:

and man feels happy only in the place which he has discovered, which has stood the test for him and with whose power his own power is associated.

The place of pilgrimage, the seat of grace, is thus a sort of home of the second power. On festival days the Jew went on pilgrimage to Jerusalem, and once in his lifetime the Mohammedan must accomplish the great pilgrimage to Mecca. In Buddhism, in fact, pilgrimage is even the sole bond of this otherwise very loose religious community. For from pilgrimage man hopes for property and prosperity, fulfilment of desires, annulment of sin, admission to the divine world and eternal bliss:—indeed for almost everything powerful that man can possibly wish for himself.[5] In this way, then, whole peoples and religious communities can have their home: the Jews, Jerusalem: Mohammedans, Mecca and Christians, Rome. The world, which can

---

[1] *cf.* Rob. Grosche, *Catholica*, I, 1932, 91 *ff.*
[2] A. de Buck, *De Egyptische Voorstellingen betreffende den Oerheuvel*, 1927.
[3] Dombart, *Der babylonische Turm.*   [4] Adriani, *loc. cit.*
[5] J. Ph. Vogel, *De cosmopolitische beteeknis van het Buddhisme*, 1931, 15.

actually only be one's own, is then found in remote regions. Necessity compels emigration and the abandonment of the powerful subsisting in one's own place. Thus the seat of grace may become the image of the other world, and all life be regarded as a pilgrimage or a crusade. But Mysticism interprets this also in quite a different way: it can believe in no holy place whatever, and transfers all salvation inwardly to the holiest of holies in the heart. One of the reasons for the execution of the famous *sufi* al-Hallaj, in fact, was his assertion that pilgrimage might possess a purely spiritual character and be undertaken in one's own room, because the true sanctuary lay within the heart.[1] And the mystic Bayazid Bastami fulfilled his pilgrimage to Mecca by walking seven times around a sage: the real sanctuary is man.

[1] Massignon, *Al Hallaj*, 227, 348.

CHAPTER 58

THE SACRED WORD

1. "I CANNOT the mere Word so highly prize",[1] says Faust, and in its stead he places the deed. But he does not realize that in so doing he is not actually restoring or replacing it, but is merely giving a different translation of the Greek term *logos*. For the world of the primitive and of antiquity, and above all the religious world, knows nothing whatever of "empty words", of "words, words"; it never says: "more than enough words have been exchanged, now at last let me see deeds"; and the yearning no longer to have to "rummage among words" is wholly foreign to it. But this is not at all because the primitive world has a blunter sense of reality than ours; rather the contrary: it is we who have artificially emptied the word, and degraded it to a thing.[2] But as soon as we actually *live*, and do not simply make scientific abstractions, we know once more that a word has life and power, and indeed highly characteristic power. For we can go to the other powers, which we have by now converted into things, repeatedly: the communion elements, the sacred ceremonial places, always remain. But the word occurs only once for all, and it entails decision. In this living speech, then, time becomes *kairos*, the "due *season*," *hic et nunc*.[3] Whoever speaks, therefore, not only employs an expressive symbol but goes forth out of himself, and the word that he lets fall decides the matter. Even if I merely say "Good Morning" to someone I must emerge from my isolation, place myself before him and allow some proportion of my potency to pass over into his life, for good or evil.

We have already discussed Givenness and Possibility:[4] it is the word that decides the possibility. For it is an act, an attitude, a taking one's stand and an exercise of power, and in every word there is something creative. It is expressive, and exists prior to so-called actuality. Of the origin of language we know nothing, but it is probable that the most

---

[1] *Faust*, Part I, 878.

[2] "The 'nominalistic' standpoint, for which words are only conventional signs, mere *flatus vocis*, is only the outcome of later reflection, and not the expression of the 'natural' and immediate consciousness of language. This regards the 'essential nature' of the object as not merely mediately indicated by the word, but as in some way or other contained and present within it." Cassirer, *op. cit.*, II, 33 *f*.

[3] Frick, *Ideogramm, Mythologie und das Wort*, 19.   [4] Chap. 23.

primitive speech consisted of terms of wishing and feeling;[1] situations and opportunities were summoned up or settled.[2] For a word is always a charm: it awakens power, either dangerous or beneficent. Whoever asserts anything "poses", and thus exerts some influence; but he also "exposes" himself. Thus to the name of the ancient Egyptian king the formula *ankh wza śnb* was regularly added, meaning "life, salvation, health", since to mention his name exposed the king, and this "salvation formula" was intended to act as a counter-charm and once more place him in security.[3] In the light of these conditions, then, are also to be understood the frequent prohibitions of speech and word which are encountered among primitive peoples and in antiquity: for dangerous things and people must not be named. This goes so far that, for example, in Northern Rhodesia it is forbidden to say "No", because of the consequences to be feared from it; to the question: "Is the beast in the kraal?" the reply is: "It is in the kraal", even when it is not there; the power of the word is feared more than that of facts.[4] Under these conditions, of course, lying is an art, a merit, rather than a sin. And from these lies of avoidance there sprang up a by no means negligible proportion of poetry: metaphor arose, indeed, from this fear of calling things bluntly by their correct names, so that it was preferable to paraphrase them and call the knife, for example, "the sharpness at the thigh".[5] From the rule *nomina odiosa*, then, arose poetic paraphrase. In Central Celebes, again, a man who is going hunting says that he intends to look for rattan or pick bananas, since otherwise he would kill nothing, and rain is called the blossom of trees, or ashes.[6] The purpose of all this concealment and lying is attained in an even surer

[1] Thurnwald, *Psychologie des primitiven Menschen*, 267.

[2] So-called "Holophrasis" (or the use of "portmanteau words", as Marett calls them), which prevails to a certain extent even to-day in primitive and child language, and according to which it is not the isolated concept, but the situation, that is equivalent to the sentence as a unit, substantiates this view; where we for example, in our languages, can locate a seal just as we please either on a block of ice or in the sunshine, *etc.*, certain Eskimo languages employ a specific expression for each situation; *cf.* van der Leeuw, *Structure*, 11. F. Boas, *The Mind of Primitive Man*, 1922, 147 *ff.* Danzel, *Kultur und Religion des primitiven Menschen*, 21 *f.*

[3] Obbink, *De magische beteekenis van den naam*, 128.

[4] R. Thurnwald, *Die Lüge in der primitiven Kultur*; in the cooperative volume *Die Lüge*, 1927, 399.

[5] Naumann, *Isländische Volksmärchen*, No. 78. H. Werner, *Die Ursprünge der Metapher*, 1919. G. van der Leeuw, *Wegen en Grenzen*, 12 *ff.* E. Nordenskiöld, *Journal des Américanistes*, N.S. 24, 1932, 6; *cf.* further Old Norse *kenningar*, Portengen, *De oudgermaansche dichtertaal in haar ethnologisch verband*; also Hesiod's expressions "housebearer" (snail) *etc.* in Rose, *Primitive Culture in Greece*, 144.

[6] Kruyt, *Measa*, II, 43 *f.*

way by silence being commanded; in Roman sacrifice *favete linguis* was a demand for silence which might not be broken by a single word, and was accompanied only by the flute.[1] Similarly in Central Celebes no one may either speak or laugh during the invocation of spirits or any other religious ceremony; whoever speaks or laughs falls ill and the rite is ineffective.[2]

2. The word, then, is a decisive power: whoever utters words sets power in motion.[3] But the might of the word becomes still further enhanced in various ways. Raising the voice, emphasis, connection by rhythm or rhyme—all this endows the word with heightened energy; and from this a broad road leads to the domain of the *Phenomenology of Art*, which however we cannot here pursue.[4] But singing, rejoicing and mourning generate greater potency than mere speaking, and the power of lamentation is sufficiently well known in the mourning customs of innumerable peoples. In the Osiris myth, again, the grieving of the two goddesses Isis and Nephthys, the original models of all professional mourners, has power to awaken the dead god to new life. Certain unusual words possess intensified power: the term *eilikrineia*, for instance, gives a holy man an "excellent feeling", and to Jung-Stilling it appears "as if it had lain in splendour",[5] while James has told us of the marvellous effects on pious souls of such words as "Mesopotamia" and "Philadelphia"![6] More important still is the vast power which always emanated from such cult terms as *Hallelujah*, *Kyrie eleison*, *Amen*, *Om*; a mystical tone-colour is attached to them, while

---

[1] G. Mensching, *Das heilige Schweigen*, 1926, 101 f.   [2] Kruyt, *ibid.*, 39.

[3] This is very obvious in the primitive pun which, in this respect radically different from our own, places two realities in mutual relationship. The Egyptian pun, for example, invokes a god in order to *greet* "in his name" the *great*. These two ideas, *greet* and *great*, *Gruss* and *gross*, which possess for us merely accidental assonance, are essentially connected by means of the name; *cf.* Chap. 17, also Hubert-Mauss, *Mélanges*, 52; Obbink, *op. cit.*, 63; H. Werner, *Einführung in die Entwicklungspsychologie*, 1926, 111; and Larock, *Essai*, *RHR*. 101, 1930, I, 42 f. "What we call a sentence is composed (for the non-civilized mind) of a series of aerial beings, exerting a subtle influence, which he understands, but of which he never sees anything at all, and which are therefore mysterious in the sense of being formidable, sinking into his body and manifesting their influence there; escaping from his lips, they spread wherever they circulate the principles of action." "Words are the material and active essences of things, and to speak is equivalent to causing these groups of living, personal and sonorous phantoms of things and beings to manifest themselves, thus forming verbal sequences."

[4] G. van der Leeuw, *Wegen en Grenzen*.
[5] H. R. G. Günther, *Jung-Stilling*, 1928, 56.
[6] *The Varieties of Religious Experience*, 383.

their very incomprehensibility enhances their numinous power. Frequently a special cult language thus arises, for which an older tongue no longer in use is usually employed: in Christian worship, Latin, and Sanskrit in the Buddhist Mass of China and Japan.[1] Finally, speaking softly, barely audible words have potent decisiveness: the priest of the mysteries *lento murmure susurrat*—slowly murmurs in a low voice his most sacred utterance about the waking of the god.[2]

3. Words, however, possess the greatest power when they combine into some formula, some phrase definite in the sound of its terms, their timbre and their rhythm. Even in the Middle Ages a request uttered not occasionally and in ordinary terms, but ceremonially intoned in the appointed words, had compelling power,[3] and almost universally in religion rhythm, pitch and sequence possess such a potency: they hold together, as it were, the power immanent in the words.[4] The best example of this is the Roman *carmen*,[5] which consisted of *verba certa*, "appointed words", none of which might be at all altered and which must be recited with a special cadence; a *carmen* was required for all services of dedication and prayer. From Roman religion the *certa verba* were transferred to the Christian; the entire liturgy is in fact a *carmen* and still, to some extent, enjoys compelling power. In ancient Christianity, too, the creed in St. Augustine's Rome was delivered "from an elevated place, in view of the faithful people, in a set form of words learnt by heart".[6] In ancient Egypt likewise the correctness of the recital was so important that the destiny of the departed depended on it; whoever could recite his formulas accurately and "had the right voice" could defy all the dangers of the other world and emerge from them victoriously. *Ma-a khrw*, "correct so far as the voice is concerned", ultimately acquired the meaning of "blessed", and was eventually added formally to the dead person's name, like our "late" or "deceased". To "know the utterances", that is the sacred *Texts* to be recited, was the most important matter for the dead,[7] *S-iakhw*, literally words

---

[1] Otto, *The Idea of the Holy*, 67. "The songs of the Salii are hardly understood correctly by their priests, but religion prohibits their alteration, and what has been rendered sacred must be observed", as Quintilian had remarked. Lehmann-Haas, *Textbuch*, 222.

[2] Firmicus Maternus, *De errore profanarum religionum*, c. 22; *cf.* on numinous utterances, Will, *Culte*, II, 150, and on cult language, *ibid.*, 135 *f.*

[3] Huizinga, *Herfstty der Middeleeuwen*, 404.

[4] G. van der Leeuw, *Wegen en Grenzen*.

[5] Examples in G. Appel, *De Romanorum precationibus*, 1909, 69 *f.*

[6] Augustine, *Confessions*, VIII, 2.   [7] *cf. e.g.* Pyramidentexte (Sethe), 855.

"that make the power of glory arise", being the name for the sacred ritual, which may be simply translated as *carmina*. In the ancient German world, similarly, the formula used in law, ritual drinking and sacrifice, was called *kvad*, and this again was a sort of *carmen*. So great was the potency of the formulas, indeed, that gods and divinities bore their names: thus *Paean* was originally a healing charm, and *Brahman* the power of the Universe, a chanted magical incantation.

H. FRICK, *Ideogramm, Mythologie und das Wort* (*Marburger theol. Stud.* 3), 1931.

V. LAROCK, *Essai sur la valeur sacrée et la valeur sociale des noms de personnes dans les sociétés inférieures* (*RHR.* 101, 1930).

G. VAN DER LEEUW, *Wegen en Grenzen. Over de verhouding van Religie en Kunst*, 1932.

H. W. OBBINK, *De magische beteekenis van den naam*, 1925.

A. J. PORTENGEN, *De oudgermaansche dichtertaal in haar ethnologisch verband*, 1915.

CHAPTER 59

THE WORD OF CONSECRATION

1. THE repetition of words, to continue, intensifies their power in the same degree as intensifying the tone and the rhythm:[1] this constitutes the Litany type.[2] "Thou must say it thrice" has always been the maxim of magic; and the accumulation of epithets in invoking the gods has the same purpose.[3] The object to which speech is directed, the power to be constrained, is thus as it were enveloped in words or, if the repetition occurs from one of several different points of vantage, for example from or towards the four points of the compass, enclosed within them.

The content of the words, also, is often expressly chosen so that power may be generated; thus among many ancient peoples lewd speaking was a sort of rite.[4] *Aischrologia*, or vituperation, as practised by the Greeks,[5] and usually indulged in by quite respectable matrons, had the same end in view. For speaking about powerful things itself generates power, and so everything referring to sex matters or to bodily secretions has always enjoyed great potency: the invective and obscenity surviving to-day sprang, in fact, from the word's powerfulness. Insult therefore is no senseless waste of words, as everyone knows who is in direct contact with life. The forcible terms of the ancient Germans also had a highly practical effect; if someone said to another person: "You lack courage for it", he was dishonoured unless he performed the action referred to, and if a woman was upbraided as a witch or whore she had to submit to the punishment for witchcraft or harlotry unless she had someone who could "avenge" her (*uphaevelse*, or setting up again).[6] Thus whether she were actually guilty or not was not at all important; the words rendered her culpable, and only some fresh manifestation of power could make her pure again.[7]

[1] G. van der Leeuw, *Wegen en Grenzen*, 60 f.

[2] It is remarkable that sufferers from mental disorders indulge in this type of repetition; the verbigeration of katatonics may be compared to magical formulas with which "the victims attempt to strengthen themselves and protect themselves against dangerous forces"; A. Storch, *Das archaisch-primitive Erleben und Denken der Schizophrenen*, 1922, 50. [3] E. Maass, *Orpheus*, 1895, 199 ff.

[4] Lévy-Bruhl, *Primitives and the Supernatural*, 295 f.

[5] Also by the Romans at the Festival of Anna Perenna.

[6] *cf*. Wagner's *Lohengrin*. [7] Grönbech, *op. cit.*, I, 101.

By means of the word, then, invective brings the person who is being abused within the power of the evil deed or detestable characteristic: it is a *word of consecration*. The reviler dedicates his opponent to those evil conditions about which he speaks;[1] and thus the curse is an effect of power that requires no gods nor spirits to execute it.[2] Once pronounced, a curse continues to operate until its potency is exhausted, and perpetually dedicates its object to the fate it has summoned into being. This was familiar not only to the primitive world, but above all to Greek tragedy, in which the persons acting are merely the instruments of the curse, of the ἀρά. The "curses", ἀραί, were conceived as personal;[3] the hereditary family curse dwelt in the house as a demon and continued to operate implacably. Certainly it lost its force as time ran on, and thus Orestes could appeal to the fact that he had already encountered so many people without this contact appearing to injure them, as a proof of the weakening of the curse.[4]

But equal in its power to the malediction is the blessing, "word-salvation" as it was called in the ancient German world.[5] It is indeed by no means a mere pious wish, but the allocation of fortune's gifts by employing words. When we were children we were astonished to find that Isaac had no benediction ready for his beloved Esau after the first had been purloined by the cunning Jacob. But Isaac was not expressing any mere wishes: he was blessing, and he could bestow the same blessing only once.[6] In blessing, also, much if not everything depends on the exactitude of the *carmen*, and in the Jewish legend an *Amen* omitted from the blessing was punished by God with a painful death.[7] All that is primitive and modern, heathen and Christian, with regard to blessing, is contained in Guardini's fine lines: "Only he who has Power can bless: only he who can create. God alone can bless. . . . For to bless is to decree what exists and is effective. . . . Only God can bless. But we are essentially suppliants."[8]

2. The word of consecration, still further, finds manifold applications. In the first place there is the *vow*, familiar in its classical form from the story of Jacob: "If God will be with me, and will keep me in

---

[1] Radermacher, *Schelten und Fluchen, AR.* XI, 1908, 11 *f.*
[2] *cf.* R. Thurnwald, *Reallexikon der Vorgeschichte, Zauber*, 497. A curse once pronounced cannot be retracted; *cf.* an Indian example in Vogel, *Meded. Kon. Akad. d. Wetensch., Afd. Lett.*, 70, B. 4, 1930, 16.
[3] Aeschylus, *Choëphoroe*, 406.   [4] Aeschylus, *Eumenides*, 285.
[5] Grönbech, *op. cit.*, I, 170.   [6] *Gen.* xxvii.
[7] Bin Gorion, *Der Born Judas*, V, 153.   [8] *Von heiligen Zeichen*, 68.

this way that I go, and will give me bread to eat, and raiment to put on, so that I come again to my father's house in peace; then shall the Lord be my God: . . . and of all that thou shalt give me I will surely give the tenth unto thee."[1] The Ewe king, again, swears to the *tro*: "If thou canst help me, so that we are not molested by any other king and always have food in our houses, then I will always serve thee."[2] But that such a contract with Power is not pure rationalism has already been observed in discussing gifts and sacrifice.[3] The vow is certainly a contract; but a contract is not governed by purely rational motives.

The Roman *votum* was a typical example of the word of consecration; and an *evocationis carmen* evoked the hostile god from his city during a siege;[4] it too bore the form of contract. A primeval formula also accompanied the *devotio* whereby the general, as simultaneously dedicator and dedicated, bound himself and the enemy's army together into a single unity and, by seeking death, consecrated both himself and the foe to ruin; if the general did not fall, then he remained impure and the prey of the under-world.[5] A similar dedication, only not of oneself, was the ancient Israelite ban חרם; if God delivered the enemy into Israel's hands, the people would lay on him the חרם (*ban*), that is destroy the enemy root and branch.[6]

The most familiar form of the word of consecration, however, is the *oath*. It actually leads us into the realm of the Phenomenology of Law, but partially, and in virtue of its essential nature, it pertains to religion. The oath, then, is an automatically effective power-word which, if his assertion cannot be confirmed, dedicates the swearer to this power. But this does not necessarily mean that the statement need even be true. Here also the word is more powerful than reality, and one may succeed in "making a matter true". In a Mohammedan story, for instance, a Christian offers a Mussulman half a banana with the words: "Sir, by the truth of thy faith, take this !" The Mohammedan is afraid

[1] *Gen.* xxviii, 20 *ff.*   [2] Spieth, *Ewe*, 107; *cf.* Heiler, *Katholizismus*, 65.
[3] Chap. 50.
[4] Lehmann-Haas, *Textbuch*, 226. Appel, *De Romanorum precationibus*, 15 *f.*
[5] The formula: "Janus, Jupiter, father Mars, Quirinus, Bellona, ye Lares, ye gods Novensiles, ye gods Indigetes, ye divinities, under whose power we and our enemies are, and ye dii Manes, I pray you, I adore you, I ask your favour, that you would prosperously grant strength and victory to the Roman people, the Quirites, and that ye may affect the enemies of the Roman people, of the Quirites, with terror, dismay and death. In such manner as I have expressed in words, so do I devote the legions and auxiliaries of the enemy, together with myself, to the dii Manes, and to Earth for the republic of the Quirites, for the army, legions, auxiliaries of the Roman people, of the Quirites." Livy, VIII, 9, 6 *f.* (Spillan). Appel, *op. cit.*, 14. L. Deubner, *Die Devotion der Decier, AR.* VIII, 1905.   [6] *Numbers* xxi. 2.

to allow the Christian's oath to become untrue, so he eats the banana, which contains a stupefying drug.[1] A modern would say: "my faith is pure independently of anyone else's assertions"; but the oath possesses the power to render true and untrue. Thus we can understand the institution of the oath of purification existing among many peoples. If someone is accused of theft, he strikes the earth with his hand and thereby has sworn an oath; but if, nevertheless, he has stolen the object, he must die.[2] Testimony on oath is thus decisive as to guilt or innocence. The oath is a "powerful word", and its potency may be intensified; for this purpose, among other things, repetition serves, frequently thrice.[3] The manner of taking the oath, again, also heightens its power; for example, in ancient German custom the oath had to be sworn naked (*ritus paganus*);[4] or the oath was reinforced by accompanying celebrations. In ancient Israel, for example, the man's genitals were touched while swearing an oath;[5] they were the seat of a powerful soul-stuff: "Pray, place your hand under my thigh, and I will make you swear an oath by the Eternal", said Abraham to his servant.[6] The most frequent method of strengthening the oath was, however, the institution of the oath-helper (compurgator), which is also the most conclusive proof that it is not an assertion in accordance with "actuality", but a power-word. In the Middle Ages the number of these "con-sacramentals" was decided according to the importance of the issue; in one case a man who had been attacked while alone took with him three straws from his thatched roof, his cat and his cock to swear to the outrage before the judge.[7] Finally, the oath, which is already in itself a form of ordeal, may be confirmed by a judgment of God,[8] for example by taking communion,[9] or by a duel. An oath, again, is false, perjury, even when broken unintentionally;[10] for the word is valid, and when it has once been spoken it produces its effect, that is it induces injury to the swearer or to the object by which the oath was sworn; thus the tree by which two persons have sworn never to part from each other withers when death separates them.[11]

---

[1] *The Arabian Nights.*

[2] Spieth, *Eweer*, 59. An Egyptian purificatory oath in E. Révillout, *Revue égyptienne*, V, 25 ff. Arabian and Israelite, Pedersen, *Der Eid bei den Semiten in seinem Verhältnis zu verwandten Erscheinungen*, 181, 186.   [3] Hirzel, *Der Eid*, 82.

[4] J. Grimm, *Deutsche Rechtsaltertümer*, I, 166. On the same custom among the Berbers: Westermarck, *The Origin and Development of the Moral Ideas*, I, 59.

[5] Pedersen, *op. cit.*, 150.   [6] *Gen.* xxiv, 2, 3 (Moffat).

[7] Grimm, *op. cit.*, 176. For Egypt, A. Wilcken, *Zeitschrift für ägyptische Sprache*, 48, 1911, 170.   [8] Chap. 54.   [9] Westermarck, *ibid.*, II, 687; I, 504 f.

[10] Hirzel, *op. cit.*, 49 f.   [11] Cretan folksong; Hirzel, *ibid.*, 35.

3. I have already observed that the similarity to a contract rationalizes neither the vow nor the oath, since the contract is not in itself a purely rational action, but a word of consecration. This it is in the form: word against word. Among the Romans a contract was a *carmen*; to all legal actions there pertained *certa verba*, *litterae* and gestures. May remarks, not incorrectly, that in legal affairs all three elements of religious dedication are represented: λεγόμενα, δρώμενα, δεικνύμενα, what is said, what is done, and what is exhibited. The law is spoken (*jus dicere*);[1] the word of consecration thus unites the phenomena of religion with those of law, and the legal relationship between persons is absolutely dependent on their own relation to Power.

R. Hirzel, *Der Eid*, 1902.

E. Maass, *Segnen, Weihen, Taufen (AR.* XXI, 1922).

J. Pedersen, *Der Eid bei den Semiten in seinem Verhältnis zu verwandten Erscheinungen*, 1914.

L. Radermacher, *Schelten und Fluchen (AR.* XI, 1908).

[1] May, *Droit romain* 20 and Note 16; *ibid.*, 34.

CHAPTER 60

MYTH

1. ACTUALLY, the myth is nothing other than the word itself. For it is neither speculation nor poem, neither a primitive explanation of the world nor a philosophy in embryo, although it also may be, and indeed frequently is, all of these. It is a spoken word, possessing decisive power in its repetition; just as the essential nature of sacred action consists in its being repeated, so the essence of myth lies in its being told, in being repeatedly spoken anew.[1] Generally, therefore, the attempt to understand myths and mythology has been far too abstract or esthetic; the type of mythology that has usually been relied on has been, to some degree, that luxuriance of myths springing up in periods during which they had themselves become dubious or indeed offensive, such as the culmination of Greek literature, together with its later phases, or in Christian-Germanic antiquity. But the living myth itself is the precise parallel of celebration; it is, indeed, itself a celebration, so that the discovery of the close relationship between myth and rite has, in recent years, led not only to the understanding of many myths which were previously enigmatic, but has also elucidated, for the first time, the essence of myth as such. And conversely, the myth certifies the ritual. "It refers to the past when the sacred action was first executed, and indeed often enables us even to prove that primitive man perhaps not merely *repeated* the incidents that had been elaborated, but that the initial celebration was deliberately and literally carried out as an actual occurrence, including everything that was then essential to it".[2] The myth is therefore not reflective contemplation, but actuality. *It is the reiterated presentation of some event replete with power*; verbal presentation, however, is quite as effective as the repetition; it is, then, verbal celebration.[3] The classical example is the repeating of the *Qui pridie*, the words of the Institution in the mass, which constantly recall anew the mighty event of the redemptive death of Christ.[4]

Mythical repetition in the form of narrative, however, conceals in

[1] Harrison, *Themis*, 328 *ff.*   [2] Preuss, *Gehalt der Mythen*, 7.
[3] Wundt, *op. cit.*, V, 24 *f.*, 48; *cf.* further Chap. 17.
[4] Examples that it is really the rite which explains the myth: Pentheus, the "man of sorrows" of the Dionysiac circle; Jephthah's daughter; the Roman Anna Perenna; the Nordic myth of Baldur, *etc.*

itself an element that does not concern other sacred words—*Endowment with form*:[1] myth not only evokes or recalls some powerful event, but it also endows this with form. In this the origins of the sacred word in magically conditioned metaphor indubitably cooperate;[2] by bestowing form the mythical utterance becomes decisive. It does not kill, like the concept that abstracts from life, but calls forth life, and thus constitutes the most extreme antithesis conceivable to pure theory. The concept, for example, refers to the "Law of Gravitation" and abstracts from every actual weight, attempting in this way to include diversified concrete events within one single dead formula. But myth speaks of "that mad and quickening rush by which all earth's creatures fly back to her heart when released".[3]

Yet the life that falls within the decisiveness of the mythical word is not ordinary reality: this requires no decision at all, since it is simply "accepted". But myth accepts nothing: it 'celebrates' reality. It does with it what it will, and deals with it according to its own laws. As a single example: it arrests time, and in this it is sharply distinguished from celebration in the form of action, which utilizes the temporal instant, the *kairos*. Myth takes the event and sets it up on its own basis, in its own realm. Thus the event becomes 'eternal': it happens now and always, and operates as a type. What occurs daily in Nature, sunrise for example, becomes in the myth something unique.[4] It must be repeated so that the event may retain its vitality. The mythical occurrence, then, is typical and eternal; it subsists apart from all that is temporal. If nevertheless we attempt to fix it in time, we must place it at either the beginning or the end of all happening, either in the primeval era or at the conclusion of time,[5] that is before or after "time".

Thus myth is no "figurative mode of expression". The image it evokes has a very real significance; it proceeds inferentially not from "reality" to the picture, but rather from the picture to reality. When, for example, it calls God "Father", it does this not on the basis of any given fatherhood, but creates a paternal form to which every given fatherhood must conform (this case has been acutely elaborated

---

[1] On this term *cf.* Note 3, p. 87.
[2] *cf.* H. Pongs, *Das Bild in der Dichtung*, I, 1927, 14.
[3] Chesterton, *The Innocence of Father Brown*, 233 (Popular Edition).
[4] A. Réville, *Prolégomènes de l'Histoire des Religions*, 1889, 153 f. Further, 155 f. "What is permanent and frequent in Nature and in humanity is derived from some occurrence which happened once for all".
[5] Chap. 87. Hubert-Mauss, *Mélanges*, 192 f.

by Frick).[1] The myth proclaims, essentially and decisively; and thus it becomes possible that for a culture in which abstract tendencies prevail, either it is no longer understood at all, as with Greek myths in the days of the sophists and Christian myths in the nineteenth century, or, in quite the opposite direction, that it becomes the expression of the ultimate and the highest, withdrawing itself from all that is merely conceptual, as in Plato's myths or the conclusion of Goethe's *Faust*.

2. In the form of the *saga*[2] the myth reverts to the temporal. The saga is a myth which, during its expansion, has become attached to some specific place or other, or to some sort of historical fact. The narrative of the saga, therefore, has not the character of a decision. In the saga an attitude is assumed which, though frequently devout, is purely contemplative. The myth is eternally present,[3] while the saga refers wholly to the past. In the Old Testament the distinction is quite clear: the myths at the beginning of *Genesis* are sharply distinguishable from the succeeding patriarchal sagas.[4] The *motif* of the saga is not historical but mythical; it attaches itself repeatedly to different historic personalities, and the principal aspect is the typical as being always more important than the historical. In 1892, for instance, some cabmen were heard discussing Queen Louise in a Berlin beer dive. One of them asked whose wife she really had been, and another expressed the opinion that "she was old Fritz's wife", since "the best king had also had the best queen".[5] Thus while the typifying myth that confers eternity overrides history, its actuality has been lost; the myth of the dragon slayer, for example, persists in Worms on the Rhine and draws within its circle occurrences in world history,[6] but thereby the dragon becomes a prehistoric monster and loses its actual dreadfulness. The *fairy tale* is therefore closer to the myth than the saga.

[1] *Ideogramm, Mythologie und das Wort.* An antithesis, referring to the Mother form, occurs in Plato, *Menexenus*, 238: "the woman in her conception and generation is but the imitation of the earth, and not the earth of the woman" (Jowett).

[2] This term is employed in a broad literary sense, as in Galsworthy's *Forsyte Saga*.

[3] The myth knows no "Time" in the Newtonian sense. "The magical 'Now' is by no means a *mere* 'Now', no simple and detached present instant but, to use Leibniz's expression, *chargé du passé et gros de l'avenir*." Cassirer, *Die Begriffsform im mythischen Denken*, II, 140 f.

[4] Here again in Galsworthy's literary sense. I can admit no difference in principle between myth and saga in the sense that in the myth only gods, and in the saga only human beings, appear, as *e.g.* H. Gunkel maintains (*Genesis*[3], 1910, xiv); *cf.* Bethe, *Märchen, Sage, Mythus*, 133.

[5] Bethe, *ibid.*, 126 f.   [6] *cf.* H. Schneider, *Deutsche Heldensage*, 1930, 21 ff.

3. "The historical saga usually adds something extraordinary and surprising, or even supernatural, to the ordinary, familiar and present; but the fairy tale stands quite apart from the actual world in a secluded and undisturbed sphere, beyond which it does not gaze; it mentions, therefore, neither name nor place, nor any definite home."[1] Fairy stories have deep significance not merely for the history of religion, since they contain much ancient religious material,[2] but for religion itself also. Telling fairy tales is therefore no affair of pure delight in fabulous narration, but has a magical effect, and the Pawnee Indians believe that relating them, by depicting man's subjugation of the buffalo, successfully militates against the decline of the herds.[3] Narrating fairy stories is celebration too,[4] in fact a *carmen*; their wording must never be changed; even children insist on this, and the art of telling such tales, which among ourselves is entrusted to "old grannies"— *e.g.* nursery stories going back to the old wives' tale, *fabula anilis*, of Apuleius—and by primitive peoples to professional story-tellers, rests to a large extent on their accurate recitation. The famous woman of Niederzwehrn, for instance, who recited fairy tales for the brothers Grimm, could correct each error immediately and never altered her wording at all, no matter how often she repeated them;[5] and Jacob Wassermann has given a clear and psychologically profound account of the cogent force of fairy story narrative.[6]

Like myth, the fairy tale too is "homeless, fluttering through the air like gossamer in sunlight". Its figures have neither names nor history: they are *the* prince, *the* step-mother, *the* vizier, or just simply Hans and Gretel, Yussuf and Ali.[7] Time stands still, as in the Sleeping Beauty's Castle. All at once the little girl is ready to be wed, while Penelope never grows any older; "once upon a time": in other words, it is eternal and ever-present, and Cinderella and Tom Thumb live to-day just as a thousand years ago. "Once upon a time: it will happen some day: that is the beginning of all fairy tales; there is no 'if' and no

---

[1] Wilhelm Grimm, in Wehrhan, *op. cit.*, 7.

[2] In their oldest forms fairy tales represent a very primitive level of human experience; I mention only the way in which the wish rules the event, the part played by animals, the frequently very ancient sayings that occur in even our modern fairy stories, *etc.* Huet, *Les contes populaires*, 71; Gunkel, *Genesis*, xxvii; Wundt, *op. cit.*, V, 166 *f*. Thimme, *Das Märchen*. On the origin of fairy tales *cf.* Bédier, *Les Fabliaux*, 42, 242 *ff*.   [3] Wundt, *op. cit.*, V, 110, 172 *f.*

[4] *cf.* P. Saintyves, *Les Contes de Perrault*, 1923.

[5] Grimm, *Kinder- und Hausmärchen, Vorrede*; Thimme, *Das Märchen*, 8; Huet, *Les Contes populaires*, 70.   [6] *Der Aufruhr um der Junker Ernst.*

[7] Bethe, *op. cit.*, 107; Thimme, *op. cit.*, 1 *f.*, 139, 147; Huet, *ibid.*, 71.

'perhaps'."[1] Neither is there any space: "Go to the Red Sea", it says, and the girl goes there: that is perfectly simple![2] Similarly there is no constancy in the phenomena, no identity; metamorphosis is something so common that if the lion continues to be a lion, while the horse changes itself into a mouse, then we are told almost apologetically: "the lion was a lion, always".[3] There is no doubt, still further, that the sphere in which fairy tales are carried on is to a great extent the realm of dreams.[4] "The cock crowed, and it was daytime": this typical ending to French fairy stories[5] stresses the dream character of the narrative;[6] and hence the marvellous in the fairy tale is nothing in the least extraordinary, but is its own characteristic world. Originally, however, this dream aspect by no means implied that something transcending reality was intended; rather what is expressing itself here is primitive mentality, which is much more realistic than theoretical and has been conserved in the fairy tale. "The man of science says, 'cut the stalk, and the apple will fall'; but the fairy tale says, 'Blow the horn, and the ogre's castle will fall' ".[7] The latter, however, is far more realistically intended than the former, which is a mere abstract statement.

4. The *legend*, in conclusion, is really the story of some saint to be read during Christian worship. It has an edifying character: it effects something and thus pertains to sacred words; but the specifically decisive power of the word has here been enfeebled. The legend then, which in any case brings with it very much that is mythical and saga-like, approaches pious contemplation.

J. BÉDIER, *Les Fabliaux*, 1893.

E. BETHE, *Märchen, Sage, Mythus*.

E. CASSIRER, *Die Begriffsform im mythischen Denken*, 1922.

G. DUMEZIL, *Naissance de Rome*, 1944.

A. VAN GENNEP, *La formation des légendes*, 1910.

G. HUET, *Les contes populaires*.

G. JACOB, *Märchen und Traum*, 1923.

G. VAN DER LEEUW, "Die Bedeutung der Mythen" (in *Festschr. für A. Bertholet*, 1950, pg. 287).

K. TH. PREUSS, *Der religiöse Gehalt der Mythen*, 1933.

A. THIMME, *Das Märchen*, 1909.

---

[1] Tegethoff, *Französische Volksmärchen*, II, No. 33; *cf.* H. Gunkel, *Das Märchen im Alten Testament*, 1921, 161.   [2] *Kinder- und Hausmärchen*, No. 88.
[3] Stroebe, *Nordische Volksmärchen*, I, No. 12.   [4] Jacob, *Märchen und Traum*.
[5] Tegethoff, *Französische Märchen*, II, 324; *cf.* O. Weinreich, *AR.* 22, 1923–24, 333 *f.*
[6] Huet, *op. cit.*, 78 *f.*   [7] Chesterton, *Orthodoxy*, 89.

CHAPTER 61

THE STORY OF SALVATION: THE WORD OF GOD

1. IF the myth concerns the introduction of some cult, the discovery or attainment of a cult image or something similar, we then speak of a *cult legend*. Such is, for example, the dream of the Pharaoh Ptolemy which induced him to have the image of Serapis brought from Sinope, just as in a dream at Jerusalem, Bishop Gualfredus heard about an image of the Lord supposed to have been made by Nicodemus. So he contrived to procure the effigy, which arrived from Joppa at the harbour of Lucca on a ship with neither sails nor rudder. At first no one could reach this ship; then when a man of God arrived, summoned by an angel, it entered the haven of itself. This is the same story as that of the arrival of the black stone of the *magna mater* in Rome in 204 B.C., for the ship bearing it ran ashore off the harbour of Ostia and was refloated only when a chaste woman seized the cable. In such cult legends as these, however, the mythical occurrence does not become actual, but remains an affair of the venerable past.

Mythical history, again, becomes actual, but impalpable, in the Hindu form of the *Jatakas*;[1] "they are prolix comedies of a hundred scenes, with the Universe as the stage".[2] The individual event, the actual powerfulness of occurrences or persons, is in the *jataka* "linked" with the timeless history of Buddha. The event is then made eternal in the form not of uniqueness, but of never-ness: it is only an illusory manifestation of eternal salvation, and the most widely contrasted representations, for example in the reliefs of the Boro-Budur temple on the Island of Java, have only *one* meaning:[3] salvation is purchased at the cost of reality.[4]

The *hieros logos* on the other hand—the "sacred story"—follows the directly opposite path. It proclaims some definite occurrence, but it also determines the hearer's salvation, and the sacred events of the mystery religions were such "salvation stories". They were not merely recited but also acted[5] and experienced, the representation of Kore's ravishing and rediscovery, of the Mithraic bull sacrifice, of Attis'

---

[1] Chap. 22.   [2] Lévi, *Les Jatakas*, 18.
[3] N. J. Krom, *De levensgeschiedenis van den Buddha op Barabudur*, 1926. Lévi, *op. cit.*, 13. Lüders, *Buddhistische Märchen, Zur Einführung*.
[4] Huet, *op. cit.*, 170 f.   [5] A. van Gennep, *op. cit.*, 114 f.

dying and resurrection, Isis' "search" for her lost spouse, all being related and represented in the mysteries either symbolically or purely dramatically.[1] Thus the representation of the myth implies the salvation of the hearer and spectator. Salvation, quiescent in the event, becomes actual in the myth. A man is ritually killed, for example; he is "the man of sorrows", Pentheus, over whose death mourning resounds, and the renewal of whose life is ultimately celebrated with rejoicing.[2] Such a *hieros logos*, as in the case of Pentheus, can lose a goodly proportion of its determinative power; then it becomes simply myth or saga (again as in *The Forsyte Saga* sense), and finally literature (Euripides!). It may on the other hand retain its vitality but gradually lose its significance: this happens when it becomes a popular custom such as driving away Winter, expelling Death *etc.* But if it remains true to its real nature it is, as it were, the focus of all powerfulness, nourishing the community's life from its glow: and thus by the dramatic representation of the "sacred story", the powerfulness that has appeared in history is transferred to the life of the community and likewise of the individual.[3] In Christian worship the *hieros logos* is in fact the focal point: for not merely the sacrament of the Eucharist but the entire system of worship, in the cycle of its ever recurring celebrations,[4] is in principle a repetition of the typical story of Christ; and in this reiteration the powerfulness of the story is transferred to the church's own life.

2. But the *hieros logos* of Christianity is not merely a myth subsisting in celebration: it is also *evangelium, Proclamation*;[5] and in the Hellenistic world an *evangelium* was the proclamation of the saviour-king's accession to the throne.[6] For Christianity, still further, it is not primarily the literary form of the life of Jesus, but first of all the joyful message that Jesus is the Lord, the Saviour. Even in the biographical form of the Gospels themselves, this is the principal feature; it is no mere affair of imparting certain facts, but of preaching Him Who is recognized as Lord. In Christianity, therefore, the repetition of the story of salvation and the announcement, the proclamation, of salvation, are intimately connected.[7]

    cf. O. Kern, *AR.* 26, 1928, 15.
    [2] An example of symbolic representation is the ear of corn in Eleusis; *cf.* Chap. 53; also P. Wolters, *Die goldnen Ähren*, in *Festschrift Loeb*, 1930, 111 *ff*.
    [3] *cf.* Wundt, *op. cit.*, V, 48 *f*. Preuss, *Gehalt der Mythen*, 31. Myth is a "necessary constituent of the cult in so far as a beginning in primeval time is held to be necessary for validity".   [4] Chap. 56.   [5] *cf.* Bultmann, *Glauben und Verst.*, 186 *f*.
    [6] Chap. 12.   [7] *cf.* Bultmann, *ibid.*, 291.

3. Associated together in this way, they are called the "Word of God".[1] This is in the first place the announcement, the message of salvation;[2] but it is also this salvation itself as it is revealed in the actual event. The preaching of the message, then, is always at the same time a priestly act, and conversely.[3] The very utterance is powerful: "to a certain extent a preacher must be one of those men of whom his hearers are compelled to say: 'Whither shall I flee from this man? his speech pursues me to every hiding-place; how shall I get free from him? for he is upon me at every moment' ".[4] Such an utterance, however, is power actually present, the direct antithesis of any mere contemplation or explanation. The Word, and indeed in this its dual meaning of announcement and actually present divine Power, thus becomes the form of revelation in general.[5] In the later Greek period, indeed, the *logos* was the veritably present and effective Power of God, as it was subsequently in Christendom. But Christianity preaches the incarnate *logos* that has appeared in historical actuality; the very "Word", by which all things have been created, took flesh and dwelt among us "full of grace and truth".[6] Thus determinative announcement and determinative event both occur in the figure of the Saviour Jesus Christ. For such a form is essential to every myth.

The idea of the Word of God, however, lives in other religions besides Christianity, and above all in Islam. The world was created by God's Word; but within this there resides no specific power whatever: it is only one attribute of God. For passionate Mohammedan monotheism tolerates no independent *logos*, and still less a figure of any kind, and wages war therefore against the Christian doctrine of the *logos*.[7] But similar tendencies sprang up much earlier also; from the earliest historical times, in fact, the so-called "Monument of Memphite theology" attests a "theology of the word" in Egypt, with reference to the ancient Memphite god Ptah: "it happened that the heart and the tongue received power over all the members by teaching that he (Ptah) is in every body (as the heart), and (as the tongue) in every mouth of all the gods, all men and cattle, all reptiles (and) what

[1] *cf.* W. B. Kristensen, *De goddelyke heraut en het woord van God, Meded. Kon. Akad. v. Wetensch., Afd. Lett.* 70, B, Nr. 2, 1930.
[2] Chap. 28.   [3] *cf.* P. Tillich, *Die religiöse Lage der Gegenwart*, 148.
[4] S. Kierkegaard, in: Ed. Geismar, *Sören Kierkegaard*, 1929, 367.
[5] Chap. 85 *ff.*
[6] *John* i, 14. On the relation of history to the Word of God *cf.* Bultmann, *ibid.*, 287.
[7] Thus *e.g.* in popular literature like *The Arabian Nights:*—*Tausend und eine Nacht* (Littmann) VI, 66 *f.*

(ever else) lives, since he (as the heart) thinks and (as the tongue) commands all things as he will" . . . "it (the heart) is what permits all knowledge to emerge or arise, and the tongue it is that repeats what the heart has been thinking" . . . "but every word of the god came into being through what the heart had thought and the tongue commanded" . . . "and thus all works and arts are carried out, the arms' actions, the legs' motion and the movements of all the limbs, all in accord with this command which was conceived by the heart and expressed by the tongue, and which constitutes the meaning of all things." The organ of creation is the mouth, "which named all things", and thus heart and tongue are the two representatives of creative power.[1]

Primitive man also knows the word as primal power: the Uitoto tribe in Columbia ascribe to the sacred words, employed in their celebrations, the original beginning: "in the beginning the word gave origin to the Father". The sacred words, remarks Preuss, subsist independently of this Father to a certain extent, and existed before him;[2] thus the word has precedence here even over the god, and makes the latter really superfluous.

[1] Sethe, *Dramatische Texte zu altägyptischen Mysterienspielen*, I.
[2] *Religion und Mythologie der Uitoto*, I, 1921, 26.

CHAPTER 62

THE WORD OF MAN: MAGICAL FORMULA AND PRAYER

1. WITHIN the stream of divine utterance there resounds the word of man; but we are very far from being able to distinguish, always and precisely, between God's word itself and human expression. For the word of Power is mighty in man's mouth just as it is in God's. Man's own word at first, therefore, is magical, creative, and so far as we can speak of "God" in this connection[1] man takes a divine word into his mouth.[2] Thus in their misery people came in hordes to Empedocles, to enquire the way of salvation and "to hear a little word bringing deliverance."[3] The magical formula and the prayer, again, cannot be kept apart; so that if in Roman prayer the rule held good, "in prayers there should be no ambiguity",[4] then it is clear that this prayer is a *carmen*, a magic formula.[5] The word, in and of itself, is powerful, so that if I pray for someone and make a mistake in his name, then the blessing will not reach him but the bearer of the name I have mentioned. In prayer, therefore, one must state as definitely as possible both name and place: an accurate filling in of all the details is requested![6] It has already been observed, too, that in Rome, the language of *precatio* and of *pactio*, of prayer and of contract, was the same;[7] in prayer, then, names are the chief features.[8]

To pray is therefore to exert power, and the Iroquois call praying "the laying down of one's *orenda*", perhaps because the act of praying presupposes the surrender of one's own power, but it may also be, quite conversely, because in the prayer power should manifest itself.[9] Similarly we find in Aeschylus that praying is "to show the force of the

---

[1] Chap. 1.

[2] It is true that this implies no historical development "from spell to prayer" in the evolutionary sense (Marett, *The Threshold of Religion*, Chap. II). Rather a prayer always subsisted side by side with the magical formula; "at first" refers, therefore, merely to the "structural relationship".

[3] In Diels, *Fragmente der Vorsokratiker*, I, 265.

[4] Servius, *ad Aen.*, VII, 120.   [5] Heiler, *Prayer*, 67 f.

[6] Plato, *Cratylus*, 400 c.   [7] Appel, *De Romanorum precationibus*, 76 f., 145 f.

[8] Usener, *Götternamen*, 335 f.; *cf.* Chap. 17.

[9] Hewitt, *Orenda*, 40. Beth, *Reiigion und Magie*, 262.

mouth for someone's good".[1] Prayer has extremely concrete purposes; the Romans prayed "for the health of the cattle",[2] and the *epithalamium* sought to ensure the fertility of marriage; the incantation, again, wrought recovery from illness. The Greek *paean*, a power-word against diseases, became even a god, while to-day there are many people who still revere the doctor's prescription as a magical incantation. Thus prayer exercises potent influence alike over men, powers and gods.[3] "Upon speech all the gods live, on speech the *gandharvas*, animals and men . . . speech is imperishable, the first-born of the (*eternal*) law (Ṛta), the mother of the Vedas, the navel of immortality", says ancient Hindu word-philosophy which is based directly on the use of the *carmen* during sacrifice;[4] to the Germanic tribesman, likewise, prayer was a weapon which he hurled against his opponent.[5] The prayer of Christians moves the house where they are assembled:[6] that of the vestal virgins roots an escaping slave to the spot;[7] saints in prayer are levitated by the power of their supplication, and hover in the air.[8] The finest example of all is provided in the legend concerning the *sufi* al-Hallaj: "Once when he heard the *muezzin* call to prayer he cried: 'Thou hast lied', and when the people were enraged with him and sought to put him to death, al-Hallaj continued: 'No, thou hast not recited the *shahada* properly'; and when he himself said it, the minaret collapsed."[9]

2. Magical prayer owes its powerfulness to precise recitation, to rhythmical sequence, to the utterance of the name together with other factors; one very important consideration, for example, being the so-called epic introduction that occurs in many magical formulas. I call this the *magical antecedent*: thus one of the Merseburg magical incantations says: "Once some *idisi* (wise women) sat down (here and there). Some were knitting fetters, others were hindering the army, others were freeing from (the strong fetters).—Break away from the fetters! Escape from the enemy!"[10] And the second: "Phol and Wotan were

---

[1] Aeschylus, *Choëphoroe*, 721.   [2] Cato, *De Agri Cultura*, 83.

[3] *cf.* Wundt, *op. cit.*, II. Heiler, *ibid.*, xiii *f.*, 53 *f.* F. B. Jevons, *The Idea of God*, 115 *ff.* Fr. Pfister in *Handwörterbuch des deutschen Aberglaubens, Gebet.*

[4] Bertholet, *op. cit.,* 9, 55.   [5] Grönbech, *op. cit.*, IV, 44 *f.*

[6] *Acts* iv. 31.   [7] Pliny, *Nat. Hist.* 28, 12 *f.* Appel, *op. cit.*, 74 *f.*

[8] J. von Görres, *Mystik, Magie und Dämonie*, 1927, 250. This was also said about Vintras, the prophet of "Vintrasism"; *cf.* J. Bois, *Les petites religions de Paris*, 1894, 122 *f.*   [9] Massignon, *Al Hallaj*, I, 449.

[10] Bertholet, *op. cit.*, 12, 70.

once riding in a wood. There Balder's foal sprained its foot. Then
Sinthgunt charmed it, (and) Sunna her sister; then Friia charmed it,
(and) Volla her sister; then Wotan charmed it, as he well knew how to
do; alike the injured bone, the damaged blood, the broken limb—bone
to bone, blood to blood, limb to limb, as though they were glued
together!"[1] Here the actuality that has been given is corrected by
means of the word, as it were by substitution; an event that occurred
in prehistoric times, and which now possesses a mythical eternity and
typicalness, is by the power of the formula rendered present in the
literal sense and made actual and fruitful.[2] This phenomenon is also
very well shown on a runic piece of wood discovered in Westeremden,
one side of which bears a runic inscription recounting a mythical
event, an "epic introduction", a "magical antecedent", as follows:
"Amlud (Hamlet) took up his position (for battle) at Upheim. The
surf bowed before his runic yew staves." This is, then, a historical
occurrence of a mythical kind and of typical power. On the other side,
in a different hand: "May the surf bow before this runic yew stave."[3]
This practical application of the myth was probably inscribed on the
wood, in some moment of dire need, by the Frisian seamen who had
bought it in Denmark, and the stave was then cast into the raging sea.
The wood of the yew, and the runic inscription, possessed magical
power; here then it was actually the runic wood itself that was the
concrete presence of the mythical event; succinctly, it may be said that
the seamen threw the Hamlet-event into the sea. Man thus transforms a
disagreeable reality by the creative induction of something better;
and we find an extreme example of this creative, event-producing
power of the word in an Indian tribe. "A telegram once came to my
bungalow. 'Baloo dead, don't worry.' Baloo was a hundred miles
away. . . ." He was, however, not dead at all; "a crow had momen-
tarily perched on his head, and his uncle had sent the wire to prevent
the fulfilment of this ill omen . . . to realize it in some way beforehand.
The crow, by perching on the boy's head, had doomed him to an
inevitable death."[4] For now Baloo *was* dead, since the word had con-

---

[1] Bertholet. Further examples: in popular custom, Usener, *Heilige Handlung*, 423 *f*.
M. L. Palès, *Revue anthropologique*, 37, 1927. C. Bakker, *Ned. Tydschrift voor Genees-
kunde*, 65, 1921. Christian, K. H. E. de Jong, *De magie by de Grieken en Romeinen*,
1921, 238. Ancient Egypt, *Pyramidentexte* (Sethe), 418. Ad. Erman, *Die ägyptische
Religion*[2], 1909, 169 *ff*.
[2] *cf*. further Preuss, *Gehalt der Mythen*.
[3] J. M. N. Kapteyn, *Dertiende, veertiende en vyftiende Jaarverslag van de Vereeniging
voor Terpenonderzoek*, 1928–1931, 72 *ff*.   [4] Chap. 54.

summated the event, and so he would not die again so soon. At all events the omen had "been exhausted".[1]

3. An intermediate form between conjuration and prayer is the *summons* which, in connection with the sacrament, has already been discussed as the *epiclesis*.[2] *Mars vigila*—"Mars, awake!"— cried the Roman general setting out for the field; that is a kind of warning cry, probably intended to remind the god of the pact that had been concluded.[3] Yet another type is the summons which invokes the saviour,[4] like the extremely ancient one of the women of Elis: "Come in springtime, O Dionysos, to thy pure temple by the sea, with the *Charites* in thy train, rushing with ox-foot (phallus). Noble bull, Noble bull."[5] Here the summons was intended to effect the epiphany of the life-bringing god: the presence of power was "bespoken". Professional magic also requires the god's presence and invokes him, often indeed in words whose sublimity far surpasses their trivial purpose: one magical papyrus in Leyden thus invokes Eros: "Come unto me . . . O thou omnipotent god, thou who hast inspired men with the breath of life. Thou, the lord of all that is beautiful on earth, hear my prayer . . . *etc.*"[6] The Christian *epiclesis* also, alike in prayer and in the sacrament, vacillates between conjuration, summons and actual prayer, while the ancient Christian *maran atha* is a cult summons. In the *Apostolic Constitutions*, again, we find the prayer: "send down thy Holy Spirit upon this sacrifice";[7] the Roman mass, however, required this *epiclesis* no longer, or placed it elsewhere because its formula of consecration (*Qui pridie*) could compel the presence of divine Power.[8]

Thus to a higher degree than the formula, the summons possesses the character of spontaneity; it is a kind of warning cry: a sort of "Hallo! Look out!" uttered to power. In its most elementary form it approaches the *exclamation*, still occurring in many prayers as a very ancient component (πομπυσμός, ὀλολυγή;[9] *hallelujah, Kyrie eleison, euoi, triumpe, etc.*), and which is similarly prominent in ecstatic forms of supplication. Similarly the Hindu syllable *om*, however much it may subsequently have been stored with speculation, was originally such a

---

[1] Lévy-Bruhl, *Primitives and the Supernatural*, 375.   [2] Chap. 52.
[3] Wissowa, *Religion der Römer*, 144. Heiler, *Prayer*, 16.   [4] Chap. 12.
[5] Plutarch, *Quaestiones graecae*, 36. Farnell, *Cults*, V, 126.
[6] De Jong, *Magie by de Grieken en Romeinen*, 157, 155 *ff.*
[7] Lietzmann, *Messe und Herrenmahl*, 68.
[8] Lietzmann, *ibid.*, 121 *f.* We find a similar vacillation in the formula of absolution (*ego te absolvo*), which was definitely changed from the deprecative to the indicative form only by the Council of Trent.   [9] Heiler, *Prayer*, 8 *f.*

"numinous primeval sound", "the long protracted nasal continuation of the deep 'o' sound".[1]

4. When man recognizes first of all Form, and later Will, within Power, then the power-word, the conjuration, changes into *prayer*; Power operates only upon power: the potency of Will requires a second will. To begin with, then, prayer is the verbal presentation of the human will before the superior, divine, Will. We cannot say, however, that prayer first arises as a practical manifestation of the will after the magical formula has served its purpose. For the latter has never completely exhausted its capacities, while prayer, as such an expression of the will, occurs even among the most primitive peoples; of this Heiler's admirable volume gives an abundance of examples. Prayer exhibits the greatest contrast in tone, from the threat to the most submissive humility, from alarmed entreaty to the most cordial trust. But wherever it appears, it is an address from man to the Will which he knows to be above him, and the reply of this Will. Essentially, therefore, prayer is a *dialogue*, usually having some very concrete aim: something definite is prayed for. Frequently, on the other hand, it is simply the expression of a pious or reverential, an anxious or some other type of mood; thus the Ana people of Atakpame in Togo daily appear before the sacred staff of the supreme god, kneel, clap their hands and say: "Good morning to-day, father".[2]

In prayer, then, the compulsion pertaining to the power-word is "transposed" to *fatigare deos*; God must be troubled; prayer should compel Him, as it were, as did the widow's request to the unjust judge in the *Gospel*.[3] The classical example of this "power of prayer", which has however completely discarded its magical character, is the story of Jacob's struggle with the angel, as conceived in the exegesis of the fervour of Christian prayer: "I will not let thee go, except thou bless me."[4]

[1] Otto, *The Idea of the Holy*, 197. On the modern interpretation of *om cf.* von Glasenapp, *Reformbewegung*, 44.   [2] Heiler, *ibid.*, 29.   [3] *Luke* xviii.
[4] *Gen.* xxxii, 26. The ascent of prayer can be facilitated; among other things, *incense* may serve for this; *cf.* Lietzmann, *op. cit.*; also the fine passage in *Paradise Lost*, XI, 15 *ff.*:

> To heaven their prayers
> Flew up, nor missed the way, by envious winds
> Blown vagabond or frustrate: in they passed
> Dimensionless through heavenly doors; then, clad
> With incense, where the golden altar fumed,
> By their great Intercessor, came in sight
> Before the Father's throne.

From an early stage, however, it was doubted that any direct inter-course with deity was possible in prayer; and while the religion of absolute Power[1] diverts from magic to the rapture of the feeling of union with God, the religion for which Power and Will subsist in the background of the Universe[2] expressly turns its back on both the delirium of unity and reciprocity between two wills; Confucius' attitude is typical: "it must be a long time since I prayed".[3] Laments over the futility of prayer, too, are not lacking;[4] they are the antithesis of the expectation that the contract between God and man will be fulfilled. Certainly this contract is just as little essentially a matter of reckoning as is *do-ut-des* in sacrifice;[5] rather is it a *demande d'avoir de quoi donner*,[6] and a readiness to give what one wishes to receive. But as soon as this attitude becomes either mechanized, or based on the pure benevolence of Power, then disillusion must arise; and this can be overcome only by that courage which creates witnesses and martyrs, the boldness, παρρησία,[7] introducing the *Pater noster* in the *Text* of the mass: *praeceptis salutaribus moniti et divina institutione formati audemus dicere: Pater noster* . . .: "Taught by the precepts of salvation and following the divine commandment, we make bold to say: 'Our Father'."[8] But this prayer is never an individual act, since it is always based upon the sacred common element; and even when it is uttered by the individual, and its object is of a supremely personal character, it still reposes on the prayer of the community.[9] Prayer bearing the character of dialogue, then, is essentially intercessory, *intercessio*; in the Christian church it is the prayer of the *church*: a mode of relation-ship between the Body of Christ and the exalted Saviour; hence prayer is only *in Christo*.[10]

5. But to the extent that the relation between Power and man is devoid of the structure of Will, prayer loses its dialogue character and becomes a monologue saturated with religious energy; and thus, for Tauler, "prayer is nothing more than an absorption of the soul in

---

[1] Chap. 21.   [2] Chap. 18.
[3] Bertholet, *op. cit.*, 6, 67. The interpretation of the text is doubtful, but the Master's scepticism is obvious from his question, when they wished to pray for him during his serious illness:—"Will it be any use?"
[4] *e.g.* Sophocles, *Antigone*, 1336 f.   [5] Chap. 50.
[6] J. Segond, *La Prière*, 135 ff. (1911).   [7] Chap. 29.
[8] E. Peterson, *R. Seeberg-Festschrift*, 296 f. The formula is very old; *cf.* the beautiful Mozarabic version (at Christmas): *tibi, summe Pater, cum tremore cordis proclamemus e terris*; C. E. Hammond, *Liturgies Eastern and Western*, 343.
[9] Will, *Culte*, 221.   [10] *cf.* Fr. Heiler, *Das Geheimnis des Gebets*, 1919, 36

God".[1] Speaking and hearing then become subordinate affairs; nothing at all is rendered definite; words are indeed actually superfluous, since silent prayer[2] is the most suitable form for "effective self-surrender".[3]

Mystical prayer, still further, begins by inverting the relationship between God and the suppliant; and then the circulation of Power from man to God, and from God to man, whose essential nature we discerned in sacrifice, is indispensable alike to God and to man: God *needs* man's prayers, as with Pascal: "He was 'made sin for' me. He is more abominable even than myself; and far from detesting me, He feels it an honour that I go to Him to help Him."[4] Still more directly Angelus Silesius affirms:

> God is so blessed, and exists free from all desire,
> Because He receives from me as much as I from Him.[5]

The relationship has thus become wholly mutual, like the primitive relations between gift and return-gift, the stream of gifts[6] now being replaced by the stream of speech: God and man carry on an intimate conversation! But prayer is always at the same time an answer; God's utterance coincides with human speech, and prayer with its hearing.[7] No longer then is "something prayed for"; prayer for something definite ceases, or at least becomes regarded as imperfect and, gradually, prayer becomes pious meditation, a monologue. It requires no recipient: one prays either to one's higher self[8] or even to oneself,[9] or regards it as a matter of complete indifference to whom prayer is offered.[10] The old "godless" religion has exchanged the magical for the mystical garb; prayer remains indeed a celebration of Power, only this has now neither Form nor Will; and just as it is devoid of Will, so must the supplicant himself become. Mystical prayer is "merging in God". He who prays must be *"comme une toile d'attente devant un peintre"*,

---

[1] G. Siedel, *Die Mystik Taulers*, 1911, 6.

[2] Chap. 63.   [3] Segond, *La Prière*, 52.

[4] *ibid.*, 144. *"Il a été fait péché par moi. Il est plus abominable que moi, et, loin de m'abhorrer, il se tient honoré que j'aille à lui et le secoure."*

[5] *The Cherubinic Wanderer*, I, 9.   [6] Chap. 50.

[7] *cf.* H. Groos, *Der deutsche Idealismus und das Christentum*, 1927, 121 *f.*, and Schleiermacher's definition of prayer: "The intimate connection of the desire to attain what is best with the consciousness of God"; § 146, 1; *cf.* further the whole Chapter.

[8] Segond, *ibid.*, 42.

[9] Romain Rolland, *Jean Christophe, La foire sur la place*, 42. Mystical prayer may also be a monologue by God; *cf.* B. M. Schuurman, *Mystik und Glaube, im Zusammenhang mit der Mission auf Java*, 1933, who quotes a Javanese *Text*: "It is Allah who adores Allah, but Allah is really only the name Allah"; 15.   [10] Segond, *ibid.*, 35.

like a burning candle consuming itself from love;[1] and thus this prayer attains its highest form in *submersion*,[2] while the dialogue type of supplication, on the other hand, always remains word and entreaty, practical demonstration of Will to will, even when it prays in *its* highest form: "not my will, but thine, be done".

[1] Segond, 37.   [2] *cf.* Fr. Heiler, *Die buddhistische Versenkung*[2], 1922.

CHAPTER 63

PRAISE, LALLATION, AND SILENCE

1. WHOEVER is deeply moved cries out: he "lifts up" his voice. Crying aloud and singing set power in motion.[1] But the most important type of profoundly emotional utterance is *praise*: the *song of praise*. It is distinguished from prayer by being, not an assumption of a position before the divine will on the part of man's will, but a "confirmation" of divine power. Of course this confirmation is by no means a sort of ratification, nor a sentimental assertion, but a "confirmation" in the literal sense, a consolidation of the power, of the will, with which man finds himself confronted; so the Botocudos repeat incessantly: "the chief, he knows no fear".[2] This is neither assertion nor poetry, but a *carmen*, a confirmation of the chief's power. To praise ancestors, again, is regarded by many primitive peoples as a means of influencing their "situation", and determining this to some result or other.[3] Praise is therefore no embellishment, no mere adornment, of intercourse with power: it is no beautiful or cordial superfluity. Whoever is deeply moved emotionally, praises: he cannot possibly avoid doing so; for in praise there lies self-forgetfulness, elevating itself above life in the powerfulness of the one who is praised. To praise, "to rejoice in the Lord", then, implies not that we desire nothing from God: on the contrary, we seek everything from Him: but rather that we relinquish ourselves and our own power, and rely wholly on God's Power. To praise is to turn away from self and towards God.

Thus we can understand that at all times, and by all religions, praise has been regarded as exceedingly important; "service"[4] is almost entirely the offering of praise,[5] and the *vita religiosa*, whether monastic, or in accord with the Reformation ideal vocational, has no other purpose

---

[1] G. van der Leeuw, *Wegen en Grenzen*.   [2] *ibid.*, 12.

[3] Lévy-Bruhl, *Primitives and the Supernatural*, 135 f. Lévy-Bruhl's concept of "Disposition" and my own term "Situation" are almost exactly identical; both may be applied alike to persons, objects and circumstances. Heidegger, *op. cit.*, 161: Speech is existentially equally original as situation and understanding; "as the existential condition of what can be inferred from Being, speech is constitutive of its existence".

[4] Chap. 53.

[5] Like other *carmina* (*Brahman, etc.*) the song of praise was transformed into a person; in the Middle Ages, for the season when the Alleluia was omitted, "the Alleluia was buried"; *cf.* G. R. S. Mead, *The Quest*, IV, 1912, 110 *ff.*

than the praise of God and the never ceasing proclamation of His glory: *gloria Patri et Filio et Spiritui sancto, sicut erat in principio, nunc et semper, et in saecula saeculorum.* The sound of praise reaches eternity, and finds an outlet in the angelic song of praise; it is a cosmic movement towards God, which is the affair not only of man but of the whole Universe. "Make a joyful noise unto the Lord, all the earth: make a loud noise, and rejoice, and sing praise. Let the sea roar, and the fullness thereof; the world, and they that dwell therein. Let the floods clap their hands: let the hills be joyful together before the Lord."[1] Roman Catholicism, as I have already observed, transferred this idea to the monastery, while the reformers, and above all Calvin, expanded it into the magnificent demand that the whole of life should be devoted only to God's glory; measured by human standards, then, the purpose of life is uselessness and superfluity; this purpose is to confess to the Lord that He is the Lord and that His name is mighty. But this implies that life finds its own fulfillment only in life's surrender, and that genuine powerfulness is attained only by relinquishing all power. Thus praise takes the place of sacrifice: the Eucharist, indeed, was always[2] a thank-offering as a return gift for God's sacrifice. But the whole life of obedience also proceeds from the viewpoint of thankfulness: to fulfil the commands is no burden, but praise.

One striking form of the expression of praise is the so-called *acclamatio.* This hail, which in the Hellenic era was made by the mass of the people on the appearance of the emperor or some high official at assemblies or in the theatre *etc.*, was a genuine "confirmation". It authenticated an event, but also had legal validity and confirmed a decision or a choice. It was praise and decision simultaneously; it was, indeed, the sole possible decision where a majority of votes possessed no power.[3] A fine example, applied to a deity, is the acclamation of the Ephesians: "Great is Diana of the Ephesians", which continued for no less than two hours;[4] in *The Epistle to the Philippians,*[5] again, there is a similar acclamation: "Jesus Christ is Lord, to the glory of God the Father".[6] At the election of the bishop in Milan, too, a little child cried out: "Ambrose, Bishop!" and they all acclaimed Ambrose as their bishop;[7] this was regarded as an election, and it is still a recognized procedure in Catholic electoral law, even though it is a survival: *vox populi, vox Dei.* Confirmation is potent.

---

[1] *Ps.* xcviii. 4, 7 *ff.*   [2] Chap. 52.
[3] E. Peterson, *ΕΙΣ ΘΕΟΣ* (1926).   [4] *Acts* xix. 28.   [5] ii, 11 (Moffat).
[6] E. Peterson, *Die Einholung des Kyrios, Zeitschrift für systematische Theologie,* 7, 1930, 699.   [7] I. H. Gosses, *Met meerderheid van stemmen,* 1929, 4.

2. Profound emotional disturbance also results in lallation. An apparent impediment is then the greatest powerfulness: ecstasy breaks forth in interrupted and spasmodic sounds. Examples of prophetic utterance have already been dealt with;[1] and the specific feature of lalling is that the speaker has no power over his own speech; it is "uncontrolled" and impulsive. We find such lallation in the glossolalia attested from early Christian times and in many religious movements, both ancient and modern—the pentecostal movement, *etc.* "The person who expresses his emotions in glossolalia speaks without desiring to do so; in many instances he appears to feel himself impelled to speak, in others perhaps even this is not the case; he speaks like a machine, or more precisely, *something speaks through him.* He knows not the content of what he says in advance, but interprets his words and understands them afterwards, as if they were those of another person."[2] Power is thus discovered in impotence; from the loss of one's own powerfulness the operation of some superior Power is inferred. St. Paul, indeed, who himself possessed the "gift" of speaking with tongues, "more than any of you", "would rather say five words with my own mind for the instruction of other people than ten thousand words" in incomprehensible glossolalia.[3]

3. Deep emotional agitation produces *silence* also; *favete linguis*, "keep silence", which was originally magically intended and supposed to overcome the power of some unpropitious word, became through "transposition"[4] the positive expression of the inexpressible, the language of the unutterable. Not man, but "it", is to speak. Glossolalia, in which "it" does indeed speak, is ultimately nothing more than verbosity; but the silence of profound emotional disturbance is the manifestation of the super-powerful itself, the wordless decision of the eternal Word.

The standard terminology of the liturgy, no detail of which can be arbitrarily changed, and which is employed with the utmost conservatism, is itself an approximation to silence;[5] and it is the experience of every celebrant and liturgist that while repeating the words of the liturgy he must himself be silent; "it", however, speaks all the more articulately through him. The strangeness of liturgical language is also

---

[1] Chap. 27.
[2] T. K. Österreich, *Einführung in die Religionspsychologie*, 1917, 60.
[3] 1 *Cor.* xiv. 18 f.   [4] [On this term *cf.* pp. 31, Note, and 610].
[5] G. Mensching, *Das heilige Schweigen* (1926), 125; Brilioth, *op. cit.*, 14.

an approach to silence: the ceremonial tones of a tongue long alien to everyday usage as with Luther's Bible, or ecclesiastical Latin and Greek;[1] while the subdued prayer of the priest in consecration also belongs to this category and leads to the complete silence characterizing the culmination of the mass.[2] This worshipful silence, however, is no lack of audibility; it has not a negative but a positive value. Exactly as with music, where the pauses often cause the most intense impression and the richest expression,[3] silence during worship not merely gives vent to the profoundest emotion, but is also the means of conveying the profoundest revelation. "Silences in worship are not the empty moments of devotion, but the full moments."[4] Silence filled by divine powerfulness corresponds to the darkness of sacred space, the numinous emptiness of Islamite holy places;[5] and by mystics of all ages the most extreme poverty is accounted as the greatest riches, emptiness as fullness, power as impotence. Mensching distinguishes a preparatory, a sacramentally unifying, a contemplative, a worshipful, an expectant and a monastic-ascetic silence.[6] From the fourth century onwards, indeed, the ancient Eastern liturgies were already familiar with silent prayer; the Quakers also practise it,[7] and so does the Roman church, apart from consecration, in the *Pater noster* and in the passion at the moment of Christ's death.[8] The Greek *bacchae*, too, experienced a sacred silence at the climax of their ecstasy.[9]

Universally, mysticism seeks silence: the strength of the Power with which it deals is so great that only silence can create a "situation" for it. This is the "paradox" of expression referred to by Jaspers: we should like to say all that could possibly be said, and much more: the greatest eloquence alternates with complete silence.[10] That mysticism has always been very eloquent is therefore only the reverse of its essential silence: the uniquely powerful is revealed only *per viam negationis*. This is the reason why mysticism usually opposes *carmina*, formal prayers, and why it cannot ultimately rest content with even free personal prayer; Muslim mysticism warns even against the praise of God: we "must forget even the praise that God has placed on our lips, in

---

[1] Will, *op. cit.*, I, 201 *f.*   Casel, *op. cit.*, 143 *f.*   [2] Will, *ibid.*, I, 201.
[3] G. van der Leeuw, *Wegen en Grenzen*, 148 *ff.*
[4] Amiel, *Journal*, 22 Aug. 1873 (Brooks).
[5] *cf.* Otto, *Aufsätze das Numinose betreffend*, 108 *ff.*   *The Idea of the Holy*, 70, 216.
[6] *cf.* further his *Die liturgische Bewegung in der evangelischen Kirche*, 1925, 47 *ff.*
[7] Will, *op. cit.*, I, 323.   [8] Heiler, *Katholizismus*, 411 *f.*
[9] Rohde, *Psyche*, II, 9. E. T. 259.
[10] *Psychologie der Weltanschauungen*[2], 1922; *cf.* van der Leeuw, *Mystiek*, 1925.

order to worship, on this side of His heart, Him Whom they praise".[1]
True worship, genuine *salāt*, is uninterrupted, in so far as he who
practises it is always pure because of the light in his heart.[2]

The injunction to "pray without ceasing. In every thing give thanks",
has certainly another basis: "for this is the will of God in Christ Jesus
concerning you".[3] The religion of Power in Will, of faith in the Form
that has actually appeared, also knows the inexpressibility of God, the
fullness of the void, the wealth of poverty and the eloquence of silence;
but it finds these in the *kenosis* of Him Who emptied Himself *by coming
into the world*.[4] Thus silence is primarily and principally a speaking to
God and being addressed by Him. The *sursum corda* was originally
spoken by the priest "in order that silence might be observed";[5] but
praise follows it.

Christian mysticism, however, speaks in Tersteegen's exquisite
Night Song, a song of praise which dies away in a silence that is the
utterance of God:

> Now let us sleep,
> And whoso cannot sleep,
> Shall with me pray
> To the great Name,
> To Whom by night and day
> The heavenly guardians pay
> Glory, honour, praise,
> Jesus, Amen.
>
> May Heaven's beauteous light
> Shine upon thee;
> May I be thy little star
> Shining here and there.
> I lay me down;
> Lord, do Thou alone
> In deepest silence
> Speak to me in the dark.

---

[1] Massignon, *Al-Hallaj*, 513; *cf.* N. von Arseniew: "On (the) heights of mystical
experience the song must again die away, since it is the realm of the inexpressible . . .",
with his further observations on the mystical *Jubilus* (*AR.* 22, 1923–24, 266 *ff.*). In
Javanese mysticism the song of praise (*dzikr*) is uttered in the first mystical stage with
the tongue and the heart; in the second and third with the heart; in the third the *dzikr*
is all that comes from the mystic's mouth, whether it is the usual formula of praise of
Islam or the mystic syllable *hu*, or the lallation: *la, la, la, oh, oh, oh,* or even "his weeping and trembling, his movement or his stillness"; Schuurman, *Mystik und Glaube*,
17 *f.*   [2] H. Kraemer, *Een Javaansche Primbon uit de zestiende eeuw*, 1921, 78.
[3] 1 *Thess.* v, 17 *f.*   [4] *Phil.* ii, 6 *f.*   [5] Casel, *op. cit.*, 149.

CHAPTER 64

THE WRITTEN WORD

1. "WHAT we have in black and white we can safely take home with us":—the tendency already discerned in Fetishism[1] becomes evident also in the valuation of the written word. Strictly, then, *writing* is a charm: written signs are charms. A *rune* (Gothic, *rûna*) is a secret, a secret decree or resolve, a mystery; the Old High German verb *rûnen* means *susurrare*, "to murmur or whisper". Thus the living word, filled with power and murmured in a subdued voice, persists in the written characters.[2] Runes originated with Odin, who in his turn received them from "the powers", and on the Stora Noleby Stone in Sweden may be read the inscription: "I write runes, *regenkunnar*, (derived from the powers)."[3] The greatest power was possessed by the system of twenty-four runes, the so-called *futhark*, itself in turn divided into three "families" of eight signs each.[4] The ancient Egyptian hieroglyphs, again, were magical beings: like all writing, they were originally pictures incorporating the essence of what is depicted; they were even called *ntr-w*, the term for "gods", and in the script certain hieroglyphic figures, representing something unfavourable or terrifying, were either suppressed and replaced by strokes or intentionally curtailed in their design.[5]

Writing, then, is magic:—one method of gaining power over the living word. The tradition of the sacred word is originally oral; it lives in being recited, and only later did oral tradition give place to graphic; in certain cases, indeed, as in that of the *Vedas*, only in our own times.[6] Committing sacred texts to writing therefore was not, in the first place, intended to render tradition exact (in antiquity, and for primitive peoples, oral tradition left nothing more to be desired!), but to attain

---

[1] Chap. 3.

[2] G. Ehrismann, *Geschichte der deutschen Literatur bis zum Ausgang des Mittelalters*, I, 1918, 46.

[3] Kapteyn, *Dertiende, Veertiende en Vyfriende Jaarverslag van de Vereeniging voor Terpenonderzoek*, 1928, 31, 53.

[4] *ibid.*, 54 f. *cf.* E. Mogk, *Germanische Religionsgeschichte und Mythologie*, 1921, 44 ff. Magnus Olsen, *Magie et Culte dans la Norvège antique* (*RHR*. 96, 1927, 1 ff.).

[5] W. Spiegelberg, *Zeitschrift für ägypt. Sprache und Altertumskunde*, 65, 1930, 120. P. Lacau, *ibid.*, 51, 1913, 1 ff.

[6] *cf.* H. von Glasenapp, *Religiöse Reformbewegungen im heutigen Indien*, 1928, V.

power, since with the written word man can do just what he will; writing is no more precise than the living word, but is more easily dealt with. Even where writing is employed the necessity for recitation still persists: unuttered, the word has no decisive power.

But with what exists in black and white we can proceed in a much more drastic way than with the merely spoken word. The crassest example of this is the *drinking* of a sentence. According to Mosaic law, for instance, a woman suspected of infidelity had to drink water with which a curse, written on a piece of paper, had been washed off; thus she literally drank the curse, of course as an ordeal.[1] In the Egyptian fairy tale, similarly, the hero drinks a whole book of magic that has been soaked in beer and dissolved in water, so that he may know everything it contains;[2] we too still swear by the Gospel to-day; not, that is, by the Word of God, but on the holy book. Scripture, again, is an *oracle*; it is opened arbitrarily to obtain instructions.[3] It had indeed the effect of a *judgment of God* when a key was placed in the Bible at *St. John* i. 1, a passage regarded as particularly sacred, in order to discover whether a woman were a witch or not; the book was tied up and suspended from the woman's finger, and if she were guilty she would let it drop.[4] At a quite early stage in the Egyptian ceremonies for the dead, also, the written magical charm played its part: persons who were ritually buried received their thousands in bread and beer; but "miserable is their flesh (nevertheless) if a written document be not there (among the sacrificial gifts)" and furnished with a great seal.[5] In China, again, the Buddhist dead receive a passport intended to open the entrance to heaven for them, and filled up with all due ceremony by the proper official; it concludes: "As soon as thou receivest this passport, thou must set out for the place of the blessed where thou mayest expect great bliss and peace. Given this eighth day of the fourth month in the sixth year of Hienfong."[6] Another remarkable example of the written sacred word is the so-called *heavenly letter*, written by God or by an angel and fallen from heaven, or obtained in some other miraculous way, and supposed to be a protection against every form of evil. The peculiar feature is that here it is a matter of a written *revelation*; the

---

[1] *Num.* v, 11 *ff. cf.* R. Kreglinger, *Grondbeginselen der Godsdienstwetenschap*, 40.

[2] G. Roeder, *Altägyptische Erzählungen und Märchen*, 1927, 145. G. Maspero, *Stories of Ancient Egypt*, 129.   [3] Chap. 54.

[4] The so-called *kaei* (key) trial. Waling Dykstra, *Friesch Volksleven*, II, 171.

[5] *Pyramidentexte* (Sethe), 474.

[6] Lehmann, *Textbuch*[1], 23 *f.*; *cf.* the small gold tablets placed in the grave with the Orphic dead, discovered in Southern Italy; chap. 47.

celestial letter is a sort of popular parallel to the Word of God.[1] Quite recently the *Book of Mormon*, the holy writ of the Mormons, as is well known, was composed by God and sent down from heaven,[2] while the sheer and pure power of letters, even though utterly meaningless, is to be found in the magical papyri of antiquity (*Abraxas*, *ephesia grammata*) and pre-eminently in the Jewish *kabbala*.[3]

2. From the oracular use of sacred writings, of which the finest example was perhaps the opening of the Sibylline books by the Romans in times of direst emergency,[4] is distinguished the utilization of holy writ in order to find in it the revealed word of God. This required that settled delimitation of the writings called a *canon*; from the abundance of sacred words and writings a certain portion is "selected" and elevated to the status of "holy writ", exactly as certain actions are given prominence as sacraments among the mass of sacramentals. This canonization may consist, in the first place, in placing the origin of the writings under consideration in some miraculous light, sacred writings, for example, being frequently "discovered", of course after having been deliberately concealed. In 181 B.C. a Roman secretary found a stone coffin with an inscription asserting that king Numa Pompilius was buried in it; in the coffin were books purporting to be Numa's writings, and dealing with the philosophy of Pythagoras; a *praetor* read them, however, and had them burnt as dangerous to the state. Here then an attempt had been made to create respect for a specific religion by means of books that had appeared miraculously.[5] Not only origin, but restriction also, pertains to canonization: then from the writings arises the sacred book within which the power of the sacred word is confined, the limits being most rigidly drawn in Islam, Judaism and Christianity. Other religions too have their more or less definitely fixed holy books: the *Vedas*, the *Avesta*, the Buddhist *Tipitaka*, etc. The Chinese Buddhist *Tipitaka* includes from 5000 to even 7000 volumes, arranged in rotating cases in the Japanese temples; and turning the case is regarded as the study of the holy writ and is a

---

[1] R. Stübe, *Der Himmelsbrief*, 1918. [2] Stübe, *ibid.*, 41 *ff.*
[3] A. Dieterich, *Abraxas*, 1891. P. Vulliaud, *La Kabbale Juive, Histoire et Doctrine*, 1923. [4] H. Diels, *Sibyllinische Blätter*, 1890.
[5] Fowler, *The Religious Experience of the Roman People*, 349. Perhaps the discovery of the "strict book of the law" by the high priest Hilkiah in B.C. 623 was also an attempt to endow the law with divine authority; *cf.* 2 *Kings* xxii. In Egypt the "process of discovery" was quite a usual affair; *cf.* R. Weill, *Les Origines de l'Égypt pharaonique*, 1908, 39 *ff.* G. van der Leeuw, *Pia fraus, Mensch en Maatschappy*, 8, 1932.

meritorious action.[1] But only Judaism, Christianity and Islam possess
one single holy book, and the last of these is pre-eminently a genuine
religion of the book. The Koran comes from God: "He it is who hath
sent down to thee 'the Book' . . . But they whose hearts are given to
err, follow its figures, craving discord, craving an interpretation; yet
none knoweth its interpretation but God. And the stable in knowledge
say, 'we believe in it: it is all from our Lord'."[2] It is precisely the
intensely passionate monotheism of Islam, which regards with suspicion
a God possessing any attributes, that leads to the crassest belief in the
letter of the writings. God speaks, and His utterance is not His attribute
in the sense of the Aristotelian philosophy that has pervaded Islam, but
pertains eternally to His essence; it is an "eternal attribute" which
"had no beginning and is never interrupted"; the utterance of the
eternally speaking God must therefore be eternal; the Koran, that is to
say, did not originate in time and was not created by God, but existed
uncreated from all eternity.[3] In the eyes of the Mutazilites, however,
this belief was too dangerous: besides God, there could be nothing
uncreated; the Koran must therefore have been created like all other
creatures, and was not the immediate language of God but only a means
of which He made use. On this question a vehement dispute ensued
with orthodoxy, forming an exact parallel to the Christian controversies
about the nature of Christ; the spoken and subsequently the written
word thus assume in Islam the place of the "Word", that is of Christ
and of the *logos*, in Christianity.[4] Scriptural orthodoxy triumphed,
however, and even went so far as the assertion: "whatever lies between
the two covers is the word of God", thereby declaring the paper and the
ink to be uncreated;[5] and these contentions are typical of the difficulties
of scriptural theology in Judaism and Christianity. Moses, again, was
supposed to have received the tablets of the law, written by God's
own hand, on Sinai; certainly the Old Testament canon was defined
only in Christian times;[6] but for the Jews holy writ was always "law",[7]
just as the law was its oldest and most essential constituent. Subsequently Christians too repeatedly sought the fixity of divine revelation:

---

[1] Clemen, *Die nichtchristlichen Religionen*, I, 107 f.
[2] *Sura* 3, 5 (Everyman's Library); *cf.* I. Goldziher, *Vorlesungen über den Islam*,
1910, 81 f.   [3] Goldziher, *ibid.*, 112 f.
[4] For a parallel between Mohammedan doctrine about scripture and the doctrine of
the two natures in Christianity *cf.* Frick, *Vergl. Rel. wiss.*, 32.
[5] Goldziher, *ibid.*, 113 ff.; *cf.* H. Frick, *Marb. Theol. Stud.* 3, 10.
[6] Hölscher, *Geschichte der israelitischen und jüdischen Religion*, 101.
[7] *cf.* further below.

"It is written!"[1] The Christian church has indeed again and again
found the way back to its essential nature, and continually discovered
anew that her "Word" is not the written word, but the living utterance
of God in the figure of Christ.[2] The church, still further, has
undoubtedly made the written word fluid and vital in its liturgy, and
actual and decisive in its preaching, although in its Roman and Greek
forms it has admittedly diminished the ascendancy of the writings by
the more supple tradition.[3] It has also, in the Greek communion, not
only read the Gospel aloud, but has rendered it living in worship and
in the church.[4] And finally, in the evangelical churches, it has returned
repeatedly to the recollection of its actual and true nature, by asserting
that it is *not* a book religion like Islam but faith in the living Word, and
by substantiating this conviction either by the power of its prophetic
utterances or by the sincerity of its experience. The Bible has nevertheless won a place for itself, as the written word of God, which is far
more important than can ever be understood from its mere character
as a document of revelation. The fact that it is *written* has exerted its
own influence, while the facility with which the word of God can be
manipulated and controlled has repeatedly attracted the Christian
mind. So far as the Protestant church is concerned, indeed, Tillich
speaks quite justifiably even of a sacrament, not of the word alone,
but of the written word, which according to him has established a new
hierarchy of pure doctrine.[5]

But on the other hand, there naturally occurs a periodical reaction as
the outcome of the formidable problem of *interpretation*. What does the
Bible say? Everything, and nothing. "When will people understand that
it is useless for a man to read his Bible unless he also reads everybody
else's Bible? A printer reads a Bible for misprints. A Mormon reads his
Bible, and finds polygamy; a Christian Scientist reads his, and finds
that we have no arms and legs."[6] The Bible, then, must be *interpreted*:
but how, and by what authority? In these difficulties a by no means
negligible proportion of the most important questions that have agitated

---

[1] In India, where sacred tradition is transmitted orally, it is usual to say "It has
been heard" instead of "It is written"; the *Veda* is called "What has been heard".
[2] Will, *Culte*, II, 335: the Bible as sacred action, and its being read aloud as the
event itself.   [3] Heiler, *Katholizismus*, 587.
[4] S. Hans Ehrenberg and Sergej Bulgakov, *Östliches Christentum und Protestantismus*
(*Religiöse Besinnung*, I, 1928). On tradition in the Eastern church *cf.* S. Boulgakoff,
L'Orthodoxie, 1932, 12 *ff.*, and on the actual procedure in reading the scriptures,
ibid., 32.   [5] *Religiöse Verwirklichung*, 141.
[6] Chesterton, *The Innocence of Father Brown*, 277 (Popular Edition). J. Wach, *Zur
Hermeneutik heiliger Schriften* (*Theol. Stud. und Krit.* 1930).

Christianity, in the course of its history, found its origin. In Islam, still further, the situation was exactly the same. Without a living faith, therefore, dictating the understanding of scripture, there can be no vitally operative holy writ. For Christianity, this implies that no living holy writ can subsist without the church; while in the case of Christianity and Islam, and to a certain extent of other religions also, as for example Hinduism, it involves the necessity of a *theology* which at all times shall render possible a new and living understanding of scripture.[1]

Holy writ, then, requires first of all a *tradition* subsisting concurrently with itself:—in Judaism the rabbinic, in Islam the *hadith*,[2] and in Christianity the παράδοσις. Its true significance, nevertheless, by no means lies in settling the meaning of the original author of the sacred text. Exegesis *e mente auctoris* is certainly frequently identified with the elucidation of the fundamental religious import; but this is always a subordinate matter, since the critical issue is that a living word of God should resound from the writ. Of course many theologians, in both ancient and recent times, assert that the *sensus strictus* of the writ is identical with the divine meaning. Moses implied what Christ taught. But this is correct only if we concede that one and the same divine meaning repeatedly manifests itself in distinctive forms and with reference to different affairs. Allegorical and typological interpretation in Christianity, like the rationalization of the ancient myths and prophetic and ecstatic utterances, find their analogy in Mohammedan theology. In the most recent developments of Protestant theology, however, there has arisen an endeavour to return to purely theological exegesis, and thus to turn from the written, settled and dead word of God to the living. It is true that the attempt simply to identify the divine meaning with the original import of the author can no longer be repeated; and so Christianity may be reverting, by a long and arduous road, to the understanding of the decisive power of the word; then it will no longer ask: "what says Moses?" or "what does St. Paul mean?" but "What is God saying to us?"[3] For the final and ultimate significance of holy writ is neither the meaning of its author, since indeed its real "author" is always God alone, nor that of its occasional interpreters; its deepest import always transcends us: it is "revealed" to us, that is to say, proclaimed at that moment when God speaks to us, without

---

[1] Chap. 84.   [2] Goldziher, *op. cit.*, 40 *f.*, 80 *ff.*
[3] Compare the history of the modern exposition of the Koran, which parallels the history of the interpretation of the Bible to an almost incredible degree. R. Hartmann, *Die Krisis des Islam*, 1928.

our therefore being able to maintain that we "have understood the mind of God".[1]

The mystics, of course, think otherwise. They compose their own holy writ. One day al-Makki was walking with the *sufi*-martyr al-Hallaj through one of the narrow streets of Mecca and reciting from the Koran: "he listened to me reciting and then said: 'I also could say such things' "; but, the orthodox Mohammedan adds, "I ceased to associate with him".[2] To cite another example from a totally different sphere of civilization: the Romantics cherished the ideal of writing not merely a cultural novel on the great model of *Wilhelm Meister*, but also a Bible.[3]

3. *Creeds*, still further, are a special type of holy writ. Like all that is written, they too are derived from the living, spoken word; and with this they fuse once again, in so far as they actually subsist only when they are recited. To be written down implies far less for them than for genuine holy writ; for in the case of creeds the principal feature is that they express the "sacred common element", and become recognized as such. They come to life, therefore, first of all in community worship, and may represent acts of trust, praise, adoration *etc.*, as for example the creed in Christian worship. Creeds, therefore, are fixed forms of a communal declaration before God: they are confessions. As such, again, they are scarcely to be separated from confessions of sin: the confession of faith and the confession of sin are indeed closely interconnected. They lead, too, to decision and systematize conduct, thus yielding the possibility of a new mode of life. This holds true especially of the confession of sin. "As long as the doer of the deed keeps it a secret, it is like a being that has issued from himself, living a life of its own, and in its turn engendering fatal consequences; if he openly confesses that he is the doer of the deed, he withdraws from it the life with which he had endowed it, and takes away its power to harm. As the Eskimo shaman put it, he 'takes the sting out' of the evil."[4] Among certain primitive peoples, similarly, before a campaign each warrior is asked to make an open and general confession; this however has nothing at all to do with repentance, only there may have been some dangerous element in the soldier's conduct that should be made good and therewith harmless; and thus once more the decisive power of the word

---

[1] Chap. 85 *ff.*   [2] Massignon, *Al-Hallaj*, I, 56 *f.*
[3] *cf.* R. Haym, *Die romantische Schule*[3], 1914.
[4] Lévy-Bruhl, *Primitives and the Supernatural*, 356.

is shown.[1] With this the confession of sin approximates to purification[2] and the apotropaic in general.[3] But such a confession of guilt requires no idea of God whatever, no moral obligation, and indeed hardly any conception of sin; it is just felt that something is not right as regards the holy, and the alleviating power of the word is realized; while with this apprehension of guilt there may also be connected the so-called "negative admission of sin" in ancient Egypt, in which adjurations alternate with the assurance of innocence: "I have *not* oppressed, *not* stolen", *etc.*[4] Certainly there can be no reference to any personal admission of guilt in all this; it is not at all an affair of the moral consciousness, but only of warding off evil consequences by means of the word.[5]

The confession of faith, also, is first of all a power-word; and a Bantu negro, who had been converted by the mission, was compelled by his relatives to abandon the Christian "faith" again by means of an emetic.[6] Somewhat similarly, during preparations for ancient Christian baptism in Rome, the "faith" was "handed over" to the *competetentes—traditio symboli*—originally together with the Gospel and the Lord's Prayer; then the catechumen "returned it" again (*redditio*)[7]. With the "faith", again, there was often associated a renunciation of evil powers, naturally in the form of a *carmen*:—in the early Christian world *abrenuntiatio diaboli*; in Mazdaism, too, both were connected together.[8] The Buddhist is a typical confession of faith: "I take my refuge in the Buddha. I take my refuge in the doctrine. I take my refuge in the monastic community",[9] which is thrice repeated and clearly exhibits the decisive character of the confession. Whoever confesses his faith, therefore, is not expounding any *Weltanschauung*, but is deciding, while a decision is made about himself also; this holds good too of those confessions that assume a quite different form, for example the assertory creed of Islam: "There is no God but Allah, and Mohammed is His prophet"; in confessing the oneness of God the confessor confesses *himself*. Similarly, the Christian creed is absolutely an act of confession, not merely an explicitly expressed conviction.

---

[1] Lévy-Bruhl, *Primitives and the Supernatural*, 348. R. Pettazoni, *La confessione dei peccati*, I, *passim* (1929).
[2] Chap. 49.   [3] Pettazoni.   [4] *Totenbuch* (Naville), *Kap.* 125.
[5] Of course this does not prevent us estimating the level of Egyptian morality from the enumeration of offences that have not been committed.
[6] Lévy-Bruhl, *Primitives and the Supernatural*, 88.
[7] Braun, *Liturgisches Handlexikon*, 350. L. Duchesne, *Origines du culte chrétien*[4], 1908, 308 *ff.*   [8] Bertholet, *Lesebuch*, I, 16.   [9] *ibid.*, II, 129 *f.*

The apotheosis of the confession of faith in Mazdaism is very important. The soul of the departed meets its own *daena* (a spiritual primeval being, and subsequently a confession of faith) in the form "of a girl, glorious and radiant, with shining arms, strong and well built, beautifully formed, with high breasts, and a splendid figure, of noble birth and high lineage, fifteen years old and as lovely as the most beautiful of creatures". To the spirit of the righteous man she says: "I am thy good religion, thine own personal confession";[1] conversely, an ugly old woman is the form of the *daena* of the wicked. Here the forms of the "external soul",[2] of the guardian spirit and of the faith (including good works) have been fused in one super-terrestrial beauteous figure.[3]

4. Religious *doctrine*, to continue, is the intellectual treatment of a given sacred word. It differs from myth because form here assumes less importance and conceptual thought predominates, while it is distinguished from the philosophy of religion by being the doctrine of some community and in originating from the "sacred common element". The occult knowledge in primitive secret societies, on the other hand, withheld from women and children but confided to neophytes, is not doctrine because what is known possesses no conceptual interconnection. Primitive religion in general, in fact, recognizes no doctrine:[4] celebration and myth constitute it in its entirety; it is related, not taught. So it was in the case of Egyptian and Babylonian, Greek and Roman religions; and similarly in the Old Testament. The first essential in the formation of doctrine, then, is a creed. This is the centre and the basis of every *development of dogma*; from which it follows, on the one hand, that dogma is never a collective philosophy, but always and essentially an act of worship, a celebration, and an act of praise. On the other hand, dogma is never purely existential, never merely concerned with reality, because it always represents some theoretical elaboration of the confession. It is the reflective contemplation of celebration, the expression of myth in logical form. But as soon as it ceases to be transparent and to exhibit its inherent confessional nature, it loses its specific character

[1] Lehmann-Haas, *Textbuch*, 162 *f.*
[2] Chap. 42. Persian, *Fravashi.*
[3] The "transposition" that has occurred here is very remarkable; it formed a creed, ligion and a thesaurus of good works out of the soul-being; *cf.* H. Lommel, *Die Religion Zarathustras*, 1930, 187 *ff.*
[4] It approaches most closely to the essential nature of doctrine when initiates in primitive communities are instructed about the existence of the gods who founded the ceremonies, the so-called originators (Chap. 18).

and sinks to the level either of some mere philosophic thesis, or religious technique; and from time to time this may well happen.

We find doctrine then, and for the first time in the history of religion, in the theological compositions of the Egyptian heretic king Akhnaton; for in the name he assigned to his god he set out the different conclusions at which he had arrived in the course of his reforming labours, and thus axiomatically fixed their relationship to the prevailing ideas of God. It is true that these dogmas were scarcely the utterance of a living community, although they were certainly so intended.[1] The doctrine of a genuine community is however to be discerned in Orphism and similar Greek spiritual movements. Here, in the form of a cosmogony and theogony, arose the doctrine of sin and salvation, based on the "story of salvation" in the death of Zagreus, in which the type of sin as original, and of salvation as release from the cycle of births, are systematically represented.

Here the form certainly remains predominantly mythical; and we must realize that doctrine can never completely discard the mythical if it wishes to avoid falling to the level of a mere philosophical thesis. The material of doctrine in general, again, is of the most various types. Precepts pertaining to worship and morality, myths, narratives about ancestors, etc., are all incorporated within doctrine, receiving a significance that is modified in accordance with the requirements of its religious theories; and this absorption of an entire religious tradition in doctrine shows, on the one hand, that this can never deliquesce into pure theory: the heterogeneity of its material constitutes the copiousness of doctrine. On the other hand, this of itself involves immense difficulties. For the entire tradition, at first preserved for centuries in verbal form, and subsequently consolidated in writing, must now be expressed as dogma and forced into one doctrinal system which, even if it is not purely conceptual, is still as self-consistent as is possible. But this never proceeds at all easily, since the fantasies of mythology, the ecstasies of enthusiasts and the pathos of prophets, chronicle and fairy story, hymn and proverb, must all be given doctrinal form which must possess power, and still at the same moment be intelligible. We should however guard against discarding, without further ado, the accompanying violation of the material as sheer falsity, since the

---

[1] cf. H. Schäfer, *Amarna in Religion und Kunst*, 1931. G. van der Leeuw, *Achnaton*, 1927. In ancient Egypt the urge towards doctrinal development of religious tradition was very powerful; cf. K. Sethe, *Amun und die acht Urgötter von Hermopolis, Abh. der preuss. Akad. der Wiss.*, 1929, *phil.-hist. kl.* 4.

completed theology which begins its activity[1] at this stage would then
be radically untrue.

Certainly we can "understand Schleiermacher's conclusion that all
expression involves the stagnation of religious experience, so that the
definition of doctrine as 'experience that has become torpid' would not
be incorrect; still, to be articulately expressed pertains to experience, as
does its utterance also, while utterance in its own turn leads logically to
reflection and doctrine. Again, we must not forget that all doctrine
sustained by the consciousness of the religious community is essentially
living and remains so, while even in the most abstruse dogma the
original experience of God may repeatedly renew itself".[2]

5. Finally the *law*, as the rule of conduct, is given with religion itself:
it is the guarantee of celebration. But it also receives a fixed mould and
becomes a formula that is spoken, and subsequently written, which as
such pertains to the category of sacred words. Traditional usage and
custom, derived from ancestors, were codified only at a certain stage
in the development of the cult and, in the course of this process, relatively new laws are recorded together with ancient observances. Of
this the Jewish *Torah*, the Iranian *Vendidad*, the Indian *Brahmanas*
and the Mohammedan *Sunna* are classical examples. The ancient Greek
laws of religious communities, also, like those of the Orphics and the
Pythagoreans,[3] were to a great extent changed forms of old tabu
regulations.[4] In these, law and custom, moral and religious bonds all
subsist together, without being distinguished from each other. The
links are precisely those of religious celebration, and it is quite immaterial
whether its content, according to our own criteria, pertains to law or
custom, to ethics or piety. The relations between religion and law, again,
are in the main of four types: (*1*) It forms an object of veneration.
Here again the Old Testament is the classical example: the law demands
not only obedience, but love; some of the *Psalms* (especially *Psalm*
119) express this conviction. (*2*) This veneration of the law as the
revelation of God may then degenerate into formal observance, such as
arose in Judaism and Parsiism. Here primitive worship of the written
word (ceremonial burial of ancient *Torah* rolls *etc.*) is associated with
scholarly endeavour, for which the study of the *Torah* is the highest
duty. On the other hand this observance may: (*3*) lead to a revolt

---

[1] Chap. 84. [2] *RGG*. Article *Lehre*.
[3] An example of *symbola pythagoraea* in Bertholet, *Lesebuch*, 4, 43.
[4] Chap. 4.

against the letter of the law, as in the case of the prophets and of Jesus, or against the law as such, as with St. Paul. The law, confined within its proper limits, is then: (4) frequently categorically disavowed by mysticism, as being at most of merely relative value when contrasted with that of religion.

Thus a rabbi in Warsaw, whom Jeremias questioned about his attitude towards Zionism, said as he raised the *Torah* roll: "Professor, we still have our country—a portable country".[1] That is legal piety at its highest power; the written word of the law replaces everything: celebration and sacred space, the "how" and the "where". The "what" of the divine word, fixed for all time, suffices in the actuality of obedience and love.

---

[1] A. Jeremias, *Jüdische Frömmigkeit*, 1927, 11. The Law may also be a power-bearer in the most primitive sense; there are miraculous laws, just as there are miraculous images; in Judaism there are accounts of miraculously saved *Torah* rolls; *cf.* Will, *Culte*, II, 311; also the *Torah* words, "Mezuza" and "Tephillin", used as amulets; W. Bousset, *Die Religion des Judentums*[3], 1926, 179.

R. PETTAZONI, *La Confessione dei Peccati*, 1920–1936.
J. WACH, "Zur Hermeneutik heiliger Schriften" (*Theol. Stud. und Krit.* 1930).

CHAPTER 65

ENDOWMENT WITH FORM IN WORSHIP

1. "WORSHIP assembles together the scattered and sporadic feelings, and transforms an indefinite religious sentiment into an individual, and at the same time collective, religious consciousness."[1] Thus everything that we have so far discovered in conduct and celebration, in time and space, in action and word, is part of this thoroughgoing self-comprehension, this confronting of the self with Power, which we call *worship*. In worship, therefore, man seeks to give form not only to individual and to collective experience, not only to the conduct of himself and his community, but also to the activities of Power, indeed to its very existence. In worship the being of man and the Being of his God are comprehended within one actual "being-thus": man's being and God's Being are interpreted, and are given form, essentially as becoming profoundly moved, and as what causes this, as what is created, and as creation, respectively. In worship, the form of humanity becomes defined, while that of God becomes the content of faith, and the form of their reciprocal relation experienced in action. This holds true of *all* worship, from richest to poorest: even the most unpretentious Calvinistic type of divine service cannot satisfy itself simply by "ceremonially proclaiming the King's advent": He must also make His entry.[2]

2. The sacred, then, must possess a form: it must be "localizable", spatially, temporally, visibly or audibly. Or still more simply: the sacred must "take place". This "taking place", however, is never and on no occasion simply the event that is given: rather, in the given, possibilities must first of all reveal themselves.[3] Eating, therefore, is not a "taking place" of the sacred, but the sacrament is. But every event may be a "taking place" of the sacred, and in such cases we speak of a "*symbol*". A symbol, that is to say, is by no means something quite inessential, as our loose modern mode of expression seems to imply,

---

[1] Will, *op. cit.*, I, 23.

[2] R. Will, *Les principes essentiels de la vie cultuelle*, *Revue de theologie et de philosophie*, Lausanne, N.S. 14 (60), 1926. In a more highly developed cult the entrance becomes a permanent place of residence, and the cult itself a "heaven on earth"; Boulgakoff, *Orthodoxie*, 179. [3] Chap. 23.

but rather the encounter, συμ-βάλλειν, between possibility and givenness, between the event and "taking place", between secular and
sacred.[1] The symbol, then, is *a participation of the sacred in its veritable,
actual, form*: between the sacred, and its form, there exists community
of essence; and the distinction between the genuine, and the modernized,
symbol is most clearly expressed in the conception of the Eucharist:
do the bread and wine "signify" the body and blood of Christ, or *are*
they these too? Community of essence, alone, constitutes the symbol;
what signifies and manifests on the one hand, and what on the other
hand is thus signified and manifested, fuse together into one single
image.[2] In Australia, for instance, flowers made from wood and worn
in the hair symbolically represent the kangaroo flesh which the totem
ancestor carried on his head during his wanderings.[3] And this is no
mere esthetic metaphor, nor is it a technical symbol in any chemical
or mathematical sense but, in its essential nature, community.[4] The
image *is* what it represents, and that which signifies *is* what is signified.

The whole of human life, indeed, should be regarded from this point
of view. "All that is transitory is a parable": in this universally familiar
dictum of Goethe's the little word "only" may quite justifiably be
omitted in this connection, since the equivalence implies community.
The situation in which we find ourselves is essentially connected with
sacredness: of this it is an image, from this it derives its own value.
Thus earthly love symbolizes God's love, and this makes it valuable
and in itself sacred: earthly fatherhood, again, is an image of the divine:
that renders it great and potent.[5] Further, it is not that our so-called
reality is there first, and only subsequently the sacred which this
symbolizes: it is rather the sacred that first and solely exists, and our
secular entities possess value and permanence only because they are
capable, in any given instance, of symbolizing the sacred and cooperating
with it. This expresses the profoundest significance of the principle
that we are created in God's image: God is the archetype, but our
"images" can witness to Him and indicate Him. We may also assert,
with Mensching, that the symbol always has a meaning determined by
the story of salvation, and is not arbitrary but necessary.[6] The sacred
becomes "fixed", or "placed", in the concrete human situation; and

---

[1] cf. Wundt, *op. cit.*, IV, 35; Déonna, *Quelques réflexions sur le symbolisme, RHR.* 88,
18 *ff.*

[2] cf. Kretschmer, *Medizinische Psychologie*, 22. Reuterskiöld, *Totemismus*, 14.

[3] R. Thurnwald, *Zeitschr. f. Ästhetik und Allg. Kunstwiss.*, 21.

[4] "Participation", Lévy-Bruhl.   [5] cf. Huizinga, *Herfstty*, 345.

[6] *Buddhistische Symbolik*, 6 *f.*, 9.

this includes persons and objects—the "things" of Chapter 3—words, actions *etc.*, all of which receive their ministerial status from the sacred and thus become symbols; while among these, "symbols" in the narrower sense such as the cross, incense, the *sacra* of the mysteries *etc.*, play a subordinate though momentous part. For it is in these that the sacred becomes actualized: in Egypt, for example, incense was regarded as "the stair to heaven";[1] and with the cross we bless. The most real symbol of all, however, is the altar, the throne or table of God, because there the sacred does in fact become "placed", and as it were establishes itself.[2] Symbols, still further, assist man in bringing the world into his own power, and with them he works magic; but in those types of religion where this impetus to exercise power over the world has yielded to being seized upon by Power, the sacred always becomes definitely "localized"; and then it is not the transient that is a "parable", but rather the creature[3] which, as such, can be a bearer of divine Power. The earthly situation implies the divine: "All creatures are shadows, echoes and pictures, mere vestiges and imitations and images."[4]

3. Upon the divine seat the god is enthroned; and now man may place his image on it. But this by no means always happens. The ark of Jahveh, for instance, was an empty throne of God;[5] and the vacant throne occurs also among primitive peoples.[6] This of course does not involve any "purely spiritual" worship of God, but merely that the deity should assume his place on the empty throne at his epiphany. The *image of the god* is a means of holding him fast, of guaranteeing his presence: thus it has the same purpose as the fetish,[7] from which it often cannot in fact be distinguished. The fetish or semi-fetish indeed, or the formless image, is usually preferred to the wholly human image;[8] and so to faith the black Madonnas have greater value than the most beautiful work of art.[9] For the dreadful and almost inhuman expresses

---

[1] *Pyramidentexte* (Sethe), 365. On the inexhaustible wealth of symbols *cf.*, together with Déonna, *op. cit.*, Danzel, *AR.* 21, 1922. A. Goblet d'Alviella, *Croyances, Rites, Institutions*, 1911.

[2] It is extremely probable that the ark of the covenant of Jahveh was also a throne of this type. The form of the sacred building, too, is symbolic: *e.g.* the cruciform church, the Hindu *stupa*, the Babylonian *ziggurat, etc.*

[3] Chap. 45.   [4] Bonaventura, *Itinerarium mentis in Deum*, 2.

[5] *cf.* H. Gressmann, *Die Lade Jahves und das Allerheiligste des salomonischen Tempels*, 1920.

[6] As on Bali Island, as Prof. J. C. van Eerde kindly informs me.

[7] Chap. 3.   [8] G. van der Leeuw, *Wegen en Grenzen*, 116.

[9] *cf.* Trede, *Heidentum in der römischen Kirche*, II, 91, with Note.

the sacred far better than does the human and is therefore preferred, since it stands closer to the "wholly other"; and Otto compares the terrible Hindu caricatures of the gods to the harsh and fearful Byzantine images of the Madonna and of Christ.[1] But still the human element breaks a way through for itself and forces itself forward, from the composite forms of Egypt and the many-limbed monsters of India to the pure humanity of the Homeric gods and the maternal form of the Madonna; so among the symbols of Power the human gains preference. The worship of images of the gods, therefore, is not founded on any error in piety towards the dead, or towards the gods of having confused them with their own images, as Euhemerism maintains:[2] "With respect to the gods too, our ancestors believed carelessly, credulously, with untrained simplicity; while worshipping their kings religiously, desiring to look upon them when dead in outward forms, anxious to preserve their memories in statues, those things became sacred which had been taken up merely as consolations."[3] By the image of the god it is essentially the *sacrum* that is indicated, the presence of the divine; and "the oldest image of the Gods", says Nietzsche, "is meant to shelter and at the same time to hide the God—to indicate him but not to expose him to view".[4] But similarly, even where fetish or semi-fetish has long yielded place to the human image, it is never a matter of mere external resemblance; for the essence of the god's image consists not in its resemblance to man but in its being filled with power, exactly as in the case of the fetish; and primitive people willingly give their fetishes to European collectors, but not their magic medicine, which is power.[5] The essential factor in the image, then, is power; hence the importance of the dedication of images, since this first endows them with potency. Arnobius represents a heathen as saying: "We too do not decide that the bronze or gold, or silver or any other materials from which images are made, are gods or divinities in themselves; but we venerate the gods in these images and worship them, whom the sacred act of dedication introduces and causes to dwell within wrought images."[6] Further, the power in the image may be either pure potency

---

[1] *cf.* the profound passage in *Human, All Too Human* (Nietzsche), II, 115 (Foulis Edition).

[2] As *e.g.* in old Arabian narrative: J. Wellhausen, *Reste arabischen Heidentums*, 1887, 14; *cf.* Negelein, *Spiegel und Schatten*. Geffcken, *Der Bilderstreit des heidnischen Altertums, AR.* 19, 293 *f.*

[3] Minucius Felix, XX, 6; similarly *Sap.* XIV, 15.

[4] *Human, All Too Human*, II, 116.

[5] A. Bertholet, *Journal of Biblical Literature*, 49, 3, 1930, 229.

[6] Geffcken, *loc. cit.*, 308.

(dynamistically) or some powerful person (Animism). In the latter case the god or spirit inhabits the image: if he is not present the image is a mere block of wood or stone;[1] thus the Egyptian *ka*[2] animated the statue of which he took possession. In New Guines, again, the spirit inhabits the *korwar*, from which he pronounces oracles and where he receives sacrifices *etc.*[3] The image is, as it were, the medium of the spirit.[4] The dedication of the image, further, may be replaced by its miraculous origin and characteristics. Thus it is the bearer of the sacred because it has shown itself to be filled with power and allocated thereto; and there are many cult legends relating to the marvellous origin of certain celebrated images of the gods. The image of Sarapis, for example, was transported from Sinope to Alexandria by divine command, given in a dream to the ruler Ptolemy, while the black stone of the mother of the gods was brought to Rome from Pessinus and worked miracles at the moment of its landing.[5] The same stories are told of many sacred images; and that these manifest their allocation to power by cures, oracles *etc.* is universally familiar; in ancient Egypt they were made to speak by means of some special contrivance, and in this way Alexander received his oracle from Amon.[6] Sacred images also bleed, descend from their pedestals, speak and cure if they are touched *etc.*[7]

Veneration of images is almost universal. It subsisted most vigorously in orthodox Christianity, which separated the altar space from the church by a wall of images—merely painted, it is true (*iconostasis*); the holy images constituted the space an *adyton* and the sacred acts a *mysterium*.[8] In the Greek church, again, the *festum orthodoxiae* designates the victory of those who revered images over those who, in the Byzantine empire, desired to abolish them.[9] This strife concerning images, however, was only a particularly violent outbreak of a conflict that is latent in all religions, and which had already aroused disturbances in Old Testament times and in the classical period.[10] In the course of this conflict the

---

[1] *cf. e.g.* R. Wilhelm, *Chinesische Volksmärchen*, 1919, No. 18, with Note.
[2] Chap. 42.   [3] Wilken, *op. cit.*, III, 190 *f.*
[4] *cf.* J. C. Lamster, *Tydschrift Ned. Aardr. Genootschap*, 2. *Reeks*, 47, 1930, 452 *ff.*
[5] Plutarch, *Of Isis and Osiris*, 28; *cf.* E. Petersen, *Die Serapislegende, AR.* 13, 1910, 47 *ff.*
[6] Maspero, *Études égyptiennes*, I, 77 *ff.* M. Weynants-Ronday, *Les statues vivantes*, 1926. O. Weinreich, *Antike Heilungswunder*, 1909.
[7] Negelein, *op. cit.*
[8] K. Holl, *Die Entstehung der Bilderwand in der griechischen Kirche, AR.* 9, 1906; *cf.* on icons, Boulgakoff, *Orthodoxie*, 461 *ff.*   [9] 842.
[10] Geffcken, *op. cit. passim.* G. van der Leeuw, *Wegen en Grenzen, passim.*

primitive awe of the image[1] was transformed, by "transposition", into the consciousness that the sacred can neither be firmly fixed nor portrayed. In this respect *Deuteronomy* provides the outstanding criterion. The ancient prohibition of images in Jewish law presupposed the concept of the real essence subsisting within the image; later, this was "transposed" into the realization of the insufficiency of every image. Jahveh speaks "out of the midst of the fire" on Sinai: "ye heard the voice of the words, but saw no similitude";[2] here the decisiveness of the word is placed above assumption of form. In the latter there is a suspicion of command over Power, whereby it may be deprived of its sacredness; awe of the numinous element in the image has been transformed into awe of the numinous in general.[3] In Greek and Roman antiquity, too, men were influenced by fear of dominating the deity by means of its image, and appealed to the absence of images (which probably had other reasons !) in the earliest religion; Varro thought that by the introduction of images religion had suffered the loss of purity.[4] And fear of the human form, of man's own work, of the no longer "*wholly* other", subsists equally in the Stoics and in Judaism: both were united by the early Christian apologists, for the first time in St. Paul's speech on the Aeropagus recorded in *The Acts of the Apostles*.[5] Subsequently, during the Byzantine agitations of the iconoclasts, political reasons combined with a fear of form that was to some degree influenced by Islam; similarly in the Reformation period, social motives united with rationalistic, and with the fear of form itself, in iconoclasm.[6] For in the image man dreads the idolizing of his own power.

But images have always found their defenders too, even as early as the classical era. Not merely as a makeshift, and pedagogically as a *Biblia pauperum*, but also as a matter of principle, images of God have their legitimate status. For as Posidonius maintained, the human body contains the *logos* and is therefore worthy of representing God. In the Byzantine dispute about images, further, this idea was rendered yet more profound by an appeal to the Incarnation:—if in Christ God has assumed human form, this form is thereby essentially endowed with

---

[1] Chap. 41.   [2] *Deut.* iv, 12.

[3] Otto. Whether there ever were images of Jahveh in Israel is a debatable question; *cf.* Obbink, *Zeitschr. f. d. altt. Wiss.*, 1929. S. Mowinckel, *Acta orientalia*, 8, 1930.

[4] Geffcken, *op. cit.*, 299. Plutarch, *Numa*, 8, 8. Fowler, *Religious Experience*, 146. Wissowa, *Religion und Kultus*, 28.

[5] *cf.* Norden, *Agnostos Theos.*

[6] G. van der Leeuw, *Wegen en Grenzen*; obedience to scripture also probably played a significant rôle; *cf. e.g. Biblioth. Reform. neerl.*, II, 1904, 601.

Power.[1] Man portrays God in human guise, then, not as a mere make-shift and because he knows not the form of God, but precisely because he does know it, in Christ. Man has not dressed God up in his own image: God has created man after His image.[2] Thus opponents of images have, often unwittingly, suppressed self-centredness and self-righteousness, while their advocates, again frequently without being aware of it, have defended the *locus standi* of God in the Universe, the "place" of God in human life.[3]

4. To the experience of the sacred, finally, *music* has also given a specific form that has in general not been regarded so mistrustfully by religion as has the visible image; musical expression of the holy occupies an extensive domain in worship. There is hardly any worship without music; and this is capable of actualizing even the most inadequate aspects of the experience. Nevertheless here too the fear of form, now in the guise of music, has not been absent, and stricter Buddhism, like Islam, has proscribed it just as Calvinism has forbidden images. But with this we encounter the formidable problem of the expression of the sacred in Art: not merely in music, but also in the word and the image, in architecture, in dance and drama; this expression always shows itself to be at once necessary and impossible. Its discussion pertains, however, to the Phenomenology of Art.[4]

W. Déonna, *Quelques réflexions sur le symbolisme* (RHR. 88, 1924).
J. Geffcken, *Der Bilderstreit des heidnischen Altertums* (AR. 19, 1919).
G. Mensching, *Buddhistische Symbolik*, 1929.

[1] Geffcken, *op. cit.* Will, *op. cit.*, II, 192.
[2] *Gen.* i. 27 probably refers to the bodily form of God.
[3] This may be carried to its extreme in the idea of images of Christ not made with hands: ἀχειροποιητοί. Will, *op. cit.*, II, 304.
[4] G. van der Leeuw, *Wegen en Grenzen*.

CHAPTER 66

ENDOWMENT WITH FORM IN CUSTOM

1. CONDUCT assumes form as *custom*. Observance of the potency of life, tabus, and purifications,[1] the obligations of worship and the other demands of Power upon life, together constitute usage, tradition and custom, whose sphere of operation is more extensive than that of law.[2] Custom then is essentially religious, because it is the endowing with form of fear and of awe before superior Power. It occupies the intermediate position between mere etiquette, good form and morality; and every now and then it changes into one of these. Good form is its empty shell; but morality may derive its own claim either from some quite independent principle, as it has been sought to do again and again in the modern world, or else it rests, exactly like custom, on the demand of Power—only not in this case, as with custom, by way of any possible endowment of life with form, but in the catastrophic type of complete failure—of sin—and of being raised up anew—of grace.[3]

Of course there already exists, in the simple fact of usage, a tendency towards this rupture which, in ethics, intersects the whole of life. For the sacredness of Power awakens the sense of distance; but conduct and custom aim at bridging this interval and rendering possible some definite and satisfactory relationship towards Power. And this usually succeeds, although failures of course occur, which must be atoned for: "no such thing ought to be done in Israel",[4] was said of such a failure. But in custom there is no question of any complete breakdown; on the contrary: life is so ordered that it accords with divine rule, whether this is simply tradition, or cosmic law (*ṛta, asha, ma-at, etc.*).[5] The state of impurity, then, has nothing whatever to do with observance of custom; it is always a condition of fullness of power, even though this may be a repletion with dangerous and undesired power. Whoever transgresses custom goes astray, and instead of celebrating as he should he sends the course of the powers off the rails; and this must be made good again. For this reason value is laid on the confession of sin[6] which sets

---

[1] Chap. 4, 49. [2] Chap. 64.
[3] Chap. 78. [4] 2 *Sam.* xiii. 12—a proverbial saying in the Old Testament.
[5] Chap. 4. [6] Chap. 64. Lévy-Bruhl, *Primitives and the Supernatural*, 352.

the stagnant stream of events in motion once more, or upon the assurance of innocence, the so-called negative confession of sin[1] which we encountered in Egypt, in a rudimentary form, as early as in the *Pyramid Texts*: "He has not reviled the king", *etc.*[2] Here, of course, it is not a matter of personal "moral responsibility" in the sense of ethical autonomy, just as little as it is a "consciousness of sin" such as we find, for example, in St. Paul or in the Babylonian penitential psalms; and the offence against custom, the transgression, revenges itself on lifeless objects, or again on animals and plants, just as on man. There are, indeed, no "lifeless" objects; for every being has power, and this power can interfere with the current of potency in some undesirable way. By the Kukis of British India, for instance, the tree that has killed a human being is destroyed; Xerxes, again, commanded the Hellespont to be scourged, while the Draconian laws punished objects just as, in the Gospel, Christ cursed the barren fig tree. Until 1846, too, the law remained in force in England that a thing that had caused death to any one should, as a *deodand*, become the property of the king as the representative of God.[3] The ground of custom, therefore, is not the moral consciousness, and still less intention, but only the quality of powerfulness which is produced by some act or other.[4]

2. Custom, still further, need not remain a mere guarantee of life's potency. It may itself also become one means of the attainment of yet greater power, and in such cases we are concerned with *asceticism*. I have previously observed that the possession of power is a quality which might be called physical, since it is placed on just the same level as warmth, heat, glow;[5] thus great power is great heat, which may become dangerous to "custom", but may also promote it. The story of the creation of Masu, for example, related that the earth (that is the Island of Sumba) in its newly created condition was still very wet; then someone brought fire from heaven, and the earth became dry and had to be cooled again with raw flesh and water; and this is still always done as soon as the earth threatens to become too warm, for example as a result of illicit sex intercourse or adultery.[6] *Transgression*, therefore,

---

[1] Chap. 64.
[2] *Totenbuch* (Naville), *Kap.* 125. *Pyramidentexte* (Sethe), 892. Ad. Erman, *Zeitschr. für ägypt. Spr.*, 31, 75 *ff.*
[3] Westermarck, *The Origin and Development of the Moral Ideas*, I, 262.
[4] *cf.* Kurt Latte, *Schuld und Sünde in der griechischen Religion* (*AR.* 20, 1920–21, 256).   [5] Chap. 1 *f.*
[6] J. P. Kleiweg de Zwaan, *Tydschr. Ned. Aardr. Genootschap.* 2. *Reeks*, 47, 1930, 195.

causes heat. But on the other hand, heat is also produced by *celebration*. Everywhere that the operation of power proceeds, whether in the beneficial or the forbidden sense, there "heat" arises: the Hindu *tapas* has previously, in the discussion of power,[1] been found to be warmth and heat. Ascetic celebrations, again, develop a powerfulness that inspires even the gods with fear.[2] Asceticism may therefore be described as a celebration which develops power exactly as does transgression, but in the opposite sense, so that it confirms custom instead of violating it; and to this the detail of ascetic practice corresponds: chastity, fasting, self-castigation, silence, holding the breath, *etc*. Thus while custom regulates the operation of powers within life, asceticism controls them *à outrance*, so that almost nothing remains of them. Custom prescribes speech *and* silence, but asceticism silence alone; custom forbids the enjoyment of certain viands, while asceticism forbids eating in general, in so far as it is not absolutely necessary for life;[3] custom ordains speaking in defined periods and according to an accepted accentuation, but asceticism regulates even breathing and limits this to what is indispensable; custom dictates definite relations in sex intercourse, forbidding this with regard to certain persons and times; asceticism, however, proscribes such intercourse altogether.

But the deprivation of power involved in this strengthening of custom is merely apparent: rather, it intensifies the ascetic's own power. The seeming weakness becomes experienced as strength,[4] since the enfeebling of certain vital functions invigorates others. So far, then, Nietzsche is quite right in his assertion that "in every ascetic morality man worships one part of himself as a God, and is obliged, therefore, to diabolize the other parts".[5] Asceticism thus presupposes a fracture within life, quite unknown to custom; and as long as life is regarded as a totality there is no question of any "diabolizing". But for the ascetic many more tabus are in force than for the ordinary person;[6] and in this way he can avoid many transgressions of which others become guilty, while by restraint he intensifies his own power. A medicine-man therefore, or a king or priest, must submit to all sorts of tabus and observe a certain degree of asceticism. But when life is dualistically interpreted and a distinction drawn between body and soul,[7] then asceticism serves

---

[1] Chap. 2.   [2] Oldenberg, *Lehre der Upanishaden*, 49; *id.*, *Mahabharata*, 119.
[3] Thus ordinary fasting, that is to say the prohibition of specific foods at definite times, belongs to custom; abstinence from eating in general, to the verge of exhaustion, pertains to asceticism.   [4] Lévy-Bruhl, *Primitives and the Supernatural*, 241 *f*.
[5] *Human, All Too Human*, I, 140 (Foulis Edition).   [6] Chap. 4, 29.
[7] Chap. 43.

to eliminate the now completely diabolized body as much as is possible, to render it harmless, to oppose its operations, chastise it and even torture it, so that the "soul" may free itself and rule absolutely: the "best" in man, his eternal element or whatever else we may call it, is to be released. Psychologically, however, this type of celebration implies a satisfaction of natural instincts in some indirect way, since the ascetic knows how to procure various pleasures even through agony and pain; and in this connection psycho-pathology provides valuable comment, and can say much about the attainment of power by means of its loss. All ascetics, nevertheless, are not deranged, nor lustful perverts; and in the contrast with the flesh the antithesis to the unholy may at all times be patent.[1] It makes a very great difference, therefore, whether the flesh be diabolïzed, or the *diabolus* sought in the flesh; certainly the propriety of this latter attitude may be doubtful, but its religious value need not be disputed.

Asceticism, however, is concerned neither with autonomous morality nor with religious ethics. For it is an extreme type of celebration—essentially an acquisition of power: to it life can never be a catastrophe. And the entire interval separating asceticism from the demand that arises from the consciousness of sin and grace is shown by placing its practice of the depreciation of life, in order to heighten life's power, side by side with the Gospel teaching that he who loses his life keeps it, but that he who desires to retain it loses it.

But all this does not mean that asceticism treats life any less seriously than does autonomous, or religious, ethics: it may indeed become intensified into the very destruction of life; we have in fact already encountered such enmity towards life.[2] But this brings no deliverance; and this has been occasionally realized even in ascetic India, where the task of effecting deliverance has so often been assigned to asceticism: "asses and other animals roam about shameless and naked near houses and forests; are they therefore free from passion? If men could be released by smearing themselves with clay and ashes, would not the dog also be released, who is continually lying on clay and ashes? Are not the jackals and mice, the gazelles and other animals ascetics, who feed on grass, leaves and water alone and live in the forest? Are not frogs, fish and other aquatic animals *yogins*, since they remain from birth to death on the banks of the Ganges and other sacred streams?"[3]

[1] K. Schjelderup, *Die Askese*, 1928.   [2] Chap. 47.
[3] E. Abegg, *Der Pretakalpa des Garuda-Purana*, 1921; here asceticism is contrasted with knowledge of truth.

3. Conduct, in conclusion, may also assume the form of worship, not merely in the general sense as representative action and ritual observance, but also as *taking sides*. In ancient Egyptian religious plays, for instance, two parties were formed, one led by the god and the other by his enemies. A mock battle broke out, which in the case of the Osiris mysteries was fought on water, the people choosing the side of the god against his adversaries: "I beat back those who were attacking the sacred barque of the god, and overthrew the enemies of Osiris."[1] Similar combats occurred in many popular customs of ancient times, as in modern days.[2] In that case religious custom develops into a "following" of the god, which we shall encounter at a later stage when discussing the idea of Imitation.[3]

MIRCEA ELIADE, *Yoga Essai sur les Origines de la Mystique Indienne*, 1936.
G. MENSCHING, *Gut und Böse im Glauben der Volker*, 1950.
K. SCHJELDERUP, *Die Askese*, 1928.
E. WESTERMARCK, *The Origin and Development of the Moral Ideas*, I, II.

[1] H. Schäfer, *Die Mysterien des Osiris in Abydos*, 1904, 22.
[2] Usener, *Heilige Handlung*, 435 ff.
[3] Chap. 73; *cf.* further Chap. 90. Schäfer, *ibid.*, 24. "I prepared the 'great departure', and followed in the god's footsteps."

B. INWARD ACTION

CHAPTER 67

RELIGIOUS EXPERIENCE

1. THE division of our subject into Outward and Inward Action by no means implies a belief in the possibility of separating the inner from the outer:

> Wouldst thou truly study Nature?
> Seek the Whole in every feature.
> Nought's within and nought's without,
> For whatever's in will out.[1]

Everything external is closely connected with something internal; and conversely, without the outer there is no inner, or if there were it would not appear. A sacred stone, a god, a sacrament, therefore, are experiences precisely as fear, love and piety are, since in both cases it is for us a question of what appears, of what makes itself known by signs. Feeling, again, does not exist without speech and gesture; thought is not present without form and action; even mysticism requires words. It is therefore never permissible to place "institutional" religion in antithesis to the inward experience of religion. For every dogma, every act of worship, can only become understood primarily as the reflection of some experience; every act, every idea, is the expression of a need or a release, of pain or bliss.[2]

2. Nor again should we contrast experience as purely "personal" with the collective or communal element in external action. We shall find, indeed, that in a certain sense everything in religion is "personal", in so far as it can never be manifested outside the actual given situation, the existential determinateness, of humanity; but also that nothing is ever "purely" personal, since nothing whatever could be manifested were it not at some time understood by others besides any one individual. Very possibly, too, the last of all to understand is the present author!

---

[1] Goethe, *Epirrhema* (Dwight).
[2] On the relation between "Inner" and "Outer" *cf.* further Scheler, *Vom Ewigen im Menschen*, 366 *f.*

Still, he has innumerable predecessors. Everything, then, must be taken into consideration in order to constitute the experience that arises.[1]

My intention in discussing "inward action", therefore, is to maintain that every experience without exception may be regarded from two quite different sides:— from the point of view of its expression, or as it were in its external aspect, and also from the angle of its impression, or in other words in its internal aspect. I say advisedly "as it were". For the outer is always and simultaneously the inner, and conversely; only our survey may be directed either more specifically to the expression, to whatever makes itself manifest, or more towards the impression, that is to those inward emotions that have occasioned the expression. Thus it may be concerned with prayer, but equally with inner questioning: with space, but also with a yearning for some definite "situation": with what deeply moves us as well as with our being profoundly affected. Of course the contemplation of the inward can never be separated from that of the outward; here the position is analogous to our field of vision: I see the garden, for instance; that is, I see the flowers in the front of the garden, and in the background the trees near the fence; alternatively, I direct my glance towards the trees and at the same time see the flowers, although I intend to look at the trees. Investigation, in other words, can never restrict itself entirely to the external nor to the internal; only on each given occasion its direction is different. In this respect an analogy, or rather a relationship, subsists with the psychological distinction between introvert and extravert, or schizoid and cyclothyme. So long, that is to say, as it is manifested within the limits of the normal mind, neither of these two types ever exists entirely without the other; but (once again) the orientation is different in each of the two cases.

Thus our regard is now directed inwardly: the outward, nevertheless, is not forgotten but always remains within the visual field. The direction of our gaze, however, constitutes an attempt to advance from the "world" which "astonishes" us, and subsequently excites our "anxiety" and our "celebrating",[2] to that ultimate solitude where man stands, absolutely alone and with no "world", in dread before God.[3] An attempt merely— for to this goal we shall never actually attain: but on the road to the inward we hope that much will be disclosed.

3. In the spiritual life of to-day, then, religious experience is to a great degree in bad repute; and this is because it is quite wrongly restricted to "feeling", its value being then estimated according to the intensity

[1] Chap. 107.   [2] Chap. 48.   [3] Schmalenbach, *op. cit.*

of such feeling. Religious experience would in that case naturally mean the utmost subjectivity; but as such it should have no place, at least in religion, wherein the Object, as has repeatedly been maintained in Chapter I and in other passages, is simultaneously the Subject. Experience, however, is in no sense either mere feeling nor, specifically, religious feeling: under no conditions whatever, indeed, can any "feeling" be separated from life in its totality, except in antiquated faculty psychology! For together with feeling, other constituents are always present: will, reason, *etc*.[1]

It would therefore be better to avoid all such terminology, and speak (as Binswanger does) of a *social* ego directed from the subject to the environment: a *solitary* ego, which tends not to disclose the subject: a *conscious* self also, including the two selves previously referred to: an *accessible* self, which is not oriented by the subject to the world and of which, too, the individual himself is not aware, but which we are able to comprehend: and, finally, an ego which we can *understand* and which implies all these selves.[2] Our path then proceeds from the social and accessible ego, by way of the isolated self, to the ideal of the last ego—the ego we can understand. But whether we call the excitations within these various selves feelings, impulses or anything else, in any case the entire ego is involved in every such activity, and the whole life is present therein which becomes experience[3] owing to the disturbance (which may eventually be intensified into being profoundly moved), and consequently exists only in so far as it is referred to the object.[4]

What the nature of an experience is will be most clearly understood if it is compared with the "event". Event and experience, then, are the same "content", in the first place as a fact, and then as meaning also. A phenomenon therefore is always related to experience, since unless this is so it would not appear to us meaningfully. But outer phenomena also possess an element constituted by fact and event, a natural aspect, which cannot be understood as such. I understand the altar, for example, as a "locality" or "position"; but I cannot understand the stone of which it is made. Thus the experience is, *idealiter*, devoid of fact and of event: it is meaning in its purity.[5]

---

[1] [The brief passage that follows, in small type, is of a somewhat technical character.]

[2] Binswanger, *Psychologie*, 272.   [3] *ibid.*, 244.

[4] This is in fact implied by the term *Er-lebnis* itself; *cf*. pp. 462, 671.

[5] Thus the experience which I have previously called "dual experience of form" would here be lacking *idealiter*; on the other hand, the fact that it is never wholly absent first renders possible the descent to the worldless depths of significance; objectively, this means that experience, apart from the world of events, does not exist; and subjectively, that there is no meaning which cannot be understood. Understanding is not a supplementary activity on the part of the investigator, but pertains essentially to life itself; *cf*. Heidegger, *op. cit.*, 164; similarly, "what the disciple of Saïs unveils is not life, but form"; Dilthey, *op. cit.*, 7, 195.

But it is therefore never completely attainable, since it must always express itself in and through something that has the character of an event: it can appear only when it conceals itself within the opaqueness of the event. *For only what is concealed can become revealed.* But the solitude we seek here is a sort of treed hedge beyond which, indeed, we do not pass, but which attracts us, as a norm, to where dread of the "world" of events has yielded to the dread devoid of any object, where pure meaning would be found if it could ever be found at all, but which would then necessarily disclose itself as madness!

4. Religious experience, further, is that experience whose significance refers to the Whole; it can therefore never be understood from the standpoint merely of the moment, but only and always from that of eternity. Its meaning is an ultimate meaning, and is concerned with "the last things";[1] its nature is eschatological, and transcends itself; while for man it implies an ultimate, a boundary. But it could not attain this significance were it not primary and initial; thus its meaning becomes experienced as "wholly other", and its essence as revelation.[2] There is always a remainder therefore, something that fundamentally cannot become understood, but which religion regards as the condition of all understanding; and thus, at the frontier of the world of appearance, understanding is exchanged for being understood.

Like all experience, nonetheless, religious experience is related to the object, and this indeed in a pre-eminent sense: "in the very expression *Er-leben* there already resounds some degree of objective orientation".[3] In religious experience, however, this orientation is a presence, subsequently an encounter, and finally a union. And in this presence not he who experiences is primary, but He who is present; for He is the holy, the transcendently Powerful.

W. JAMES, *The Varieties of Religious Experience*, 1902.
R. R. MARETT, *Faith, Hope and Charity*, 1932.
F. SCHLEIERMACHER, *Über die Religion*, 1799 (*Ausg.* RUD. OTTO, 1913; Eng. tr., *On Religion*, 1958).
H. WERNER, *Einführung in die Entwicklungspsychologie*, 1926.

[1] Chap. 87.   [2] Chap. 85 *ff.*
[3] Spranger, *Einheit der Psychologie*, 175.

CHAPTER 68

THE AVOIDANCE OF GOD

1. WE have already[1] observed how isolated objects, actions *etc.*, that are "excepted" from the entire world of experience, become declared tabu; and this "excepting" then becomes a "selection" manifested in times and spaces, in persons, objects and words *etc.* In their totality, again, these "selected" factors constitute the realm of the *sacred*, as this detaches itself from the unselected and secular world, while the contrast between sacred and secular showed itself increasingly to be fundamental. With this, too, from the inner aspect or from the side of experience, awe is correlated (to use Marett's fine term) which has been compared by Murray to the Greek *aidos*;[2] and on its own part this awe appeared as ambivalent, as involving the *fascinans* just as it does the *tremendum*.[3] Thus man fears the sacred, but loves it also: he attempts to elude it, yet seeks for it too. In *fear* therefore, which we are now about to examine, we shall discover not avoidance alone, but within and about this always a simultaneous attraction: "Half drew she him, half sank he in."[4]

2. By "fear", however, we understand not reasonable alarm nor dejection due to some concrete danger.[5] Essentially, this has nothing whatever to do with religion. By fear I wish rather to indicate exclusively that experience which Kierkegaard calls "dread", and which I shall myself distinguish as *primary fear* from the first mentioned, *secondary fear*.[6] This primary fear, still further, is not based on any rational set of conditions, for it exists prior to every experience: such fear is a mode of the very state in which one subsists. "Prudence perceives what is to be feared because it is itself within the existential mode of fear; and fear as a slumbering possibility of the existential 'being in the world', faintheartedness, has already understood and appreciated the world in so far that from it something akin to the terrifying may approach." But "what arouses dread is 'being in the world' itself".[7] Thus the child's

---

[1] Chap. 4. [2] Murray, *The Rise of the Greek Epic*, 104, 109 *f.*
[3] Otto. [4] Goethe, *The Fisher*.
[5] On what follows *cf.* Heidegger, *op. cit.*, 140 *ff.*, 184 *ff.*
[6] Ribot, *The Psychology of the Emotions*. [7] Heidegger, *op. cit.*, 141, 187.

dread of the dog, about which it knows nothing, the boy's dread regarding the domain of sex, just because of his ignorance, the undefined dread that may seize us when we are alone, on a moor or in the forest, and whose echoes vibrate in many legends and fairy tales, horror in the dark:—all this is fear in the specifically religious sense. Or to state this bluntly once and for all: in the secondary sense, already indicated, I fear the car which threatens to run me down, but in the primary sense I fear the motorless world of the steppes; secondarily, again, I dread the idea of being attacked in the forest; primarily, I dread the very feeling of the forest's uncanniness and would on that account greet the appearance even of robbers with joy! The fear here referred to, therefore, is not some annoying disturbance, like the secondary type of fear, that should be subdued. On the contrary, it has a positive value and is intimately related to religion, as is shown by the Greek expression *deisidaimonia*, and above all by the Jewish "fear of God". There always persists in it something of that instinctive and irrational fear which is occasionally manifested without any concealment in the Old Testament itself, to whatever degree the Old Testament idea, in the course of time, may have accumulated ethical content; thus it was in the case of the "panic" of Jahveh which he sent before Israel.[1] The vision of the prophet Isaiah is the most vivid expression of this fear; and here it is precisely ambivalence that is very clearly exhibited, since the awe becomes the consciousness of sin, the terror becomes worship.[2] Similarly in the New Testament, when it is concerned with the appearance of Jesus, not only astonishment but fear also is present; thus in the marvellous description in *St. Mark* x, 32, where the Lord is on the way to Jerusalem and His disciples are following Him in terror and fear; and again in the profoundly penetrating passage in which Peter falls at Jesus' feet: " 'Lord, leave me; I am a sinful man'. For amazement had seized him and all his companions at the take of fish they had caught."[3] Thus the primitive amazement, and later fear, produced by the extraordinary and miraculous, here appear at the very centre of religious experience, where its ambivalent aspect is presented as worship.

It seems then that the ancient dictum: "Fear was the first creator of gods in the world",[4] is absolutely true; and desiring to express the practical character of his religion, an Eskimo shaman said: "we do not believe: we fear."[5] But this dread, which we have already learnt to

---

[1] *Exodus* xxxiii. 27; *cf. Isaiah* viii. 13; "let Jahveh be your fear and your dread".
[2] *Isaiah* vi.   [3] *Luke*, v, 8, 9 (Moffat).
[4] Statius, *Theb.* iii, 661.   [5] Lévy-Bruhl, *Primitives and the Supernatural*, 22.

recognize as the primeval experience in religion, is not mere slavish fear, and still less feeble despondency;[1] it is essentially ambivalent, a condition intermediate between being repelled and being attracted. And long before Freud and the psychology of the "Unconscious", Kierkegaard dealt most profoundly with this primal experience: the dread to which he refers is that of Nothingness. The unrestricted possibility of the unformed feeling of life causes the "vertigo of liberty". Thus dread is not consciousness of guilt; it is rather the essential condition therefor. In itself, indeed, it is innocence: "that is the profound mystery of innocence, that it is at the same time dread", a hesitation between hastening towards the object and escaping from it, attachment and anxiety, fear and love. The development of youth during puberty shows this dread of Nothingness in its clearest form, while many neuroses also provide examples. But these are merely the extreme types of a universally human experience, which awaits all men in the hour of death, when Nothingness confronts us: "The father and mother of all fears being the fear of death."[2]

This dread, however, is not correlated with unpleasant feelings, as an earlier psychology maintained. On the contrary, it is connected with feelings of pleasure just as frequently as with the unpleasant. Thus man loves his dread and becomes fascinated by it, like one who after staring into the water for a long time is captivated by the horror of destruction by the stream, or like Goethe's fisherman's fascination by the water-sprite. This dread, still further, may be almost completely resolved into terror, in which a considerable proportion of the fear of demons and spirits persists; but it may also traverse the entire range of human feeling, from terror through horror, awe, reverence and the sense of distance, to trust and love; and in love there is always something of horror, in horror always some degree of love. Dread itself, however, is no haphazard feeling, but the primeval experience aroused by the unlimited possibility lying at the base of all religions without exception, and also of life beyond the merely given in general; this dread indicates the tension of the relationship between Power and man. It is a "sympathetic antipathy and an antipathetic sympathy",[3] so that in fear there is always an element of love, however feeble this may be, and in love an element of terror, however refined it may have become; and there

---

[1] In his own day Varro drew the distinction, "saying that the gods are feared by the superstitious man, but are reverenced by the religious man as parents, not as enemies"; in Augustine, *The City of God*, 6, 9.

[2] Marett, *Faith, Hope and Charity*, 41.

[3] Kierkegaard, *Begrebet Angest* (*The Concept of Dread*).

are no religious ideas from which awe, as corresponding to the primeval experience of dread, is wholly absent.[1] Only thus, in fact, can we understand that to fear God, to love and to serve Him, appear as related concepts;[2] and we all realize, in truth, that we not only hate our dreads, but also, in secret, love them. The religious element in awe, then, is given with its inexplicability and irreducibility on the one hand, and on the other with its limitlessness extending over the totality of life: "everything is possible: I stand before the Nought".[3]

3. Dread, again, is the condition of the experience of *guilt*, which will be discussed later;[4] but it is already clear that the tension of ambivalent dread has caused a rupture in the recesses of human nature. For it confronts man with himself, divides him, as it were, into two egos, one of which desires to comply with the terribly-sweet demand of the sacred, while the other strives to escape from it. One self longs to conform to the sacred, whether this self-accord be a hastening away from, or towards, the sacred; the other self attempts to place life above the infinite possibility, to survive the gnawing dread, to ignore the demand; and we may call the first ego *conscience*, provided we apply this term in its original sense and not in connection with so-called autonomous morality. For the word *conscience*, *conscientia*, συνείδησις, presupposes a schism within the self; it is derived not from a theoretic-ethical, but from a mythical-religious idea, as a result of which our inner psychic life stands confronted with itself as with something foreign. It is my conscience that says something to me; but it could say nothing at all to me if it were myself; and thus it is a *foreign* being, a sort of demon within me.[5] A Bechuana tribesman was once asked if he had a conscience: " 'Yes, all have one', he said in reply. 'And what does it say to them?' 'It is quiet when they do well and torments them when they sin '."[6] From this it follows that the inner voice, the inward judge, usually denies and seldom or never affirms, as we also know indeed

---

[1] *cf.* Söderblom, *Gottesglaube*; similarly for Ribot, *The Psychology of the Emotions*, who will accept *primus in orbe* only if a moment of attraction is recognized in repulsion; for Marett (*Faith, Hope and Charity*), who includes in *timor* the feelings of wonder, admiration, interest, reverence and love; for Grönbech (*op. cit.*, II, 77), who concedes fear as a primeval feeling in religion only if this implies "wanton gaiety as well as despair". (Marett observes that fear is founded in hope: "hope is of superior importance, since ultimately we fear because we hope, and not *vice versa*". *loc. cit.*, 22, 40. In the end this is nothing but a different way of emphasizing ambivalence.)

[2] *Deut.* x, 12.   [3] Chap. 67.
[4] Chap. 78.   [5] *cf.* A. Vierkandt, *Naturvölker und Kulturvölker*, 1896, 179 *f.*
[6] Westermarck, *The Origin and Development of the Moral Ideas*, I, 125.

from experience, despite much ethical theory, while even children are already aware of it. The conjoined knowledge cries out to knowledge, the associated self to the self, that man must undertake something with respect to the sacred, and that he may not live in disregard of it. The most celebrated example of this is Socrates' Demon, which ethics, but for its too positive and too moral conception of conscience, would not so frequently have refused to identify therewith; the Demon, this "revenge of the irrational" on the rationalist Socrates, as Joël says,[1] also expressed itself negatively, as is well known. "This voice, which emerges from unknown depths, appears as something foreign that does not pertain to the self, and this precisely at the moment when it arises to prevent something. For where it operates positively, *currentum instigans*, the voice of conscience is unheard in the din excited by consciousness and therefore not observed as something particular."[2] But in so far as it represents the alien and the sacred, it appears to be a god; the ancient Egyptians, indeed, called conscience, which they regarded as the heart, the god within us: Intef performs all his good works under the leadership of his heart: "I was excellent by virtue of what it told me to do: I was distinguished under its guidance; people say: it is a decree of the gods residing within everybody."[3] Paheri again: "I knew the god who dwells within man: I recognized him; I distinguished this way from that, *etc.*";[4] and there follows an assurance of honesty. Now it is possible, certainly, with Nietzsche and Freud, to ascribe the "strangeness" of the voice, which warns us to avoid, to infantilism; "not the voice of God in the heart of man, but the voice of some men in man".[5] We may however prefer the Egyptian description; on this point phenomenology has no decision to make. But this much is certain: a rupture (to repeat) manifests itself here which cleaves human personality. The self, which desires simply to live, is compelled to "avoid" by the other self which interrupts it. "Avoidance", then, means observance, *religio*; it may become flight, but it may also become a passionate seeking; in both cases alike "avoidance" reveals itself in the fact that distance is recognized together with dread. And if man simply continues to live in spite of his conscience, then it will torment him even when he is unconscious of any fault; in

[1] *Geschichte der antiken Philosophie*, I, 1921, 816 *f.*

[2] M. P. Nilsson, *Götter und Psychologie bei Homer*, AR. 22, 1923/24. 380; *cf.* Windelband, *History of Philosophy*, 98; *Präludien*, I⁶, 1919, 77 *f.*

[3] Sethe, *Urkunden*, IV, 974.

[4] *ibid.*, 119; *cf.* 117. Ad. Erman, *Die ägyptische Religion*², 1909, 123.

[5] *Human, All Too Human*, II, 224.

this respect "psychoanalysis confirms what the pious were wont to say, that we are all miserable sinners";[1] this confirmation, though coming somewhat late in the day, should nevertheless be welcome. On the other hand the recognition of the inner voice, either as foreign or as divinely experienced, gives to human conduct a firmness and a calm, outstanding examples of which we can perceive at the end of Socrates' *Apology* and in Luther's declaration at Worms, that "to act against conscience is neither safe nor advisable".

4. To him therefore who is seized by dread, subsequently by awe, and compelled to "avoid", different paths stand open other than the easiest way of continuing to live while ignoring all this, which has just been referred to. The first is that of presumption, of autocratic seizure of power, and with this attitude of mind we have already become familiar in countless magical customs; at a later stage I shall discuss its background[2] in turning away from the world, which is overcome only in appearance, but which in reality is abandoned. The experience accompanying this frame of mind is often an almost wanton arrogance; we find it in pure magic—for example in the Hindu idea that the *tapas* (warmth) of ascetic fulfilment of duty makes the throne of the great god in heaven hot;[3] and thus dread is overcome in a mighty trial of strength, which makes matters hot for the gods on their thrones. A titanic mood may also colour this experience; in myth the type is Herakles, who threatens Helios, appears terrible before the throne of Hades, instils fear into its mighty ruler and himself attains divinity. In the fairy tale, again, it is Strong Jack who thrashes the devil and sets out, but all in vain, to learn what fear is. The Greeks called such an arrogant disregard of awe *hubris* and looked upon it as the great sin, although they themselves could never renounce it: to render oneself like the god, not to esteem the god rightly, is *hubris*, the human element being altogether discarded; and so Aias calls down divine anger on himself, "thinking things not fit for man".[4] The ecstatic likeness of the *bacchae* to the god was likewise described as "bacchic frenzy".[5] This Titanism, however, is by no means the same as that living in disregard of Power, that failure duly to observe the sacred, which we have already encountered. On the contrary: Power is here frankly recognized, and

---

[1] Freud, *Totem and Taboo*, 121; *cf.* O. Pfister, *Die psychoanalytische Methode*, 1913, 87 *ff.*   [2] Chap. 82.
[3] Lüders, *Buddhistische Märchen*, No. 53.   [4] Sophocles, *Ajax*, 776 *f.*
[5] Euripides, *The Bacchae*, 779; ὕβρισμα βακχῶν.

then a hostile attitude is adopted amounting to contempt; and thus man turns away from the Power that arouses dread towards himself, towards his own powerfulness, under the impression that his own likeness to the god will excite no alarm. In its other aspects too Goethe has expressed the religion of *hubris* in its finest form (and has at the same moment provided its keenest criticism!) in his *Prometheus*:—

> Here sit I, fashion men
> In mine own image,—
> A race to be like me,
> To weep and to suffer,
> To be happy and enjoy themselves,
> All careless of *thee* too,
> As I![1]

Similarly, *Postilion Kronos*:—

> So that Orcus may know we are coming,
> And the mighty ones below
> Are rising from their seats.[2]

This is *Herakles redivivus*! and the same heroic victory over dread is very finely portrayed, especially with reference to conscience, in Ibsen's *Master Builder*; Hilda's demand, that the Master Builder should equip himself with a "robust conscience", is pure *hubris*. The Master Builder attempts to do so and—here too criticism closely accompanies the challenge—falls from the tower he has himself constructed. In fact, a tower became the classical type, and also the warning example, of this heroism: the tower of Babel!

In the second place, against dread man may come to rely on *habit*. Alarm, or care, may lead to man gaining dominance, but also to habit, either with respect to what has been acquired, or to the impossibility of such acquisition. A child, for instance, wonders at some object in its environment and tries to seize it; then he becomes quite accustomed either to the thing he possesses or to the fact that he cannot have the object. So out of his relation to Power man forms a habit which becomes firmly established in the various rites and customs we have encountered, but which also represents an inner attitude. It is "justice towards the gods", *justitia adversus deos*,[3] in which Cicero found the essence of piety: the correct behaviour that never surpasses the limits imposed on man and involves an equally unmoved outlook with regard to both

---

[1] Dwight's translation.   [2] In the original version.
[3] Cicero, *De Deorum Natura*, I, 41.

possibilities and impossibilities; the *justus*, in other words, is he whose demeanour is correct.[1] The Romans, indeed, placed great emphasis on practical conduct; so did the Greeks but, in accordance with their characteristic temperament, they expressed themselves more freely about the experience connected with this. It is then this spiritual condition which, as the antithesis to *hubris*, runs through so many Greek concepts about God and the Universe—*sophrosyne*. The magicians were "crafty", ὀλοόφρονες; they had pernicious ideas, while whoever was *sao-phron* had saving and healing thoughts. The mood of *sophrosyne* was related to the Apollonian calm of the soul of the Delphic god, to "Nothing in excess": μηδὲν ἄγαν.[2] It was a highly prized possession, a sort of sea-calm of the soul, which did not however prevent it being regarded by profounder minds as inferior when compared with Dionysiac ecstasy, nor hinder a poet like Euripides from putting its glorification into the mouth of the petty *bourgeois* and the philistine.[3] And no less a thinker than Plato extols the "madman", μαίνεσθαι, at the expense of the "sane man", σωφρονεῖν, in his celebrated eulogy of "mania".[4] But as regards the "Wholly Other", habit is always very foolish: in three days, just when the horse became used to eating nothing at all, it died; and when man has completely lost his capacity for surprise, he too is as good as dead! For in dread we may be blessed, or we may realize that we are damned; but in the easy-going calm of the man who has altogether forgotten astonishment and amazement there is neither blessedness nor damnation.

The third way of escape from dread is faith.[5] Dread, says Kierkegaard again, enfolds the point at which the spirit breaks through, alike in the fall and in deliverance. Then every attempt to elude astonishment or care is abandoned, and the dreadfulness of Power is not merely unreservedly acknowledged, but experienced as part of one's very own existence. This experience is vividly expressed in the passage from Luther's sermon on *Exodus* xx. 1, which Otto quotes: "For therefrom can no man refrain: if he thinketh on God aright, his heart in his body is struck with terror: yea, he would escape out of the world."[6] It lives too in the sixth chapter of *Isaiah*, in *Job*, in the Babylonian peni-

---

[1] *cf. ibid.*, II, 4, 10, and the formula of the fetial on the *hostis* who was, as such, *injustus: illum injustum esse neque jus persolvere.*

[2] G. van der Leeuw, *Goden en Menschen*, 87 *ff*.; *cf.* Murray, *The Rise of the Greek Epic*, 48. Samter, *Religion der Griechen*, 74.

[3] Euripides, *Medea, e.g.* 1078 *ff. The Bacchae*, 1150 *ff.*

[4] *Phaedrus*, 245.   [5] Chap. 80.

[6] *cf. The Idea of the Holy*, 103, and Calvin, *Institutio*, I, 1, 3.

tential Psalms and in all the horror of the Hindu experience of God in the *Bhagavad-Gita*.[1] Dread, however, finds its end in God, from Whom it emanated: "the mothers do not tell us where we are: they leave us quite alone; where dread ends and God begins we too may be allowed to be".[2] Again: "There is no fear in love; but perfect love casteth out fear: because fear hath torment."[3] Or: "That is perfect fear which is born of love and expels ordinary fear."[4]

S. F. H. J. Berkelbach van der Sprenkel, *Vrees en Religie*, 1920.
S. Kierkegaard, *Begrebet Angest* (*Samlede Vaerker*, IV), 1923 (Eng. tr., *The Concept of Dread*).
A. Mosso, *Die Furcht*, 1889.
Th. Ribot, *The Psychology of the Emotions*.

[1] Especially 11, 15 *ff.*
[2] Rainer Maria Rilke, in P. Zech, *Rainer Maria Rilke*, 1930, 64.
[3] 1 *John* iv. 18.
[4] Abbas Dorotheus, in Nik. von Arseniew, *Religiöse Besinnung*, I, 1928, 109.

CHAPTER 69

SERVITUDE TO GOD

1. THE opposite Pole to titanic insubordination, and different also from habit as discussed in the previous Chapter, is servitude to God, wholly resigned and unreserved submission to the rule of Power. Man, realizing his own dependence on Power and compelled to assign to this dependence a form in his religious consciousness, has here chosen the form of a servant to express his unrestricted recognition of this subjection. The bodily posture associated with this recognition is προσκύνησις (הִשְׁתַּחֲוָה), prostrating oneself: before Power man humbles himself. God is *Lord*, not only of the earth like the Semitic *baalim*, but also of those who live on it and who are His slaves: He is the king who owns the land and whom all men must serve. And in his own divinity the earthly king is by no means the prototype of this "Lord" God, but is His shadow or His son;[1] thus the Hebrew expressed himself:—"I am thy slave, the son of thy female slave"[2]; in the New Testament too the designation recurs in relation to Christ: "the slave (δοῦλος) of Christ Jesus".[3] Slavish servitude may certainly be implied here, but it may equally well be the expression of awe before the sacred; this it is already in very many passages in the Old Testament. In such a spirit of serving God, for example, Abraham says to Him: "Here am I venturing to speak to the Lord, I who am mere dust and dross".[4] On the other hand, even such slavish humiliation may facilitate an excessive intensification of self-respect in being the servant of such a master,[5] just as to serve, with the *arrière pensée* of being able to rule all the more effectively, repeatedly appears in human experience.

2. The designation "servant of God" involves, however, not only complete submission but also readiness for service, obedience; here[6] servitude borders on the imitation of God, with which I shall later on deal in fuller detail.[7] Obedience is hearkening to God's decisive word. Life becomes viewed as fulfilment of this word: its whole significance

---

[1] Chap. 13, 25.
[3] *Phil.* i. 1; *cf. Tit.* i. 1.
[5] There is a good example in Günther, *Jung-Stilling*, 93.
[7] Chap. 73.

[2] *Ps.* cxvi. 16.
[4] *Gen.* xviii. 27 (Moffat).
[6] Chap. 53.

lies in decision. This is shown very beautifully in Parsiism; obedience (*sraosha*) is there one of the sacred beings which surround Ahura Mazda; and at a later period *sraosha* was assigned to the soul, as a psychopomp, on the road to the judgment of the dead—that is of decision.

All volition, in fact, has obedience as its presupposition: "A man who *wills* commands something within himself which renders obedience, or which he believes renders obedience."[1] Thus the will to power presupposes obedience, which indeed may also be one attitude of the man who listens to himself; and in such a case we have the parallel to prayer as monologue. But it may also be the disposition accompanying prayer as dialogue,[2] in bowing before the word of the Wholly Other encroaching upon life; here power is found in a voluntary powerlessness, which is however neither weakness nor hostility towards life, but simple acknowledgment of the validity of the word that has been heard. In this sense Jesus is said to have "learned obedience by the things which he suffered",[3] and in this way too He is the realization of that ideal of service which prevailed in Israelite prophecy:

> "He was despised and shunned by men,
> a man of pain, who knew what sickness was; . . .
> He was ill-treated, yet he bore it humbly,
> he never would complain,
> dumb as a sheep led to the slaughter,
> dumb as a ewe before the shearers.
> Yes, many shall hold my servant blameless" (saith God)
> "since 'twas their guilt he bore.
> Therefore shall he win victory,
> he shall succeed triumphantly,
> since he has shed his life-blood,
> and let himself be numbered among rebels,
> bearing the great world's sins,
> and interposing for rebellious men."[4]

---

[1] Nietzsche, *Beyond Good and Evil*, 26 (Foulis Edition). [2] Chap. 32.
[3] *Hebrews* v. 8. [4] *Isaiah*, liii (Moffat); *cf.* Chap. 13.

CHAPTER 70

THE COVENANT WITH GOD

1. JUST as it is possible for men to enter into a covenant, and in association with one another to discover the sacred common element,[1] so too they can conclude a covenant with Power, with Deity. Certain rules are, as it were, laid down according to which the game between God and man is to be played;[2] man and Power both alike pledge themselves to some definite course of conduct. "Peace" must prevail between them; and in ancient Rome the entire life of the community was based upon a pact, *pax deorum*. This "peace" was a legally concluded covenant maintained by varied means, and when calamities fell on the people, when *portenta* occurred, *etc.*, it was a sign that the *pax* had been infringed; while the *pax* was preserved, the *status quo* assured, by sacrifice and prayer, the fulfilment of vows, purifications, conscientious investigation of the "situation" and attention to whatever was "unseasonable". In all this, however, there was no reference to trust in the gods; the Romans believed merely that correct words and acts securely determined the powers. Were this not the case, the reason was that some incorrect celebrations had been carried out; these were then corrected, or some new methods tried, for example a great repast of the gods: "For the purpose of imploring the favour of the gods there was a *lectisternium*, the third time since the building of the city."[3] The *pax* thus required a "conscientious observation" of the divine powers (*pietas*);[4] and with this the Germanic concept of "peace" may be compared.[5]

From the Old Testament, again, we can trace how the covenant with God arose from that between men, and was originally identical with this.[6] The human covenant was contracted on holy ground in the presence of the gods, and in this compact the deities of both parties were

---

[1] Chap. 33 *ff.*

[2] This comparison is in no degree depreciative, since there is scarcely anything in life more serious than play, especially child's play; *cf.* "the maturity of man—that means, to have recognized the seriousness that one had as a child at play". *Beyond Good and Evil*, 89 (Foulis Edition). [3] Livy, VII, 2.

[4] Fowler, *Religious Experience*, 431; *cf.* 169*ff.*, 261; also H. Wagenvoort, *Pietas*, 194.

[5] Grönbech, *op. cit.*, I, 20 *ff* [6] On what follows *cf.* Pedersen, *Israel*, 201 *ff.*

included. The covenant rite was a communal meal (בְּרִית perhaps means "food") of which gifts also formed part;[1] and the compact inaugurated peace, *shalom.* Later there arose the idea of a covenant between Jahveh and the people; and here the remarkable and typically Israelite feature was that Jahveh himself concluded the covenant; a covenant with Noah is referred to, with Abraham also, and later still with the whole people, whose intermediary was Moses. The compact demanded man's obedience to the divine commands (the Tables and the Book of the Covenant), while on His part God pledged Himself to conquest of the promised land and victory over their enemies. Here too the rite was sacrifice, or the dismemberment of the sacrificial animals,[2] while circumcision was regarded as the covenantal sign.

As has already been observed,[3] contract is never a merely rational nor even advantageous affair; and the covenant, as it became apprehended in Israel, was quite different from this. On the one hand trust in God's word and on the other obedience to His commands became more and more intensely, and at the same time more and more inwardly, experienced: in this respect indeed the covenant approximates to the relation of friendship, which will be discussed later;[4] it stood firmly grounded in Jahveh's *truth* to eternity:

> He never forgets his compact,
>   the pledge given for a thousand generations,
> the compact made with Abraham,
>   the oath he swore to Isaac,
> confirming it as a decree to Jacob,
>   for Israel as a lasting compact,
> that he would give them Canaan's land,
>   to hold it as their own possession.[5]

The contrast with earlier ideas of the covenant was clearly perceived and a "new" covenant distinguished from the "old": a new compact having in the first place an eschatological significance: "I will remember my compact with you in the days of your youth; I will ratify a lasting compact with you";[6] while as the mediator of this renewed deliverance *Deutero-Isaiah* presents the Servant of Jahveh, the obedient.[7] But

---

[1] Chap. 50.
[2] *Gen.* xv. For other examples of the idea of covenant, *inter alia* in Japan, *cf.* Jevons, *The Idea of God in Early Religions*, 1913, 92 *ff.*   [3] Chap. 50.
[4] Chap. 71.   [5] *Ps.* cv. 8 *ff.* (Moffat).
[6] *Ezekiel* xvi. 60 (Moffat); *cf. Isaiah*, lv, 3; lxi, 8; lxvi, 22.
[7] *Isaiah* xlii. 6; xlix. 8.

Jeremiah places beside its wide range into eternity its deep roots in experience: Jahveh declares that the new covenant consists in that

> I will put my law within them,
>   and write it on their hearts;
> and I will be a God to them,
>   and they to me a people.[1]

In this the significance of both the old and the new covenants is clearly exhibited, and the direction taken by the New Testament made possible; man recedes completely into the background: the covenant means solely the saving act of God in history, and His faithfulness means only His grace.

[1] *Jer.* xxxi. 33 (Moffat); *cf.* xxxii. 39 *f.*

CHAPTER 71

FRIENDSHIP WITH GOD

1. THOSE associated in any covenant are friends;[1] and thus the god who is accepted in the compact, or even concludes this, is a friend too. This friendship with the god, further, may awaken the sense of some likeness between god and man, and so we can well understand that in the sphere of religion man has been very chary of employing the title of friend. Peterson has discussed the genesis of the idea of friendship with the god in the Greek-Semitic world,[2] and has found it predominantly in Hellenistic circles or in those influenced by Hellenism. Previously employed by Plato, the concept of friendship with God was occasionally objected to,[3] but in later philosophy it became highly esteemed as one title of the sage. The designation of the patriarch Abraham also, as the friend of God,[4] probably originated from Hellenistically influenced quarters, while besides Abraham, Moses also appears as God's friend. For friendship with God, again, there were two conditions, the first being the possession of divine knowledge; and in this sense too St. John's *Gospel* speaks of the friends of Jesus: "Henceforth I call you not servants; for the servant knoweth not what his Lord doeth: but I have called you friends; for all things that I have heard of my Father I have made known unto you."[5] Thus friendship with God takes the place of service of God. In the second place, fulfilment of the commandments pertains to this: "Ye are my friends, if ye do whatsoever I command you";[6] obedience, which we have already discerned to be the presupposition of service, now becomes the condition of friendship also. Certainly St. John referred not to God but to Christ, as God revealed. The ultimate ground of this friendship, then, is divine love which expels fear: and this love is

---

[1] cf. Pedersen, *Israel*, 201 ff.
[2] On the original meaning of $\phi\iota\lambda\sigma\varsigma$ ($\theta\varepsilon\sigma\hat{\upsilon}$) as "sanctified, dedicated" cf. Fr. Pfister in Pauly-Wissowa, *Realenzykl. d. klass. Alt., Kultus*, § 5, 5. On $\phi\iota\lambda\sigma\varsigma$ as a title at the court of the Ptolemies cf. A. Deissmann, *Bibelstudien*, 1895, 159 ff. On the Israelites as friends of God: Strack-Billerbeck, *Kommentar zum N. T. aus Talmud und Midrasch*, II, 1924, 564 f.
[3] E. Peterson, *Der Gottesfreund* (*Zeitschr. für Kirchengeschichte*, 42, N. F. 5.), 166 f.
[4] *James* ii. 23.   [5] *John* xv. 15.   [6] *ibid.*, 14.

2. The mystical being and existing *"in Christo"*, which finds undying expression in the parable of "The Vine and its Branches". All these features—the contrast with servitude and fear, the mystic community (with reference even to the sacrament!) and the knowledge of God, occur in the passage cited by Peterson from Origen:[1] "At first Christ the shepherd leads the sheep to pasture, but now the friend invites his friends to his table. 'For', he says, 'I no longer call you servants, but friends.' The fear of the Lord makes servants, but knowledge of the mysteries of God makes friends."

Friendship, to continue, includes a certain degree of intimacy; and this becomes stressed in mysticism; as al-Ghazali says: "When the mystic is overcome with joy at the nearness of God and the contemplation of what is imparted to him in revelation . . . a blissful mood arises in his heart; and this mood is called intimacy."[2] In *Sufi* mysticism, too, God is the friend, just as in fourteenth century German mysticism.[3] Conversely, man's turning towards God is friendship. "Thus man has turned to the best part, which is God . . . and then they are called the hidden friends of God";[4] the "cherubinic Wanderer" (Angelus Silesius) goes still farther: "Whoso would embrace him must be not merely his friend, but must even be his child and mother."[5]

In friendship love becomes visible, the blissful intimacy with God, while mysticism esteems it as the prologue to complete union: so in the words from *The Imitation of Christ*, with which Peterson also concludes: "That Thou alone wouldst speak to me and I to Thee, as a lover talking to his loved one, a friend at table with his friend. This is my prayer, my longing, to be made one with Thee. . . . Ah, my Lord God, when shall I be quite one with Thee, drawn in to Thee, myself utterly forgotten, Thou in me, I in Thee? Grant us to stay thus —one."[6]

---

[1] 191.   [2] A. J. Wensinck, *Semitische Mystiek* (De Gids, 83, 1919), 289 f.
[3] *cf.* E. Lehmann, *Mystik in Heidentum und Christentum*[2], 1923. Grete Lüers, *Die Sprache der deutschen Mystik des Mittelalters im Werke der Mechtild von Magdeburg*, 1926, 181.
[4] Lüers, *ibid.*, 182 (*Das Buch von geistlicher Armut*).
[5] Silesius, *Cherubinischer Wandersmann*, III, 17.   [6] IV, 13, 1.

CHAPTER 72

KNOWLEDGE OF GOD

1. POWER always requires knowledge; this has already been evident in our discussion of the close relationship between the ideas of Power and of capacity.[1] Whoever desires to exercise power must know something about both the sources of his potency and the object to be controlled; and although knowledge is not identical with ability, yet nevertheless capacity is always intimately linked with knowledge. Acquaintance with those formulas that induce power, therefore, becomes highly esteemed, and the knowledge of any tradition, preserved by elders or priests, determines the powerfulness of the community. At all times then, even under most primitive conditions, knowledge plays some part in religion.

If however there is to be any *knowledge of God*, not only must ability imply some degree of knowledge, but knowledge must *ipso facto* involve ability. Knowledge is power: to comprehend is to seize. But the validity of this dictum of liberal and optimistic learning, as we are familiar with it particularly in the nineteenth century, has in the present connection an altogether different character. For the knowledge implied here refers neither to the world in the technical sense, nor to the ego in the psychological sense, but solely to salvation: How am I to participate in Power? Whether I wish to assure myself of it, as being superior to it, or whether I kneel before it in fear and trembling, in any case I must know where it is to be found and how it is constituted. And I may also believe that this knowledge is the really essential matter, and that it of itself effects salvation. In that case, I am seeking the path of *the knowledge of God*, or theosophy. So pious Jews recognize the sacred duty of studying *Torah* and *Talmud*; in Warsaw, Jeremias found that among them every trade, bakers, coachmen, cobblers, *etc.*, had its "little room", in which the intervals between work were utilized to study the *Torah*.[2] The way to salvation, then, is study.[3]

To a far greater degree than this, however, we find the knowledge of God in India. For the brahmin, acquaintance with the sacred sacrificial formulas procures world-power.[4] He only, because of his know-

---

[1] Chap. 1.
[3] Chap. 64.
[2] A. Jeremias, *Jüdische Frömmigkeit*, 1927, 26.
[4] *cf.* Oldenberg, *Die Lehre der Upanishaden*, 6 f.

ledge, is competent to perform the sacrifice which sustains the world and upon which the gods depend, which indeed actually first of all produced both world and gods. "The dictum that knowledge is power has a completely different meaning from our own, since it implies not what we understand by it—that is the capacity for acting rightly—but rather that, in some mysterious way, it effects an immediate connection between the knower and his knowledge. . . . Here therefore it is not a matter of the intellectual ability to comprehend, but of some mystic equipment for accommodating knowledge and for protection against the hazardous powers dwelling therein."[1] The essential nature of the knowledge of God cannot be better expressed than in these words of Oldenberg; and he indicates a fine example in a *Brahmana Text*: "It (the sun) never actually sets." This, according to our views, is knowledge of a fact. But the *Text* continues: "Whoso knows this never sets, but attains to community with (the sun) and similarity thereto, and to life in its world."[2]

2. Magical knowledge, in the next place, becomes "transposed" *mystically*; and again we find this mystical transposition primarily in India. The realization that world and self are ultimately one[3] effects salvation; and the whole of Buddhism reposes on insight into the essence of the Universe and of man. Knowledge of the "four noble truths" brings with it the salvation of the cessation of births: "In me", says Buddha, "arose the knowledge and the conviction: the liberation of my spirit is assured; this is my last birth, and now for me there is no being reborn."[4] Certainly this insight is not "theoretical" in our sense; it is still magical-mystical, since it does not simply render man capable of attaining salvation, but actually imparts it; and the amalgamation of Hindu knowledge of God with the rationalist scientific consciousness of to-day was reserved for modern theosophy.

Knowledge of God, still further, is wholly mystical whenever it refers to the apprehension of the mystery of union with God. This also, of course, holds true of Hindu speculation, and in this respect Brahminic knowledge of God, as well as Buddhist, is absolutely mystical; and no less so was Hellenistic *gnosis*. "I proclaim the mystery of the sacred path: I call it knowledge", says the *Naassene Hymn*.[5] And it effects salvation through deification: "The high destiny of those who

---

[1] *cf.* Oldenberg, *Die Lehre der Upanishaden*, 6 f.   [2] *ibid.*, Note 1.
[3] Chap. 2.   [4] Bertholet, *Lesebuch*, 11, 40.
[5] Bertholet, *ibid.*, 5, 57.

have gained knowledge is to become divine".[1] This is very finely expressed in a gnostic thanksgiving prayer: "We thank Thee, Most High! for by Thy grace we received this light of knowledge, Thou unnameable, Whom we invoke as God and praise as Father, because Thou showest to each and all of us fatherly affection, benevolence and blessing power, favouring us with thought, reason and knowledge, that we may rejoice in knowing Thee. . . . We perceived Thee, the light apprehensible by thought alone: we have known Thee, life of human life: we apprehended Thee, the womb of all, imparting life in maternal generation; we knew Thee, the eternally enduring bestower of life. Worshipping Thee thus, we ask nothing of Thy goodness but that Thou mayest preserve us in Thy knowledge and that Thou mayest vouchsafe to let us never lose the life we have thus won."[2] Here too, then, knowledge bestows power, unites man with God and procures for him some portion of divinity. Again, it was no presumptive rationalism nor intellectualism to which the Christian church objected in Gnosticism, and which inspired the warning in *Timothy*: "avoid the profane jargon and arguments of what is falsely called gnosis".[3] Far more does this rejection, on the part of Christianity, apply to that essentially magical feature in all knowledge of God that *my* knowledge effects salvation and ultimately, indeed, creates God. In this sense therefore we understand the warning: "Knowledge puffs up, love builds up. Whoever imagines he has attained to some degree of knowledge, does not possess the true knowledge yet; but if anyone loves God, he is known by Him."[4] Thus love, and in fact the love of God, is placed at the very foundation of "true knowledge": nothing at all is permanent except what is erected on this basis.[5] And knowing itself reposes on a being-known.

3. Mysticism[6] attempted to remove the magical element from the knowledge of God by the fusion of subject and object: God then becomes apprehended by the God in man: or in Goethe's words, "were not the eye itself a sun, no sun for it could ever shine"; (this will be considered at a later stage).[7] To what has already been said there need be added only that the knowledge of God, although assigned its proper limits, is of course not absent from Christianity, and this indeed precisely as participation in God. St. John's *Gospel* is thoroughly imbued with the importance and the excellence of knowledge; but here

---

[1] Bertholet, *Lesebuch*, 74.   [2] *ibid.*, 5, 85.
[3] 1 *Tim.* vi. 20.   [4] 1 *Cor.* viii. 1 *f.* (Moffat).
[5] *cf.* 1 *Cor.* xiii. 8 *f.*   [6] Chap. 75.   [7] *cf.* p. 494.

"to know" is neither a matter of theory—in the modern sense—nor—in the primitive manner—an affair of the will to power. It is an imparted life. "And this is life eternal, that they might know thee the only true God, and Jesus Christ, whom thou hast sent."[1] But for St. Paul the apostle "knowing in part" is transformed into: "then shall I know even as also I am known"; and this will at some time render love possible.[2]

[1] *John* xvii. 3.   [2] i *Cor.* xiii. 12; *cf.* R. Bultmann, *RGG.* "Paulus".

CHAPTER 73

THE FOLLOWING OF GOD

1. IF Power possesses a form, and if it moves in some direction comprehensible by man, then he can *follow* it. This following, however, is not the non-obligatory and arbitrary attitude such as is often referred to (for example) in Protestant circles, when "merely following Jesus" is censured, as this is advocated by the modernist group. "To follow" always implies the union of the follower's life with that of him he follows: if I follow after someone I resolve to share his life, to make his fortunes, his victory and defeat, his gain and loss my own: to join my life to his and to allow my own powerfulness to be merged in his. Even when I decide to observe the instructions of the policeman, for instance, to "follow" the tram lines, I surrender to a specific powerfulness: that is to the direction, the ultimate goal, the turnings *etc.* of the route. But then I must be able to *see* how the line runs; it must have shown me an intelligible direction and this, again, in some fixed and permanent form. I cannot "follow" an airship because it immediately disappears from sight; I must have some support, some visible road.

There is therefore nothing remarkable in our encountering "following", or imitation, in connection with the mystery ideas about human life being concealed within the life of the saviour.[1] There was indeed in ancient Egypt a reference to the king "doing what Osiris does", and leading a life imitating or "following" the god; there too the basic idea of sacred drama was always "to repeat the life, death and resurrection of the god in dramatic form".[2] Not only was worship itself such a "repetition", but also the life of him who took part therein; we have already observed how the participant in the Osiris mysteries took the side of the god and fought for him,[3] and we know also that the essence of the Hellenistic mysteries consisted in the members "taking part" in the life and death of the saviour-god. The power of mystery consecration, in fact, lay in the initiate assimilating his own life wholly to

---

[1] Chap. 12. [2] Junker, *Stundenwachen,* 2.
[3] Chap. 66. Do the primeval *šmsw Ḥr*, the "followers of Horus", owe their names to this type of "Imitation"? The determination of the expression by the ship in the oldest period seems to indicate a connection with the (mock) water combats; *cf.* Flinders Petrie, *The Royal Tombs of the First Dynasty*, I, 16, 22; II, 8, 5; 12, 1. Sethe, *Beiträge*, 67 *f.*

that of the god, as may be seen from one of the best known exhortations, probably taken from Attis worship: "Be of good cheer, ye initiates, for the god has been saved; and you also shall be saved after toil":

$$\theta\alpha\rho\rho\epsilon\hat{\iota}\tau\epsilon \ \mu\acute{\nu}\sigma\tau\alpha\iota \ \tau o\hat{\nu} \ \theta\epsilon o\hat{\nu} \ \sigma\epsilon\sigma\omega\sigma\mu\acute{\epsilon}\nu o\nu.$$
$$\check{\epsilon}\sigma\tau\alpha\iota \ \gamma\grave{\alpha}\rho \ \dot{\eta}\mu\hat{\iota}\nu \ \dot{\epsilon}\kappa \ \pi\acute{o}\nu\omega\nu \ \sigma\omega\tau\eta\rho\acute{\iota}\alpha.^1$$

In just the same way, St. Paul also preached following after Christ in the sense of practice of worship: "We believe that as we have died with Christ we shall also live with him."[2] And still more clearly in relation to baptism: "Our baptism into his death made us share his burial, so that, as Christ was raised from the dead by the glory of the Father, we too might live and move in the new sphere of Life. For if we have grown into him by a death like his, we shall grow into him by a resurrection like his, knowing as we do that our old self has been crucified with him in order to crush the sinful body and free us from any further slavery to sin."[3] Alike in the New Testament and in the Hellenistic mysteries of Isis and Mithra this following is occasionally conceived as military service, and as a sacred *militia*, fidelity to the god being compared to the soldier's loyalty;[4] in the service of Mithra, indeed, this idea found very fine expression in the refusal of the crown. The initiate who claims the rank of *miles* was presented with a crown as the symbol of victorious power; but he had to refuse it, saying that Mithra was his only crown. Later he had again to decline it, even when offered to him as a military honour, since it rightfully belonged only to his god, *invictus*.[5]

2. Following appears not only in worship, however, but in religious custom also, where the outstanding example is the Persian type. There the commandment of life is man's own participation in the great contest which Ahura Mazda has to sustain against the evil Power. This partaking, still further, is wholly practical: it is deed, virtue, and may be realized even in tilling the soil. For agriculture was regarded as a struggle against the malicious Power: cultivated land belonged to Ahura Mazda, desert country to the demons;[6] in the labour of civilization, therefore, man participates in the combat of the god, and thus

---

Firmicus Maternus, *De errore prof. rel.* 22.   [2] *Rom.* vi. 8 (Moffat).
[3] *Rom.* vi. 4 *ff.* (Moffat).   [4] Reitzenstein, *Hell. Mysterienreligionen*[3], 192 *ff.*
[5] F. Cumont, *Die Mysterien des Mithra* (Gehrich)[3], 1923, 143 *f.*
[6] Chap. 57. Lommel, *Religion Zarathustras*, 250.

culture, morality and worship (*yaz*) find their unity in following the fighting god. "He who cultivates the grain crop cultivates the law, he promotes in the most advantageous way the religion of the Mazda worshippers . . . when there is grain the *devs* sweat (with dread)."[1] Among the Greeks, on the other hand, the idea of imitation in custom was quite rare; we find it however in Pythagoras, who demanded as the condition of deliverance a "Pythagorean life" which he described as a "following of the god".[2]

3. Mysticism, again, transfers imitation and following wholly into the realm of the inward, even when some external means are utilized such as the cross with the nails or meditation on the stations of the cross. The suffering and death of Christ must then be repeated within the soul of the faithful: like Christ, the mystic commences with mere humanity, in order by pain and death to rise to divinity. Mysticism of course found its starting-point in the New Testament itself: with Christ it desired to be crucified and raised again. In this, however, it not only proceeds to the complete effacement of all limits without exception, but it also regards following more as a salvation to be attained, to be won by asceticism, than as being imparted. Union with God, still further, is expressed even physically: we may recall the stigmata of St. Francis and of many other saints, while the self-sufficiency of following is manifested, according to the great schema of Dionysius the Areopagite, by the self-alienation of God (in the Incarnation) being regarded as a realization of man. The single foundational act is thus accomplished in two phases, "one of which ascends to the Trinity and the other descends to humanity";[3] and so God's act has a human, together with a divine, aspect. The existence of Christ thus becomes a paradigm of divine-human unity: in His ascension Christ has "shown all mysticism the path to the ultimate goal".[4]

4. For Christianity, however, imitation or following is practical in worship and custom; it is mystical also, and yet at the same moment something quite different, since it signifies that very self-renunciation which is the essential feature of the figure of Jesus; the path He indicates is precisely that of impotence, and at no time whatever that of the grasping of power: "Treat one another with the same spirit as you

---

[1] Bertholet, *op. cit.*, I, 37.
[2] G. van der Leeuw, *Goden en Menschen in Hellas*, 157.
[3] Thus *e.g.* Görres, *Christliche Mystik*, I, 168 *ff.*   [4] *ibid.*, 172.

experience in Christ Jesus. Though he was divine by nature, he did not snatch at equality with God but emptied himself by taking the nature of a servant; born in human guise and appearing in human form, he humbly stooped in his obedience even to die, and to die upon the cross."[1] Here then it is not divinity that is the stake, the goal, of following God, but obedience: not power but impotence: participation in God is not a triumph but a cross: "If anyone wishes to follow me, let him deny himself, take up his cross, and so follow me."[2] The single ground-colour then breaks out, in the history of the church, into an entire colour spectrum: the martyr is the follower of Christ in sacrificing his life—the monk by overcoming the world—the humble, because they have taken Christ's *humilitas*—the voluntarily poor, because they have accepted His poverty—the virtuous, because they have taken His obedience as an example. But in whatever way it is particularized, such imitation always remains a community of life which never elevates itself to God as its own example, but on the contrary humbles itself as did God Himself in Christ. So it is expressed in Zinzendorf's hymn, in which the way is indicated:

> Jesus, still lead on,
> Till our rest be won;
> And, although the way be cheerless,
> We will follow, calm and fearless;
> Guide us by Thy hand
> To our fatherland.

But this is to be found also in the New Testament, which shows the road not to him who would storm heaven, but to the little child: "Be ye therefore *followers* of God, as dear *children*; and walk in *love*, as Christ also hath loved us, and *hath given himself* for us an offering and a sacrifice to God for a sweet-smelling savour."[3]

---

[1] *Phil.* ii, 5 *ff.* (Moffat).   [2] *Mark* viii, 34 (Moffat).   [3] *Eph.* v, 1, 2.

CHAPTER 74

BEING FILLED WITH GOD

1. IN discussing Shamanism,[1] rapture was found to be one method of enhancing life's powerfulness. Somewhat crudely, it is true, this may be described as a radical evacuant, undertaken, however, with the intention of a no less thorough replenishing. In order to participate in higher and more potent life man attempts to suppress consciousness completely, whether by drugs of various kinds, by exercise and asceticism, or finally under the urge of his own psychical constitution or, again, some mental derangement.

Whether or not this inspiration is ascribed to demonic possession it is in any case an affair of decreasing one's own, and increasing a foreign, numinous and demonic life; the ancient Israelite judges, for example, led their people to victory because the spirit of Jahveh had come upon them.[2] This exaltation, this fullness of God, confers mighty power: we need think only of how Samson slew a thousand with the jawbone of an ass.[3] Similarly the old Germanic *berserkr*, who became beside themselves in battle, hacked their enemies to pieces in frantic exaltation and then, feeble and quite exhausted, once again became normal. The *Egils Saga* expresses this characteristically: "In their deeds they became so strong that nothing could resist them. But when their rage ceased they were weaker than usual."[4] It appears then that the emptying produces not mere power but a veritable power to attack: the man beside himself attacks others: he feels the urge to manifest his power destructively. This is true even when the struggle is carried on with spiritual weapons: Fox describes his appearance at the Court of King's Bench in London in a particularly impressive way:—"I was moved to look round, and turning to the people said 'Peace be among you'; and the power of the Lord sprang over the court."[5]

In ecstasy, therefore, there is an element of violence, equally in the

---

[1] Chap. 26.
[2] Schwally, *Semitische Kriegsaltertümer*, I, 100. *Judges* iii. 10; vi. 34; xi. 29. I *Sam.* xi. 6 *ff*.   [3] Schwally, *ibid.*, 101.
[4] *Die Geschichte von Skalden Egil* (Niedner), 1914, 84; *cf.* also the psychosis of *amok* and *latah*, peculiar to the Malays; F. H. G. van Loon, *Revue Anthrop.* 37, 1927, 109 *ff*.   [5] *Journal* (Parker), 313.

emptying and in being filled with God. To be beside oneself confers extraordinary powerfulness: even Nature becomes dominated by this frenzy: "Bacchic maidens draw milk and honey from the rivers when they are under the influence of Dionysus, but not when they are in their right mind."[1] It is as though, in rapture, closed doors are opened and all hindrances disappear, particularly those of the body: lightly and freely the ecstatics soar away. The transport due to chloroform, for instance, is described thus: "Simultaneously with the loss of taste and hearing, the body had completely lost its sense of orientation. It seemed as though it were nowhere at all, but were simply hovering in space."[2] The power thus acquired may involve either calm and serene happiness, destructive rage, mystic illumination, extraordinary energy, or productive capacity and intelligence. I should not, however, derive this wholly from loss of power on the side of the body, together with reinforcement on the side of the soul, as (among others) Leuba has suggested;[3] of course it may involve this also, and certainly ecstatic experience has played its own part in psychological theory. But here we are concerned with something more:—the enfeebling of life in general; all the senses are weakened, but at the same moment normal consciousness also. On the other hand, the newly acquired and foreign powerfulness affects both body and soul alike; the body is not lost merely in order to sustain the soul: both alike are lost, and a new body and a new soul gained.[4] We do not walk, but soar: nor do we think, but revelation comes to us; and as has already been observed, there is a harmonious, and a discordant, state of being beside oneself, pure happiness and also delirium; but the foundational experience is always the shrinking of one's own power and the becoming filled from without. Hence, too, the feeling of the expansion of life, of the collapse of all limitations, so that it seems as though the whole world were moving within oneself.[5]

As means of procuring ecstasy alcohol, opium, hasheesh, tobacco and other poisons have played a great part; while wine is the drink of the gods too, enhancing life. It addresses man:

---

[1] Plato, *Ion*, 534 (Jowett).

[2] J. H. Leuba, *Extase mystique et Révélation* (*Mercure de France*, 36, vol. 172, 1925), 673; for what follows, *cf*. Achelis, *Ekstase*.

[3] Chap. 42 *ff*.

[4] Were ecstasy dependent on the dualism between body and soul it would never occur among primitive peoples. Klages expresses the same opinion in *Vom Kosmogonischen Eros*[2], 1926, 63 *ff*., although in other respects his assertions are very sweeping.

[5] Baudelaire, *Les paradis artificiels; cf*. Jaspers, *Allg. Psychopathologie*, 75.

En toi je tomberai, végétale ambroisie,
Grain précieux jeté par l'éternel Semeur,
Pour que de notre amour naisse la poésie
Qui jaillira vers Dieu comme une rare fleur![1]

The ancient Hindu *soma* was a drink of this kind which found its way into myth;[2] it conferred divine power: "Now we have drunk *soma*, we have become immortals, we have attained to the light, we have found the gods."[3] Here all the factors occur together: rapture elevates to divine existence, to immortality, but it also facilitates inner illumination. It is well known how, in mysticism, above all in its Mohammedan form, rapture became the stimulus, and the symbol also, of the fullness of God:

> Knowest thou the cup-bearer who gives drink to spirits?
> Knowest thou the beverage which the cup-bearer pours forth?
> The cup-bearer is the beloved, who pours out for thee annihilation,
> The drink is fire, wherein thou drinkest illumination.
> Drink the draught of ecstasy, burn in the glow of love!
> Gladly the droplet seeks extinction in its mighty flood.
> The whole Universe is a wine lodge: every thing a goblet;
> It is our friend who holds the chalice, and we are the drinkers.
> Even wisdom is drunken and completely sunk in rapture.
> Heaven and earth are drunken: every angel is drunken.[4]

And still more clearly: "In the drunken, my friends, you can see plainly that there is a link with God, where there is no being of one's own."[5]

In the case of the *sufis* it is usually not quite clear whether wine is still actually taken, or whether this has already become symbolical, but in any case the ecstasy is very real; it can also be attained by practice, asceticism, exercise, methodical meditation *etc*. In all this, too, dance and music exercise their functions equally with concentration and the greatest possible degree of immobility: there are ecstatic maenads as

---

[1] Within thee I shall plunge, ambrosial plant,
   Most precious grain cast by th' eternal Sower,
   So from our love shall poesy be born,
   As a rare flower that rises up to God.
                              Baudelaire, *L'âme du vin.*

[2] Chap. 52.   [3] Bertholet, *op. cit.*, 9, 57.

[4] Lehmann-Haas, *Textbuch*, 376; Mahmud's *Gulshan I Raz.*

[5] F. H. G. Tholuck, *Blütensammlung aus der morgenländischen Mystik*, 1825, 219; *cf.* also *Gulshan I Raz.*

well as ecstatic *yogis*. Mental derangement also, either individual or
epidemic, may entail the emptying of the self. No precise diagnosis is
possible here, and depersonalization, the collapse of the limits separating
the individual from the external world, the rapturous state, *etc.*, occur
in several forms of mental disorder.[1] We are concerned, however,
not with the causes of the ecstatic condition, but with the fact that it
affords us a very characteristic understanding of man in his relationship
to Power.

2. Fullness of God, "the state of being filled with God", is not of
course "enthusiasm" in the modern sense of the word, not even when
this is so acutely elaborated as it has been, for example, by Jaspers.[2]
The term must rather be understood in its original significance, derived
from Dionysiac mysticism. This experience is distinguished from mere
rapture and psychosis, since the ecstasy, the being beside oneself,
is at the same moment connected with fulfilment; and the fulfilling
element is Power, God. The enthusiast then, in the full sense of this
word, knows that he is being swept away by some overruling power
which lifts him completely out of himself and fills him with new insight,
new strength, new life. We are familiar with the marvellous apologia for
frenzy in Plato's *Phaedrus*:[3] "madness" is an excellent state, "the
special gift of heaven", without which neither ecstatic mantic can be
attained, nor dedication nor expiation, bringing release to the sick
and the insane; nor is poetry possible in the absence of frenzy, since
"he who, having no touch of the Muses' madness in his soul, comes to
the door and thinks that he will get into the temple by the help of art—
he, I say, and his poetry are not admitted"; "and his sane poetry is
completely effaced by that of the mad poets". But more than any other,
it is he who possesses the memory of the divine that he once saw who
may speak about this frenzy; "as he forgets earthly interests and is
rapt in the divine, the vulgar deem him mad, and rebuke him"; "for
the many are not aware that he is full of God" (*enthousiazon*)[4]. This
"madness" is the love of divine beauty, while for Plato it is the rapt

[1] It would be altogether too simple to connect ecstasy with manic-depressive
derangement, or with the cyclic type of psychosis, although the conduct of the maenads,
for example, at first abandoned and then apathetically silent, would accord with this.
But hysteria, epilepsy, *etc.*, also exhibit ecstatic features, and identification with the
environment is characteristic of the schizophrene or schizoid type; *cf.* Storch, *Archaisch-
primitives Erleben*. Jaspers, *Psychologie der Weltanschauungen*, 1922, 137.
[2] *ibid.*, 117 *ff.*   [3] *Ion* 534 must also be considered.
[4] *Phaedrus*, 245, 249 (Jowett).

love of wisdom, *philosophia*.[1] But Platonic philosophy, as is well known, is no mere theory about life but rather life itself as, impelled by Eros, it rises to the gods. The idea therefore remains exactly the same as in Dionysiac mysticism: "The ekstasis, the temporary *alienatio mentis* of the Dionysiac cult was not thought of as a vain purposeless wandering in a region of pure delusion, but as a *hieromania*, a sacred madness in which the soul, leaving the body, winged its way to union with the god. It is now with and in the god, in the condition of *enthousiasmos*; those who are possessed by this are ἔνθεοι; they live and have their being in the god. . . . The ἔνθεος is completely in the power of the god; the god speaks and acts through him. The ἔνθεος has lost his consciousness of himself."[2] The person in the grip of ecstasy is himself a god, a βάκχος or a βάκχη. Hence there are but few of these: "For 'many', as they say in the mysteries, 'are the thyrsus-bearers, but few are the bacchoi'."[3]

3. Thus ecstasy is the condition of mysticism and being filled with God its goal.[4] Here too it may appear with a greater or less degree of turbulence; but the violent element is always retained, "for with a violence it is done, and as it were against nature", as Richard Rolle asserts.[5] Connected with this trait of violence, too, is the recoil that the ecstatic mystic experiences as soon as his transport ceases: a short time ago he was filled with God, and now it seems as though God has forsaken him again. It is like a bitter taste in his mouth, and he feels himself twice as impotent and abandoned as before.

> O dreadful is the check—intense the agony—
> When the ear begins to hear, and the eye begins to see;
> When the pulse begins to throb—the brain to think again—
> The soul to feel the flesh, and the flesh to feel the chain.[6]

In conclusion, I cite a Hindu and a modern example of emptying and filling. The Hindu poet Manikka Vachakar, in the first place, thus

---

[1] *Symposium*, 218; "madness and passion in your longing after wisdom" (Jowett).

[2] Rohde, *Psyche*, II, 19 *f*. with Note. E. T. 259, 275. He also cites Proclus: ἑαυτῶν ἐκστάντας ὅλους ἐνιδρῦσθαι τοῖς θεοῖς καὶ ἐνθεάζειν.

[3] *Phaedo*, 69.   [4] Chap. 75.

[5] In *Mysticism*, 440 (Underhill). The distinction drawn by Rolle between ecstasy (*raptus*, "ravishing"), as being "ravished out of fleshly feeling", and the "lifting of mind into God by contemplation", again shows that ecstasy essentially affects the whole man; *ibid*.

[6] Emily Brontë, *The Prisoner*. We may compare Tholuck's prosaic observation (*Blütenlese*, 115 *f*.), referring to a beautiful description of ecstasy by Jalaluddin Rumi: "intoxication remains intoxication, and after each debauch there follows a headache".

describes ecstasy: "I can neither comprehend it nor utter it. Miserable me, ah! how can I bear it. I do not understand what He has done to me. I do not know what Thou has given Thy slave; I taste it and am not satisfied: I drink it and do not retain it. As surging waves swell on the milk-white sea, so has He moved deep waters in my soul. Indescribable ambrosia penetrated my every pore: this is His gracious work! In each limb of my miserable body He filled me with honied sweetness. At His command ambrosial showers miraculously drenched my being. With loving soul He fashioned for me a form bestowing grace, as though He were making me like to Himself: and as an elephant seeks through a field of sugar cane, so sought He me and found me and brought me to life. He poured the pure honey of mercy into me, and in His grace gave me heavenly food—He whose nature not even Brahma knows."[1]

Similarly, Stefan George:

> White and soft as whey, the Earth is shaking—
> I mount above frightful chasms:
> I feel that I am swimming beyond the topmost clouds
> In a sea of crystal splendour—
> I am just a spark from the sacred Fire,
> I am but a murmur of the sacred Voice.[2]

[1] Lehmann-Haas, *Textbuch*, 148.   [2] *Der siebente Ring, Entrückung.*

CHAPTER 75

MYSTICISM

1. IN mysticism man, desiring to becoming dominant and to exercise power, breaks down the barriers alike of the self and of the external world. He ceases to experience anything whatever as objective, and likewise to be influenced or determined by anything as an object; both object and subject blend in formless and contentless fusion. Ecstasy, as we have just seen, induced the emptying of the self and the possibility of its being filled with some "Other". In mysticism, also, an evacuating has its place, but equally of object as of subject. Ecstasy, therefore, is certainly inherent in every mystical experience; but mysticism always goes still further than ecstasy, beyond all frontiers, beyond even the primeval relationship in which man himself subsists; to use the expression coined by Jaspers: in mysticism the schism between subject and object is in principle abolished. Man refuses not only to accept the given, but he also opposes care, strangeness and foreignness, and every possibility; he needs no rites whatever, no customs, no forms: he does not speak, he no longer bestows names and no longer wishes to be called by a name: he desires only "to be silent before the Nameless".[1]

Thus it is in "extreme" mysticism. Most mystics, however, either remain half-way, or return thence. Nevertheless in all mysticism, and essentially, the division between subject and object is suppressed, since its very essence lies in the yearning for this abrogation. And in this respect, too, the mystic differs from primitive man who also, like himself, restricts the whole world within the realm of the internal as in "magical" experience.[2] The mystic, however, not only transforms the entire external into the internal, but equally all that is internal into the external: only the completely void, the desert, remains:

> Where is my biding-place? Where there's nor I nor Thou.
> Where is my final goal towards which I needs must press?
> Where there is nothing. Whither shall I journey now?
> Still farther on than God—into a wilderness.[3]

[1] Mehlis, *Die Mystik in der Fülle ihrer Erscheinungsformen*, 13. Jaspers, *op. cit.*, 84 *ff.* Hofmann, *Rel. Erlebnis*, 45; *cf.* Jaspers, *Allg. Psychopath.* 262: "that primeval phenomenon—personality transcending itself".

[2] Chap. 82. On the distinction between magic and mysticism *cf.* Kraemer, *Javaansche Primbon*, 110 *ff.* Contrast Underhill, *Mysticism*, 85.

[3] Angelus Silesius, *The Cherubinic Wanderer*, I, 7.

2. Mysticism, again, is international and interconfessional; in this too it knows no limits. But in Neo-Platonic mysticism it has acquired a typical form that has shown itself most clearly, on the one hand in *Sufism*, and on the other in the Christian and partly ecclesiastical mysticism which began with Dionysius the Areopagite.[1] In these, too, it has developed a specific theory of knowledge which, derived originally from a sentence of Plato,[2] was given its classical expression by Plotinus and received from Goethe its most beautiful form:

> Were not the eye itself a sun,
>   No sun for it could ever shine:
> By nothing godlike could the heart be won,
>   Were not the heart itself divine.[3]

Sufism speaks exactly the same language: "He who discourses of eternity must have within him the lamp of eternity. . . . The light of intuitive certainty by which the heart sees God is a beam of God's own light cast therein by himself; else no vision of Him were possible", says Bayazid Bastami.[4] God is known by God.   In the Thomist system, again, in which man knows by means of "likeness" (*similitudines*), the *lumen gratiae* must render the image of God visible; according to St. Thomas this is a created light, but for the genuine mystic Tauler it is uncreated. The conclusion, at which the scholastic halted, is then drawn that in man God loves and knows as both subject and object; but for St. Thomas, too, in the contemplation of God the divine essence was both that which is seen and that by which one sees (*et quod videtur et quo videtur*).[5]

The mysticism of the church is a restrained mysticism, that of Tauler unrestrained: St. Thomas desires to behold God through God, Tauler to enjoy Him, to make Him useful as it were (*visio essentiae Dei*, as contrasted with *fruitio Dei*).[6] St. Thomas halts at the divine barrier: Tauler breaks it down simultaneously with his own. Only the God Who is within knows the God Who remains without. Or better: where God becomes known, both without and within, here and there alike, are abolished. In the act of knowledge God and the self cannot be distinguished. "Cognition presupposes similarity between knower and known and produces equality."[7]

Here also, then, knowledge is powerfulness. Mysticism is nearer to

---

[1] On his reception by the Roman Catholic Church *cf.* A. Merx, *Idee und Grundlinien einer allgem. Geschichte der Mystik,* 1893, 24; *cf.* further H. Dörries, *Erigena und der Neuplatonismus,* 1925.   [2] *Republic,* VI, 508*b*.
[3] Dwight's translation.   [4] R. A. Nicholson, *The Mystics of Islam,* 51, 50.
[5] G. Siedel, *Die Mystik Taulers,* 1911, 22 *f.*   [6] *ibid.,* 20 *f.*
[7] Eckhart, in Lasson, *Meister Eckhart der Mystiker,* 96.

omnipotence than is magic, but of this truth it makes no use; its know-ledge is a divine act, but in a "modeless mode", since the self which is to harbour God must make room for Him. Here therefore "emptying" assumes a specific and mystic form which, with ancient German mysticism, we may call "deprivation of being" (*das Entwerden*).

3. Nothing is more characteristic of mysticism than the description of the *path* which man must traverse in order to attain his goal. This road is divided into *stages, stadia*; their designations are widely different, but the fact remains unaltered.[1] There may be seven steps which, as in *Sufism*, must be ascended: repentance, abstinence, renunciation, poverty, patience, trust in God and satisfaction. There may be four, like the Buddhist *jhanas*; or six, as with de la Badie: *touchement divin, illumination, élévation, union divine, quiétude, sommeil*;[2] but it is always the toilsome way from fullness of life to the sublime void of non-Being, of dying in God. This mystic path might certainly be called asceticism,[3] not however in the sense hitherto employed, but with its literal meaning of "exercise"; and among its adepts mysticism counts Hindu *yogis*, who have attained almost to immateriality, as well as emaciated Christian saints, Persian epicureans and Dionysiac orgiasts. But all these *practise*, and practise repeatedly, the loss of the self, either in self-indulgence or in fasting; here there opens out the path of the deprivation of being, the Neo-Platonic ἅπλωσις, *annihilatio*.[4] Fasting, rapture, control of

[1] *cf.* Field, *Mystics and Saints of Islam*, 124 *ff.*; Fr. Heiler, *Die buddhistische Versenkung*[2], 1922.

[2] H. Heppe, *Geschichte des Pietismus und der Mystik in der reformierten Kirche*, 1879, 294 *f.* Javanese mysticism distinguishes four stages, which it characteristically designates by images borrowed from the indigenous drama: I. *scharé' at-Wajang*-play (the creature puppets act only through the creator—*dalang*-puppet player); II. *tarékat-Barongan*-play (unity between the actors and their leader, but concealed; for this reason the players wear animal costumes); III. *hakékat-Topéng*-play (unity between the actors and their leader, hidden merely by an animal mask); IV. *ma' ripat-Ronggèng*-play, the dance girl (henceforth there is only *one* actor; the *ronggèng* appears unmasked; complete unity between creator and created). Schuurman, *Myst. u. Glaube*, 22.

[3] Chap. 66.

[4] Heiler, *ibid.*, 10; *cf.* Mme Guyon:

> Ah! How happy is his fate
> Who has a self no more!
> How wretched is the soul
> When it lives ever within itself! . . .
>
> By ever dying to oneself
> No longer know we our own will:
> And then the Will of the Supreme
> In truth becomes our own.
> (Segond, *Prière*, 107.)

breathing, contemplation, meditation, prayer—all these and yet more have only the one purpose, to induce unconsciousness, to reduce the self to nothingness. In the language of scholastic mysticism this is expressed by saying that the "images", which are the media of ordinary knowledge, must here yield ground: *Fili mi, tempus est, ut praeter-mittantur simulacra nostra*:—"My son, it is time to leave our images behind", says the youth in Dante's dream.[1] Here imagination fails and form disappears.

> Would ye know how I came forth from *images*?
> When I perceived the unity within me.
> That is true unity
> When nothing startles us, neither love nor sorrow:
> I *ceased to be*.
>
> Would ye know how I came forth from Spirit?
> When in myself I perceived nought whatever,
> Nought but *sheer unplumbed Deity*;
> Then no longer could I keep silence: I must proclaim it:
> I *ceased to be*.
>
> Since thus I have been lost in the *abyss*
> I would fain speak no more: I am dumb:
> Thus hath Deity
> Manifestly absorbed me in Itself . . .
> I have been *annihilated*.[2]

Or, again, in these lines from Strassburg:

> Whoso would love
> The Good that hath no ground,
> Must rise above the senses;
> Thus a splendid courage is gained.
>
> *Oh modeless mode!*
> Thou art so truly fine.
> Thou soarest o'er the senses,
> There is thy proper place.[3]

---

[1] *La Vita Nova.*

[2] In Merx, *Idee und Grundlinien*, 12 *f*. Here and in what follows the typically mystical expressions are in italics.

[3] In H. A. Grimm, *Von Gottes- und Liebfrauenminne*, 40.

Similarly in Konrad Immendorfer's *Hymn to the Trinity*:

> Around Him circles
> What Spirit hath never encompassed.
> There the *path* leads
> Into a strange *waste*,
> Immeasurable, endless,
> Where is *nor Time nor Place;*
> So unique is its Being.
>
> This *desert path*
> No foot hath trod.
> Created thought
> Came never there.
> *It is.—What?* No one knoweth.
> 'Tis here, 'tis there,
> 'Tis far, 'tis near,
> 'Tis deep, 'tis high!
> Yet have I lied:
> For 'tis *nor this nor that.*
>
> Become a child!
> Be deaf! Be blind!
> Let thy heart forget
> All that is!
> What is, what is not—let it be!
> Leave Place! Leave Time!
> Leave *image* far away!
> *Go with no road*
> Along the narrow path.
> So wilt thou find this desert track.[1]

Here both Deity and man alike become a waste, a qualitiless, unnameable Nothingness, the *ground*, of which German mysticism speaks so fluently. In other words, the abrogation of the division between subject and object, the fusion of God and man, are possible only when practice, deprivation of being, *annihilatio*, have reduced both man and God together to the same Nothingness: void meets void. And now, after it has dispensed with all images, mysticism speaks in images of such great beauty and impressiveness that they have never been forgotten.

---

[1] In Will Vesper's *Deutscher Psalter*, 43 *ff.*; *cf.* Siedel, *Tauler*, 99. On the images and the ground in Thomas and Eckhart *cf. ibid.*, 56: "The Deity hath nowhere wherein to secure a proper position except in the ground of annihilation" (Eckhart).

One is the simile of the *butterfly*, seeking the love-death in the flame. From al-Hallaj to Goethe it speaks the same language:[1]

> Tell it the wise alone, for when
> Will the crowd cease from mockery!
> Him would I laud of living men
> Who longs a fiery death to die.[2]

The *raindrop* also, happy in its dying as it strives toward the Ocean:

> The raindrop mourns: Far from the sea am I!
> But Ocean laughs: in vain is all thy grief!
> For we are all One: we all are God—
> Nought parts us but the tiny point of Time.[3]

Similarly:

> Drink the draught of ecstasy, burn in the glow of love!
> Gladly seeks the droplet extinction in its mighty flood.[4]

Again: "As the rivers flow to their rest in the ocean, released from form and name, so the knower, liberated from form and name, passes onward to the divine, supreme Spirit."[5] Or finally, Madame Guyon in her *Torrens spirituels*.

Love too is a metaphor of the mystic path, but always a love that leads to death: however sensuous its content, however richly coloured its portrayal, ultimately it is always a submersion in the beloved, a dissolution, a death:

> Upbraid me not for my love! Always do I offer myself to Death;
> For whenever love was true, Death was the loved one's fate.[6]

For the merging of God in man, of man in God, is possible only when the indescribable unites itself with the indescribable, and nothingness with nothingness. Mysticism therefore turns first of all inward, to seek therein the secret chamber, the *fundus animae*, the "ground of annihilation": for without, the lover has nought to search for. Thus when Madame Guyon complained to a Franciscan monk about her

---

[1] Massignon, *Al Hallaj*, 473. For Saadi *cf*. Tholuck, *Blütenlese*, 247 *ff*.; further, Field, *Mystics and Saints of Islam*, 128 f.

[2] *West-Eastern Divan*, 19; "Blessed Yearning" (Dowden).

[3] Omar Khayyám, in Lehmann, *Textbuch*[1], 296.

[4] Mahmud's *Gulshan I Raz*, in Tholuck, *Blütenlese*, 218; *cf*. Field, *op. cit.*, 180.

[5] Oldenberg, *Lehre der Upanishaden*, 147; *Mundaka Upanishad*.

[6] Saadi, in Tholuck, *op. cit.*, 248.

difficulties in prayer, he replied: "That, madame, is because you are
seeking outwardly what you possess within. Accustom yourself to search
for God in your heart, and you will find Him there"; words that wrought
a change in her life.[1] The modern mystic, also, directs us inwards:

> If you seek evil around you,
> If you strive to seize salvation without,
>   You are but pouring into leaky vessels,
> You only strive for what is valueless.
>
> You yourself are all and in all:
> The ecstatic note of prayer
>   Blends into one with all love,
> Calls it God, and Friend, and Bride.[2]

From the Inward the road leads to the Innermost, to the ground,
the *scintilla*, the "spark", the very soul of the soul. And this is no mere
abstraction, not some kind or other of "pure consciousness", but the
only real element in man, his nothingness which is his all. Brahminic
mysticism need coin no new concepts here: it employs the *ātman*, which
is really the ground of the soul rather than the soul itself: "It is the
ātman, which is called: No, No! It is impalpable, for it cannot be
seized: indestructible, since it cannot be destroyed: not clinging, since
it does not cling: unbound: it wavers not, and suffers no harm."[3] The
fundus animae, then, is precisely as inexpressible as is the essential
nature of God, with which it is one. "It is the place lying beyond this
contrast (between subject and object), where God and the soul are one
and the same."[4] The Buddhist mystic too knows that he "advances
completely beyond the place where neither consciousness nor unconsciousness subsists"[5]. Tersteegen's sensitive lines on the Ground may
be cited:

> Why is all so well with the soul
> When it finds its long sought Good
>   So *near its heart?*
> Now has it all, whate'er it will.
> Embraced, beloved, *it lies still*,
>   With its God, *in the ground*.[6]

[1] *Vie de Mme Guyon*, 1791, I, 78.   [2] Stefan George, *Der Siebente Ring*.
[3] Oldenberg, *Lehre*, 63; (*Brihad-Aranyaka Upanishad*).
[4] Fr. Delekat, *Rationalismus und Mystik, ZTh K.* N. F. 4, 1923, 280 *ff*.
[5] Heiler, *op. cit.*, 28; *cf.* Lasson, *op. cit.*, 101 *f*. Underhill, *Mysticism*, 120.
[6] *Geistliche Lieder*, 1897, 17.

In forcible and numinously primitive tones, again, Ruysbroek speaks
of "eternal emptiness" and of "wild, *desolate and formless nakedness*":

> Call out, all ye with hearts open:—
> O! vast *abyss*!
> That hast *no orifice*,
> Lead us into thy *depths*,
> And proclaim to us thy love.[1]

And here too, even where it is a matter of the complete absence of
image and form, we find an abundance of imagery: the colourless being
described in glowing tints and the void as the greatest treasure. As has
already been observed, the "ground" is the desert,[2] while the next
image is silence. "Someone asked, 'Teach me Brahman, O exalted
one!' But he (the wise Bāhva) remained silent. The other besought
him a second and a third time. Then he spake: 'I teach it thee indeed,
but thou perceivest it not. This *ātman* is silence.' "[3] Tersteegen again:

> By silence are they known
> Whose hearts are God's abode.[4]

Here the "paradox of expression" appears, as Jaspers calls it. For
the very essence of mysticism is silence: in the ground mute silence
rules. But this silence becomes apparent only in speech, and indeed in
excessive and overhasty speech, one image being annulled by another
which then, like its predecessor, is outstripped and suppressed. Behind
the radiant splendour of the images stands the majestic bareness of the
imageless: behind the diversified form of speech the fearful power of
silence.[5] The mystic must be silent: but this he cannot be: he must

---

[1] In Huizinga, *Herfstty*, 375 *ff*.
[2] Tersteegen, *e.g. Geistliche Lieder*, 21.

> Into the waste I am enticed,
> Where God and I exist alone,
> And Spirit with spirit communes:
> O! Solitude, so far, so far
> From creature, space and time!
> The best loved stands without.

> *Man lockt mich in die Wüste ein,*
> *Da Gott und ich nur sind allein,.*
> *Da Geist mit Geist umgehet:*
> *O Einsamkeit, so weit, so weit*
> *Von Kreatur und Ort und Zeit!*
> *Das Liebste draussen stehet.*

[3] Oldenberg, *Lehre*, 133.   [4] *Geistliche Lieder*, 23.   [5] Chap. 63.

speak, "jubilate", break forth in "silent music".[1] "What the grace *jubilus* is, that ye shall observe. It is a grace exceedingly great: so great that no one can keep it secret, and yet no one can utter it completely," says the *Kirchberg Monastery Chronicle*.[2] Meister Eckhart, too, tells us that the "secret word" is born "in the Ground . . . there is profound silence, for thereto neither creature nor any kind of image has attained" . . . in this silence "are space and rest for that birth, that God the Father may speak His word there".[3]

Together with silence, sleep is the analogue of the mystical state; thus the *sufi* is like the seven sleepers of the legend,[4] while the quietist describes how her peaceful soul "often falls into mystic sleep, wherein all powers are silent".[5] Wholly devoid of will, man surrenders quite passively just like a tool, some instrument for writing or for music:

> Lutes are we, and Thou the player sounding through them;
> Art Thou not He who groaneth in our groaning?
> Flutes are we; but the breath, O Lord, is thine;
> We are the hills: the echo is still thine.[6]

Rapture, likewise, that renders possible deprivation of being.[7] "I mean by the chalice the wine of Eternity", asserts Hafiz; "and for me the meaning of this wine is the surrender of the self, the suppression of selfhood."[8]

4. But mysticism is most rapturous, and also most loquacious, when the long road ends, when perfect union is attained and the *unio mystica* completed. When the *sufi* mystic Rabi'a was asked how she

---

[1] St. John of the Cross.   [2] In N. von Arseniew, *AR.* 22, 1923–24, 271, 279.
[3] *ibid.*, 269.   [4] Tholuck, *op. cit.*, 62 *f.* Field, *op. cit.*, 161.
[5] Mme Guyon, *Moyen court et très facile de faire oraison*, 12, 5.
[6] Jalaluddin Rumi in Tholuck, *op. cit.*, 66; *cf.* 62 *f*; Oldenberg, *Lehre*, 140 *f.*
[7] Chap. 74.
[8] In Merx, *Idee und Grundlinien*, 7; *cf.* Omar Khayyám (Lehmann, *Textbuch*[1], 296):

> I drink from no mere pleasure in carousing,
> Nor just to violate the Koran's teaching,
> But for the brief illusion of Non-Being—
> The ground of all the revels of the wise.

Similarly Jalaluddin Rumi: "Men incur the reproach of wine and drugs that they may escape for a while from self-consciousness, since all know this life to be a snare, volitional thought and memory to be a hell." Nicholson, *The Mystics of Islam*, 67.

achieved this union she answered: "By losing in Him all that I had found"; and again asked how she had gained her knowledge of God, she replied: "Oh Hassan, thou knowest in a certain way and manner, but I with no way nor manner."[1] This, once more, is the "modeless mode" of German mysticism, the overflowing of God into man characteristic of French mysticism: two mystics indeed, Madame Guyon and her friend Fénelon, did not *speak* of God at all, but between them "there went on an almost continual flowing of God".[2] "There are only these two truths: the All, and nothingness. Everything else is a lie. We can honour the divine All only by our own annihilation, and immediately we are annihilated God, Who can endure no void without filling it, fills us with Himself";[3] God is thus a sort of fluid which directs itself everywhere where room has been made for it. The *mirror* image is also employed here:

> Only one task the *sufis* have on earth—
> That their hearts may become clear mirrors of God.[4]

Here then negation preponderates, although it certainly remains a metaphorical negation, and must so remain: richness in poverty, a form obliterated again and again, a nullity that is nevertheless repeatedly endowed with form. Or can there be a crasser and more metaphorical description of the unity, which at the same moment more sharply stresses its inadequacy, than the Mohammedan *fana*, "evanescence", a depiction, however, immediately contradicted in the expression *fana al-fana*, the evanescence of even the consciousness of evanescence also?[5] The Buddhist, again, speaks of the "lonely island", of *Nirvana*: "In this state, rapture consists just in there no longer being any feeling in it."[6] Such too is the bliss of the concluding song in *Tristan and Isolda*:

---

[1] In Tholuck, *op. cit.*, 32.

[2] M. Masson, *Fénelon et Mme Guyon*, 1907, XXXVII.

[3] Guyon, *Moyen court*, 20, 4.

[4] Jalaluddin Rumi in Tholuck, *op. cit.*, 115; *cf.* Ghazali in Field, *op. cit.*, 16 *f.*

[5] The expression is probably of Indian origin, and was first employed in *Sufism* by Bayazid Bastami; *cf.* Nicholson, *op. cit.*, 17 *ff.*, 60 *f.*; also Schuurman, *Myst. u. Glauben*, 17 *f.*

[6] Heiler, *Versenkung*, 36 *ff.*; *cf.* the beautiful lines:

> No standard can measure him who is at rest,
>   There are no words wherewith to speak of him;
> All that thought could grasp has passed away,
>   And every pathway's closed to human speech.

> Shall I sip them, dive within them,
> To my panting breathing win them,
> In the breezes around,
> In the harmony's sound,
> In the world's driving whirlwind be drowned?
> And sinking,
> Be drinking,
> In a kiss
> Highest bliss.[1]

And even when no other term is admissible except simple negation, and when "nothing" becomes the name for the best and dearest, then too the word has a resonance that promises inexpressible wealth, the "rich nothing" as it was called by the Christian mystic of the seventeenth century, Louvigny.[2]

In this respect, further, that man is God implies that God is man, and conversely. In so far as perfect union is possible only to man "deprived of his being" and emptied, mysticism's claim to divinity need be no presumption whatever. This had already been adduced in vindication of Mansur Hallaj, the fettered mystic, who had to pay for his bliss with the most fearful tortures. He said: *Ana' l-Haqq*, "I am the truth": that is, according to Muslim belief: "I am God". Hallaj himself, however, does not say this, but God by the mouth of the selfless Hallaj.[3] Certainly the prosaic al Junayd was not incorrect when he thus replied to him: "Nay: only through truth dost thou exist! What a gallows wilt thou stain with thy blood";[4] to the consciousness of the mystic himself, however, he is nothing more than "the hand that serves God as an instrument".[5] This effacing of limitations even proceeds so far that he can pray: "Oh my God, Thou knowest that I am powerless to offer Thee the prayer of thanksgiving Thou requirest. Come then, in me Thyself to thank. That is the true thanksgiving prayer! there is no other."[6] The mystics also outstrip and outbid each other just as mystic images do; so Bayazid Bastami asserts with mysterious profundity: "I went from God to God, until they cried out from me in me, 'Oh thou I'."[7]

Union then is submersion, that is to say dying. All the dreadfulness of delight in death lies in the celebrated lines in which al-Hallaj described his relations to God when, dancing in his chains, he was led

[1] Corder.
[2] Heppe, *Quietismus*, 90.
[3] Nicholson, *op. cit.*, 152.
[4] Massignon, *Al Hallaj*, 62.
[5] *ibid.*, 260.
[6] *ibid.*, 116.
[7] Nicholson, *op. cit.*, 18.

to the place of judgment;[1] when asked: "Oh master, how camest thou into this condition?" he replied: "Through the caresses of His beauty which attracts so intensely those who long for union." Then he recited:

> My host, in order not to seem to offend me,
> Has made me drink from the bowl from which he himself has drunk: like the host who honours his guest.
> Then, after the bowl has passed from hand to hand, the scourge and the sword are brought forth.
> Thus it befalls him who drinks wine with the dragon in Midsummer.

Here one primeval human experience is manifested in the sublimest and tenderest mystical stirrings; a yearning for death is united with the will to power, and forebodes the highest powerfulness in extinction. The "thirty birds", similarly, whose pilgrimage is described by the *sufi* Fariduddin Attar, at the goal find only themselves: *Simurgh* (a term meaning "thirty birds"). God is a mirror in which everyone views himself: "So they vanished in Him for ever, as the shadow disappears in the sun."[2] Thus the ray that Deity emits is a "ray of darkness".[3] Fear and the voluptuousness of death lie close beside each other: they become one, indeed, in the fearful bliss of annihilation.

5. Since mysticism is essentially silent, for that very reason it speaks all languages; it is fundamentally tolerant:

> Pagoda and ka'ba are the place of the pious,
> The music of the bells their melody;
> The Parsee's girdle, church, rosary and cross
> Are all, forsooth, the tokens of the pious.[4]

To mysticism therefore everything individual, distinctive and historical in religion is ultimately quite indifferent. For the deprivation

---

[1] Massignon, *op. cit.*, 9, 301. The French Text as follows:

> *Celui qui me convie, pour ne pas paraître me léser,*
> *M'a fait boire à la coupe dont il a bu; comme l'hôte qui traite un convive.*
> *Puis, la coupe passée de mains en mains, Il a fait apporter le cuir du supplice et le glaive.*
> *Ainsi advient à qui boit le Vin, avec le Lion en plein Été.*

cf. Tholuck, *op. cit.*, 322 *ff.* Field, *op. cit.*, 68 *ff.*

[2] Field, *op. cit.*, 131 *ff.* On union *cf.* further Tholuck, *op. cit.*, 64 *f.*, 87 *f.*, 105 (Jalaluddin Rumi). Oldenberg, *Lehre*, 126, 142, 181. Kraemer, *Primbon*, 72 (on the so-called *kawula-gusti* of Javanese mysticism, "the truth of Lord and servant", *cf.* also Schuurman, *Mystik und Glauben*, 15).

[3] Dionysius Areopagita in Merx, *Idee und Grundlinien*, 20, 71.

[4] Omar Khayyám, in Merx, *op. cit.*, 26.

of being affects also all images, ideas and thoughts that religion regards as important; and while mysticism speaks the languages of all religions, no religion whatever is essential to it. The void remains void, the nought nought, whether in Germany or India, in Islam or Christianity. The mystic may be a faithful Muslim or a true son of the Christian church: at bottom that counts for little. At best the particular symbols, rites and ideas of the individual religions can assist him on his path towards annihilation; but in the end they too must pass away like all else. The true *Ka'ba*, says Jalaluddin Rumi, is a sorrowful and broken heart;[1] and Bayazid Bastami, who wished to complete the sacred journey around the *Ka'ba*, discovered a sage who said to him: "Give me the two hundred pieces of gold thou needest for the journey, and walk around me seven times"; Bastami did what he had been told to do, for man is the true *Ka'ba*, the house of God.[2]

Christian mystics, indeed, often pay scant attention to scripture and sacrament; the saints, and even the Virgin, must rest content with the disappearance of their figures.[3] For the mystic even the very core of Christianity, God assuming flesh, may be ultimately merely a symbol of his own personal history: incarnation becomes *generatio aeterna* in the hearts of men. And the remarkable feature is that, in this respect, Mohammedan mystics hold quite similar views to Christians, and even praise Jesus in passionate terms—of course as the Christ eternally born in the heart.[4] The saviour can be only a messenger; and what does he, who knows the sender, care for messengers?

> He who lies hidden in the sultan's bosom
> Demands no embassies nor documents.[5]

Celebration can no longer help, now that there is no support. Custom, too, can no longer avail, when no conduct whatever can make any difference in the indistinguishable. Thus mysticism has always been hostile to every code of morality, not however from any immoral tendency but simply because law and order attempt to bind where

---

[1] Field, *op. cit.*, 151.   [2] *cf.* Chap. 57. Field, *ibid.*, 54.

[3] Mme Guyon: "I could no longer perceive the saints and the Virgin apart from God, but saw them all in Him, without being able to distinguish them from Him except with difficulty." Heppe, *Quietismus*, 161. For Eckhart, Lasson, *op. cit.*, 323.

[4] St. Teresa, Molinos; *cf.* Heppe, *Quietismus*, 20. Eckhart, *cf.* Lasson, *op. cit.*, 129 *f.*, 120, 9, 12. Fénelon, Heppe, *ibid.*, 394 *ff.* For a modern parallel, Inge, *Personal Idealism and Mysticism*. Jalaluddin Rumi, *cf.* Field, *op. cit.*, 159, 161, 211.

[5] Jalaluddin Rumi in Tholuck, *op. cit.*, 167. A remarkable parallel from heathendom: late Hellenistic mysticism made the Attis myth the type of the history of the soul also, as in Sallustius, in Murray, *Five Stages*, 246; *cf.* Gnosis generally.

there is no longer anything at all to be restrained. For he who has attained the *unio mystica* need give no further heed to any instructions. From Jalaluddin Rumi, who sets himself above the law:

> He to whom licence has been given
> May eat whate'er he will: he has permission,[1]

to the English mystic Blake, who permits heaven (good) and hell (evil) to marry,[2] and Browning, who infuses a naturalistic element into his mysticism:

> Type needs antitype:
> As night needs day, as shine needs shade, so good
> Needs evil: how were pity understood,
> Unless by pain?

the tone is ever the same. Not only what is hurtful, but also what is evil, loses its peculiar position; for there can be no special position whatever in the wholly undifferentiated divine.[3] Nothing therefore but complete repose, immersion, evanescence, can avail for the mystic: the ethics of mysticism is quietism: "Accustom thyself to absolute immobility, and lay not thy hand on the ark if thou seest it totter, as did Uzzah; for although this would be a good deed for another person, for thee, whom God desires to be completely passive, it is worthless."[4]

Thus mysticism is a hasty attempt at self-liberation through self-destruction, an endeavour to render the self powerful by death. "God is born as man, that I may be born as the same God . . . God's 'ground' is mine and my 'ground' is God's";[5] or in the language of the *sufi*:

> Yea, Jalaluddin, thou art the ocean, and the pearl art thou,
> Thou art thyself the secret of the Universe;
> Observe no other ceremonies.

Finally in the semi-naturalistic, semi-mystic Omar Khayyám:

---

[1] In Tholuck, *op. cit.*, 153.

[2] Spurgeon, *Mysticism in English Literature*, 141 *ff.*

[3] Julian of Norwich, for example, in *Revelations of Divine Love*, 26. Mme Guyon and the French quietists: E. Seillère, *Mme Guyon et Fénelon*, 1918, 32 *f.*, 217, 71. Masson, *op. cit.*, 55, 58, 227. Eckhart: Lasson, *op. cit.*, 8 *f.* The *sufis*: Field, *op. cit.*, 65. 188. Tholuck, *op. cit.*, 81, 96 *ff.*, 120 *f.*, 130, 159 *f.*, 212 *f.* Nicholson, *op. cit.*, 88, 99. Dionysius Areopagita: Merx, *op. cit.*, 19.

[4] Mme Guyon in Masson, *op. cit.*, 277; *cf.* Tersteegen, *Geistliche Lieder*, 19 *ff.* Siedel, *Tauler*, 118. A modern instance in Amiel's *Journal*, April 6, 1851.

[5] Lasson, *op. cit.*, 205.

> Heav'n but the Vision of fulfill'd desire,
> And Hell the Shadow from a Soul on Fire.[1]

Thus mysticism circles around the impenetrability of the ego itself:[2] at any moment it may become the most extravagant self-glorification but also, at any time, the most abysmal consciousness of nullity. In Meister Eckhart, for instance, self-deification turns into a "forceful doctrine of grace",[3] just as universally in mysticism, even in its Mohammedan type, predestination plays a prominent part. For both a "Cherubinic Wanderer" and a Rainer Maria Rilke, again, self-annihilation changes into the dependence, indeed into the nullity, of God:

> What wilt Thou do, O God, when I shall die?
> I am Thy tankard: (what if I should break?)
> I am Thy potion: (what if I should spoil?)
> I am Thy raiment and Thy calling,
> In losing me, Thou wouldst lose Thy significance.[4]

God is a fledgling that has fallen out of the nest! Human sonship, similarly, is converted into a fatherhood, or rather motherhood:

> I love thee as a dearly loved son
>   Who once forsook me when he was a child,
> Because Destiny had called him to a throne,
>   'Fore which all lands are as valleys.[5]

Still more audaciously, and with the tone of concise finality, in Angelus Silesius:

> Deep calls to deep. My spirit's Deep doth cry amain
> To Deep of God: say, which is deeper of the twain?[6]

But we should not regard mysticism as one specific type of religion and raise the question, for example, whether Christianity and mysticism can be reconciled. Mysticism is a definite tendency in religion that may arise, and has indeed arisen, in every religion. It is a form of self-direction, of autism, of "living inside oneself"; not however the magical

---

[1] On Omar Khayyám and the various sources of his *Rubá'iyát* cf. A. Christensen, *Critical Studies in the Rubaiyat of Umar-i-Khayyám*, 1927.

[2] Hofmann, *Rel. Erl.* 47.

[3] cf. Otto, *Zeitschr. für Theol. und Kirche*, N. F. 6, 1925, 425.

[4] *Das Stundenbuch.*

[5] *ibid., cf.* A. Faust, *Der dichterische Ausdruck mystischer Religiosität bei Rainer Maria Rilke, Logos*, 11, 1923.   [6] *The Cherubinic Wanderer*, I, 68.

form[1] in which man transfers the world into himself, but a still more radical type in which man, by way of nothingness, constitutes himself the All. Mysticism, in other terms, is a forcible exaggeration of the consciousness of power, which finds its satisfaction in the omnipotence of death: no one can harm the dead, not even himself. Therefore, indeed, every religion can and must include mystical elements; but it can incorporate these within itself only in so far as they do not contradict its own essential character. Thus in primitive religion the boundary or frontier of mysticism is magic with its own practical aims; in Islam and Judaism, the overruling command of God; in Christianity, love.[2] With justice, then, has a "restrained mysticism" been discussed;[3] for except in such extreme cases as Angelus Silesius, Madame Guyon, Jalalludin Rumi, *etc.*, mysticism is almost always "restrained". Even "pure" mysticism is never wholly "pure". The mystic never suffers a complete loss of identity, just as little as does the schizophrene or the primitive, whose experience is similarly based on the abrogation of the division between subject and object, although it does not therefore attain the mystic's passionate level. Mysticism, then, is like Dante who, wholly absorbed in contemplation of Beatrice, immovably gazes at her. But life itself, its possibilities and faith also, resemble the three theological virtues which divert the poet's steady gaze with a *troppo fisso*—"too fixed a gaze"—and recall him to consciousness.[4] And it is no accident that it is precisely the theological virtues that pronounce this *troppo fisso*.

W. J. AALDERS, *Mystiek*, 1928.

K. BETH, *Frömmigkeit der Mystik und des Glaubens*, 1927.

F. HEILER, *Die Bedeutung der Mystik für die Weltreligionen*, 1919.

F. VON HÜGEL, *The Mystical Element of Religion* I, 1908, II[2], 1924.

K. JASPERS, *Die Psychologie der Weltanschauungen*[2], 1922.

A. LASSON, *Meister Eckhart der Mystiker*, 1868.

G. VAN DER LEEUW, *Mystiek*, 1925.

E. LEHMANN, *Mystik in Heidentum und Christentum*[3], 1923.

J. H. LEUBA, *The Psychology of Religious Mysticism*.

G. MEHLIS, *Die Mystik in der Fülle ihrer Erscheinungsformen*.

R. OTTO, *West-östliche Mystik*, 1926 (Eng. tr., *Mysticism East and West*, 1937, 1957).

C. F. E. SPURGEON, *Mysticism in English Literature*, 1913.

E. UNDERHILL, *Mysticism*.

[1] Chap. 82.   [2] Chap. 76.
[3] E. Brunner.   [4] *Purgatorio*, 31, 32.

CHAPTER 76

THE LOVE OF GOD

1. IN our discussion of fear we have already seen that religious experience is ambivalent: the relationship to Power is always simultaneously a being attracted *and* a being repelled whenever it attains any marked intensity: both *tremor* and fascination. Love in the religious sense, therefore, is by no means a purely harmonious attitude in life, since it never exists wholly free from its apparent opponent, fear, just as fear, on its part, is never present quite apart from love. Even hatred is closely connected with love: "everyone who hates is an unhappy lover without knowing it".[1] In this sense, then, the Power encountered in human life is always loved even when there is no implication of the love of God in any strict sense. This ambivalent experience of love may even be regarded as the basic experience in religion; for without the attraction there would be no fear, no celebration, indeed no religion whatever. Membership within some definite powerfulness, too—in the community or the covenant—is one form of love; being drawn to one's neighbour, to one's brothers or companions, the going forth from oneself, or rather the fusion of oneself with another, all repose on the common potency.[2]

2. Apart from this quite general sense, however, love appears as *surrender*. "In the purity of our hearts there surges the endeavour willingly to surrender, out of gratitude, to some higher, purer and unknown Being: thus unriddling the eternally unnamed One. This we call Piety!" Surrender thus implies the gift of oneself; while the gift which, as has been seen,[3] is itself always to a certain extent a surrender, is therefore the outward act pertaining to the inward experience. In the total experience, then, sacrifice and love are united; whence it follows that love always presupposes love in return, exactly as the gift presupposes a counter-gift. Or rather: as man's gift is always a counter-gift, so too his love is always a love in return.

It is thus that we find love in the Old Testament. There, originally, it pertains to the covenant in virtue of which Jahveh chose his people; in

---

[1] Künkel, *Einführung in die Characterkunde*, 16.
[2] Chap. 32 *ff*. cf. Marett, *Faith, Hope and Charity*, 178.   [3] Chap. 50.

Deuteronomy, indeed, love of God is an explicit commandment: "And thou shalt love the Lord thy God with all thine heart, and with all thy soul, and with all thy might";[1] this love of the people, and later of the individual also, is as it were the answer to Jahveh's love. His love is true and steadfast, even when that of the people (or of the individual) is deceitful. Hence the repeated parable of the faithless wife whose infidelity, however, never causes her husband's love to vacillate. Hosea, again, opposes love, as God's demand, to sacrificial ceremonial: "For I desired mercy, and not sacrifice; and the knowledge of God more than burnt offerings."[2] Jahveh loves his people, and among the members of the community especially the righteous, the obscure and the miserable,[3] while the people and its members requite his love by the praise of their reciprocal love. Here therefore there is no place for that antithesis found in Islam, where love to God plays a conspicuous and occasionally central rôle only among mystics and heretics, and where man's attitude towards God must therefore exhaust itself above all in the praise that he owes to God, because here too man rightly feels that all love is reciprocal even while, at the same moment, he cannot attribute to the exalted Creator any human and self-surrendering love.[4]

For religious sentiment in India, on the other hand, matters are altogether different; wherever Form and Will become manifested in Power, the otherwise preponderating celebration, even when it assumes the guise of asceticism, and also knowledge of God, yield place to surrender, *bhakti*. Here too, however, it is God's attitude, His deed of love, that first evokes man's love; and in *Mahayana* Buddhism surrender to the god Buddha replaced self-liberation in accordance with Buddha's own example—"I take my refuge in the Buddha". Buddha's vow not to desire to enter into *Nirvana* until all shall have been released is here regarded as the proof, the practical demonstration, of God's love which challenges surrender.[5] In Hinduism, then, the *Bhagavad-Gita* unites the two paths, of knowledge and of works, in the higher way of *bhakti*, of surrender; a personal lord, *Isvara*, who draws to himself man's love, is the focus of religion.[6] And the essence of this love and love in return is very beautifully expressed in the eighteenth song of the *Bhagavad-Gita*:

[1] *Deut.* vi. 5.   [2] *Hosea* vi. 6.
[3] *Ps.* cxlvi.   [4] *cf.* Massignon, *Al-Hallaj*, 161 *f.*
[5] This, and other aspects of the subject, are lucidly discussed in Tiele-Söderblom, *op. cit.*, 187 *ff.*
[6] "Love" and "surrender" appear to be more adequate renderings of *bhakti* than "faith"; *cf.* Chantepie, *op. cit.*, II, 148.

"The Lord abides in the heart of all things, O Arjuna, making all beings revolve mounted on a machine by his magic power.

Go even to him as refuge with thy whole being, O Bharata; through his favour thou shalt win the highest peace, an eternal abode.

Thus has knowledge more secret than the secret been declared to thee by me; examine it fully, and as thou wilt so do.

Listen again to my highest word, the most secret of all: dear art thou to me most surely; therefore I will speak what is for thy good.

Have thy mind on me, be devoted to me, sacrifice to me, do reverence to me. To me thou shalt come; what is true I promise; dear art thou to me."[1]

Here it can be very clearly observed how the knowledge of God, the most essential of all religious values in India, is gradually transformed into a love of God; and in this change the lord, from being a teacher, a supreme *guru*, becomes more and more an all-sufficing God: "Abandoning all (other) duties come to me, the one refuge; I will free thee from all sins; sorrow not."[2]

By the poets *bhakti*, although it hardly ever completely loses the subsidiary meaning of knowledge, is expressly opposed to rites and ascetic exercises:

> Why chant the *vedas*? why listen to the *sastras*?
> Why be taught moral principles every day?
> Why learn one *anga* (an auxiliary science) or all six?
> To bear the Lord in our hearts alone brings salvation.
> Why torment ourselves? Why observe fasts?
> Why chastise ourselves on high mountains?
> Why wander to and fro to sacred streams?
> To confess the Lord continually alone brings salvation.[3]

3. For the Greek, whom we must now consider, every experience bore a divine countenance. He spoke therefore not of love for God, and still less of God's love, since love itself is the god, indeed the oldest of gods:—Eros, the primal impulse of the Universe. And the entire life-movement, alike in its most sensuous as in its sublimest moments, whether directed to the beautiful, the good or the true, is for Plato an upward striving urge, Eros:[4] the Orphic primeval world-principle, the Sophoclean victor "resistless in fight", becomes love, highest and ultimate, the Idea. This Idea itself, however, cannot love. "God loves

---

[1] E. J. Thomas, *The Song of the Lord.*
[2] *Bhagavad-Gita*, 18, 66. (E. J. Thomas).
[3] Bertholet, *Lesebuch*, 14, 55.   [4] Chap. 95.

(Plato's Ideas do not love). Out of love to man God sent His Son to earth. Christ is the loving one: the man who loves God and God Who loves man. The dynamic of love no longer has one direction only, as in antiquity—from man to what is higher; but a dual course—also from what is higher to man; and Christ unites in Himself both tendencies."[1] "In Christianity, and wholly unplatonically, not only is loving central but also" (I prefer to say: essentially) "being loved . . . For antiquity Eros was a cult creation: for Christianity Eros is deliverance."[2] In this respect, then, a radical contrast exists between the Greek spirit and that of Christianity. Certainly Eros was surrender, but as instinct and subsequently as possession; as a sacred lunacy, but also always as the enhancing of power. The Christian *agape*, *caritas*, is however the surrender to Him who has surrendered Himself; neither instinct nor impulse therefore, but grace; neither possession nor increase of power, but pure gratitude.[3] In Christianity, then, the closest approach to Platonic love is shown in mysticism; for the similes of bridal love and of death from love are often nothing more than a transformation of childlike gratitude into a powerful impulse.

4. For Christian faith, then, love is not a god, but God is love.[4] And the Christian concept of love is not "spiritual," as the antithesis of "sensuous", love; rather does it subsist as "equally foreign to spiritual reality as to corporeal reality";[5] it implies a complete inversion of all the conditions of life without exception. Christians, in fact, sought their own specific term for love, *agape*, and rejected the various current expressions;[6] and the fundamental meaning of this word is "to receive, to welcome, to embrace". It already presupposes, therefore, the gift of a love; and in this it differs from φιλέω and ἐράω. In principle, therefore, *agape* is reciprocal love. It is neither instinct nor impulse, but readiness, preparedness, responding to God's act; and in this it is therefore not man's own conduct that is intrinsic, but the attitude of God. "I ask not for love in general and occasionally, but for that love with which I am loved";[7] and in this sense the striking assertion of the

---

[1] Marcuse, *Über die Struktur der Liebe*, *Jahrbuch der Charakterologie*, 5, 279.
[2] *ibid.*, 280.
[3] It is no accident that Islam, while rejecting love, was able to accept Platonic love; *cf.* Massignon, *Al-Hallaj*, 176.
[4] 1 *John* iv. 6, 18.   [5] Marcuse, *loc. cit.*, 283.
[6] Lohmeyer, *Rel. Gemeinschaft*, 59. Tromp de Ruiter, *Gebruik en beteekenis van* AGAPAN *in de grieksche literatuur*, *passim.*
[7] Bultmann, *Glaube und Verst.*, 242; *cf.* also 237.

so-called anti-Christian Nietzsche holds good, in which he distinguishes love from *pity*:[1] "all great love is above all its pity: for it seeketh— to create what is loved!"[2] God's love, then, is creative, while love for God is the creature's own gratitude. It is not even in the first place a giving, but rather a permitting oneself to receive.[3] "Love lies in this, not in our love for him but in his love for us—in the sending of his Son to be the propitiation for our sins. . . . We love, because he loved us first."[4] God descends to man: that is real love; and human love exists only as response. Christian love, therefore, is dynamic, for it is an activity of God and a reciprocal activity of man. Kierkegaard has referred to its "dialectic" and discussed this with ardent profundity: "the higher one stands above another whom he loves, the more, in human terms, will he feel inclined to raise him up to himself; but all the more, divinely speaking, will he feel impelled to descend to him. That is love's dialectic."[5] In Christianity, therefore, love can assume the central position because it coincides with God's act, with God becoming man. It is never merely a fine sentiment, a praiseworthy feeling, but an absolute deed; and as man's love for God it has its being only in God's powerfulness. "This impotent One then, who can save neither himself nor others, but brings misery to all who attach them- selves to him, is the absolute. Who can believe that? man cannot. For he has an ineradicable idea of what Power is; and this impotence is not Power, and still less the Power of the Absolute."[6] We have become sufficiently familiar with this "ineradicable idea" in our previous discussions! In Christian love it is directly controverted: both the relationship between God and man, and that between man and man (community of love, the community grounded in the love of Christ) rest upon a Power which is neither a property nor an attribute of man, but a gift to him, a gift from the Father to the child. About this love, finally, the apostle Paul composed his great hymn, which is the very reverse of praise of any human excellence. For it is the song of the gift of God, of the absolutely indispensable, of the eternally existent:

> I may speak with the tongues of men and of angels,
>   but if I have no love,
>   I am a noisy gong or a clanging cymbal;
> I may prophesy, fathom all mysteries and secret lore,

---

[1] Chap. 97.   [2] *Thus Spake Zarathustra*, 105 (Foulis Edition).
[3] Scholz, *Eros und Caritas*, 51 *ff.*   [4] 1 *John* iv. 10, 19 (Moffat).
[5] Geismar, *Kierkegaard*, 193; *cf.* 115, 194 *ff.*, 497 *f.*
[6] Kierkegaard, in Geismar, *op. cit.*, 412.

I may have such absolute faith that I can move hills from their place,
            but if I have no love,
                I count for nothing;
I may distribute all I possess in charity,
I may give up my body to be burnt,
            but if I have no love,
                I make nothing of it.

.   .   .   .

Thus "faith and hope and love last on, these three", but
    the greatest of all is love.[1]

L. MARCUSE, *Über die Struktur der Liebe* (*Jahrbuch der Charakterologie*, 5), 1928.

H. SCHOLZ, *Eros und Caritas*, 1929.

S. TROMP DE RUITER, *Gebruik en beteekenis van* AGAPAN *in de grieksche literatuur*, 1930.[2]

[1] 1 *Cor.* xiii (Moffat)

CHAPTER 77

CHILDREN OF GOD

1. THE Orphic, appearing in the underworld before the gods, refers to his origin:

> Say: "I am a child of Earth and of Starry Heaven:
> But my race is of Heaven. This ye know yourselves."

Again:

> For I also avow me that I am of your blessed race, ye gods.[1]

The Homeric hero, too, boasts of his divine descent, and among numberless primitive peoples the link with Power is at the same time the relationship with divine, or at least extremely potent, ancestors. In all these examples, then, man advances this claim to common origin and common potency with the powers: among these, as it were, he includes himself. The Old Testament, still further, in addressing the people of Israel or the Messiah as the son of God, shows that an intense feeling of dependence may accompany this. For the son is intimately associated with the Father, obeys and trusts him; the Father's figure is perfectly familiar to him;[2] and in this sense the speech on the Areopagus can quote the words of the Greek poet: "For we are also his offspring."[3]

But in adopting this idea Christianity changes filiation to God, from being a matter of relationship, into one of *faith*.[4] For Christ alone and uniquely is "Son of God" in the sense of relationship. Man therefore is not the child of God, but he may become so. Or rather, because here least of all does any purely temporal relationship subsist, he is not the child of God in the tranquillity of immutable being, but in the agitation of faith. This sonship is a gift: "For the sons of God are those who are guided by the Spirit of God. You have received no slavish spirit that would make you relapse into fear; you have received the Spirit of sonship. And when we cry, 'Abba! Father!' it is this Spirit testifying

---

[1] (Cornford.) Gold tablets from Petelia and Thurioi, in Diels, *Vorsokratiker*, II, 175; Olivieri, *Lamellae orphicae*; *cf.* K. Kerenyi, *AR.* 27, 1928, 322 *f.* Kern, *Orph. Fragm.* 105 *f.*

[2] Chap. 20. [3] *Acts* xvii. 28. [4] *cf.* Piper, *Ethik*, I, 121.

along with our own Spirit that we are children of God";[1] similarly in the Johannine trend of thought: "Think what a love the Father has for us, in letting us be called 'children of God!' That is what we are."[2] We are children of God, therefore, not in virtue of descent nor origin, but of the selfless love of God that has chosen us.

[1] *Rom.* viii. 14 *ff.* (Moffat).   [2] 1 *John* iii. 1 (Moffat).

CHAPTER 78

ENMITY TO GOD

1. THE subject of this Chapter is enmity to God. We are no longer, therefore, discussing the infraction of Power which sets free a reaction, nor the observance of tabus. Nor again are we now concerned with celebration and conduct; or in other words, there is no reference whatever to custom.[1] But when we realize that, in the second half of. this Section, *inward* action comes to the fore, this in no sense means that not custom, but an autonomous morality, is to be dealt with. Certainly morality too will appear in its diversity from religion, but only in a restricted aspect. For enmity against God has nothing whatever to do with moral failures; it refers to God alone. Nor can the various defences of morality that have been advanced in the course of centuries assist us at all. Thus it can by no means imply, for example, that experience which induced the Orphic, and subsequently the Christian also, to find his guilt in the captivity of the soul within the prison of the body: that would be misery, perhaps failure, but certainly not enmity.[2] Equally little can result from any utilitarian explanation of moral good in terms of the usefulness it serves. In accordance with the Old Testament and with many primitive peoples, we too assert "good" equally of a character, an action, of food and a nap;[3] but it never occurs to us that the lack of this type of goodness implies enmity. Neither does the grounding of inward action in Nature, nor in human caprice, assist us here. It is not at all a matter of man departing from Nature nor operating in opposition to his normal growth ($\phi\acute{v}\sigma\iota\varsigma$) nor, again, of his transgressing any universal principle ($\theta\acute{\epsilon}\sigma\iota\varsigma$). Rather does the issue concern his guilt. And "being guilty does not first of all result from some fault, but conversely: this itself is only possible on the ground of an original state of guilt".[4] This guilty condition, therefore, has nothing to do with either habit or custom, law, commandment or "Ought". It is not the absence of any kind of deed or disposition. As Heidegger finely

---

[1] Chap. 66.

[2] Brunner remarks that sin originates not in corporeality, but in the freedom of the spirit; *Gott und Mensch*, 84.

[3] Westermarck, *The Origin and Development of the Moral Ideas*, I, 132 *f*.

[4] Heidegger, *op. cit.*, 280 *ff*.

states this: man is not merely laden with guilt: he is guilty. The state of being " laden with guilt" originates in the circle of celebrations and cares; but guilt itself has no specific origin whatever: rather it pertains to the very being of man.

Sin and guilt, then, are related to the deepest element in man, to the ground of his being, just as he is, without any kind of possibility arising, or any sort of celebration producing any change.[1] As long as man clings to possibilities, as long as he celebrates his experience, he may continue to suppose that his power will never be entirely lost. But behind these possibilities there still lies nothingness; and in this nullity there subsists not only impotence but guilt. And as soon as conscience calls to man,[2] he becomes aware of this threatening nullity at the very ground of his being. How this comes about, however, it is difficult to say. For dread, which we have already encountered as dread of possibility, cannot explain guilt, although it "points towards it", as Kierkegaard has so impressively shown.[3] He who, standing on high, has become dizzy in his dread, falls and rises guilty. Between dread and guilt, however, there is a profound chasm, something not to be understood, something that is not apparent. Guilt therefore, with faith, falls quite outside the realm of Phenomenology.

Into experience, still further, this nullity enters as *enmity*. Regarded non-religiously, there is nothing whatever in his "being dust and ashes" with which man could be reproached. Religion, however, is never concerned with actions or dispositions that may deserve praise or blame, but with the very ground of being. And the nullity of this reveals itself as enmity against God. Conscience cries out to man that he hates God. The will that is hostile to God arises from man's deepest being. He will accept nothing as a gift, but will himself be God and bestow something on his God. But that is sin against God's very essence, against love. Even sacred actions are taken into his own service by self-sufficient man: in order to surmount his dread, celebration must help him to ignore the voice of conscience and to attain power in spite of everything. But then his conscience hurls him back into the nullity of impotence, which hates God. Awe, or primitive avoidance, may therefore be said to approach much more closely than does moral

---

[1] This is also the meaning of *original* sin; *cf.* G. Mensching, *Die Idee der Sünde* (1931), 50: "The distinctive peculiarity of the Christian idea of sin is to be perceived in the concept of general sin as original guilt"; *cf. ibid.*, 51 on the Vishnuite parallel to the parable of the Prodigal Son, and its characteristic distinction from this in its concept of sin.

[2] Chap. 68.   [3] *Begriff Angst (The Concept of Dread).*

failure to the consciousness of guilt, although it is by no means identical
with it.

2. Sin, to continue, is enmity against God. But God cannot be
measured by any human standards, however highly moral they may
be. He is *holy*: that is, He is eternally superior, remote, incomprehensible: "For my thoughts are not your thoughts, neither are your
ways my ways."[1] We do not even require to grasp the sublime idea of
God in *Deutero-Isaiah* in order to realize the profound contrast between
sin against God and every form of transgression, of lack of goodness or
insight, *etc.* For this the moving prayer of a simple Egyptian workman,
addressed to the "mountain peak", may quite well serve: "I am an
ignorant man with no understanding, and cannot distinguish between
good and evil. Once I transgressed against the mountain peak, and it
has punished me: day and night I am in its hand. I sit on the tile
like a pregnant woman; I call to the wind, but it does not come to me.
I prayed to the mighty mountain summit, and to each god and goddess:
'Behold', I say to great and small among the workers: 'be humble
before the summit of the mount, for there a lion dwells; it strikes
just as does the fiercely glaring lion, and it pursues him who offends it'. I
called to my mistress, and then I found that she came to me as a refresh-
ing wind. She was gracious to me after she had let me see her hand
(Providence). Graciously she turned to me and enabled me to ignore
my suffering; she was like a breeze to me. Truly the mountain peak in
the West is charitable, if we call upon it. Nofer-Abu says, and speaks:
'Truly, hear all ye with ears who live on earth: be humble before the
Western mountain-top'."[2] It is probably but rarely that we discern the
very essence of religion in such a simple garb as in this prayer of the
worker thirsting in the desert. Deepest despair and the most blissful
release lie close together, both being grounded in the essential nature
of the god. That this is a grim mountain-top does not at all affect the
issue; it is far nearer the essence of religion than the enlightened,
rational and benevolent Lord God of so many Christian sermons! And
this fully confirms Kierkegaard's dictum that the antithesis of sin is
not *virtue*, but *faith*.[3] The Egyptian workman's prayer touches the
same chords as do the profoundest terms of the Christian consciousness
of sin. For "Lord, I am not worthy", "I am no more worthy to be

[1] *Isaiah* lv. 8.
[2] In G. Roeder, *Urkunden zur Religion des alten Ägypten*, 1915, 57.
[3] In Geismar, *op. cit.*, 328.

called thy son", refer to no sort of vice nor series of transgressions, but to the very nature of man as estimated by the absolute majesty of God: "Thou art worthy, O Lord."[1]

The essence of guilt also appears very clearly in the Babylonian hymns, the so-called penitential psalms; and here again primitive avoidance is very much nearer the religious consciousness of sin than is moral failure. For the Babylonian *Texts*, which are all spells, start from this avoidance. The lament is occasioned by illness or some other misfortune; and from the decline of his powers the sufferer infers the wrath of God, and his own unconscious guilt. Without being aware of it he has come into contact with Power and bears the consequences; and this is certainly never thought of as being at all a moral issue. But the poet's religion has, in this connection, a particularly suitable opportunity to appear.[2] The sick man allows himself to be exorcised and prays for the cure of his sickness; and both the spell and the cure are for him identical with divine liberation. But in this practical attitude he begins to realize the divine holiness and the depth of his own guilt; for although he is not immediately aware of his fault, still he is conscious of his guilt and unworthiness. His error may indeed have been a ritual one or—in our sense—moral. The god's anger, sickness, impurity, sin: it all amounts to the same thing: we offend God, even when we ourselves neither know nor desire this;[3] we are enemies of God, and indeed for no other reason than that He is our enemy. This appears most explicitly in the celebrated hymn that has been compared with the *Book of Job* (I have italicized the significant passages): "Just when I had almost *recovered* the (critical) moment passed. However I sought it was evil, very evil; my *agony* ever more increased; my right I found nowhere. If I called to my god, he vouchsafed me not his countenance; if I prayed to my goddess, she raised not her head to me. The *sacrificial diviner* could not decide the reason for things after an inspection, nor could the *dream interpreter* form a judgment about me by means of an incense offering. I approached the *soothsayer*, but he opened not my ear; the *exorcising priest* could not appease the *gods'*

---

[1] *Matt.* viii. 8; *Luke* xv. 19 ; *Rev.* iv. 11. Mark Connelly's modern Negro drama, *The Green Pastures*, is a very fine example of the genuinely religious consciousness of sin, especially Act I, Scene 4.

[2] *cf.* Morgenstern, *The Doctrine of Sin in the Babylonian Religion*, 1905. A. H. Edelkoort, *Het zondebesef in de babylonische boetepsalmen*, 1918. Ch. F. Jean, *Le péché chez les Babyloniens et les Assyriens*, 1925; *cf.* also A. van Selms, *De babylonische termini voor Zonde*, 1933.

[3] *cf.* Jastrow, *Religion Babyloniens und Assyriens*, I, 1, 68 *ff.* Paul Dhorme, *La religion assyro-babylonienne*, 1910.

wrath by his magical performance. Whence the changed actions everywhere? If I looked behind me, persecutions and afflictions! Like a man who has not dedicated the gift to the god, and has not invoked the name of the goddess over his food: who has shown no humility and known no submission: in whose mouth supplication and prayer had ceased and for whom the day of the god had ended: by whom feast days were neglected: who laid his arms in his lap, disregarded the gods' will, and has not taught his people the fear and adoration of the god: has not called to his god, and has devoured the repast intended for him: has abandoned his goddess, and has not offered the regular sacrifice: has neglected everything, forgotten his lord and has lightly sworn by his holy god—so I appeared.

"And yet *I myself remembered supplication and prayer*; prayer was my thought, sacrifice my rule; the day of the god's worship was the joy of my heart, the day of the goddess's procession was gain and wealth to me. My joy was to honour the king, and my pleasure to play on the harp for him. I ordered my country to esteem the god's name, and commanded my people to exalt the name of the goddess. The king's worship I treated like that of a god, and taught the people to show reverence before the palace.

"For I knew that such actions are acceptable to the god. *Yet what appears beautiful to man is abominable to the god, and what is odious to man's heart is most pleasing to the god.* Who has learnt (to understand) the will of the gods in heaven, the gods' plan, full of wisdom? who can comprehend it? *When have stupid mortals ever understood the ways of the gods?* He who was alive yesterday, to-day is dead: suddenly he is plunged into darkness and quickly dashed to pieces. One moment he is singing and playing, and in a trice he is howling like a mourner. Their wills are as different as light is from darkness." Again, of God: "His *hand is too heavy*, I cannot bear it; his fearfulness is all too great . . . His *word of wrath* is a storm flood—mighty is his stride. . . ." Finally, the sick man is rescued by the god Marduk, who purifies him by leading him through the twelve gates of E-sagila.[1] Here, therefore, in this magical conception of sin, its true and essential character is admirably manifested.[2]

An equally profound consciousness of guilt is to be found in the

---

[1] Lehmann-Haas, *op. cit.*, 312 *ff. cf.* Jastrow, *op. cit.*, I, 2, 124 *ff.*

[2] In the so-called *Shurpu-Texts* the type of offence is exhaustively investigated (a complete list of vices is compiled) in order that it may be "set free"; Lehmann-Haas, *op. cit.*, 317 *ff.*

Hindu hymns to the god Varuna. This god pertains to those superior beings in the background of the Universe[1] who, as we have seen, are intimately linked with morality; but he is also the confessor of those who know that they must acknowledge actual sin: "I take counsel with myself about it: when shall I ever be in favour again with Varuna? Will he accept my sacrifice without anger? When shall I confidently see his grace? I examine myself closely about my sin, O Varuna. I go to the wise to enquire of them; and the sages tell me the same thing: Varuna is wroth with thee. What then was this most wicked sin, O Varuna, that thou wilt destroy him who praises thee, thy friend? Tell me that, thou infallible one, thou self-sufficient one! With obeisance and freed from guilt I would entreat thy pardon, anticipating this. Forgive the sins of our fathers: forgive us what we ourselves have done!".[2]

In the Old Testament again, as everyone knows, the same tone repeatedly resounds in the *Psalms* and elsewhere. And in the *Book of Job* the religious consciousness of guilt has certainly detached itself completely, not merely from its prior magical conditions, but also from the success of the prayer for deliverance. While Job is still plunged in abject misery, he places his hand over his mouth and is silent: from beginning to end God is here the first and the only One. But considered in its entirety, it is the *Book of Psalms* that exhibits the true nature of sin and guilt more clearly than perhaps any other literature; and in this respect it certainly pictures a situation in most marked contrast with current moral preaching. Here again misery is the revelation of God's wrath: "Remove thy stroke away from me; I am consumed by the blow of thine hand. When thou with rebukes dost correct man for iniquity, thou makest his beauty to consume away like a moth."[3] "Lord, be merciful unto me: heal my soul for I have sinned against thee."[4] (But this is not the moral soul!). Misery, however, and above all sickness, are directly referred to Jahveh; they manifest his wrath, but to the contrite penitent, his mercy also:

> Oh the bliss of him whose guilt is pardoned,
> and his sin forgiven!
> Oh the bliss of him whom the Eternal has absolved,
> whose spirit has made full confession!

[1] Chap. 18.
[2] Bertholet, *op. cit.,* 9, 51; *cf.* Oldenberg, *Religion des Veda.*
[3] *Ps.* xxxix. 10, 11.
[4] *Ps.* xli. 4; *cf.* xxxviii. 19; cvii. 17.

> So long as I refused to own my guilt,
>   I moaned unceasingly, life ebbed away;
> for thy hand crushed me night and day,
>   my body dried up as in summer heat.
> Then did I own my sin to thee,
>   uncovering my iniquity;
> and as I vowed I would confess,
>   thou didst remit my sinful guilt.
> So let each loyal heart pray to thee in trouble:
>   the floods may roar,
>   but they will never reach him.[1]

Here confession[2] and prayer have taken the place of the spell. Sin is a matter that man must fight out with his God. Our own consciousness of guilt still leaves avenues of escape open to us, but God's wrath only the sole remedy of His grace. For the ground of guilt is not transgression but the opposition between two wills, the divine and the human. So from the marvellously gracious word of God's compassion His anger, too, is not absent:

> The Eternal is pitiful and gracious,
>   slow to be angry, rich in love;
> he will not always chafe,
>   he will not hold to his anger for all time;
> he treats us not according to our sins,
>   he deals not with us as our guilt deserves;
> but, high as heaven is over earth,
>   so vast his love is to his worshippers.[3]

Sin therefore is hostile contact with God; but nevertheless it is an encounter with *God*; subsisting in the deepest essential being of man, it brings him close before God, where will opposes Will, and Power, power:

> It is against thee I have sinned,
>   I have done evil in thy sight.
> Yes, thou art just in thy charge,
>   and justified in thy sentence.
> Ah! 'twas in guilt that I was born,
>   'twas in sin that my mother conceived me.[4]

---

[1] *Ps.* xxxii (Moffat).   [2] Chap. 62.   [3] *Ps.* ciii. 8 *ff.* (Moffat).
[4] *Ps.* li. 4 *ff.* (Moffat). Kautsch observes with justice that it is not here a question of the adulterous origin of the community (as for Hosea) and still less of the sinfulness of sex relations, but solely of the fact that sin pertains to the essential nature of man.

Here too then, as in Babylon, sin is so deeply hidden that it is concealed even from the sinner, while God alone knows of it.[1] All this is apparently accompanied however, and this with no difficulty, by the consciousness of righteousness:

> Right me, O thou Eternal, for my life is right . . .
> blamelessly I wash my hands.[2]

For sin lies wholly elsewhere; and this is precisely its dreadful aspect:— that man is guilty without himself doing anything whatever towards it. Nor can he amend anything in his own conduct: just as Jahveh alone can avert his wrath, so Jahveh alone can pardon the guilt and "conceal it from view".

> If thou didst keep strict tally of sins,
>   O Lord, who could live on?
> But thou hast pardon
>   that thou mayest be worshipped.
> So I wait in hope for the Eternal,
>   my soul waits hoping for his promise;
>   my soul looks for the Lord
>   more eagerly than watchmen for the dawn,
>   than watchmen for the dawn.
>
> Put your hope in the Eternal, Israel,
>   for with the Eternal there is love,
>   there is a wealth of saving power;
>   'tis he who shall save Israel
>   from all their sins.[3]

For the marvellous mystery of guilt, of sin, of enmity against God, is that in it man discovers God:—certainly as an adversary, but nevertheless in the closest proximity. Thus the: "My God, my God, why hast Thou forsaken me?" of *Psalm* xxii is an expression not merely of estrangement, but equally of nearness. The God Who can "forsake" is a God Who has first been near. In the Confession of Faith of the Dutch and French reformed churches, being forsaken by God, the profoundest solitude, was made equivalent to the "dread of hell". But the grace of God then becomes heavenly joy. And precisely for this reason, both misery and bliss can transcend all else, reaching to the supreme height

---

[1] *Ps.* lxix. 6; xc, 7 *ff.*   [2] *Ps.* xxvi. 1, 6 (Moffat); *cf.* vii, 9; xi, 4 *ff.*
[3] *Ps.* cxxx (Moffat). On forgiveness as the act of God *cf. Theol. Wörterbuch z. N. T.*, "ἀφίημι" (Bultmann).

as to the profoundest depths, because it is not man who forsakes or finds the way back, but rather God Who forsakes or finds. Forcible and tender, regardlessly pressing on and almost inaudibly entreating, the prayer for the nearness of God resounds from the *Psalms*:

> Bestir thyself, Eternal One! Why sleep?
>   Awaken! ah, discard us not for ever!
> Why art thou hiding thy face,
>   forgetting our woe and distress?
> For our soul is bowed to the dust,
>   our body lies low on the ground.
> Come to the rescue!
>   For thy love's sake, oh save us.[1]

Here there is no longer any reference to piety or human weakness: everything is grounded in God: God alone remains important:

> The deer is panting for a stream,
>   and I am panting, O God, for thee.
> I am athirst for God, the living God.[2]

This is yearning. But fulfilment is proclaimed in the marvellous *Psalm* lxxiii, which advances from the enigma of the unrighteous course of the world to the praise of Jahveh; only his honour, his nearness, matters:

> Yet I am always beside thee;
>   thou holdest my right hand.
>
>   .   .   .   .   .
>
> Whom have I in heaven but thee?
>   On earth I care for nothing else.
> Body and soul may fail,
>   but God my strength is mine for evermore.
> Those who leave thee are lost;
>   all who are faithless to thee, thou destroyest.
> But to be near God is my bliss,
>   to shelter with the Lord
>   that I may tell of all thy works.[3]

Here God's mercy is His essence, and His essential nature is to be near, while His being near is His own deed: *He* forsakes man, but *He* also finds him again. Always *He* alone, and again *He*.

---

[1] *Ps.* xliv. 23 *ff.* (Moffat); *cf. Ps.* lxxxviii. 15; lxxxix. 47; cxliii. 7.
[2] *Ps.* xlii. 1 *ff.* (Moffat).   [3] Moffat.

From here the path leads the believer into the dizzy fear of *quantus tremor est futurus*, to terrified adoration of *rex tremendae majestatis*, but also into trust: "Who savest whom thou savest free": *qui salvandos salvas gratis*. In this light therefore we can understand Peter's words: "Lord, leave me; I am a sinful man", together with the *miserere nobis* of the liturgy; but in the same spirit, "Who giveth joy to my youth": *qui laetificat juventutem meam*: of this liturgy, and the *felix culpa* of the church Father.

3. In view of this essential constitution of sin and of guilt, still further, a conflict between religion and morality is undeniably possible. This contest expresses itself now as a defence, on the part of religion, against an exaggerated morality, and again as an attempt at protection, by an "independent" morality, against the encroachments of the religious mentality. Thus Schleiermacher, in his second *Discourse upon Religion*, and later Rudolf Otto, have each in his own way detached morality in principle from religion. For according to Schleiermacher, religion is not at all concerned with man's practical activities; religious feeling should rather "accompany all human action like a sacred music, so that he should do everything together with religion, and nothing because of religion". Otto, indeed, distinguishes the holy, in the sense of moral perfection, from the holy as a purely religious quality, but afterwards unites the two once again in a composite category *a priori*. The group of problems raised by this relationship pertains however, with very few exceptions, to the Phenomenology of Morality, but on the other hand the remainder have already arisen in connection with my previous remarks about the essential nature of sin as being enmity against God. Here I need add only that the merging of religion within morality, as we are familiar with this in Confucianism, or our own eighteenth century, ultimately abolishes religion unless, as was the case with Kant, the moral law assumes on its own part a genuinely religious status and declares itself to be ultimate and unconditioned, and equally to be the Wholly Other.[1] Apart from this, "ethical culture"[2] remains mere "culture"; that is to say, it is religion only in so far as all culture is religion. Existence must be made a matter for "care", and this "caring for" can become a celebration equally in the sense of ritual

---

[1] On the essentially religious character of so much "mere" moralism *cf.* Otto, *Zeitschr. f. Rel.-Psych.*, 4, 1931, 9.
[2] Felix Adler founded his "Society for Ethical Culture" in 1875.

as of custom. But this does not reveal the deepest ground of the being of the "Other". So long as man still has something to care for, faith cannot for him acquire ultimate significance; so long as he still has something that he himself must do, he cannot completely become dust and ashes in his relation to God; and in this sense the saying which is often applied in altogether too edifying a way, "casting all your care upon him; for he careth for you",[1] becomes a terrifying, yet bliss bestowing, main commandment of religion.

The opposition between morality and religion, however, need by no means lead to any moral indifference. For in the obedience of faith, moral commands themselves find both their abrogation and their fulfilment. It is true that St. Paul, in the *Epistle to the Romans*, is striving for the correct understanding of sin, and his repeated: "Never!" when he alludes to the possibility of sinning in order that grace may "much more abound", discloses to us a forcible tension between the urge to care on the one hand, and on the other the tranquillity of justification by faith: "Sin increased, but grace surpassed it far. . . . Now what are we to infer from this? That we are to 'remain on in sin, so that there may be all the more grace'? Never! . . . Are we 'to sin, because we live under grace, not under law'? Never! Do you not know you are the servants of the master you obey, of the master to whom you yield yourselves obedient, whether it is Sin, whose service ends in death, or Obedience, whose service ends in righteousness?"[2] Here there opens out before the apostle the path of mysticism,[3] which eludes all care but also at the same moment knows nothing whatever of obedience. And St. Paul himself chooses the way of faith.

4. This commences with *repentance*. "It is the holy sorrow of the forgiven that places us in the most vital contact with the loving work of the Redeemer. It is the holy that appreciate the Holy One, and the conditions of His love. But I mean the holy of the swift and piercing conscience, the holy of the passionate and tragic soul, the holy who are forgiven much—it is they rather than those white flowers of the blameless life, the angelic purity, and the mystic mood; it is regenerate Launcelot more than noble Arthur."[4] These words of an English dogmatic theologian have precisely the same significance as the poet's lines:

[1] 1 *Peter* v. 7.   [2] *Rom.* v. 20; vi. 1, 15 *ff.* (Moffat).
[3] Chap. 75.   [4] P. T. Forsyth, *The Expositor*, X, 1915, 354 *f.*

> God speaks to me and I to Him;
> With the same voice we speak.
> Yet what He means to say to me
> Is clearly manifested in His creation;
> And what I wish to say to His forbearance
> Lies deeply guarded in my guilt.[1]

Obviously it is here not a matter of repentance in the moral sense.[2] We are not concerned with grief over transgressions that have been committed; and repentance "first assumes its full significance when it is aroused no longer by evil alone, but by that evil in the eyes of God which is called sin";[3] and this repentance is "sustained by God's love", which first grants us the power to repent. "This impulse of love first appeared to us as our love; then we perceived that it was already reciprocal love."[4] Thus repentance leads immediately to conversion and to faith.

---

[1] Roel Houwink, *Strophen*, 1930, 12.   [2] *cf.* Piper, *Ethik*, I, 101.
[3] M. Scheler, *Vom Ewigen im Menschen*, I, 50 (1921).   [4] *ibid.*, 58.

CONVERSION. REBIRTH

1. IN the previous discussion of human life[1] it was observed how its distinctive periods, indicated by rites, displayed on each of these occasions as it were a new life. Every transition, then, is a *rebirth*: the *rite de passage* designates a new beginning. Thus we found, for example, that in primitive initiation ceremonies the neophytes were greeted as just born and their adult life regarded as wholly new; in Greece, also, those adopted by the deity in the mysteries were looked upon as *deuteropotmoi*, "those to whom a second destiny was given".[2] As we then saw, too, life can be renewed either after death,[3] or previously in this existence; the initiate in the Mithraic mysteries called himself *renatus in aeternum*:—reborn in eternity. Christian baptism likewise effects a rebirth.[4] In all these cases, therefore, acquisition of power is a complete renovation.

We know nothing at all, however, about the psychical undercurrents of these outward events. But it is obvious that in every instance alike some inner experience corresponded to the outer process, so that when the Egyptian Pharaoh declared of himself that he *whm ankh*, that he was "repeating and renewing life", this certainly referred not merely to any definite rites subserving this renewal of life, but also presupposed an inner experience of which, however, we are quite ignorant. But this ignorance by no means releases us from the duty of depicting the inner structure of the external event as soon as this makes its appearance. And this happens in those occurrences which we call conversions, in which the main emphasis falls on the inner event, though not without this becoming outwardly observable also.

But an intermediate form between what we, with our inadequate means of expression, call "outward", and what we term "inner", is found in what Lévy-Bruhl has called "dispositions".[5] These are the "positive aspects" of affairs, about which man must know something before he can successfully apply himself to any kind of undertaking whatever. Are the beings with whom he has to deal beneficently, indifferently, or even perhaps inimically disposed? Here relations are

---

[1] Chap. 22.
[3] Chap. 47.   [4] Chap. 52.
[2] Rohde, *Psyche*, II, 421. E. T. 602.
[5] *Primitives and the Supernatural*, 65.

involved that are to our own minds completely incomprehensible and imperceptible, such as the "disposition" of a weapon *etc*. But it is also a matter of peculiarities that we too would call disposition or mood, such as quarrelsomeness and the like; and the remarkable feature is that these "dispositions" are conceived not as being subject to any psychological influences, but precisely as being as objectively physical as are magical attributes. Primitive man, in fact, drew no distinctions at all in situations where we ourselves clearly differentiate. We can understand how an attempt is made, by some concrete method, to prevent a physical event happening, just as we can understand the endeavour to influence a person's disposition by psychical means. But we cannot at all comprehend anyone persuading a storm or a tree in a friendly manner, and attempting to change someone's opinion by a rite.[1] On the other hand, primitive man completely fails to understand our stressing so heavily the differences between these two procedures. We know, again, that men become baptized for their salvation, and we can understand men being converted to the same end; but we scarcely comprehend how baptism and conversion can both be the same. For us the one is objective and pertains to ritual, the other subjective and a matter of psychology. Essentially, however, they are both in the same category: for inner and outer experience should not thus be separated from each other. Here again our fatal predilection for the "spiritual" (which is usually, nonetheless, merely something psychical!) has destroyed our insight into the phenomena themselves. Conversion is new birth, and new birth a conversion.[2]

2. But before considering conversion as this is familiar to us in the great revivalist movements, it is worth while glancing at one example of "inward-outward" conversion; and the story which Apuleius narrates, in his celebrated romance about his hero Lucius, is in its final chapters undoubtedly a genuine account of conversion. The way in which the unfortunate hero, after so many excesses and afflictions, dedicated himself to the service of the goddess, broken in spirit, repentant and contrite, indicates a unity between the outward and inward occurrences which finds unequivocal expression in the exhortations of

[1] We may say, in brief, that we ask a maid for her love, but we "make use of" a house in which to live with her; primitives, on the other hand, "make use of" a love charm for the girl, while they implore the house for its blessing.

[2] The entire problem of the relationship between conversion and rebirth in systematic theology may be understood in the light of this false "modernization" of viewpoint.

the priest of Isis. For initiation, then, three conditions are laid down that supplement each other: the summons of the goddess in accordance with her "providence"; the neophyte's own readiness; and the rites that must be performed by and on the latter. These three together constitute rebirth, whose occurrence nevertheless depends not on any devout attitude of man, but solely upon the decision of the deity. "The day of each man's initiation", said the priest, "was fixed by the" nod "*of the goddess*, and the priest destined for her service was likewise chosen by *her providence*, and a like instruction appointed the sum required for the expenses of the ceremony. He bade me like others await all these ordinances with reverent patience, warning me that it was my duty to beware with all my soul of over-eagerness and petulance, to avoid both these faults, and neither to delay *when summoned* nor to hasten unbidden. 'There are none', he said, 'of all the order of priests of Isis so abandoned in spirit, or so given over to death, as to venture rashly and sacrilegiously to undertake the service of the goddess without *her express command* and thus to contract mortal guilt. For the gates of hell and the power of life are in the hands of the goddess, and the very act of dedication is regarded as a *voluntary death and*" salvation by grace, "inasmuch as the goddess is wont *to elect* those whose term of life is near its close and who stand on the threshold of the night, and are moreover men to whom the mighty mysteries of the goddess may safely be committed. These men the goddess by *her providence brings to new birth* and places once more at *the start of a new race of life.* Therefore thou too must await the command of heaven although long since appointed and ordained, by the clear and evident choice of the great deity, to be highly favoured in thy service at her shrine. And to that end thou like other servants of the goddess shouldst henceforth refrain from impious and unlawful foods, that so thou mayest more righteously win thy way to the secret mysteries of the purest of faiths.' "[1]

Only thus can we understand the far-reaching correspondence that exists, even in the expressions employed, between rites of initiation, and the experience of conversion. The initiates, whether primitive negroes or Hellenistic Greeks, are "new men" with new names, "newly born", *etc.*; and this holds good of converts too. In the first case however it is the outer, and in the second the inner aspect of the process that is presented to us. The fundamental experience, nonetheless, is the same: a new powerfulness enters into life which is experienced as "wholly other", so that life receives a new basis and is begun afresh. In other

---

[1] Apuleius, *Met.* XI, 21 (modified from Butler).

respects the rite is certainly absent from conversion, but by no means its external definiteness; on the contrary: conversion is fixed to a certain date, often indeed to some definite hour and minute. But instead of all the famous and the less well-known accounts of conversion, I shall cite here the marvellous document in which Blaise Pascal has recorded the experience of the night of his own conversion, the concise form of which brings us very close to that experience:

Mémorial de Pascal. † *L'an de grâce 1654 Lundi 23 Nov. le jour de St. Clément Pape et m.-veille de St. Chr. Depuis environ dix heures et demi du soir jusques environ minuit et demi.—Feu—Dieu d'Abraham, Dieu d'Isaac, Dieu de Jacob, non des philosophes et des savants. Joye certitude sentiment vue joye. Dieu de Jésus Christ. Deum meum et Deum vestrum. Jeh. 20. 17. Ton Dieu sera mon Dieu. Ruth. Oubly du monde et de tout hormis Dieu. Il ne se trouve que par les voyes enseignées dans l'Evangile. Grandeur de l'âme humaine. Père juste, le monde ne t'a point connu, mais je t'ay connu. Jeh. 17. Joye Joye Joye et pleurs de joye. Je m'en suis séparé. Dereliquerunt me fontem. Mon Dieu me quitterez-vous? que je n'en sois pas séparé éternellement.—Cette est la vie éternelle qu'ils te connaissent seul vrai Dieu et celuy que tu as envoyé. Jésus Christ. Jésus Christ. Je m'en suis séparé, je l'ay fui renoncé crucifié. Que je n'en sois jamais séparé, il ne se conserve que par les voyes enseignées dans l'Evangile. Rénonciation totale et douce. Soumission totale à Jésus-Christ et à mon directeur. Eternellement en joye pour un jour d'exercice sur la terre. Non obliviscar sermones tuos. Amen.* †.[1]

---

[1] "*Mémorial de Pascal.* † This year of Grace 1654, Monday, November 23rd, day of Saint Clement, pope and martyr; Eve of Saint Chrysogonus. From about half past ten at night, to about half after midnight. Fire. God of Abraham, God of Isaac, God of Jacob, not of the philosophers and the wise. Security, Feeling, Joy, Peace. God of Jesus Christ. *Deum meum et Deum vestrum. John* xx. 17. Thy God shall be my God. *Ruth.* Forgetfulness of the world and of all save God. He can be found only in the ways taught in the Gospel. Greatness of the human soul. O righteous Father, the world hath not known thee, but I have known thee. *John* xvii. Joy, joy, joy, tears of joy. I have separated myself from him. *Dereliquerunt me fontem.* My God, why hast thou forsaken me? That I be not separated from thee eternally. This is life eternal: That they might know thee the only true God, and him whom thou hast sent, Jesus Christ. Jesus Christ. I have separated myself from him; I have fled, renounced, cruci-fied him. May I never be separated from him. He maintains himself in me only in the ways taught in the Gospel. Renunciation total and sweet. Complete submission to Jesus Christ and to my confessor. In eternal joy for one day of affliction on earth. *Non obliviscar sermones tuos. Amen.* †." The French Text in *Pascal, Œuvres, Pensées* (C. Brunschvicg), I, 3 *ff.*, 1904: *cf.* the typical account of Stilling's conversion, Günther, *op. cit.*, 48., and of Sicco Tjaden, who called the year of his conversion the "miracle year 1716" (Heppe, *Pietismus*, 418). For Brakel, *ibid.*, 174 *f.* H. Martensen Larsen, *Zweifel und Glaube, Volksausgabe*, 1916, 114. The latter also gives on p. 271 a remark-able conversion document, a kind of gift of the self to the Lord. B. H. Streeter and A. J. Appasamy describe the Sadhu Sundar Singh's conversion in *The Sadhu*, 5 *ff.* Apart from Christianity *cf.* Lehmann-Haas, *Textbuch*, 147 *f.* (Manikkavasagar). Field, *Mystics and Saints*, 19 *ff.* (Hasan Basri), *etc.*

This experience of conversion is almost always the same in all religions: a second self stands over against the first: a completely new life begins: everything has become different. Thus Frick was able to place the conversion of St. Augustine and that of al-Ghazali in almost literal parallel.[1]

The cause of conversion is in itself not infrequently quite trivial: it may be some text often heard that suddenly appeals to the mind with extraordinary force, as in the celebrated instance of St. Augustine and of many Mohammedan mystics; it may be a vision or some other ecstatic state, as in the no less famous case of the apostle Paul. In his classical work on religious experience William James advanced a theory about conversion which, so far as it refers to the psychological process, probably deals with the essentials. He compared the process to the condition in which we find ourselves when searching our memory for some word or name or other; we exert ourselves in vain, but as soon as we discontinue the attempt and quietly settle down, then the word for which we sought suddenly occurs to us. It is exactly the same in the case of the solution of a scientific problem or musical composition *etc.* Conversion would then be an eruption of what has for long been accumulating beneath the threshold of consciousness, which finally and forcibly makes its way into the open. Hence the coerciveness and suddenness in the course of conversion; hence too the consciousness of something wholly new which overwhelms the convert; and thus we can also understand that conversion may occur in the reverse direction, from faith to unbelief. Of this also James quotes examples, while one that is extremely characteristic occurs in Romain Rolland's autobiographical romance *Jean Christophe.* Here the tones have the genuine ring: "Christopher woke up. He looked about him startled . . . He knew nothing. Around him and in him everything was changed. There was no God. . . . As with faith, so the loss of faith is often equally a flood of grace, a sudden light. Reason counts for nothing: the smallest thing is enough—a word, silence, the sound of bells. A man walks, dreams, expects nothing. Suddenly the world crumbles away. All about him is in ruins. He is alone. He no longer believes."[2] Thus conversion is a psychical eruption which, prepared for beneath the threshold of consciousness, is as it were incubated.

3. But although this theory of conversion is most pertinent psychologically, and phenomenologically also gives a satisfactory account

[1] H. Frick, *Ghazalis Selbstbiographie, ein Vergleich mit Augustins Konfessionen,* 1919.
[2] *John Christopher,* II, 27.

of the absolute reorientation in life, it is nevertheless insufficient as a description of what is here revealed. For in conversion it is a matter not merely of a thoroughgoing reorientation of Power, but also of a surrender of man's own power in favour of one that utterly overwhelms him and is experienced as sacred and as "wholly other". Of course we are not here discussing the possibility of any divine influence in the experience of conversion: that pertains to theology. But we cannot describe the structure of conversion in itself without taking this divine influence into account as one factor in our comprehension. Estimated by this criterion then it is, comparatively speaking, a matter of complete indifference whether or not conversion is connected with any definite rites, and indeed whether in general it becomes externally perceptible or not. For religion still continues to speak of conversion when it has completely relinquished equally rites and definite seasons, and even the character of suddenness. Thus it is not man who converts himself, but God Who converts him: God bestows new life; and with this, therefore, we revert once again to the basic conditions; primitive rites remain far closer to the essence of the situation than does modern psychology: *conversion, essentially, is rebirth.* God renews life, substitutes sanctity for wickedness, and makes possible a "repetition". Thus to begin life anew is wholly impossible for man: but what is impossible for him is possible to God; and in conversion it is a matter solely of this divine possibility. Exactly as in the case of celebration, we find ourselves confronted here also by the great possibility of "repetition"; "to renew life" was the ardent desire of the ancient Egyptian. Faith itself implies this very repetition. And the primeval yearning to return to the maternal womb becomes experienced here not as any natural process, but as an act of God, of the Father.[1]

[1] *cf.* Geismar, *Kierkegaard*, 185.

CHAPTER 80

FAITH

1. FAITH is in the first place a conjecture. In saying: "I believe", we mean that we do not really know, but that we suppose something or other about the matter in question. Whoever believes in God, then, turns away from knowledge about Him; but he is conscious that he has an awareness (*Ahnung*) of God. The believer, however, has something more than a mere awareness. If someone tells me what at first sight appears incredible, I may eventually reply: "I believe you"; this by no means implies, however, that now I know about the fact told to me, but only that I accept its correctness from the narrator. Once again I know nothing (otherwise of course I need not believe it!), but I accept a truth from another person. To say: "I believe in God", therefore, is to admit the fact of God's existence; it has been declared to me, and has been believed. Thus in the structure of faith *obedience* to truth appears as a contrast to and in relation with, awareness (*Ahnung*). To speak of faith, then, is to speak of *truth*, in the sense not of correctness but of the authentic, valid, ultimate, conclusive and complete. And we observe immediately that we cannot speak about this truth, cannot say anything at all about it, until we have been seized by it, until we believe it: I have believed, and therefore I speak.

Finally, faith is *trust* also. Some affair, or task or person, demands our faith: that is to say, we must have confidence in them. I believe for example in the future of my own people: or I lack faith and can feel no confidence whatever in the matter: "I certainly hear the message, only I lack faith." But as trust, still further, faith presupposes will: we rely not upon a thing, but on a will. Whoever therefore believes in God has an assured sense of Him, obeys His truth and trusts in Him; and this again means that he does something of which no man, of himself, is ever capable. To know about God is easy: but in order to have this awareness of God, to obey Him, to be able to trust in Him, He must arouse some awareness of Himself, permit Himself to be apprehended, confide in man. The surrender involved in faith, therefore, presupposes surrender on the part of God: faith must be bestowed upon man; he can never give faith to himself. We say this even about quite ordinary affairs, and it is essentially correct. Faith is always a gift; even the faintest awareness of God can be the outcome of no human reflection alone. And here we forsake the domain of appearances and of inward experiences. Faith "appears" to us just as little as does guilt.[1]

2. With faith, therefore, an entirely new element enters into the religious life; although, taken quite literally, it does not "enter into" this life, since it would in that case be a phenomenon. Rather it bears upon life and indeed, in the first place, as a judgment passed on life, and then as its liberation. To the religious man who refuses simply to "accept" life and is troubled about it (in other words), three different ways are open: (*1*) *Domination*: man then finds his *locus standi* (*a*) magically, *locus standi in loco Dei*; or (*b*) theoretically: within the totality of his ideas he assigns a place to certain aspects of life, by means of which he presumes to dominate life; the Greeks adopted this course; (*c*) experience: so far as is possible, life becomes exhausted to its very foundations in feeling:—the path of Romanticism. (*2*) The second main course lies in *conduct*:—either in (*a*) rites, regulating life into an attained whole; or (*b*) custom; or again (*c*) prayer, which overcomes nothing whatever, but only expects, entreats, hopes:—and all this comprehends almost everything that precedes.

But now a further consideration arises: for life does not belong to us at all. It belongs to God, Who has created it. We can therefore neither overcome it nor beg for it, since it always belongs to God alone, and any possibility it possesses lies in whatever we receive. Bustling about then, whether externally or internally, is quite futile; God's deed alone sets us free. God, Who created us, creates us anew, and makes us into a "new creation".[2]

Salvation, therefore, at which all religion without exception aims, is here no longer something to be won, but is simply a gift of grace; thus, indeed, it first becomes salvation in any actual sense. For life as such, even at its very highest power, is never genuine salvation.[3] Salvation is never something attained nor effected by man himself, not what has grown into his life or has become visible therein. It is the

---

[1] cf. Boulgakoff, *Orthodoxie*, 5.   [2] Chap. 45. καινὴ κτίσις.
[3] Scheler, *Rel. Erneuerung*, 335; Hofmann, *Erlebnis*, 12 ff., 34 f.; cf. Piper, *Ethik*, I, 111.

hidden ground of life in God: it is the contrary, or rather the reverse side, of guilt. In truth, nothing becomes visible here: everything remains concealed.

Thus we can understand how it is that Christian *preaching* expounds the liberation that is trusted in as *forgiveness* of guilt, and as *atonement* for sin; and still more deeply does the idea of *election* penetrate, which arises in both Judaism and Islam and subsequently becomes the central idea in Christianity. Faith therefore is not a human sentiment, not a human deed, feeling nor volition, but man's state of being elected from the very beginning; out of His own free and incalculable grace God has chosen the believer, and imparted to him the *donum fidei*. And thus man's salvation lies wholly outside his own life (forensic justification, so-called), in God. The powerfulness of life in itself has utterly disappeared: only He has all Power; "with force of arms we nothing can". Involuntarily, we are here speaking the language of that religious movement, the Reformation, which constitutes faith the central point of all religion; and Luther's and Calvin's *sola fide* must be understood from this point of view. "For (faith) is the (Christian's) life, righteousness and bliss, which preserves the very self and makes it acceptable, and imparts to it all that Christ has, as has been previously observed, and as is confirmed by St. Paul in the *Epistle to the Galatians* ii, where he says: 'and the life which I now live in the flesh I live by the faith of the Son of God.' "[1]

---

[1] Luther, *Of the Liberty of a Christian.*

CHAPTER 81

ADORATION

1. FAITH itself and as such, therefore, does not "appear", nor become visible. But there is one phenomenon which, although it is certainly not the "appearance" of faith but its consequence, does reveal its presence. This is *Adoration*. Whoever believes, adores. He does not merely pray, since prayer originates from care.[1] Need teaches prayer but not *adoration*, as Scheler finely asserted.[2] Whoever adores has therefore forgotten his prayer and now knows only God's glory.

> God reveals His presence:
> Let us now adore Him,
> And with awe appear before Him.
> God is in His temple:
> All within keep silence,
> Prostrate lie with deepest reverence.[3]

Adoration, then, is the very culmination of worship, where inner and outer wholly coincide; and its almost muted tones resound not in Christianity alone, but also in Israel, in Islam and in India; Otto has compiled a wonderful selection of "numinous hymns" that give expression to adoration. Nevertheless the volume of sound is at its fullest where the worshipping community bows down before the presence of the Lord: "Lift up your hearts! We lift them up unto the Lord."

2. It is not only celebration, however, that culminates in adoration: custom also finds its ultimate fulfilment here; it too is transformed into praise and gratitude. Then the sole task of life is to extol God; and from this all moral conduct, as such, arises spontaneously. Thus the mystery of guilt sinks engulfed within the deeper mystery of God's love: only hope remains. And these notes too resound quite apart from Christianity (we recall the *Bhagavad-Gita*), although they were in fact most forcibly struck by the Reformers, and particularly by Calvin. All these elements united, then, reverberate in the church's hymn of adoration: *Te Deum Laudamus*:

---

[1] Chap. 62.   [2] *Rel. Erneuerung*, 300.   [3] Tersteegen.

We praise thee, O God: we acknowledge thee to be the Lord.
All the earth doth worship thee: the Father everlasting.
To thee all Angels cry aloud: the Heavens, and all the Powers therein.
To thee Cherubin, and Seraphin, continually do cry,
Holy, Holy, Holy: Lord God of Sabaoth;
Heaven and earth are full of the Majesty of thy Glory.
Vouchsafe, O Lord, to keep us this day without sin.
O Lord, have mercy upon us: have mercy upon us.
O Lord, let thy mercy lighten upon us, as our trust is in thee.
O Lord, in thee have I trusted: let me never be confounded.

PART FOUR

THE WORLD

WAYS TO THE WORLD. CREATIVE DOMINATION

1. IN Chapter 8 I showed that for primitive man the modern concept of "world" does not really exist, and that far from regarding his environment as an object, he immediately constitutes it his own "conjoint world"; and in this principle the essential feature of the religious *Weltanschauung* has already been expressed. I may now repeat this, however, in the sense that a "religious *Weltanschauung*" is never merely a "point of view", but is always a *participation*, a *sharing*. For out of his own particular environment everyone constructs a world for himself which he believes himself able to dominate; there is therefore no *one* single world, but just as many *worlds* as there are human beings. Thus what holds good of the child is true universally: and "it should be the fundamental principle of every psychology, as contrasted with theories of knowledge, that for conscious experience reality is never a constant, but that it changes with the individual's psychical organization, and indeed with his stage of development; it must then be definitely stated, at the outset, that every child lives in a world quite different from ours".[1] In this sense the world is "objective mind";[2] the human spirit does not direct itself towards a world that is given to it, but allows what meets it to become part of itself, after it has sufficiently modified it. The "world" is therefore an essentially "celebrated", not merely an "accepted" but a dominated world.[3]

2. Herein lies the truth of the principle of participation, of sharing, advanced by Lévy-Bruhl. Things do not encounter each other "solidly in space", but have some share in one another and may mingle with, and appear in place of, each other. Accordingly, man does not conduct himself "objectively" towards the "world": he participates in it, just as it does in him. His path to the world, therefore, is neither that of contemplation, nor reflection, nor presenting himself as a subject and so forming a "substratum", but of existing as oriented *towards* the world. Man's domination of the world is thus a domination exerted always from within.

---

[1] Spranger, *Psychologie des Jugendalters*, 32.
[2] *cf.* Spranger, *Lebensformen*, 17 *f.*   [3] *cf.* Heidegger, *op. cit.*, 87.

This participation, still further, is an attitude deeply rooted in human nature; it is not a disposition that requires to be overcome, but is the perfectly natural mental outlook even of "modern" man, thoroughly accustomed as he is to theoretical and practical knowledge and to objective observation and experiment.[1] As Lévy-Bruhl himself profoundly observes on this subject: "Now the need of participation assuredly remains something more imperious and more intense, even among peoples like ourselves, than the thirst for knowledge and the desire for conformity with the claims of reason. It lies deeper within us and its source is more remote."[2] This mental attitude, therefore, which neither dissects nor abstracts, neither infers nor analyses, but deals with the whole, grasps it concretely, connects together its essentials and experiences "participation", is ours to-day just as much as it is that of primitive man. In the case of the latter, certainly, it has a wider range of control, although so-called "primitives" are obviously "modern" also, and are quite familiar with analytical and logical thought! But for us too it is the actual way to the world:[3] not indeed as "lazy thinking", as Thurnwald would regard it, but existing as oriented towards the world in contrast to merely observing it. The self, that is to say, is a partner with the world and the world with the self.[4]

This relationship (to continue) results in events in the world, equally with man's own activities, being dominated by "mystical" factors; I shall employ this expression, which was coined by Lévy-Bruhl, although I believe myself that it involves some misapprehension, and I would therefore prefer to restrict the terms "mysticism" and "mystical" to the phenomenon previously described in Chapter 75.[5] As regards the facts, however, Lévy-Bruhl is perfectly correct. When, for example, Gräbner attempts to invalidate his assertion by showing that "the Australian does not conceive the natural as supernatural, but conversely the supernatural as natural", and that the magic power he employs is

[1] cf. Marett, Faith, Hope and Charity, 86.
[2] How Natives Think, 385; cf. the remarkable discussion of Lévy-Bruhl's ideas in Bulletin 29, Société française de Philosophie, 1929, No. 4. Nothing is more significant of the low philosophic level of the historical and ethnological sciences than the misunderstanding of Lévy-Bruhl's views, exhibited by investigators in the most diverse fields. In this respect the urgent necessity becomes obvious of an understanding between Psychology and Phenomenology on the one hand, and on the other the so-called pure historic, anthropological and ethnological sciences, which to-day, almost without exception, set out, without being aware of so doing, from the most extraordinary epistemological, psychological and metaphysical principles.
[3] Thurnwald, Bequemes Denken.   [4] cf. Danzel, Grundlagen, 432.
[5] cf. Werner Entw. Psych. 270.

thought of as "grossly material",[1] this only indicates that the ethnologist has failed to perceive how our own antithesis between supernatural and natural, as this has gradually developed in Western European thought, does not exist at all in primitive and religious thought. That the primitive mind understands everything supernatural in some natural sense is indeed quite correct; but then his "naturalness" is far more "supernatural", more "mystical" or (still better) more numinous, than our "supernaturalness". And that Power is conceived as material is equally true; but we observed much earlier that the contrast between the material and the spiritual is far from being so fundamental as our current popular psychology would gladly believe it to be.[2]

I can influence the world therefore, just as the world can affect me, in a way that is justified by neither logic nor facts, but which constitutes a very real struggle at the closest possible range. I shall call this contest the *magical attitude*; and the armistice that follows the struggle, which is itself however also one kind of domination preluding a new combat, I shall call the *mythical form-conferring attitude*. The former is concerned with Powers, the latter with Will and Form, but both alike are conditioned by participation. For without participation there is no struggle: and similarly without proximity. This magical attitude, however, is not a structure of the spiritual life merely of the past, of which only meagre vestiges now persist for us; nor, again, is it a degeneration nor childish malady; it is neither "primitive science" nor elementary technique.[3] It is, on the contrary, a primal attitude very deeply grounded in human nature, as vital among ourselves as it ever was, in fact an eternal structure. This is evident, too, in the recurring predominance under certain conditions of the magical attitude. Children will be considered later, while Storch has discussed the reasoning of the mentally disordered and compiled remarkable examples of the magical attitude of mind, and has explicitly placed these parallel to "primitive" data. "As an underlying current of waking day-thinking there lies ready prepared, in every man, magical-archaic experience; but this comes into serious

---

[1] *Weltbild*, 16.

[2] K. Hidding has recently given an excellent description of so-called primitive mentality in his *Gebruiken en godsdienst der Soendaneezer, De Opwekker*, 1933, 3.

[3] Of a completely different opinion are Allier (Magic is degeneration), Lindworsky (primitives think rationally, but know nothing about the conditions of natural processes: magic is ignorance), Boas (feeling predominates among primitives), Bartlett (predominance of the play instinct); I have discussed these views elsewhere in my *Structure*. Closely akin to my own ideas is W. Mayer-Gross, *Zur Frage der psychologischen Eigenart der sog. Naturvölker*, VIII *Int. Congress of Psychology, Proc. and Papers*, 1927, 206 ff.

conflict with ordinary rational thinking only in specific schizoid types";[1] thus to victims of schizophrenic megalomania "the world, from being a differentiated objectivity, again becomes the immediate content of his own existence[2] . . . instead of being an object of objective consciousness, the world of things then becomes a mere modification of self-feeling."[3] One patient, for instance, "calls herself 'the goddess', relating how she has been placed in the domain of the sun and that the end of the world has been revealed to her, but that her joy in life could not be killed, as she wished to devour the time following the end of the world". We curtly describe this mental attitude as megalomania, but we must not forget that this mania subsists in the blood of us all without exception—this mania to dominate the world—and that anyone who had entirely relinquished this madness could no longer live. It is essentially human not to accept the given world, but to manipulate it until it has been adjusted to one's own life. "The world was not, till it I did create."[4] Thus a condition of struggle always prevails, whose victorious conclusion implies the decline of world power into that of the individual.[5]

3. He who thus assumes the magical attitude, according to Salomon Reinach's fine simile, resembles the conductor dominating his orchestra; and it may well be that he believes that he himself produces the uproar! The best parallel to the person who is magically disposed, however, is Chanticleer, who thinks that his crowing makes the sun rise, and who suffers the most tragic disillusioning when, one morning, the sun is there "of itself!" So man too assumes the offensive against the powers:[6] he overcomes them by the main force of his own will: he creates them as it were. The purely magical attitude, which of course nowhere actually exists, is therefore that of God, of the Creator:

> At my command, upon yon primal Night,
> The starry hosts unveiled their glorious light.[7]

In magic, then, the dictum *eritis sicut Deus*—"ye shall be as gods"— attains full reality; and in truth magical thinking is not literally thought "but willing".[8]

---

[1] Storch, *op. cit.*, 88 *f.*   [2] *ibid.*, 74.
[3] Storch.   [4] *Faust*, Part II, Act 2.
[5] Cassirer, *op. cit.*, II, 194: "Thus the ego exercises an almost limitless domination over reality in the magical world survey; it draws all reality back into itself."
[6] Reinach, *Orpheus*[2], 32 *f.* E.T. 23.   [7] *Faust*, Part II, Act 2 (Swanwick).
[8] Prinzhorn, *Bildnerei*, 311.

It is, therefore, never legitimate to set "religion" and "magic" in any definitely adverse relationship, as though religion were the successor of magic, the latter being non-religious and the former never magical. Magic itself is religion simply because it is concerned with powers; certainly it requires no "god", but a "godless" act may very well be religious. Magic differs, however, from all other forms of religion in that the desire to dominate the world belongs to its essential nature. Not every religion has this aim; nevertheless it is adopted by very many non-magical religions, only with other methods. Thus I can concede neither the antithesis between religion and magic as social-antisocial, nor as ethical-scientific, nor again that magic is anterior to religion:[1] wherever there is religion there is magic, even though the magical stream does not always follow the main channel of religion; similarly, wherever there is magic there is religion, although it can be only one specific type of religion. Saintyves, therefore, is quite correct: magic is an art, knowledge, a cult, only it deals with mystery.[2]

The magical attitude, then, is certainly religious: nevertheless it demands nothing "supernatural"; and the extent to which scholars of to-day take for granted the application of modern concepts to primitive religion, and in fact to religion in general, is astonishing. If I shoot an arrow at an enemy directly opposite me, this is to our modes of thought certainly a disagreeable, but perfectly logical, action. But if I aim my arrow at an opponent who is in another town a hundred miles away, then our logic ceases and we speak of an action grounded on the "supernatural", for whose results the supernatural may well be responsible. In primitive consciousness, however, these two acts are by no means so different: in any case we require a superior and numinous power for the success of both alike.[3] This is the truth in those theories of magic which emphasize the close relationship of ordinary *technique* to magical processes,[4] although the derivation of magical activity from primitive *technique*, attempted by Vierkandt,[5] has little force; and with his usual keen penetration Nietzsche has perceived the essential feature here: "when one rows, it is not the rowing that moves the boat, but rowing is only a magical ceremony by which one compels a *daemon* to

---

[1] *cf.* W. Otto's admirable observations on these problems: *AR.* 12, 1909, 544 *ff.*; *cf.* Clemen, *Wesen und Ursprung der Magie, Arch. f. Rel.-Psych.*, II-III; Beth, *Religion und Magie*; Bertholet, *op. cit.*, 23; Thurnwald, *Zauber*, 485, 498 *ff.* Vierkandt, *Die Anfänge der Religion und Zauberei, Globus*, 92, 64.

[2] *Force magique*, 9, 14.   [3] *cf.* Arbmann, *op. cit.*, 352.

[4] Söderblom, *Gottesglaube*, 68 *ff.* Vierkandt, *loc. cit.*, 21 *ff.*, 40 *f.*

[5] *cf.* Beth, *op. cit.*, 84.

move the boat" (I should myself substitute a "power"). "All maladies, even death itself, are the result of magical influences. Illness and death never happen naturally; *the whole conception of 'natural sequence' is lacking* . . . when a man shoots with a bow, there is still always present an irrational hand and strength . . . man is the *rule*, nature is irregularity."[1] To this I need add nothing.

But what really lends the magical attitude its intrinsic human interest is its character of protest: Preuss has observed how, in magical thinking, man opposed animal *instinct*, and so rose above himself; how too, in magic, lie the roots of all idealism and the possibility of the liberation of the human spirit.[2] Magical man, then, makes a "world", his own world, out of the "environment" of the animal; and thus magic was the earliest mode of uniting individual objects within one all-inclusive world-picture.[3]

This magical attitude, still further, appears even more clearly in the simplest examples than in complicated magic rituals. Lévy-Bruhl alludes, for instance, to the rite of reversing an action (*renverser un acte*): in certain tribes stepping over anyone is strictly prohibited and whoever inadvertently does so must nullify his action by once again stepping over the person concerned, only this time "in the reverse direction".[4] That is a magical action which many of us will recognize from our own youthful experience: a compulsive action consisting, for example, in not striking the right foot with the left without making this good immediately by touching the left foot with the right one. In this simple act, however, there lies a mastery of the world which permits whatever has happened to be modified, or even to be made retrogressive. Here then man raises his protest, utters his "Nevertheless", tenses his own will against what is simply given to him. It is thus not at all astonishing that a certain relationship exists between idealism and magic. We have already quoted the Bachelor in Goethe's *Faust*; we can also cite Amiel, who correctly discerned a magical tendency in Schleiermacher's *Monologues*: "The tameless liberty, the divine dignity of the individual spirit, expanding till it admits neither any limit nor anything foreign to itself, and conscious of a strength instinct with creative force."[5]

This domination of the world by will has, however, one essential condition:—before the world can be thus controlled it must be transferred inwards, and man must take it into himself: he can actually

---

[1] *Human, All Too Human*, I, 117, 118 (Foulis Edition).
[2] *Geistige Kultur*, 8.   [3] Kretschmer, *Medizinische Psychologie*, 34.
[4] *Primitives and the Supernatural*, 381.   [5] *Journal*, 1 Feb. 1852 (Ward).

dominate it only when it has in this way become an inner realm. For this reason all magic is autism, or "living within oneself".[1] "From the sensuous data of the environment the autistic-self-sufficient schizophrene makes for himself a totally different and more abundantly filled world, which he does not secure nor bring into accord with other people by means of any logical conventions, but which remains just raw material for his own fancies, caprices and needs. The actual environment, as such, is depreciated; it demands no recognition—it may be either utilized, or excluded, wholly at will."[2] And what is here asserted about mental disorder holds good almost precisely for magical man in general.[3] Man does not trouble himself at all about "reality": he dominates it creatively, since he immures himself against it; he erects a kingdom internally, a divine service in his own soul. Wherever any settled limits are given between man and the world, between object and subject, severe conflicts arise as in mental disease, or again in the contest between the artist and the world; and wherever these do not exist, as with primitive peoples, the magician receives his own official status, while everyone participates somehow or other in magical procedure. As Kretschmer correctly observes, myths and dogmas do not consider the world as it actually is, but deal with it wholly at will and make it into a world as it should be. In the fairy tale the idea that simultaneously expresses, and fulfils, a wish holds good even to-day, and the entire rite, the celebration, is quite incomprehensible apart from this autistic attitude: it is man himself who settles his own conditions. Thus primitive man firmly believes that unless certain words are recited and certain actions performed, it will not rain; and quite similarly, "only if you tidy up your chest of drawers now will you get your summer holiday", thinks the magically disposed child, who likewise lives in her own world. "When my dearest friend was very ill", said the same child, "I believed I could save her only by going up and down the street six times every day", and naturally with a most scrupulous avoidance of the gaps in the paving-stones![4] "Children stand nearer to the world of magic: the problem of the possibility of things does not

---

[1] In fuller detail *cf.* my *Structure*.

[2] Prinzhorn, *Bildnerei der Geisteskranken*, 55.

[3] In my *Structure* I have discussed the problem, which is scarcely pertinent here, of how it is that the same attitude arises in so widely diverse types of people as the mentally deranged, primitives, children, artists, *etc.* In any case we must be most cautious in making phylogenetic generalizations.

[4] Additional examples in Zeininger, *Magische Geisteshaltung im Kindesalter und ihrer Bedeutung für die religiöse Entwicklung.*

torment them, and although their thoughts are not debarred from the experience of reality, still they remain outside its domain; they are autistic, and live within themselves, not because they are turned away from the world but simply because they have not yet attained an adequate relationship to the real." In these terms H. C. Rümke[1] presents the essence of this mental attitude and, at the same time, reveals the reason why the norm that governs the life both of children and of primitives leads among modern adults to illness.[2]

When it is considered from the standpoint of its object, the world, the autistic "living within oneself" that characterizes the subject of experience appears as "catathymia"—a term employed by Kretschmer to describe that state of mind in which everything is perceived in accordance with one's own subjective mood, so that objective reality is to that degree distorted. Consequently the "world" becomes regarded entirely as one's own domain and experienced merely "in accord with human subjectivity", with its desires and demands. One catatonic patient, for example, crawled under his bed and tried to lift it with all his strength: that was the way in which he wanted "to lead the earth nearer to God",[3] while another person similarly afflicted would fall out of bed "in order to keep the world rotating, so that the wheel should go on turning".[4] For in all such cases the "world" lies within while, conversely, nothing whatever is perceived outside except the self: another patient felt fatigued and thought that her own strength was exhausted by the farmers working in the fields![5] I cannot agree with Kretschmer, however, in seeking the principle of this "catathymia" merely in feeling;[6] while this view is certainly not wholly incorrect, still in the wish for domination, in the emotional craving, the will is also manifested, and this has formed itself on the lines of the "wholly other". Once again then: magical man *protests*.

This "catathymic" attitude, again, extends to the entire Universe: the "underworld" becomes Hades, hell: heaven the abode of the blessed, the desert the resort of demons;[7] in all conditions, and in every event,

---

[1] *Geneeskundige Bladen*, 25. *Reeks*, X, 1927, 329; *cf.* also *Psych. und Neurol. Bl.*, 1928, 5–6, 29.

[2] Prinzhorn, *op. cit.*, 298 *f.* This by no means implies that primitive thought corresponds in every respect to that of children.   [3] Storch, *op. cit.*, 73.

[4] *ibid.*, 8; *cf.* 69, 80, and the characteristic case in Jaspers' *Psychopathologie*, 400.

[5] Storch, *ibid.*, 41.

[6] According to Kretschmer, causal thought connects things together in accordance with the principle of frequency, but magical thinking on the basis of the principle of community of feeling; *op. cit.*, 34.

[7] *cf.* Danzel, *Psych. Grundl.*, 436 *ff.* Werner, *Entwicklungspsychologie*, 62.

man perceives himself. He is Power: he is God. It may be, however, that in him Faust's yearning is manifested:

> Could I my pathway but from magic free,
> And quite unlearn the spells of sorcery,
> Stood I, Oh Nature, man alone 'fore thee,
> Then were it worth the trouble man to be![1]

This indeed the Greeks were able to do, since in the Homeric structure of their spirit they were the first to discover "Nature" in its modern sense.[2] Their religion (so far, of course, as it was Homeric and not mystical-Platonic) was that of the given, of quiescent Being, and as such it maintains a quite specific position among religions.[3]

A quite different victory over magic consists in the idea of *creation*. Magic is certainly by no means disavowed: but God, Who utters His creative word, is now the sole magician; and man's word, which is essentially an answer, can never possess magical power. But God speaks "So let it be!" and it is: He speaks again, and a second creation consummates the marvel of rebirth: He speaks "the word only, and my servant shall be healed".[4] Here, then, there is neither "acceptance" nor self-sufficient "celebration", but only receiving.

4. The second mode of creative domination, as has already been observed, may be understood as a quiescent pause following on the convulsive magical attainment of mastery. Man now retires from the world to a certain distance; and at first he seems to desire only to contemplate. Hence the static aspect of the mythical world: it wholly disregards time and, as it were, immobilizes it;[5] its forms are eternal, immutable. Every human passion, every desire, every thought, has there, in the realm of myth, its "eternal aspect".[6]

But this apparently contemplative domination is nonetheless control: man endows the world powers with form so that he can overcome them more effectively, even though in a manner wholly different from his magical attitude. Thus the form-imparting individual,[7] who invokes and evokes events as myths,[8] has adopted an attitude directly opposed to that of the magical individual. The latter absorbed the world within himself: but the other type of man ejects the world from himself. He projects experienced power into the external world; his own love assumes the form of the Cyprian goddess, his yearning becomes the

---

[1] *Faust*, Part II, Act 5.   Otto, *Götter Griechenlands*, 47.
[3] Chap. 95.   [4] *Matt.* viii. 8.   [5] Chap. 55, 60.
[6] Otto, *op. cit.*   [7] Chap. 17.   [8] Chap. 60.

Garden of Eden and his guilt the fall.[1] His death again, together with his hope of resurrection, he experiences "dually" (the dual experience of form!) in the myth of Light, and his dread in demonic figures.

Flight from the self, still further, corresponds to autism, to the passionate search for the self. "The poet draws the world within himself, in order to transfer it 'outwardly' afresh in the manifold forms of his work: the youth who has withdrawn from the world, into the depths of his own soul, attempts to bring its riches to light once more by writing poems."[2] Similarly, "primitive man has created a world for himself which, although it is for us only a product of imagination, implies for him a very concrete reality; but he thus elicits from his own soul all the possibilities that he has experienced. He peoples field and forest with the figures of his desires, his dread, his hope and his woe."[3] This is the animistic tendency of humanity, which here we encounter afresh, and in this sense spirits and gods are indeed "exponents of feeling".[4] "Under the pressure of a hostile world man, unsatisfied with a refuge in his inner being, creates a life apart from his own, a 'thou', in which he finds anew his own hate and his own love. Thus the two tendencies, of magical autism and of mythical endowment with form, correspond to and complete each other. They are both present simultaneously: now the one, and again the other, predominates. Only the attitude of the mentally disordered (the schizophrene) halts at the magical method, and hence it turns into a blind alley. But we too are just as much 'mythologists' as 'primitive man' ",[5] and are distinguished from him only by being conscious of the abyss separating our "primitive" from our logically grounded knowledge. It is true that Storch maintains that poetical images and metaphors hold their place in our own thought only as parallels or comparisons, or that these figures emerge only when our ideas relax.[6] But I believe that when Chesterton describes the Law of Gravitation as "that mad and quickening rush by which all earth's creatures fly back to her heart when released", he is expounding a genuinely vital "animistic" idea[7] which, despite its lack of scientific precision, exactly expresses the essence of the situation. For the time is past when poetry could be disposed of as merely playful comparison and religion as a similarly playful notion.

The form of myth, therefore, is that of experience; and whoever wishes to understand myth must first of all discover in it not any

---

[1] cf. Danzel, *Psych. Grundlagen.*   [2] cf. Spranger, *Psych. des Jugendalters*, 68.
[3] My *Structure*, 19 f.   [4] Wilamowitz.
[5] cf. Tillich, *Rel. Verwirkl.*, 96 ff   [6] *op. cit.*, 11.   [7] My *Structure*, 20 f.

"explanation" of certain natural phenomena, but an attaining of mastery over the world which, although certainly less forcible than the magical method, would still wrest from the "thou" what magic had extorted from the powers. In this connection, too, the newer mythological method is fully justified in its endeavour to understand the cult, in the first instance, in order to comprehend myths.[1] For what lives in myth subsists already in sacred action, in the "celebration" of the event, and conversely!

Like magic, still further, the mythical endowment with form comes to an end that is, however, never ultimate. Probably, therefore, we shall never be able to remove magic completely from our path, just as we are scarcely ever likely to discontinue spontaneous creation of form or ignore the traditionally given. Essentially, however, mythical endowment with form does reach its end where nothingness is the goal of all powerfulness. Mysticism, particularly the Hindu type, can instruct us on this point.[2] For where the void, or nullity, is to be attained in a "modeless mode", there every form without exception disappears. But the mythical form also comes to an end where an all-embracing form is given to faith,[3] which is not intended to subserve any acquisition of power but is itself that of a servitor. The belief in Incarnation, therefore, may essentially (that is, theologically and eschatologically) dispense with every form.

5. The two paths to the world, finally, with which we have thus become familiar, are actually only *one* road with two rails. Once again, however, this does not involve humanity following this road to its end until it notices that it raises a dilemma, and then striking another road such as that of science, of mysticism or of faith, as evolutionists and phylogenists are inclined to maintain. For we travel both roads now, just as previously and as always. But we are not restricted to them; and at this point the simile of the two roads ends: it must now be replaced by that of strata. The spiritual life of man then consists of different levels, one of which is at the same moment the most deeply situated and the most important:—that is the dual level of autism and myth, wherein "participation" is the fundamental law. Above this stratum others are deposited that are more or less based upon it.

To these other levels (to continue) the magical-mythical domination of the world is related in the same way as is dream life to waking consciousness. From recent psychology, then, we learn that dream experi-

[1] Chap. 60.   [2] Chap. 75.   [3] Chap. 80.

ence is in no degree less "real" than is daily life. The study of dreams is in fact a no less reliable path to the secret of life than is the investigation of waking consciousness; and Wilhelm Raabe observes that "we raise a corner of the curtain over the great mystery of the world when we reflect, and carefully consider the fact that stupid people and the poor in spirit may have the most marvellous and the most intelligent dreams; just as talented and strange as those of clever people, equally by day and by night".[1] Here again, therefore, we approach more closely to primitive feeling than to that of the nineteenth century when we regard dream facts as being valid of life, though not of waking life, just as Kamchadale tribesmen do who tell a young girl whom they desire that they have already won her favours in their dreams, whereupon the girl yields.[2] Similarly for primitive man his wife's infidelity, of which he has merely dreamt, is regarded as established;[3] while in Gaboon "a dream is more conclusive than a witness".[4] We must concede then that here a consciousness of reality is experienced, and this not only in the magical attitude. Thus the dream differs from waking consciousness in three respects: (*1*) "the supporting pillar of conscious experience, while we are awake, the tension between subject and object" disappears;[5] (*2*) the dream orders events in a way which compared with the experience of the day is asyntactic:—it has a loose or "diffuse structure",[6] its images being arranged in accord with the feelings, anxieties and desires of the dreamer, as in the previously defined "catathymia";[7] (*3*) the dream world is sharply separated from daily reality: it is mythical, having neither past nor future.[8]

The dream itself, of course, is not within the religious category; nevertheless it is life: life is a dream, the dream a life. And it displays life to us in rendering the domination of the world first of all possible in the magical-mythical manner; and also by the way in which it appears in its profoundest depths at the very frontier of the mechanized consciousness. In Prospero's words:

> We are such stuff
> As dreams are made on, and our little life
> Is rounded with a sleep.

[1] *Das Odfeld (Sämtl. Werke*, 4, 90).   [2] Lévy-Bruhl, *Primitive Mentality*, 115.
[3] R. Thurnwald, *Die Lüge in der primitiven Kultur: Die Lüge*, edited by O. Lippmann, 1927, 398.   [4] Lévy-Bruhl, *ibid.*, 101.
[5] Storch, *op. cit.*, 25; not however in the manner of mysticism, since the dream lacks the element of passion.
[6] Werner, *Entw. Psych.* 41.   [7] Kretschmer, *op. cit.*, 57 *f*.
[8] Kretschmer, *ibid.*, 64 *ff*.   Binswanger, van der Leeuw, *Structure*.

R. Allier, *Le non-civilisé et nous*, 1927.

F. C. Bartlett, *Psychology and Primitive Culture*, 1923.

A. Bertholet, *Das Wesen der Magie (Nachr. der Ges. d. Wiss. zu Göttingen, Gesch. Mitt.,* 1926–27).

L. Binswanger, *Wandlungen in der Auffassung und Deutung des Traumes von den Griechen bis zur Gegenwart,* 1928.

F. Boas, *The Mind of Primitive Man.*

C. Clemen, *Wesen und Ursprung der Magie (Arch. f. Rel.-Psych.* II–III, 1921).

A. K. Coomaraswamy, *De la Mentalité Primitive (Études Traditionnelles,* 44, 1939).

Th. W. Danzel, *Kultur und Religion des primitiven Menschen,* 1924.
Die psychologischen Grundlagen der Mythologie (AR. 21, 1922).

F. Graebner, *Das Weltbild der Primitiven,* 1924.

E. Kretschmer, *Medizinische Psychologie*[2], 1922.

J. Lindworsky, *Die Primitiven und das kausale Denken (Int. Woche für Religionsethnologie,* IV. *Tagung,* 1926).

H. Prinzhorn, *Bildnerei der Geisteskranken*[2], 1923.

A. Storch, *Das archaisch-primitive Erleben und Denken der Schizophrenen,* 1922.

R. Thurnwald, *Zauber (in Lexikon der Vorgeschichte).*
Bequemes Denken (Inst. intern. d'anthropologie, III *Session,* 1927).

A. Vierkandt, *Die Anfänge der Religion und Zauberei (Globus,* 92, 1907).

K. Zeininger, *Magische Geisteshaltung im Kindesalter und ihre Bedeutung für die religiöse Entwicklung,* 1929.

CHAPTER 83

WAYS TO THE WORLD. THEORETICAL
DOMINATION

1. SIDE by side with the domination of the world by means of magic and of the creation of form appears that achieved by *thought*. "Thought is one of the powers of Being, in which fate breaks loose from itself; it is an existential power."[1] But by the term "thought" alone the type of world domination referred to here is quite inadequately characterized. For the magical and the mythical form-creating attitudes also presuppose thinking.[2] We must therefore add that in specifically *theoretical thought* man frees himself so far as is at all possible from the environing world, and moves as far as he can from it, in order to *observe* it from a suitable distance as disinterestedly as possible. Both the magical and the mythical attitudes, again, always eliminate the contrast between subject and object: here, on the contrary, it becomes strictly observed: I *direct* my own thoughts towards the world, and therefore we speak of *directed thought*.

This has the same relation to the magic-mythical as waking experience has to the dream; but after what has been said in the preceding Chapter it need hardly be added that this by no means implies a relation like that between reality and appearance. For both waking thought and dream thought are ways to the world; there is a day-dream just as there is a night-thought, the distinction being that in waking thought man directs himself expressly towards an object and reflects upon this, so as to elaborate some *theory*, while in the dream there is no absolute object whatever, and equally little any stable subject. We discover a transitional stage, however, in those sciences and modes of knowledge which certainly elevate man expressly above the totality of the world, yet nevertheless contemplate him too as a sort of "world" that is, as it were, the reverse of the external world. We have previously discussed

---

[1] Tillich, *Philosophie und Schicksal*, 310.

[2] This type of thought is very finely characterized by Pedersen, *Israel*, 75: "For the Israelite, thought is not the solution of abstract problems. It is not connected link by link, and does not elaborate principal and subordinate sentences in order to draw conclusions therefrom. *For the Israelite, to think is to make a totality his own.* He directs his soul towards the principal factor, the decisive element in the totality, and takes this into his soul, which is thus set in motion and led in a definite direction."

astrology, which allots man the status of a microcosm over against the Whole as a macrocosm;[1] I may also allude further to Indian thought, which certainly gives prominence to the human mind as the *ātman*, but only in order immediately to identify it again with the spirit of the Universe. This type of theory I call, in Oldenberg's term, "prescientific science";[2] and within these relationships astrology falls in virtue of its casting life into fixed cosmic rhythm, and Hindu speculation because of its magical type of knowledge: "knowledge is power".[3]

Thought however, even directed thought, is of course no prerogative of culture. Primitives also think: "thinkers think, they who dwell here in their world. Behind their fires those present speak together: what are we to do with our thoughts? how are we to speak with our words?" say the Cora Indians.[4] But civilized thought also, on the other hand, is never without primitive-magical-mythical elements: man can never wholly succeed in abstracting his own mind from the world. Indeed he often feels, and quite justifiably, that in this intellectual activity he is abusing his actual life.

Science, in our modern sense of the term, was born in Greece; and it is very remarkable how the magical-mythical attitude only gradually receded before that of theoretic knowledge. Thus for Pherecydes cosmogony fashions itself, imperceptibly and *quasi*-spontaneously, into the myth of the marriage of Zeus and Chthonia; the entire Ionian monism reposes, in fact, upon the idea of participation: one thing participates in another, otherwise it could have no influence whatever on it; primeval power again, the *arche*, sought by the Ionian philosophy of Nature, is essentially related to the *mana*-power that primitive peoples believe in;[5] the philosophy of Nature (and, with this, science in general) is indeed "born from mysticism".[6] But later, with Socrates and the sophists, the great change appeared. Man discovered himself, that is to say, his own spirit; and then he began to objectivize the world: Protagoras' dictum πάντων χρημάτων μέτρον ἄνθρωπος:—Man is the measure of all things—becomes the criterion of all knowledge.

[1] Chap. 7, 54.

[2] cf. *Vorwissenschaftliche Wissenschaft. Die Weltanschauung der Brahmann-Texte*, 1919.

[3] Oldenberg, *Lehre der Upanishaden*, 6 f. In *Begriffsform*, 15 ff., Cassirer gives an excellent and comprehensive description of mythical thought and prescientific science.

[4] Preuss, *Nayarit-Expedition*, I, 88; cf. A. Titius, *Der Ursprung des Gottesglaubens*, 357 f.   [5] Chap. 2.

[6] Joel, *Der Ursprung der Naturphilosophie aus dem Geiste der Mystik, passim.* cf. K. Kuiper, *Mythologie en Wetenschap*, 1919, 16, 27 f.   O. Gilbert, *Griechische Religionsphilosophie*, 1911, 29 ff., 36.

Man learns to form concepts, and from these he soon fashions the eternal Ideas. In Plato's magnificent myth at the end of the *Republic* "the entire force of mythical endowment with form is once more manifested"; nevertheless "we no longer stand on the territory of the myth. For in opposition to the ideas of mythical guilt and mythical destiny there arises here that fundamental Socratic principle, the concept of moral self-responsibility: the significance and essence of human life, and that which constitutes man's actual destiny, are transferred to his inner self."[1] But in the Socratic love of wisdom this moral self-responsibility is primarily knowledge of virtue:—insight; and thus man has erected his own power of judgment as the supreme Power.

2. "The purely theoretical person is only a construction":[2] theoretic form is always the receptacle of non-theoretic content, and knowledge is always far more than merely theoretical knowledge.[3] Even in the mental process of geometrical knowledge all the others cooperate, the esthetic in perceiving spherical form and the religious in the appreciation of its perfection, *etc.*[4] "In every psychical process mind in its entirety participates."[5] The theoretical attitude towards the world is therefore not merely a construction but is also a compulsion, equally of the spirit which refuses all too impetuously to accept what is given to it, and of the world, which in this way is conquered too conveniently; and it has quite justly been pointed out that in all the basal concepts of natural science the pale and faded anthropomorphisms are still apparent: —in other terms, they are all mythical.[6] With equal correctness it has been shown that philosophy does not spring forth from the categories of reason alone, but expresses a total life experience[7]. At the basis of all knowledge, then, there lies a faith;[8] and the theoretical path to the world is a way around faith or belief which takes its start, however, from precisely the same crisis of Power that aroused faith. Thus instead of the celebrated Fichtean dictum: "Science supersedes all Faith, and changes it into Sight",[9] it should be said that the faith that evoked

---

[1] Cassirer, *op. cit.*, II, 166.   [2] Spranger, *Lebensformen*, 122.
[3] *ibid.*, 92 f.   [4] *ibid.*, 48.
[5] *ibid.*, 48.   [6] Joel, *op. cit.*, 57.
[7] Grünbaum, *Herrschen und Lieben als Grundmotive der philosophischen Weltanschauungen*, 2 f.
[8] *ibid.*, 62, 121; *cf.* Brunner, *Gott und Mensch*, 6: "All metaphysics, and all philosophical belief in God, is the descendant of some religion, and lives much more from its impulses than from its own grounds."
[9] Fichte's *Popular Works*, II, 375 (W. Smith): "The Way Towards the Blessed Life", Lecture V.

science also abrogates it once more. Science itself, therefore, exists only in virtue of faith.

The Greeks, who invented the theoretic conquest of the world, were nevertheless not ignorant of this dependence of science upon faith. Not only was calm submission commended:

> The world's Wise are not wise,
> Claiming more than mortal may;[1]

but the mystic ground of all science was disclosed also: "For it does not admit of exposition like other branches of knowledge: but after much converse about the matter itself and a life lived together, suddenly a light, as it were, is kindled in our soul by a flame that leaps to it from another, and thereafter sustains itself."[2]

A. A. GRÜNBAUM, *Hersschen und Lieben als Grundmotive der philosophischen Weltanschauungen*, 1925.

K. JOËL, *Der Ursprung der Naturphilosophie aus dem Geiste der Mystik*, 1906.

[1] Euripides, *Bacchae*, 395 f. (Murray): τὸ σοφὸν δ'οὐ σοφία, τὸ τε μὴ θνητὰ φρονεῖν.

[2] Plato, Letter 7. Harward, *The Platonic Epistles*, 135.

CHAPTER 84

WAYS TO THE WORLD OBEDIENCE

1. EITHER by mythical-magical methods therefore, or theoretically, man transforms the world into *his* world, and himself into its sovereign: this is the profound religious basis of all culture.[1] But faith[2] is essentially hostile to every form of domination of the world without exception, since it regards this as rivalry with God, as *pseudo*-creation whether magical, mythical or rational, and opposes itself also to culture, even to that which is recognized as essentially religious, seeking its own way to the world.[3] It questions, in principle, all human control: even its own pronouncements, so far as these necessarily participate in culture, are immediately disqualified again by faith.[4]

The path of faith, then, is *obedience*. This implies that to speak about the Universe is first and foremost to speak about God: or in other words, *theology*. For antiquity the term "theology" indicated systematic, though not theoretical, discourse about deity, as this was carried on by poets and teachers; in this sense Hesiod, in his *Theogony*, and Orpheus were theologians.[5] The *logia* was a logically connected utterance—neither doctrine nor theory, however, but myth; while later, as we shall observe, myth intellectualized itself into dogma, and form became theory. But by this the peculiar character of all theology was scarcely changed in its essentials; and in any case man's spirit must discuss the uncontrolled, and the never to be controlled, formatively and rationally, explanatorily and abstractly. Theology then is no theory of the non-theoretic, and just as little an imparting of form to the formless: it involves speaking about the unspeakable. This is its own essential

---

[1] *cf.* Fichte: "The acquisition of this skill—partly to subdue and eradicate the improper tendencies which have arisen within us prior to the awakening of Reason and the consciousness of our own independence—partly to modify external things, and alter them in accordance with our ideas—the acquisition of this skill, I say, is called Culture." *Popular Works* (W. Smith), I, 181: "The Vocation of the Scholar", Lecture 1.   [2] Chap. 80.

[3] On the relative justification of the hostility between faith and theory *cf.* E. Spranger, *Der Kampf gegen den Idealismus*, 20.

[4] *cf.* Tillich, *Rel. Verwirklichung*, 13 *ff.*

[5] *cf.* Plato, *Republic*, 379a: "what is said about the gods"; *cf.* F. Kattenbusch, *Die Entstehung einer christlichen Theologie* (*Zeitschr. f. Theol. und Kirche*, N. F. 11, 1930), 163 *ff.*

and specific tension, whose ground consists in having salvation as its goal instead of domination, and faith as its starting-point instead of its own potency.[1] Whatever theology produces is indeed either form-endowment or theory, both being essentially myths, as I have already observed: but an impalpable form, a "form of grace".[2] In other terms: theology never has its object at its disposal; all that it deals with is questionable, and whatever it controls vanishes away; what is given to it with and in its object is impalpable, yet discernible. Here also a "dual experience of form" is attained, now as a controlled object, myth or theory, and again as a "form of grace".

2. Theology, further, is one form of preaching. The earliest Christianity had no theologians at all, but contemporary antiquity was quite familiar with them, in fact as the official festival preachers; in the cult associations the sermon or address was called *theologia*.[3] And theology has always preserved this character of being proclamation; in the knowledge of sacred objects (knowledge of God),[4] of rites and formulas of worship, its task was already declared; then it became an attempt to regulate these affairs and effect their mutual adjustment. Actually, however, such theology is only theogony: it is the product of the poets and thinkers of polytheism. Thus we can—in somewhat loose terms—speak of a Heliopolitan theology in ancient Egypt, because attempts were repeatedly made by the ancient city of Heliopolis to subject the whole world of the gods to the sun-god, and to draw every myth into the realm of the light-myth; the distinctive feature of this theology being syncretism. Examples of this adjustment are provided principally by the exegesis of the ancient traditional formulas, or of sacred writings.[5] "The Egyptian king Akhnaton summarizes his sun-theology in the name he assigns to his god. The old god *Shu* is at first retained, but identified with the new god *Aton*. Later he is eliminated; and in his place we find the elaboration of the 'father of *Ra* who has returned as *Aton*'."[6] This is theological reinterpretation and adjustment; and in its seventeenth Chapter the ancient Egyptian *Book of the*

---

[1] *cf.* Boulgakoff, *Orthodoxie*, 197: "This astonishment when confronted with the divine mysteries, which manifest themselves in the church, is also the principle animating theological activity, whether theoretic or practical."

[2] Tillich, *Rel. Verwirkl.* 51, 53, *cf.* 50.   [3] Chap. 27. Kattenbusch, *op. cit.*, 201 *f*.
[4] Chap. 72.   [5] Chap. 64.
[6] *cf.* H. Schäfer, *Amarna in Religion und Kunst*, 1931. G. van der Leeuw, *Achnaton*, 1927. Harnack has discussed the dangers of this theology of compromise: *History of Dogma*, IV, 341 *ff*.

Dead provides a very old commentary, which yields new meaning to the still older *Text*. Similarly the Zarathustrian *Avesta* gives fresh significance to the old god of the dead, Yima, "for whom it had no use", as the fatherly protector of the oldest humanity.[1] So, too, in the New Testament words from the Old were repeatedly introduced with new constructions. This interpretative activity of theology is of long standing; we discover it at a very early period operating in the practice of delivering oracles, and Plutarch calls the interpreters of the utterances of the Pythia οἱ Δελφῶν θεολόγοι—the theologians of Delphi.[2] More remote from the genuine essence of theology is the scientific contemplation of religion, which applies to it general philosophical ideas; and frequently it seems as though theology is nothing more than the adaptation of religious data to the prevailing philosophic world-view. Of this, in antiquity, the Stoics provided the clearest example, and in modern times the so-called liberal theology, which is almost completely oriented to Kantian philosophy. The path to the world is then literally the same as that of theoretical contemplation: religion is taken into account only in so far as is compatible with attaining the goal of world domination; and for this very reason faith, as the renunciation in principle of all world control, can find no place here.

The precondition of genuine theology is the existence of the church :[3] the church is the place for logically connected utterances about faith. Whatever has been displayed, or is being exhibited, in religion, is then investigated for its redemptive content. Myth, doctrine, law, rite, are all examined as to their significance for human salvation. "From the mass of myths there then stands forth the ἱερὸς λόγος, the sacred story of salvation;[4] of the many rites, sacrament and sacrifice come forward into full light; and the community becomes regarded as the church bringing salvation. From the sacred writings a canon is demarcated; each individual factor that has been received is tested for its connection with revelation. A theology, in this comprehensive sense, exists only where there is a church, in Christianity, although tendencies towards it appear in many places."[5]

3. The path to the world, therefore, is here a road by way of God; and thus it must be an approach to the world in obedience, starting from what God has done for the world. In Christianity therefore, as the

---

[1] Chantepie, *op. cit.*, II, 215.
[2] *On the Cessation of the Oracles*, 15; *cf.* Chap. 54, and *RGG. Theologie*, I.
[3] Chap. 36.   [4] Chap. 61.   [5] *RGG. Theologie*, I.

sole religion possessing a theology, this is in the first place creation, and secondly re-creation, liberation through the Incarnation of Christ. These two principles may certainly be distinguished, but not separated.

To seek the world in this manner, still further, is to discover history. If it be true that "the powers of history forbid an objective and commanding attitude to whoever sets out to know the world",[1] it is no less true that the attitude of obedience renders these historical potencies accessible. In its profoundest sense history is always the history of God. "There is such a thing as a human story; and there is such a thing as the divine story which is also a human story . . . every short story does truly begin with creation and end with a last judgment."[2] Historical contemplation of the world, then, begins only with the experience of the facts of salvation. Primitive peoples know merely a primal event in the background of the Universe;[3] the Hindu attitude to the world is completely unhistorical, and a timeless knowledge conditions salvation. For the peoples of antiquity, again, all events were accommodated within one settled and typical scheme: the king can do nothing but overthrow his enemies; on his gravestone an official's life is always described as exemplary in one and the same way; and whenever man reflects on the contemporary world, it is always a time of adversity in comparison with the past,[4] while the Greek spirit was by far the most thoroughly unhistorically attuned.[5] History commences with Abraham, for in his story God's saving Will manifests itself for the first time; subsequently, the festivals of the eternal periodicity of life are changed into celebrations of God's deeds. The Feast of the Passover celebrates the deliverance from Egypt, while in *Psalm* cxxvi the "salvation" produced by the harvest is transformed into the historical salvation of the return from exile.[6] Jahveh is the God of history, of his own history, which he experiences with his people.[7] Christianity is Israelite also in the sense that its God is a God in history (whose antithesis would be Power, such as is found in India, arising from a complete lack of the historical vein, and crushing life completely).[8] Windelband acutely remarks that the historical consciousness displays itself for the first time in the Christian representation of the world, which sets the facts of the fall and of liberation at the focal point of

[1] Tillich, *op. cit.*, 73.   [2] Chesterton, *The Everlasting Man*, 284 f.
[3] Chap. 18.
[4] cf. A. de Buck, *Het typische en het individueele by de Egyptenaren*, 1929.
[5] Cassirer, *op. cit.*, II, 151 f.
[6] Chap. 56.   [7] Söderblom, *Nat. Theologie*, 97 ff.   [8] Chap. 22.

world events;[1] and thus Christianity refuses to regard the significance
of the world as detached from salvation.[2] What is disclosed in history
therefore, and what proclaims itself to conscience as God's Will, are
ultimately the same; this, it is true, is revealed only to faith; and its
purpose is the "rendering the historic eternal, and making the eternal
historical".[3] But this is a miracle, and indeed the miracle of the assumption of human form, of *Incarnation*.

4. Just as little as man is a dominating soul in a controlled body[4]
is the Universe a ruling spirit in a world-realm that would be, as it
were, its kingdom, its stuff. Like man, the Universe too is a *creation*,
creatura. When man reflects upon himself, he certainly appears to
himself as one advancing along a path to the world; but he knows full
well that it is not he but God Who is traversing this road; God is
the actual subject of all theology.[5] So when man himself desires to seek
his way to the world nothing remains for him but following after God:[6]
and for this he stands in need of *revelation*.

---

[1] *Präludien*, II[6], 1919, 156. The idea of a criticism of our own times (*Zeitkritik*),
also, "has its root in the Christian concept of the whole of history as coordinated in
accord with a plan of salvation". K. Jaspers, *Die geistige Situation der Zeit*[2], 1931, 7;
cf. further Ad. Bauer, *Vom Judentum zum Christentum*, 1917.

[2] Frick; *cf. Rel. Gesch.* 25.   [3] Kierkegaard.   [4] Chap. 45.

[5] *cf*. Piper, *Ethik*, I, 252, Note 1.   [6] Chap. 73.

CHAPTER 85

GOALS OF THE WORLD. REVELATION. MAN AS THE GOAL

1. BEFORE revelation Phenomenology comes to a halt. It may seem strange that what is "revealed" can never "appear"; and yet this is not so remarkable as we might anticipate. For the "appearance" of any phenomenon as such, that is in the sense of the familiar contrast between Appearance and Reality, must undoubtedly be essentially different from that Self-disclosure of God with which revelation is concerned. In part, experience is an affair of phenomena;[1] and this holds true equally of the experience of revelation. Yet this itself, and in principle, remains wholly withdrawn from our view: it is no making known, no manifestation nor exhibition. "Only what essentially is concealed, and accessible by no mode of knowledge whatsoever, is imparted by revelation. But in thus being revealed it does not cease to remain concealed, since its secrecy pertains to its very essence; and when therefore it is revealed it is so precisely as that which is hidden."[2] Tillich's extremely apposite words are sufficiently clear; and to adopt religious phraseology, in revelation something is disclosed to me that no eye has ever seen—not even mine! I hear something that no ear has ever heard—not even my ear! Something is prepared for me which has entered no human heart—not even my own heart! Only the phenomenon, as such, can appear to my reason;[3] but it is impossible, owing to the essential conditions of the situation, to understand revelation,[4] since a revelation comprehended would not be one. Any "insight" I may have, even if it comes to me suddenly and with coercive clearness, is therefore far from being a revelation, but is at best the "appearance" to me of some phenomenon; so that all reports about "illumination", or of connections disclosed to us "like a revelation", are mere metaphor, and a bad one at that. With the data of so-called occultism,[5] again, revelation is still less concerned; at most these could yield an expansion of our knowledge,

---

[1] Chap. 67.
[2] Tillich, *Die Idee der Offenbarung, Zeitschr. für Theol. und Kirche*, N.F. 8, 406.
[3] *cf.* further Chap. 107.
[4] "To understand" means here, of course, "rational or intellectual comprehension"; *in faith* the revelation is certainly understood, only not as any insight attained by man but as illumination bestowed by God.
[5] Or, as it appears to be termed to-day, Parapsychology.

but in no degree any deepening of our understanding, to say nothing of imparting what surpasses our reason. Neither does the appeal to some sort of religious *a priori*, nor to some religious fundamental principle, avail: it may certainly account for man's own religious predisposition, but not for the "Wholly Other" communicated in revelation. Finally, the distinction between a "general" revelation to everyone, and a "special" revelation bestowed upon the faithful alone and in some particular way, is very mischievous. For in so far as it is always originally given to myself, revelation is never "general" but always "special". When therefore we refer to some universal revelation, for example in Nature or history, this implies only that Nature and history appear to the majority of mankind as media of revelation simply because they have already become an actual revelation to so many. But someone or other must have been the first, and for him revelation was in no sense "general", as little as it is so for me if I do not regard Nature or history as mere modes of revelation, but actually experience them. As phenomenologists, therefore, we must regard as valid revelation whatever presents itself as such. We can attempt to differentiate solely between genuine and spurious *experience* of revelation, and to separate the derived or the counterfeit from the original and essential type. *Revelation is the act of God.* Only he to whom something has been done, or something has happened on the part of God, may speak of it: "for he that is mighty hath done to me great things".[1] The phenomenologist can only discuss what is reported to him; he can listen for the authentic sounds and describe the objects wherein, according to the believer's own statements, revelation has for him been effected.

2. For revelation is consummated in an *object*: it has its proper medium. This however does not become some kind of divine entity by thus subserving revelation, just as little as the self-revealing loses its essential secrecy by so revealing itself in an object, or committing itself to some medium.[2] Here we meet once more almost all those objects which, in variegated procession, have already passed before our eyes: a *thing* or *place*, a *time* or *person*, is *sacred* precisely by virtue of its relation to revelation. In all these objects some Power reveals Itself which, however, does not display Itself, because essentially It always remains concealed, "Wholly Other".

We have seen[3] how primitive man, in his characteristically empirical fashion and without any theory whatsoever, experiences Power; *mana*,

---

[1] *Luke* i. 49.   [2] *cf.* Tillich, *loc. cit.*, 409 *f.*   [3] Chap. 1.

in objects. Some object, for example, becomes tabu in virtue of its character as a medium of revelation and, whenever this relationship to revelation is permanent, eventually a fetish. Here the experience of revelation occurs, as it were, from moment to moment and has no further consequences. The chief, for instance, has power, and some extraordinary fullness of the sacred "reveals" itself in him: but when age enfeebles him, then he has obviously lost his power and is therefore no longer a bearer of revelation.

Revelation through *oracles*, in the next place, is no longer entirely "primitive".[1] For primitive man all occurrences may be oracles and indicate a road to him; but to those no longer wholly primitive the way is shown only at definite places, and oracles are then consulted in some locality that has been proved to be sacred. This behaviour therefore involves some relaxation of the purely empirical consciousness of revelation: man no longer discovers the way by himself; neither powerful persons nor potent events (rites) suffice to discover the correct path. The oracle, then, is something special, set apart, which surprises him a little; the great mass of objects, actions, persons, *etc.*, is no medium of revelation, and indeed hardly can be such. Thus to the genuinely primitive individual any stone on which he steps is in certain circumstances an oracle[2]; he who is no longer wholly primitive, on the other hand, must journey to some special stone, perhaps to the *ka'ba*, in order to find the essential revelation. Here, still further, there arises the idea of miracle as something markedly exceptional. For from the primitive mind the sense of the completely impossible is absent: "what we should call miraculous appears to primitives commonplace, and though it may cause them emotion it does not readily surprise them. . . . We might say that he lives in miracles, were it not that it is essential to the definition of a miracle that it shall be something exceptional. To him, miracles are of daily occurrence, and his medicine-man can make almost as many of them as he likes."[3] In the realms of semi-culture and of civilization, however, conditions are different, although in antiquity everything that happened "could be conceived as a miracle, even when it followed a wholly natural course". At that period therefore the boundary line between miracles and the non-miraculous was very unsettled, and the decision on the matter was left to man;[4] but still

---

[1] Chap. 54. For the Hebrew *Bath-Kol*, which comes from heaven like the ark, table and lamp, *cf.* A. Marmorstein, *AR.* 28, 1930, 286 *ff.*
[2] Chap. 3.   [3] Lévy-Bruhl, *Primitives and the Supernatural*, 5, 34.
[4] Weinreich, *Ant. Heilungswunder*, VII *f.*

it was arrived at in accordance with the criterion of revelation:—what does an event declare about the god or about divine activity? Thus the miracle is really a "sign": the element of astonishment (wonder, miracle, τέρας, Egyptian *bja-t*, Hebrew פלא) accompanies the significance of powerfulness (δύναμις, ἀρετή) and token (σημεῖον, Hebrew אות). For the primitive mind, then, even the simple fact that it is raining may be a "marvel" of God;[1] it is merely a matter of the facts themselves declaring that they are media of revelation. The word goes forth to man:

> Listen to this, O Job, stand still,
> Think of the wonders of God.[2]

"At its deepest roots belief in miracles declares nothing other than: 'there is a living God' ":[3] certain objects, events and persons are, as it were, given prominence as against the world as a whole. Space for example, at some definite spot, becomes for man a "position" in the sense of Chapter 57; and from this viewpoint it may be said that certain experiences are thrown into relief within the experiential whole and called miracles, in the sense of being acts of God.

It is in itself, then, no prejudice whatever to the essence of miracle that it becomes conceived more and more as a rarity, and ultimately as a fact directly opposed to the course of the world and contrary to Nature. For this transposition is connected with the general transformation from the magical-mythical attitude to the theoretic, which has been previously discussed.[4] To primitive man, once again, everything can be a miracle, to the modern almost nothing; if however he does believe in miracles is his faith then all the more passionate. But a real injury to belief in miracles is done as soon as the rarity and the amazing element in miracle outweigh its character as a sign, for then miracle entirely loses its revelatory content, and therewith its very essence. The founders of great religions, therefore, warn against the mania for miracles, as in the case of Jesus and Buddha;[5] the marvel, in this its miraculous sense, may certainly still remain a medium of revelation, but it may also involve an obstacle to faith, equally in

[1] *Job* v. 9 f.   [2] *Job* xxxvii. 14 (Moffat).
[3] Joh. Wendland, *Der Wunderglaube im Christentum*, 1910, 1; *cf.* 60.
[4] Chap. 82, 85.
[5] *Mark* viii. 12. "When an *arhat* flew through the air, Buddha is represented as rebuking him: 'This will not conduce either to the conversion of the unconverted, or to the increase of the converted, but rather to those who have not been converted remaining unconverted, and to the turning back of those who have been converted'." J. A. MacCulloch, *ERE.* VIII, 676 *ff.*

theory as in practice; and of the second possibility Björnson's drama *Beyond Human Power* constitutes an impressive example:[1] Pastor Sang rests all his faith on the required miracle: but in this only human will, increased to colossal proportions, is manifested:—the will "beyond human power", the magic will. And when the miracle proves to be a failure, this betrays itself in the childlike words of the miracle priest: "But this was not the meaning of it—?"

As miracle becomes more and more strikingly exceptional, again, the objects in which Power reveals itself recede into the ever more remote and immaterial distance: solid fetishes become fleeting images of the dream, of illumination, of the vision. The dream has already been discussed;[2] and in Greek antiquity dream revelation was something very ordinary.[3] We have previously seen, too, how the young Red Indian, prepared by a prolonged fast, goes into solitude in order to become acquainted with his *nagual*, his individual totem, in a dream-like vision,[4] while the illuminations and visions of Buddha, Mohammed, St. Paul and of many other minor founders and reformers are universally known. As the type of vision in general that of Moses may serve:—the burning bush which becomes the medium of revelation.

In all these cases, then, the steadily expanding theorizing emphasizes the exceptional character of revelation. But just as happens in worship, man can attempt to regulate revelation too: in celebration, for instance, the god reveals himself to his people at specific times; he has his epiphany and his *epidemia*; "for an angel went down at a certain season into the pool, and troubled the water".[5] Thus in sacrament[6] or sermon,[7] at this or that definite place, man can be sure of the self-imparting of God; and almost all religious phenomena, in fact, subsist in relation to the experience of revelation. Among these, revelation in *words* occupies a very prominent place. And this is frequently flight from the burdensome concretely material into some rarer sphere which is apparently closer to the immaterial and is, still further, personal. But this is merely "apparently" since, even at its very highest, revelation in words cannot actually dispense with the object. Similarly in spiritual-evangelical Christianity, however passionately it may seek the spiritual-personal, some vestige is disclosed which is not merged in the word itself, and which leads to the doctrine of the sacrament. But neither is the word itself immaterial. For it presupposes a speaker[8] who personally exercises

[1] Act I.   [2] Chap. 82.   [3] Weinreich, *Heilungswunder*.
[4] Chap. 8.   [5] *John* v. 4.   [6] Chap. 52.
[7] Chap. 28, 61.   [8] Chap. 27.

his function, and appeals therefore not to the visual but to the auditory, and subsequently to man's intellectual and moral capacities. Here, therefore, the more man relinquishes the primitive, the more does everything become inward: even the voice coming from heaven, as in St. Paul's vision, and the general hallucinatory condition of being directly spoken to, are still too "material". Thus the "inner voice", frequently associated with conscience,[1] and also the "inner light", are intended to be media of revelation that are wholly invisible and immaterial; and in this an inclination to mysticism manifests itself. The object must now be excluded: any medium is burdensome; revelation, as it were, must hover in the air. Of course there are various transitional forms here, in which inward perception of God's voice is associated with an outward one, and even with an objective vision: in the revelation of God upon Sinai, for instance, while the whole stress of the narrative falls on the intellectual and moral content of the revelation,[2] nevertheless Moses and Aaron "see" the Lord. But however this may be, flight from the material never succeeds completely and—what is more important—it never actually becomes flight from the objective. Human experience is—perhaps!—less "material" than the "life of sense". But it is no less objective—expressed in religious terms: no less on "this side", no less earthly and transient. Man cannot wholly elude the medium of revelation.

3. But he does his best! In Pietism and its related tendencies, for example, the miracle *par excellence* is the believer's own inner *experience*:

> Mercy has come to me,
> Mercy of which I was unworthy;
> And this I account *miraculous*.[3]

But the great, indeed the sole, miracle is *conversion*,[4] the experience of salvation; and Günther is quite correct in suggesting that this "transposition" of miracle was necessitated by pietism having passed through the period of the Enlightenment.[5] This was certainly one of the conditions: but the fundamental reason lies in the tendency towards spiritualizing, towards the exclusion of the object of revelation, a tendency wholly independent of historical conditions which has influenced theology too. One of its typical representatives is Wilhelm Herrmann. Seeberg had asserted that "to experience this miracle of

---

[1] Chap. 66.   [2] *Exodus* xxiv.   [3] Ph. Fr. Hiller.
[4] Chap. 79.   [5] *Jung-Stilling*, 76.

rebirth and conversion is to enter into the sphere of the miraculous by virtue of *one's own individual experience*";[1] and Herrmann adds: "Our true aim is that the person to whom the redeeming love of God in Christ appears *should find his own life becoming more and more a miracle*."[2] For this tendency towards the non-objective, then, special "revelations" ultimately become quite indifferent:—the written word, the locality which has become a "position", sacred time *etc*. But those to whom such "experiences" occur readily forget that they too are objective. Thus in pietistic and methodist circles the idea of guidance is cherished; but this guidance can reach men only by means of certain events which must then be regarded as the media of revelation. Self-deception, which looks on whatever is gratifying as guidance while all that is disagreeable is temptation, is certainly not excluded here, and not infrequently leads to tragic conflicts. It cannot therefore be sufficiently emphasized that revelation is concerned not with any antithesis between external and internal,[3] but with that between man and God, or what is essentially rational and comprehensible on the one hand and what is essentially irrational and incomprehensible on the other.

4. Here, however, a certain rationalization obtrudes itself; for we must necessarily speak of the unutterable, and discuss the essentially concealed, as though it had not been genuinely revealed but displayed or demonstrated. Thus dogma, doctrine and law are frequently regarded as imparting definite religious content, and so cause man to forget that the content of genuine revelation can always be only God Himself. So it was that the great revelation systems arose, whatever rites, myths and customs already subsisted in a community being proclaimed anew as "revelation". This certainly never happened without an actual revelatory experience of some great founder—of a Moses, Mohammed, Zarathustra—enriching whatever had been previously received and invigorating this with fresh energy, and often indeed with a new spirit; and in this connection the extremely important task of the *mediator of revelation* is disclosed.[4] This mediator, still further, may ultimately himself become the content of revelation, as in Christianity.[5] His figure then constitutes the object of revelation, the miracle, the pre-condition of all other secondary "revelations".

---

[1] W. Herrmann, *Offenbarung und Wunder*, 1908, 53.
[2] *ibid.*, 63; *cf.* 49, 57 f., 70; further, Bultmann, *Glaube und Verst.* 220 ff.
[3] Chap. 67.   [4] Chap. 101, 106.   [5] Chap. 106.

Conversely, again, the object of revelation may become extended over the whole of Reality. Monism and pantheism follow this direction, and then primitive conditions return to a certain extent. Certainly theory rules here without any restraint: not every object *can* be an object of revelation, but every object *is* so in virtue of the divinity residing within it. We have only to contemplate it from the correct angle, that is in its own divine aspect, and then miracle is "the religious name for whatever happens".[1] An extreme, but very characteristic, type of this experience of revelation is the great poet Whitman:

> I find letters from God dropt in the street.
> These with the rest, one and all, are to me miracles,
> The whole referring, yet each distinct and in its place.
> Why, who makes much of a miracle?
> As to me I know of nothing else but miracles.[2]

N. Söderblom, *Offenbarung* (*Int. Wochenschrift* 10. Dezbr. 1910).

P. Tillich, *Die Idee der Offenbarung* (*Zeitschr. für Theol. und Kirche*, N. F. 8, 1927).

O. Weinreich, *Antike Heilungswunder*, 1909.

[1] Schleiermacher.
[2] *Leaves of Grass*. "Song of Myself", 48; "Autumn Rivulets", "Miracles".

CHAPTER 86

GOALS OF THE WORLD. REVELATION.
THE WORLD AS THE GOAL

1. WE have previously observed how sacred life pursues a cycle and renews itself periodically.[1] The world too can revolve in one and the same orbit: it then includes its goal within itself and reveals to man its own powerfulness.

The fairy story, for example, reckons with periods of a century: the wight who has been all but released says sorrowfully to the fairy tale hero, who has just missed saving him: "now I must wander about for another hundred years"; and a century later the event is repeated. Between these critical points, however, fairy tale time is quite empty: nothing at all happens: nothing begins and nothing ends. It runs: "once upon a time", not: "there was at that time", and concludes: "they lived happily for a long time, and if they are not dead then they are still alive to-day", not: "and then at last they died". The self-revealing world, then, has neither beginning nor end: it is a circle.

So it was to the Greeks. The Greek mind dared to conceive the idea of eternal *repetition*, not merely of the individual life as in Orphism, but of the life of the Universe. So in Stoic doctrine the worlds, which are absolutely identical with one another, follow each other eternally, and the rhythm from the primeval fire to the world conflagration (ἀποκατάστασις) remains eternally the same.[2] As in Heracleitus: "This world (cosmos) the same for all, was not made by any god or man, but was always, and is, and shall be an everliving Fire, with measures of it kindling and measures being extinguished."[3] Here, therefore, the Universe cannot be the "object" of a revelation, it can "mean" nothing whatever: it is only itself.

Astrology, again, proceeded in just the same way. It derived all events without exception from the eternal movement of the Universe, destroying all that is specific and significant in favour of the eternal sameness subsisting at its base. To the ancient Babylonians, indeed, the writing of the heavens was a revelation; but it revealed merely itself. In India, finally, revelation is completely merged in insight

---

[1] Chap. 22. [2] *cf.* Windelband, *History of Philosophy*, 178 *ff.*
[3] *Frag.* 30, Diels (Cornford).

into the void, the unreality of the Universe. Here too the fairy story is completely divested of all its historical vestiges; Buddha narrates fairy tales: "When the master had imparted this instruction, he explained the truths and connected the Jataka (birth story); at that time Ananda was the Brahman (from the fairy tale), Sariputta was the divinity, the Buddha community was the assembly, but the wise Senaka was myself."[1] Here "then" and "there" have completely disappeared and all meaning become impossible. The Universe reveals itself, that is to say, its impotence; and Chesterton, who here as so often shows profound phenomenological insight, has observed somewhat inexactly, but on the whole appropriately: "To the Buddhist or the eastern fatalist existence is a science or a plan, which must end up in a certain way. But to a Christian existence is a *story*, which may end up in any way."[2] In other words: in the one case the Universe displays itself as a story, in the other as a process: on the one hand as the object of revelation, the sign of transcendent Power, on the other as revelation, as Power itself . . . or as impotence!

2. In revealing itself as a circle, further, the Universe is eternal. It can have no purpose of any kind: it can merely exist, and in it all Power is amassed. Man is then a part of the Universe: more he cannot become; he can only become aware that he pertains to the world, and can "celebrate" it in thought and imagery, though scarcely in worship. "What foolish person will appeal to some external and outer motive force? Who will assert that these limbs move of themselves? Who will be content with any prior or intermediate entity, subsisting between the soul and that which is moved? As for the soul itself, though it is an incorporeal substance, it is yet wholly contained within the whole and in every part thereof, just as the voice and the word are in each of the senses of those whom it reaches."[3] The tendency towards this revelation of the Universe as Power was already evident in the thought of the ancient Ionian philosophers; their *archai* or "origins" were regarded as the living, divine, primeval substance of the world, and its manifold activities derived from the eternally unchanging and immutable.[4]

[1] Lüders, *Buddh. Märchen*, 75 *et passim*. Chap. 22, 61.
[2] *Orthodoxy*, "The Romance of Orthodoxy", 250.
[3] Giordano Bruno, *De Immenso*, XV; *cf.* Goethe's lines, p. 185:
    What were a God, who outward force applying . . .
[4] *cf.* Rohde, *Psyche*, II, 142 *f*. E. T. 364 *f*. Joël, *Naturphilosophie*.

Here there certainly is revelation, because the actual divine essence of the Universe never unveils itself: it remains mysterious and essentially concealed. Euripides expresses this very finely in the marvellous prayer of which we have already spoken:[1]

> Thou deep Base of the World, and thou high Throne
> Above the World, whoe'er thou art, unknown
> And hard of surmise, Chain of Things that be,
> Or Reason of our Reason; God, to thee
> I lift my praise, seeing the silent road
> That bringeth justice ere the end be trod
> To all that breathes and dies.[2]

Thus the world is "the living garment of God"; this no longer has its own powerfulness, distinguished from the Universe, but is nothing more than just the Power of the world.[3] It no longer has a name of its own: a name is "sound and smoke" and by a colossal "transposition" the hymn phraseology, which adds name to name and as a precaution includes at the close the unknown god,[4] becomes the pantheistic apostrophe of Aeschylus: "Zeus, whate'er he be".[5] The impenetrable mystery of the Universe is certainly recognized; but he who sustains its "deep Base" is the same as he who has his "high Throne above the World"; he is the god, Zeus, and the world-reason. Again to return, in conclusion, to Bruno-Goethe:

> He from within lives through all Nature rather,
> Nature and Spirit fostering each other;
> So that what in Him lives, and moves, and is,
> Still feels His power, and owns itself still His.[6]

3. Against this fine faith, however, there repeatedly opposes itself that religion which seeks purpose wholly apart from the Universe, in God;[7] thus the religion of creation strives with the religion of birth:

---

[1] Chap. 2.

[2] *The Trojan Women*, 883 *ff.* (Murray); *cf.* Joel, *op. cit.*, 112 *f.* Diels, *Vorsokratiker*, I, 423 *f.* on the *arche*, here referred to, of Diogenes of Apollonia. Wilamowitz, *Gr. Trag.* III, 282 *f.* H. Diels, *Zeus*, AR. 22, 1923–24, 14. L. Parmentier and H. Grégoire, *Euripide* IV, 1925, 63, Note 3. Joel, *Geschichte der antiken Philosophie*, I, 637. Ferd. Dümmler, *Kl. Schriften*, I, 1901, 163, 174, 190, 209. G. van der Leeuw, *Een dramatische geloofsbelydenis, Hermeneus II*, 1929.

[3] *cf.* Marie Gothein, *AR.* 9, 1906, 337 *ff.*   [4] Chap. 17.

[5] *cf.* Kurt Latte, *AR.* 20, 1921–22, 275 and Note 2; further: Wilamowitz, *Gr. Trag.* III, 283.   [6] *Prooemium.* "God, Soul and World."   [7] Chap. 85.

the religion of the Father with that of the Mother.[1] "The main point of
Christianity was this: that Nature is not our mother: Nature is our
sister. We can be proud of her beauty, since we have the same father;
but she has no authority over us; we have to admire, but not to imitate.
. . . Nature was a solemn mother to the worshippers of Isis and
Cybele. Nature was a solemn mother to Wordsworth or to Emerson.
But . . . to St. Francis, Nature is a sister, and even a younger sister:
a little, dancing sister, to be laughed at as well as loved."[2] But apart
from the Jewish-Christian sphere, creation is not at all creation in the
literal sense, but a birth. Life generates itself: the deity is a mother,
eternally giving birth and eternally bringing back the living again into
her womb.[3] Still more logical is the primeval Egyptian myth of the
self-espousal of the god Atmu.[4] He is the god "who satisfied himself
by his own hand", and even this extremely offensive idea involves a
highly important value for a *Weltanschauung*: as Schäfer justly remarks,
self-espousal is a crude conception of the maternal earth, a figure in
other respects unknown in ancient Egypt.[5] The idea of self-espousal,
indeed, is even more appropriate than that of the eternally bearing
mother: for everything occurs in the mighty god-world-being itself;
the one who conceives is also the impregnator.

The various myths which regard the Universe as emerging from
the body of some primeval giant present yet another *Weltanschauung*,
and an attempt to fix a "beginning" where essentially there can be
no beginning.[6] In the *Edda* Ymir, in Babylon Tiamat, in China Pawn-ku
and in India Purusha are the original beings whose limbs form parts of
the world. In India, still further, this origin of the Universe is conceived
as a mode of sacrifice, the giant being sacrificed and his limbs ritually
dissected.[7] Prajapati, again, the world creator in the *Brahmanas*, brings
forth the world from himself; first of all the waters emanate from him,
and then he lays his seed therein which becomes the golden egg
from which he himself is born.[8] Thus everything here happens wholly
"of itself", from its own nature, as birth or at best as emanation, not
as creation. "Separation or emanation emphasizes the relationship
between the originator and man, and is therefore preferred by a

---

[1] Chap. 15, 25.   [2] Chesterton, *Orthodoxy*, "The Eternal Revolution", 205.
[3] Chap. 10.   [4] *Pyramidentexte* (Sethe), 1248.
[5] H. Schäfer, *Ägyptische und heutige Kunst und Weltgebäude der alten Ägypter*, 1928,
107. The expression *ḥtp–dt*, "satisfied by his own hand", was applied to the creator
Ptah; *cf.* A. Wiedemann, *AR.* 21, 1922, 448.
[6] Alviella, *op. cit.*, 236 ff.   [7] Oldenberg, *Religion des Veda*, 270.
[8] J. S. Speyer, *De indische Theosophie en wy*, 37.

mysticism and pietism for which it is above all a matter of a fusion of humanity and divinity; while fabrication and creation stress the free act of will of the originator, and commend themselves to a belief in God which is profoundly agitated by the personal operation and Power of Deity."[1]

[1] Söderblom, *Gottesglaube*, 151. Chap. 21.

CHAPTER 87

GOALS OF THE WORLD. REVELATION.
GOD AS THE GOAL

1.   Among men I discovered this to be the highest knowledge—
              That the Earth was not, nor the Heaven above,
              Nor tree nor mountain,
              Nor any star, nor shining sun,
              Nor radiant moon, nor glorious ocean.
              When there was nought of limit and boundary,
              Then existed the one almighty God,
              The gentlest of men, and with him
              Many glorious spirits, and holy God.[1]

This so-called "Wessobrunn Prayer", an Old German poem from
a MS. of the ninth century, speaks in Christian language of the time
when there was "nought of limit and boundary", when the "Universe"
did not yet exist and God alone was there with His holy spirits. Here
therefore a *beginning* is assigned to the world in contrast to God; at
one time the world was not: not so with God. Consequently man rises
here to an *eschaton*, to an uttermost boundary of the Universe in its
entirety: he disregards both his own existence and that of the world,
seeking his goal neither in himself nor in the Universe. The "history"
in which he lives is certainly his own peculiar element, from which he
cannot disengage himself; but it began at some time or other. There
existed something "before" this commencement, and there will be
something "after" its end. And the description of the primeval condition,
in which whatever we know as existent was not yet present, frequently
occurs in the myths of all peoples. Usually too it includes a dim presage
of some better state of things, nearer to the divine. But the world that
preceded the world is also described without this longing for a better
Universe; in the myth of the Maya people, for example: "there were
neither men nor animals, no birds nor fish, no crabs, no trees and no
stones; there were neither caves nor gorges, neither plants nor forests.

---

[1] G. Ehrismann, *Geschichte der deutschen Literatur bis zum Ausgang des Mittelalters*,
I, 1918, 133; *cf.* K. Müllenhoff and W. Scherer, *Denkmäler deutscher Poesie und Prosa
aus dem VIII. bis XII. Jahrh.*[3], 1892, II, 1.   W. von Unwerth and Th. Siebs, *Geschichte
der deutschen Literatur bis zur Mitte des elften Jahrhunderts*, 1920, 149.

The heavens alone existed. The face of the earth was not yet visible, and the sea alone lay silent there under the wide expanse of heaven. There was not yet anything that coagulated or cohered, nothing which formed itself into strata nor formed a thread, nothing that had caused a rustling or a sound under the heavens. There was absolutely nothing there. . . . Everything was calm and motionless in darkness and night. One alone, Tepeu Gucumatz, existed: at once builder and generator, mother and father. . . ."[1]

Now the concept of the absolute non-being of what exists is altogether beyond human power; the Maya example is instructive also in this respect, since heaven and the sea are already present, and the earth too, although it is not yet visible. Creation therefore presents here the character of *arrangement* or *ordering*, of stratification of material which somehow or other is already present, a building up from stuff already provided; and thus the world creator is the demiurge,[2] the director, who overcomes chaos. Even the Old Testament, which places creation at the very beginning, does not escape the idea of chaos and describes the work of creation as a labour in several stages which, out of chaos, gradually forms the cosmos; while in other Old Testament allusions to creation (the struggle with the monster of chaos, *etc.*)[3] there survives the idea found elsewhere, according to which the demiurge subdues chaos. In this respect, still further, the light myth[4] has deeply influenced the creation myth: Marduk, who slays Tiamat, and Ra, who kills the Apap serpent, are light-gods who expel chaotic darkness. A different conception of the work of the demiurge is the Egyptian:— the potter making vessels, which occurs in the Old Testament also; here too there is some sort of foundation material that is utilized by the creator.

In these creation myths man struggles, as it were, with what is given apart from his own cooperation,[5] with the world just as he happens to find it, and tries to rise to belief in a deed which itself may be not "of this world". Certainly he cannot exclude himself and his world; but he does his utmost to follow the path of obedience to its end, to place the world's end and goal in God alone, and to experience revelation as a genuine act of God. In this connection, however, dogma can speak more clearly than myth; and in dogma *creatio ex nihilo* is asserted,

[1] W. Krickeberg, *Märchen der Azteken und Inkaperuaner, Maya und Muisca*, 1928, 121.

[2] Similarly in Plato's well-known account of creation, *Timaeus*, 30 ff.

[3] H. Gunkel, *Schöpfung und Chaos, in Urzeit und Endzeit*[2], 1921.   [4] Chap. 7.

[5] Chap. 21.

certainly in despite of all that is discernible.[1] For as soon as Will and
Form receive their due recognition, the "Nought" gives way and the
creator again becomes a demiurge. Thus the truly creative deed, as
the self-surrender of God, is given to *faith*—neither to reason nor to
utterance.

In all this, however, creation is never any explanation of the origin
of the Universe. Or rather: the "origin" of the world is never a *causa*
in religion, and least of all a *prima causa*. For a God-cause, as Brunner
observes, would be itself part of the Universe;[2] but the idea of creation
purports to assert something about what is not at all of this world. In
this respect, then, the situation is exactly the same as with the so-called
aetiological myth, which tells us why the raven is black and the heavens
above the earth; all this is not some kind of primitive natural science,
and from it every attempt at theoretical domination of the world is
remote.[3] It is rather a grounding of the Universe in the numinous, in
the mysterious and powerful primeval ground; and creation also is an
aetiological myth, grounding the world in the primal ground of the
divine Will.[4] Or in other terms: God is the sole magician: the magical
attitude[5] pertains to Him alone; He has thoughts that are at the same
moment deeds. The world is His *creatura*, and exists solely by virtue
of His Will bringing it into existence.

2. If now the Universe has a beginning and an end, if it is both
begun by God and by Him brought to its conclusion, then it must also
have a *centre*.[6] If again its course is no eternally enduring process, but a
drama, then the drama must have one focal point from which the whole
reveals its significance; for when any phenomenon "appears" to man,
he seeks for the point, the "centre", from which he can understand
the whole and from which its meaning becomes perceptible. The
Universe, however, is no "phenomenon"; and man cannot simply
observe it, because he himself pertains to the Universe and can never
think himself away. Nevertheless he can discuss its significance: but
this he can do only in *faith*. For the Universe does not "appear" to
him, but God reveals its meaning to him at its historic centre. In other
words: that which, in the "phenomenon", is *significance* and is *comprehended*, is in the Universe *salvation* that is *bestowed*. *At the centre
of history, therefore, God reveals the meaning of the world as salvation.*

---

[1] *cf.* Cassirer, *op. cit.*, II, 261.   [2] *Gott und Mensch*, 9.   [3] Chap. 83.
[4] *cf.* H. Frick, *Theol. Rundschau*, N. F. 2, 1930, 86. Piper, *Ethik*, I, 114 *ff.*
[5] Chap. 82.   [6] Tillich, *Rel. Verwirkl.* 116.

We can here, however, disregard the question (which falls within systematic theology) whether or not all history is the history of salvation.[1] The principle suffices that for the believer who seeks the goal and purpose of the Universe in God, the course of the world is in fact the *history of salvation*, from its beginning in God's creation to its end in His consummation. This is possible to him because on him, at the centre of this history, salvation was bestowed. In history, therefore, man seeks the history of God, that is to say, what is superior to himself, exactly as he did in the case of the soul. To him history first becomes living, and indeed becomes history proper, because of salvation; for just as history exists for us all solely in virtue of its meaning, which at first is only our own meaning but ultimately that of God, so it subsists for the believer only in virtue of salvation, which to begin with is his own powerfulness, but is in the last instance the saving power of God. History, then, is always dogmatized history: the Israelites fought the "wars of Jahveh", just as the Egyptians attacked the barbarians who were actually the mythical enemies of the sun-god. The king, again, stands as a god in the midst of a cosmic contest; his victory, still further, can never be in question, since he must conquer even if the enemy "in reality" has overcome him.[2] The history of the patriarchs in *Genesis* is indeed extremely "unnatural"; in other terms, it is a history of salvation. The birth and rescue of Isaac and Jacob's superiority over Esau, Joseph's status among his brothers, the favour shown to Ephraim and, conversely, the sinful self-assertion of Adam, Lamech and the Babylonian builders of the Tower—all this, as Lehmann has acutely described it in one of the last Articles he wrote,[3] is historical construction which we should not reject as childish nor as wanton forgery, but should rather apprehend as an attempt to depict the salvation which was given to man at the centre of history. In exactly the same way, the Synoptic *Gospels* provide no chronicle of Jesus' life but a recital of the historic salvation imparted in Him, while the fourth evangelist goes so far as almost to forget history altogether as compared with salvation.

In Christianity, to continue, this "centre" of history is the *Incarnation of Christ* and, as Tillich maintains, so far as the conception of history in general is Western European and Christian, all interpretation of

---

[1] Tillich, *Rel. Verwirkl.* 131.

[2] *cf.* R. Weill, *Les Hyksos et la Restauration nationale dans la tradition égyptienne* (*Journal asiat.* 16, 1910; 17, 1911). de Buck, *Het Typische en het Individueele.* G. van der Leeuw, *Historisch Christendom*, 1919.   [3] *La pensée du Jahviste, SM.* 3, 1927.

history leads in fact to Christology.[1] The Christian, then, has found in history the "concrete locality" where salvation is given to him. The beginnings of this religio-historical conception, however, are found in the people of Israel which not only, like all the peoples of antiquity, constructed its history in accordance with a scheme of salvation, but regarded the deeds of its God as direct leadership, as deliverance and guidance towards a goal which was nothing other than this God himself and his "service".

3. In this structure of the spiritual life, therefore, the world is the scene of a magnificent drama, whose redemptive history is disclosed to us in God's revelation:[2] a *divina commedia*. But with such a history we are already quite familiar: it is the "sacred story", *hieros logos*, which we have previously exhaustively discussed.[3] In the *hieros logos*, then, history becomes the *history of salvation*. The drama of the Cross is produced for us with the exhortation: *tua res agitur*—"thou art concerned". Now, however, the connection with Nature which we discerned in the "sacred story", of the mystery religions, for example, is absent. For the history of salvation is pure history, and salvation does not grow up for us "in the course of the world" from the eternal maternal womb, but is bestowed upon us by the divine Will. For this reason salvation, still further, can here mean *deliverance* also: the deed of salvation takes the world and man out of the "course" of the world and subjects them to a Will that transcends the world. Christology, therefore, is soteriology. Man no longer desires to make Nature bear the burden of his power, nor any longer to render her power serviceable to his own: he wishes neither to be himself a creator nor to live supported by the "given" potency. But he bows in obedience before the Creator, the Almighty, and receives deliverance from His hands alone.

4. But just because deliverance lies wholly in God's hands it must penetrate to the deepest element which, in man and in the world, opposes the tendency towards God; that is to *guilt*. Thus over against: "Look! At whom? At the bridegroom!" we find: "Look! Whither? At our guilt!" From the world, therefore, God produces something wholly different from what we ourselves find therein, even if we dig down to its profoundest ground. In other words: God changes the

---

[1] *ibid.,* 110 f.
[2] "To us":—that is to say "to our faith"; for to our understanding, as apart from faith, nothing "appears" here!   [3] Chap. 34, 61.

very essence of the world: deliverance is nothing less than *re-creation*.
And God does not simply fit out a new world from the fragments of
the old; here also He works with no material whatever; His creation is
again *creatio ex nihilo*, from what is to the human intellect quite incon-
ceivable—what exists, when nothing exists: or expressed in religious
terms, from *grace*.[1]

In other words: deliverance and new creation are *atonement*: God
sets the "bearing of guilt" in the very centre of history, and the Christian
prays: *agnus Dei, qui tollis peccata mundi.*

5. The new creation, which has a beginning of the world as its
condition, and a centre of history as its situation, must also fix an end
to the world; and thus we enter the domain of *eschatology*. The renewal
of the world, and its end, condition each other reciprocally. Of course
we cannot contemplate exhibiting here all the pictures of the end of
time as these have been painted at various periods in different religions,
especially by Parsiism and Christianity, Judaism and Islam, and also
among the Germanic peoples.[2] Instead of this, I shall attempt to sketch
a few of the main features, together with some of the most important
types, of eschatology.

It must be observed, first of all, that the *eschaton*, the uttermost limit,
is not conceived merely in some remote future, but equally in a distant
past: primeval time and the end of time, as we have already found, are
associated. Man thus attempts to deal with his world as his nought and
as God's All; but this he can do in mythical form, only at a time removed
as far as possible from his own, in the earliest yesterday as in the farthest
to-morrow. And this time is *God's time*. A golden age lies behind us:
an eternal realm of salvation confronts us.[3] Some primitive peoples,
indeed, can describe the primeval conditions when community between
heaven and earth still subsisted, and they were united by a long liana—
the Toradja of Celebes, for example.[4] The description in the *Rig-Veda*,
again, has a typically acosmic tone: "The non-existent was not, the
existent was not then; air was not, nor the firmament that is beyond.
What stirred? (Was there any wind?) Where? Under whose shelter?
Was (then) the deep abyss (of the sea) water? Death was not, immortality
was not then; no distinction was there of night and day. That *One*

---

[1] The Orthodox church perceives in redemption-re-creation a *theosis*, a deification
of humanity, but adopts therewith the mystical paradox of a "new creation, that is, an
ultimate *creation* of man *as God*"; Boulgakoff, *Orthodoxie*, 153.
[2] A. Bertholet gives an excellent survey in *RGG. Eschatologie*, I.
[3] Lietzmann, *Weltheiland*, 44.   [4] Adriani, *Animistisch Heidendom*, 5.

breathed, windless, self-dependent. Other than That there was none beyond.''[1] This sounds, it is true, like a *Wessobrunn Prayer* with an Indian tinge, while the Greek myths of the golden age transpose the primeval world definitely nearer the divine.[2] Here too primeval time and ultimate time come into contact, while from these ideas the country of the soul[3] cannot be separated. Paradise lies at the beginning, as at the end; and in Egypt the same conception occurred: "the time of the eight primeval gods, which according to its actual nature is supposed to have been a period of nothingness devoid of all life, is nevertheless a happy past, a golden age, for this later Theban cosmogony", observes Sethe characteristically.[4] Similarly Yima's kingdom, according to Persian ideas, lasts without frost or heat, sickness or death, until it must retire into its stronghold before the advancing Winter of the world.[5]

The general scheme of this course of the world, from primeval time to its end, is at first the retarded and unified rhythm of periodicity.[6] In this train of thought, indeed, every new year was a fresh harvest, every sunrise a victory over darkness; the growth of vegetation a re-creation, the recommencement of life in Spring a repetition of the world's creation; the king too was the saviour of his own period.[7] To begin with, then, eschatology is only one "special case" of this periodic cosmology.[8] Later, however, all world history is comprehended within one single period, the many cyclic time series consolidated into one unique course: Jahveh, the god who overcomes darkness at the commencement of each year, then becomes the lord of the world who creates at the beginning and conquers at the end.[9] The many *peripeteiae* or recurring crises are now reduced to two only: initial creation and concluding, consummating victory; and in a quite similar way, the periodic change of Winter and Summer is in the North "transposed" into the idea of an extraordinarily long Winter, *Fimbulwinter*, which is nothing else than *Ragnarök*, the decline of the world.[10]

And thus the scheme of eschatology dogmatically intrudes into the everyday world: Egyptian wisdom-literature depicted a condition of

[1] Bertholet, *Lesebuch*, 9, 88. E. J. Thomas, *Vedic Hymns*, 127 (modified).
[2] L. Preller, *Griechische Mythologie*, 1, 1894, 87 f. Hesiod, *Works*, 109 ff.
[3] Chap. 46.
[4] K. Sethe, *Amun und die acht Urgötter von Hermopolis*, Abh. der Wiss., 1929, Phil. Kl. 4, 63.   [5] Lehmann, *Zarathustra*, 1, 95 f.
[6] Chap. 22, 55.   [7] Chap. 13.
[8] Wensinck, *Semitic New Year*. Mowinckel, *Psalmenstudien*, II.
[9] cf. F. M. Th. Böhl, *Nieuwjaarsfeest en koningsdag in Babylon en Israel*, 1927.
[10] A. Olrik, *Ragnarök, die Sagen vom Weltuntergang*, 15 ff. (1922).

crisis in which everything was in a state of revolution; its features were certainly taken from some actual crisis, which need not however have been at all present for the poet himself, since it must occur in any case. The crisis is a genuine crisis, that is to say, not fact but judgment. The Jewish-Hellenistic apocalypse, for instance, is entirely filled with this scheme of crisis, following a period of happiness;[1] and ancient Greece also knew the "race of iron" and their era of misfortune.[2] Finally, the New Testament is familiar with a crisis that must inevitably come, and be proclaimed at a time when nothing whatever indicates it; and in this it conforms to the prophetic announcement of the "day of the Lord". But in the *Gospels* this schematism is not merely an apocalypse of the world (though it is this *also*, *St. Mark* xiii, *etc.*), but is in the first place the basis of belief, in accordance with which the life of the Messiah develops itself. For He must suffer, and His disciples with Him: a time of distress will arise: brother will deliver up brother, the father his child, and all natural relationships will be reversed.[3] Thus the course of the life of Jesus, as also the future which He described to His disciples, is intelligible only on the basis of this dogmatic-eschatological experience of history: afflictions must come so that glory may dawn.[4] The scheme of belief—this will be the world's fate—is applied by Jesus, as the mediator,[5] to Himself, and thus He makes the crisis the judgment upon Himself: "The Son of man came to give his life a ransom for many."[6]

This dramatization of history in the basis of faith desires, as it were, to "destroy" the world and time, so that the kingdom and era of God may dawn: it disowns to-day for the sake of "the day of the Lord". The *eschaton*, however, is not a nullity in the sense of the void, but in that of a violent reversal of all conditions with no exception. So man believes even with regard to Nature: "the sunshine will darken and evil winds blow in future Summers. Know ye still more? Mightily Garm barks at the mouth of the Gnipa-cave: the chains are broken, the wolf escapes. I know the tidings, I see far and wide: the mighty *Ragnarök* of the gods."[7] But the revolution concerns custom and culture also: "brothers will fight till both fall, cousins destroy their relatives; the world is dissolute, they commit adultery; there is no one who spares another."[8] Precisely the same too in the New Testament:

[1] Kampers, *Kaisermystik*, 102.
[2] Hesiod, *Works*, 174 *ff*. Murray, *The Rise of the Greek Epic*, 102.   [3] *Matt.* x.
[4] Probably the permanent significance of Schweitzer's *The Quest of the Historical Jesus* lies in this insight.   [5] Chap. 106.
[6] *Mark* x. 45.   [7] *Völuspå*; Lehmann-Haas, *Textbuch*, 245.   [8] *ibid.*

the sun will be darkened
and the moon will not yield her light,
the stars will drop from heaven,
and the orbs of the heavens will be shaken.[1]

But further: "Now the brother shall betray the brother to death, and the father the son; and children shall rise up against their parents, and shall cause them to be put to death."[2] But when everything has been thus reversed God's sovereignty begins: "Now learn a parable of the fig tree; When her branch is yet tender, and putteth forth leaves, ye know that summer is near: So ye in like manner, when ye shall see these things come to pass, know that it is nigh, even at the doors."[3]

According to its nature the end may be described as a dying, a decline, but also as a deed of God: the first type occurs in many places, being however most beautifully expressed in the Germanic myth of *Ragnarök*. There gods become heroes, while for the poet of the *Völuspá* the gods perish together with the world,[4] the essential traits of this description being probably taken from the typical decay of a tribe;[5] exactly like a clan, the gods and their world too are destroyed by impotence and unrighteousness. The world dies. And the gods also. Kahle has acutely perceived that this end of the world is directly contrary to the Christian conception. For in the former the gods are defeated: in the latter God triumphs; in the first the world passes on to its end: in the second God brings the world to an end.[6] Upon this Germanic picture of the world's collapse, however, there falls a gleam of magnificent tragedy: the tragedy of the sunset from which it arose. Man postulates the nullity of his whole world, and within the world he includes his gods.

Of the second type there is an abundance of examples: the many legends of a flood,[7] in which the god makes an end of the world because of guilt, already tend towards it; it is, however, seldom completed. In Persia, on the other hand, the "course of the world" was regarded as a path to a goal, and its periodicity as an ascent to the god's victory;[8] the will of the wise lord governs the whole. Subsequently, in Christianity, this Will, which in later Judaism was also the beginning and the end of the world, received the form of Him Who in His whole life posited an

---

[1] *Mark* xiii. 24 f. (Moffat).   [2] *Mark* xiii. 12.   [3] *Mark* xiii. 28, 29.
[4] Olrik, *op. cit.*, 51; *cf.* also his *Nordisches Geistesleben*[2], 1925, 101.
[5] Grönbech, *Folkeaet*, I, 176 f.
[6] *cf.* B. Kahle, *Der Ragnarök-Mythus*, AR. 8, 1905, 444 f.
[7] H. Usener, *Die Sintflutsagen untersucht*, 1899. G. Gerland, *Der Mythus von der Sintflut*, 1912. R. Andree, *Die Flutsagen*, 1891.
[8] *cf.* Lommel, *Zarathustra*, 130 ff.

end of the world. "For it is characteristic of Jesus that He looks forward, beyond the perfection and bliss of the individual, to a perfection and bliss of the world and of a chosen humanity. He is filled and determined by the will and hope for the kingdom of God'."[1] He proclaims the time of the end and brings this about. "The kingdom of God is at hand": and with the conclusion of His own history, in the final voluntary act, when He sends down His spirit on the disciples, the time of the end finally appears; for ever since then the world subsists only in an interim, and has lost its intrinsic value.

First of all, then, this end of the world is a *judgment*. Again Parsiism vigorously stresses this feature: the *frashokereti*, the world completion, is in the first place a *purification*, a judgment; and it is well known how closely the concepts of the end and of judgment are connected in Christianity too: the end is nothing but the nearness of God, judgment: no historical fact of the remote future therefore, but a revelation, a self-impartation of God. God's approach to the world is in itself the judgment and the end.

But again: the end of the world is also the commencement of God's sovereignty, of the *kingdom of God*:[2] the βασιλεία θεοῦ becomes actual. The world's completion begins: the goal of the world in God is realized. Dominion is linked with judgment; "judgment is the decisive characteristic of the event, perceived in the *eschaton*"; and conversely: "only from the point of view of the *eschaton* can the judicial nature of time be understood".[3] But dominion consists in the fact that the world exists solely in God:—that God is with the world, "*Emmanuel.*" The kingdom of God, therefore, may also be called the kingdom of *the Spirit*: the third kingdom. But at no time whatever should it be severed from historic reality, as the sects have done repeatedly since the time of Joachim of Floris.[4] The world ever remains the world: and without the centre of history there can be neither beginning nor end. But the revelation of the world, as in its deepest ground belonging to God, comes to us from the *eschaton*, and with this the circle becomes completed of those "phenomena" which are not actually such, because they do not "appear" to us but are revealed only. Below the sphere of phenomenological transparency, therefore, is *life*; above it: *guilt, faith, the world* as God's sovereignty. Below and above, half understood, half believed in: the *church*.

[1] Schweitzer, *Leben-Jesu-Forschung*, 634; cf. 636 f.
[2] A parallel in Hindu Varuna-religion: R. Otto, *Das Gefühl des Überweltlichen (sensus numinis)*, 1932, 168.   [3] Tillich, *Rel. Verwirkl.* 139, 136.
[4] Em. Gebhart, *L'Italie mystique*[3], 1917, 75 f.

H. GUNKEL, *Schöpfung und Chaos*, in *Urzeit und Endzeit*, 1921.

A. OLRIK, *Ragnarök, Die Sagen vom Weltuntergang*, 1922.

R. OTTO, *Reich Gottes und Menschensohn*, 1934 (Eng. tr., *The Kingdom of God and The Son of Man*, 1938).

PART FIVE

FORMS

A. RELIGIONS

CHAPTER 88

RELIGIONS

1. "RELIGION actually exists only in religions", as Heinrich Frick very justly asserts with reference to Schleiermacher's fifth *Discourse upon Religion.*[1] This means that religion does not, as such, appear to us; what we can observe, therefore, is always only *one* concrete religion: in other terms, only its prevailing historical *form* appears to us.[2] From this it follows that "primeval religion" is here disregarded.[3] The primeval ground of religion, that is in the ontological or metaphysical sense, is in principle concealed. But the historic primeval ground of religion is merely a myth; it is obviously not prehistoric religion, about which, as it is, we know very little![4] but Adam's religion. Now either Adam is the first man, whose religion is plainly quite inaccessible to us: or he is "Everyman", and then the enquiry into his religion subdivides into two others: first, that concerning the awakening of the religious consciousness in everyone without exception, which would be the problem for psychology; and that into the revelation of God in every man: and to answer this question, again, would be the task of theology. The "primeval", then, altogether eludes our comprehension; and "primeval experience"[5] can neither be renewed nor observed. Certainly we may say that the origin of religion lies in God; but that is a theological assertion which (phenomenologically) scarcely assists us at all. For from the viewpoint of revelation every religion is primeval, because in order to be revealed[6] the content must be original and never previously perceived.

Research has attempted to arrive at primeval religion, however, in four different ways: (*A*) by advancing the idea of a *"natural religion"*, which the essentially divine element in every human being discloses, either through creation (or Nature) or in conscience. On this general

---

[1] *Vergl. Rel. wiss.* 62.   [2] *cf.* Wach, *Rel. wiss.* 50 *f.*
[3] *cf.* H. Frick, *Theol. Rundschau*, N.F. 2, 1930, 72.
[4] C. Clemen, *Urgeschichtliche Religion*, I, 1932.
[5] Chap. 107.   [6] Chap. 85.

foundation the dome of historical religion may then be erected (in theological terms, as special revelation); and although this pallid abstraction has already been disposed of by Schleiermacher, nevertheless it repeatedly emerges. But with this Herder's fine maxim should be contrasted:—that every religion has "the focal point of its bliss in itself".[1] (B) Primeval religion, in the next place, was originally *one* and preceded all the current divisions. Specific religions are thus only specializations of the primeval, the various "idioms"[2] in which it addresses us. This romantic view still persists to-day in theosophy, which perceives in the actual religions the symbolic disguises of some primeval religion scrupulously guarded by initiates. (C) Primeval religion, again, is the germ of an unequivocal, unilinear *development*, being styled animism by some scholars and dynamism by others.[3] We find another modification of this in the French sociological school, for which primeval religion is supposed to imply a worship of humanity.[4] But in all these attempts at solution the common aim is to derive the plurality of actual religions from one simple origin in the sense of evolutionism. (D) Conversely, the so-called theory of degeneration tries to explain this plurality as being a descent from an original monotheism; while this monotheism, which is supposed to have comprised the essential features of belief in the creator and a morality sanctioned by God, closely approximates to (A), so-called natural religion.[5]

2. Now it is certainly not sufficient to reject primeval religion from the very outset; and the consistent advocacy of our own principle that religion exists only with and in *religions* unquestionably finds itself confronted with considerable difficulties. There is first of all the objection that the copiousness of religions cannot be surveyed adequately because, strictly speaking, each individual has his own religion. Thus my Christianity is often Poles apart from that of my nearest neighbour, and to a far higher degree is this true of a peasant's Christianity or that of a converted primitive, *etc*. It is of course undeniable that religion assumes some specific form in each person's own mind, so that just as my attitude in prayer diverges, however slightly, from my neighbour's, even when our general deportment during prayer corresponds, similarly my entire religious behaviour differs from his even when we belong to the same church and conform to the same type of piety. But this objection also concerns those cultures dealing with subject matter other

---

[1] *cf.* Wach, *Rel. wiss.* 84.   [2] Creuzer.
[3] Chap. 9, 1.   [4] Chap. 32.   [5] Chap. 18.

than religion:—esthetics, jurisprudence and ethics. Each artist, for example, has certainly a style of his own, and each individual his own mode of artistic appreciation. Nevertheless we all agree that there is no art purely in itself, and that in his creations every artist, and in his esthetic appreciation every individual, must submit to an objective ideal from which he began, within which he lives, and in whose construction or improvement he assists. There subsists a style, a consciousness proper to the period, an *objective spirit*:[1] it is quite impossible to begin the history of spirit entirely anew. I certainly have "my" religion, then, but I must nonetheless admit that it is "mine" only very conditionally; for in my own experience religion receives a special form which is, however, merely one specific form of the vast historic formation wherein I myself exist. In my own narrow sphere I assist in preserving the life of this historical religion; if I happen to be a "great man" then it is perhaps permitted to me to cooperate in its transformation, and ultimately in its dissolution and replacement by a new form. But even so this "new" religion could never be entirely "mine", but would always be simultaneously the perpetuation of what has been already given. All great founders, therefore, are essentially reformers.[2]

3. But objective spirit, still further, is so infinitely differentiated that the necessity of a *typology* is absolutely imperative; we must, then, attempt to attain an understanding of the historic forms of religion by appealing to certain ideal types. This typology may, however, follow two different courses. In the first place, and so far as is possible, it may disregard the historic and try to apprehend the specifically historical, to the highest attainable degree, under quite general points of view. Now not only is this typological method thoroughly justified: it is, still further, precisely that which has been pursued in my own investigation. Under these conditions, therefore, nothing more need be done except to draw the general conclusion from our specific considerations, in which case no new aspects whatever would come into view. But at the same time, in order to understand religions actually as forms, we must adopt a different course; and the ideal type that we discover must then be the result of the closest cooperation between phenomenological comprehension and the investigation of all that has been historically given. It follows that we are not concerned, for example, with any religion of compassion, but with Buddhism as the historically living form of this religion.

[1] Spranger, *Lebensformen;* Dilthey, *Werke, passim.*   [2] Chap. 94, 102.

Thus a general typology could be elaborated from the most varied points of view: I cite merely a few instances.

(*A*) A *collective* type becomes distinguished from an *individual* and personal type; and the whole of primitive religion then falls within the collective type. Well developed state religions rank as particularly characteristic instances of this; for example, the Roman, in which the entire social organization stood in a definite legal relationship to the powers, involving reciprocal obligations. To this the antithesis would be, for instance, the devoutness of pietism:

> If I only have Him
> Gladly will I leave all else behind
> And follow, leaning on my pilgrim's staff,
> In true devotion, my Lord alone;
> Content to let others
> Travel the wide, bright, crowded roads.[1]

(*B*) A *higher* religion is distinguished from a *lower*. Primitive religions then occupy the lowest level of all, and the advance proceeds by way of the religions of semi-culture, subsequently culminating in Christianity, or again in Judaism. But the unfortunate aspect of this typology, which is still very frequently advocated, is (first) that it estimates the historical religions exclusively from the standpoint of to-day; as the norm it presents Christianity, and in fact usually a modernized Christianity, to which all else must then be adapted. Secondly, again, this involves the error that the relatively lower and higher grades of religious development are evaluated exclusively in the light of the prevailing culture. The more closely, therefore, the scientific, moral and philosophic concepts of any given religion approach our own, so much the "higher" that religion is taken to be; a typical example of this is Tiele's classification of religions into "The Lowest Nature Religions, The Highest Nature Religions, and The Ethical Religions".[2] Quite differently, however, must this sort of typology be judged when the inadequate terms "high" and "low", which either convey nothing at all or are adopted from a shallow evolutionism, are replaced by the expressions "*primitive*" and "*modern*", provided always that these are not taken to involve stages or periods in the history of religion but eternal structures, and that they also serve to classify the historic religions according to the degree in which they participate in one or the other of these structures.

---

[1] Novalis, *Geistliche Lieder*.　　　　[2] *Elements of the Science of Religion.*

(*C*) Still more hazardous than *B* is racial typology. We have already observed[1] that it is comparatively easy to contrast, for instance, a "Semitic" concept of God with an "Indo-Germanic". But the mere facts that "race" is an extremely dubious category, and that the religion with which we ourselves are most familiar has essential affiliations with the religions of at least two "races", should be a warning to us and induce us rather to describe the intrinsic features, which appear to us as typically "Semitic" or even "Aryan", in accord with their actual nature, and to represent them for example in the light of their relations either to Will or to impersonal Power.

(*D*) A very serviceable typology has been advanced by Frick,[2] distinguishing between the religions of *works* and those of *grace*, and exhibiting this contrast not merely within Catholicism and Protestantism alone, but in Hindu tendencies also. Whether any religious "original phenomenon" becomes perceptible here we may very well leave undecided; in any case this typology is inapplicable to the whole of religion, and primitive religion in general never draws this very momentous distinction.

(*E*) Typology in terms of form characteristics, however, is extremely important; the *religion of the father*, for example, contrasts sharply with that of *the mother*; but this has already been exhaustively discussed.[3]

(*F*) Söderblom's triple division of religion into *animism, dynamism* and the *religion of originators* (in my own terms: the religion of will and of form: that of formless Power: the religion of half-formed Power in the background) has the outstanding merit that it comprises the entire history of religion; and Söderblom himself has brilliantly demonstrated this by exhibiting the characteristic features of his own three types in all the great cultural religions alike: Judaism, Christianity and Islam— Indian religions—Chinese religions and Deism.[4]

(*G*) Reliable typologies may also be based on the character of the religious sentiment of each religion: I may refer here to Heiler's classification into mystical and prophetic piousness, with which many investigators have concurred. The two classical typologies of this type, however, are Hegel's and Goethe's. Hegel distinguished an objective stage, wherein God is the power of Nature, from a subjective, for which God appears as spiritual individuality; the third grade is Christianity, wherein God reveals Himself as Absolute Spirit.[5] It is true that the question may arise whether philosophic construction has not dis-

---

[1] Chap. 20. [2] *Vergl. Rel. gesch.* [3] Chap. 10, 20.
[4] *Gottesglaube.* [5] Hegel, *The Philosophy of Religion*, III, 107 ff

placed phenomenological observation. Far less is this the case with Goethe, who advanced *reverence* as the original phenomenon. In the first instance, this is felt towards whatever is superior to us; and this forms the religion of heathendom as a primary release from fear. In the second place, reverence is experienced with regard to what is equal to ourselves: that is philosophical religion. The Christian religion, on the other hand, involves reverence for what is inferior to us, for the weak and lowly, even the repulsive; it is the religion of suffering and of death. This is the ultimate and highest form which, it is true, then becomes once more apprehended as one of three special forms of higher religion, which consists in man's respect for himself.[1]

4. But all these typologies[2] bring us hardly any nearer to religions *as historical forms*. They are, undeniably, generalizations in definite guise of the data provided by the phenomenology of religion; nevertheless they do not constitute the phenomenology of *religions*. I can, for example, write the phenomenology of hero or saint, but I can also write that of Gustavus Adolphus or of St. Francis; and at present the latter must be our task—of course in its most abbreviated form. Hegel's much derided classification (not the general one already referred to, but that according to historic types) should be esteemed as a most necessary effort that well deserves consideration. Historical typology is a quite indispensable and essential subdivision of the phenomenology of religion. This typology excludes the non-historical and predominantly unhistorical (that is, the primitive) religions; and I need not repeat the contention that every religion is more or less primitive. Nevertheless there are religions which possess a sharply outlined historic form distinguishing them from all others. But this category does not include the religions of so-called primitive peoples, while extensive sections of so-called higher religions are omitted too: those, namely, which are also found in other religions, and thus possess no specific form of their own.

[1] *Wilhelm Meister's Apprenticeship*, II, 1.   [2] *cf.* Frick, *Vergl. Rel. gesch.* 10 *ff.*

CHAPTER 89

RELIGIONS OF REMOTENESS AND OF FLIGHT

1. HISTORICAL form, then, is presented first of all by the *religion of remoteness*, the essential nature of which has already been dealt with in Chapter 18, where it has also been pointed out that it received its historic form first of all in China and predominantly, in fact, in Confucianism. This form however, as indeed must be the case in any religion of remoteness, is extremely indefinite. It is not at all remarkable, therefore, that the advocates of so-called natural religion have sought their historical justification principally in that country.[1]

In China the mystical connection between objects, which is a form of the "participation" previously discussed,[2] becomes intersected by a marked disposition to consider Power only from a distance. But the immediate proximity of countless potencies in all the affairs of ordinary life, in every situation and at every moment, presents a remarkable contrast to this remoteness from Power in general, while the scrupulous observances by no means exclude an indifference approximating to flight. Observance then becomes morality and custom, the latter being omnipotent. "The master said: he who governs by virtue is like the Pole star: he stands immovably in his place and is therefore honoured by the mass of the revolving stars."[3] The leading virtue, however, is filial love (*hsiao*) in the sense of piety. "The master said: if the father is living, consider his will; if he is dead, then think of his conduct. Whoever follows his father's ways for three years may well be called *hsiao*, full of filial love."[4] This filial love is, in the first place, the guarantee of the potency of life taking its course in accord with custom; but it also expands into a universal love of mankind which shows powerful humanistic tendencies. This great-hearted philanthropic morality is restricted only by sagacity and by *li*, that is by propriety which, however, for Confucian sentiment coincides with the rites.[5] These are intended to make it possible for man to devote himself to an aristocratically tinged love of humanity, tranquilly remote from all that is exciting: "the master was not accustomed to speak about extraordinary things

---

[1] Söderblom, *Natürliche Theologie*, 30.
[2] Chap. 82. De Groot, *Universismus*.
[3] Bertholet, *Lesebuch*, 6, 68.
[4] *ibid.*, 6, 69.
[5] *ibid.*, 6, 71.

(miracles), about deeds of strength, rebellions or demons".[1] Custom is invariably observed; thus gods and spirits receive their rightful due, so that we may peacefully devote ourselves to mankind: "To be earnestly occupied in rendering full justice to man, to show reverence for demons and gods, but to keep oneself at a *distance from them*, may well be called wisdom."[2] Power is influential, then, only in its regulated, celebrated, human form; everything else causes alarm, so that both violent deeds and all that is specially sacred should alike be avoided: "To see a saint was not permitted to me. To be allowed to see a noble person would be sufficient for me."[3] "The master said: Is it not true, Shen, that all my teaching is expressed in a single principle? Yes: was the answer. When the master had gone out his disciples asked: what does that mean? and Master Dseng replied: our master's teaching is fidelity towards oneself and kindness to others: in this everything is included."[4] Here, therefore, nothing whatever is obligatory except custom and the virtue which springs from this; the encounter with a powerful will is in principle avoided. This will is certainly recognized, together with the wills of the many demons: nevertheless man remains at a proper distance, as God does also. Here, then, God is Power and Will in the background.[5] His proximity would involve violence, excitement, inhumanity. He is therefore circumvented; for He is just the God of heaven, and heaven is very far away.

2. A second historical form of the religion of remoteness is eighteenth century deism which, indeed, appealed to China; and exactly the same tendency existed in antiquity: "the gods attend to great matters; they neglect small ones".[6] In Western European eighteenth century culture, however, this attitude implies flight from God. Being so remote and so sublime, He is certainly praised; but it is believed to be just as well that He cannot observe us too closely, because we can manage very well without Him! Man says: "God is very far off", however, simply because he has withdrawn himself. In its most pious form, in the *Profession de foi du Vicaire savoyard*, where a sincere and warm feeling for divine reality unquestionably predominates, it nevertheless runs: "The first return to self has given birth to a feeling of gratitude and thankfulness to the author of my species, and this feeling calls forth my first homage to the beneficent Godhead. I worship his Almighty power and my heart acknowledges his mercies. I need no instruction in this religion,

---

[1] Lehmann-Haas, *Textbuch*, 19.   [2] *ibid.*, 19.   [3] *ibid.*, 21.
[4] *ibid.*   [5] Chap. 18.   [6] Cicero, *De Deorum Natura*, II, 167.

which *Nature herself* dictates to me. Is it not *a natural consequence of our self-love* to honour our protector and to love our benefactor?"[1] Great love as well as great defects come from man himself: let us then return to Nature; and even if Lisbon is devastated, that is not the fault of God for sending an earthquake, but of man for building Lisbon! And in a totally different spiritual climate the religion of the remote God becomes perceptible as the religion of remoteness from God:

> Pride! And nought but pride!
> The pot of iron wants to have been lifted
> With silver tongs from out the fire, that so
> 'A may think himself a pot of silver.—Pah!
> And what it harms, thou askest, what it harms?—
> What helps it? might I ask thee in reply:—
> For, for thy "nearer consciousness of God",
> 'Tis either nonsense or flat blasphemy.
> But harm it does:—yes, harm it does most surely![2]

Miracle, however, that is to say the direct and immediate presence of God, is the crucial issue upon which this religion of remoteness begins its struggle against other religions. The nearness of God in miracle and sacrament, in sacred word and church, fades away; God becomes the God of the unforgotten, but not very vivid, background:[3] He is recognized simply because man cannot dispense with Him entirely:

> This sublime mystery is indispensable to man.
> It is the sacred bond of society,
> The primal basis of sacred equity,
> The curb of the villain, the hope of the just.
> Should the heavens, despoiled of His august imprint,
> Ever cease to reveal Him—
> If God did not exist—then man must invent Him.[4]

The essential distinction between this religion of remoteness and the religion of love is most clearly discerned when we fully realize that the most essential characteristic in the parable of the Prodigal Son—the father hastening to meet him—must be completely excluded if the parable is to illustrate the first of these two religions.

---

[1] *Emile*, Book IV (p. 240, "Everyman's Library" Edition); my italics.
[2] Lessing, *Nathan the Wise*, Act I, Scene 2.
[3] Chap. 18; van der Leeuw, *Höchstes Wesen*.
[4] Voltaire, *Epître à l'auteur du Livre des trois Imposteurs*, XCVII, *Œuvres complètes*, XIII, 1785, 226. In this connection Balzac's dictum is not too severe: "*Le déiste est un athée sous bénéfice d'inventaire*" (Ursule Mirouet).

3. The religion of flight, to continue, is *atheism*. But it has never, under any conditions whatever, acquired historical form. Certainly there are again and again individuals who run away from God; nevertheless it is impossible for them to elaborate a religion from their flight. For no sooner have they escaped from one Power than they run into the jaws of the next; they can certainly desert from God to the devil; but then the devil too is (phenomenologically speaking) a sort of "god". Or they may return from God to man or to humanity; but again, in so doing, their flight only leads them back to one of the most primitive of all potencies. Obviously too there are religions opposed to any definite experience of God and any definite idea of God: (original) Buddhism, for example, recognized no gods at all as such.[1] There are indeed modern scholars who would refuse, for this reason, to call it a religion, presumably on the ground that it does not spring from the experience of a personal God. But this is merely to assert that Buddhism is neither Judaism nor Christianity, which we knew quite well already! Earlier investigators similarly denied the presence of religion among primitive peoples, because they served no "gods"; but this contention, fortunately, has now been abandoned; there are no peoples without religion: even at the very dawn of history there is no historic form of atheism. Religion exists always and universally. Even the explicitly atheistic systems of India are nevertheless religions; *Samkhya* is the religion of the soul and its liberation, while Jainism attains a *Nirvana* without the help of gods; and to a still greater degree is the religious character of so-called atheism apparent in some modern systems, such as the presumptive atheism of deism, naturalism and idealism.[2] For in all these cases alike some different god appears instead of the gods hitherto served:—morality, humanity, Nature, the Idea. And in each case its essence is powerfulness, always in the religious sense of this term. In modern communistic atheism, again, it is precisely the same: here the dream of a kingdom of God and the religion of humanity have been united in a new religious ideal, which is atheistic only when compared with the old religion, but which in itself is a search for God rather than a flight from Him.

Actually, however, we might well have omitted atheism altogether from our discussion of the historic forms of religion. For there is no religion of atheism: there is only the individual fleeing from God— long ago described by the believer as "the fool (who) hath said in his

---

[1] *cf.* Chap. 19.
[2] He also who "speaks of God in general truths" is essentially an atheist—that is to say, he flees from God. Bultmann, *Glauben und Verst.*, 27.

heart, There is no God".[1] And the reason why atheism is nevertheless adduced here is that there is no historical religion quite devoid of atheism. No religion, in other words, is the religion of atheism: nevertheless every religion without exception is atheism. For every religion recognizes the element of flight from God; and atheism, that is to say, the deepest doubt, induces in religion a radical tension and thus preserves it from stagnation.[2] As long as a religion is living, therefore, it will include among its adherents fools who say in their hearts, "There is no God". And these fools will not be the worst among the pious! For the existential doubt, concerned with reality, allied to guilt[3] and manifesting itself in flight, is at the same moment an acknowledging of God, even though it is repressed.

[1] *Ps.* xiv. 1; liii. 2.   [2] Tillich, *Rel. Verwirkl.* 102.   [3] Chap. 78.

CHAPTER 90

THE RELIGION OF STRUGGLE

1. PREVIOUSLY, in Chapters 19 and 21, we dealt in detail with the plurality and the unity of Powers; and unity implies either the victory of absolute Power (Monism), or that of Form (Theism). Powers, however, may be reduced in number to two which struggle with one another:—*Dualism*. Religion then becomes the contest between these Powers, and man's own participation therein.

Dualism subsists in many places, and we have already observed how, in the ancient Egyptian cult, persons assumed the part of the god against his enemies.[1] The Egyptians, indeed, possessed a perfect passion for dualism and divided everything—heaven, earth, the kingdom, the provinces and temples, *etc.* They regarded the whole world as, in principle, divided, the representative gods of the two hemispheres being usually Horus and Set.

But the historic form of dualism appears in the Persian religion of Zarathustra, in which the vision of a great founder and reformer has constituted a dualism of action out of that of Nature: the entire life of the Universe, as of man, being a ceaseless struggle.

Zarathustrian dualism, however, was concerned not with the antithesis of spirit and body, as was its Greek counterpart—although it certainly recognized this distinction—but with the still more penetrating dualism of good and evil. To the "wise mind" is opposed an "evil mind", and "bad" thought to "good": to "truth" the "lie," *etc.*,[2] while the antithesis to Zarathustra and to devout mankind is the inhuman, to domestic animals the wolf, to water drought, and to plants blight, *etc.*[3] Thus the whole world is apprehended, from the standpoint of the religious experience of conflict, in terms of contrasted pairs: "In this house obedience shall triumph over disobedience, peace over discord, generosity over parsimony, submission (resignation) over revolt (pride), the truthful word over the false, truth over the lie."[4]

---

[1] Chap. 53.
[2] H. Lommel, *Die Religion Zarathustras nach dem Awesta dargestellt*, 1930, 111. In this and the succeeding chapters no Bibliography of specific religions has been given; only the most valuable as regards Typology are cited; *cf.* also H. S. Nyberg, *Die Religionen des alten Iran*, 1938, 263, 372 *ff.*

[3] Lommel, *ibid.*, 120.
[4] *Yasna*, 60, 5; Lommel, *ibid.*, 86.

2. For the Persians, then, as for Northern peoples, "life is a struggle. But the Persian has the luminous faith of the worker that the effort will be useful; the Northerner dreams that everything will be destroyed."[1] The Persian himself was conscious of the positive struggle called work, and in this connection Zarathustra is typical: "He is to be elected as lord, even as master in the part of the law (*asha*), who prepares works of the good disposition (of *Vohu manah*) for Mazda in (this) life and the (future) kingdom for Ahura."[2] The sacred labour of agriculture is the practical form in which the struggle is sustained: "He who cultivates grain cultivates the law, and advances the religion of Mazda worshippers in the best possible way; he strengthens this religion by a hundred pillars, by a thousand supports, by ten thousand prayers. If there is grain the *devs* perspire (in dread); if there are ears of grain the *devs* are wetted; if there is flour they howl, and if there is dough they act extremely rudely."[3] Persian religion, again, did not distinguish "spiritual" work from this "corporeal" labour; on the contrary: all work based on agriculture is in the lord's service; virtue, also, is work, conflict.

This conflict, in fact, arises even before birth. For duality lies in the first cause of things, and the *daena* (spiritual primeval beings) of men choose between good and evil, exactly as the two great spirits themselves decide the world's destiny in one primeval choice. The kingdom of God too is called "what man should choose", *varya*, and the term for faith means not conviction nor its analogues, but "taking the part of, voluntary decision".[4] Religion is conflict. √

This struggle finds its extreme limit, still further, not in the fact that Ahura Mazda is the lord, the creator, whose power is essentially and ultimately victorious. For theism, even the monotheism of Parsiism, does not exclude conflict, and the spirit of the lord is precisely the good spirit, the fighter opposing the evil spirit. But the contest finds its extreme limit in the monism of so-called *Zarvanism*, in the doctrine of infinite time, a factor of dissolution in the religion of Zarathustra, since the belief that Ahura Mazda and Ahriman both alike arose from *Zarvan Akarana*, from infinite time, takes the sting from the struggle and completely stultifies its moral aspect.[5]

3. Manichaeism, finally, which emerged from Zarathustrianism, can scarcely be regarded as a historic form of the religion of conflict. For

[1] Olrik, *Geistesleben*, 25.   [2] Bertholet, *Lesebuch*, 1, 7.
[3] *ibid.*, 1, 37.   [4] Lommel, *op. cit.*, 156 *ff.*   [5] *ibid.*, 24 *f.* Nyberg, *op. cit.*, p. 388.

in this the world is abandoned as lost, in principle, only the individual soul being the goal of effort, this again being reinterpreted as asceticism; and the dualism concerns the antithesis between spirit and matter. But this also appears to abrogate conflict as being the basic essence of religion; and thus the religion of struggle subsides into that general dualism which we discern primarily in Greek Orphism and the gnostic religions: God is no longer the God of the world, and conflict has lost its standing.

H. LOMMEL, *Die Religion Zarathustras nach dem Awesta dargestellt*, 1930.
H. S. NYBERG, *Die Religionen des alten Iran*, 1938.

CHAPTER 91

THE RELIGION OF REPOSE

1. THE religion of repose has already been repeatedly discussed. It has, however, no historic form; nonetheless it must be referred to here because, like atheism and the religion of unrest, which will shortly be dealt with, it is an important element in all historical religions. It is, indeed, no other than mysticism.[1]

Whoever has experienced the *fascinans* of Power too intensely to withdraw from it or flee before it, but on the other hand shrinks from conflict, or at least cannot regard struggle as the characteristic element in his life, longs for calm, for repose, that shall rule both in the divine essence and within himself, between God and humanity as among men; and if he conceives this repose either as being essentially achievable, or as fully attained, then he possesses a religion of repose. But associated with it he always has a different religion also, the religion of repose being then at best one leading component. For not only do the religions of conflict and of will counteract repose, but the religions of infinity likewise do not leave it altogether unaffected. In the first place, a perfect religion of calm would abolish itself completely as a historical form, since without some activity there is no religion whatever; while (secondly) calm itself cannot be attained without struggle, and indeed severe struggle. Repose, therefore, is the goal of longing; nevertheless it may dominate a religion completely, and then monistic and pantheistic systems arise. But it may also be incorporated within the active tendencies of a religion, either as the ultimate human goal or eschatologically as the ultimate activity, the ultimate deed of God. An example of this second type would be St. Paul's declaration: "And when all things shall be subdued unto him, then shall the Son also himself be subject unto him that put all things under him, that God may be all in all."[2] This is certainly repose, but neither pantheism nor monism: it is the yearning for the unity in God called love, which is bestowed ultimately by God Himself. Hölderlin's fine pronouncement, again, would be an instance of the first kind: "The discords of the world are like lovers' quarrels. Reconciliation is to be found in the midst of strife,

---

[1] Chap. 75.   [2] 1 *Cor.* xv. 28.

and there all that has been separated is again united. In the heart the arteries part and meet once more, and all becomes one single, eternal, glowing life."[1] In these words, though unquestionably as longing, as prospective, is depicted the union which *must* follow alienation.

[1] *Hyperion.*

CHAPTER 92

THE RELIGION OF UNREST

1. HERE also the religion of unrest, theism, must be assigned its specific position because it too is one element of every historic religion, although it never receives a proper form of its own. It is, then, neither conflict nor calm: it is ruled neither by the ethos of strife nor by the longing for peace. It is in fact the religion of a God Who rests not, Who "shall neither slumber nor sleep",[1] nor ever leave His people in repose. This, however, excludes neither conflict nor calm; for struggle is one form of unrest, while repose is its Pole and its aspiration. Still, disquietude ever remains the essential element in humanity. The conditions of conflict, too, are unambiguous. It may be that his God summons man to the contest; but it may also be a different unrest into which He plunges him, since he may be so good a fighter that he finds his peace in the very conflict itself; and this he must not do. For peaceful calm beckons as the final aim: we recall the familiar words, "our hearts are restless until they rest in Thee"; while every anticipation of this goal appears as sin.

Thus God is never-resting *Will*, which governs all human life. This is to be discerned at its best in the Old Testament, where God troubles and consoles, forsakes and seeks, punishes and shows compassion, is angry and loves:— but never for one single moment rests.

> Thou hast discarded us, crushed us in anger, O God;
>> restore us to power:
> thou hast shaken and shattered the land;
>> repair its tottering breaches.
> Hard times thou hast given to thy people:
>> and a cup to drink that has dazed them.
> Hast thou given thy worshippers a flag,
>> only that they might fly from the archers?
> To the rescue of thy dear folk!
>> Save by thy right hand, answer our entreaty,
> O thou Eternal who hast discarded us, shamed us,
>> who would'st not march out with our army.

[1] *Ps.* cxxi. 4.

> Help us against the foe,
>   for man's help is in vain.
> With God we shall do bravely;
>   he will trample down our foes.[1]

The religion of unrest, however, is not restricted to the historic form of Israel. It appears indeed not only in the closely allied religions of Islam and Christianity, but in all religions for which, however intense the element of calm may be, God is nevertheless a disquieting factor also. For Power, in the first place, is always the force that prevents man accepting life and indulging himself;[2] and this too finds its most pointed expression in the *Psalm*:

> Where could I go from thy Spirit,
>   where could I flee from thy face?
> I climb to heaven?—but thou art there;
>   I nestle in the nether-world?—and there thou art!
> If I darted swift to the dawn,
>   to the verge of the ocean afar,
> thy hand even there would fall on me,
>   thy right hand would reach me.
> If I say "The dark will screen me,
>   the night will hide me in its curtains",
> yet darkness is not dark to thee,
>   the night is clear as daylight.[3]

This we find to be repeated more or less in all religions with no exception, from the most primitive, in which the fear of God predominates, to the most mystical wherein the love of God consumes the devout. It is true that in these religions that foundation is absent which, in the religion of Israel, sustains the stirring drama of God and man:

> For thou didst form my being,
>   didst weave me in my mother's womb,[4]

and which constitutes the essence of Judaism as a historic religion. For there, and in Christianity also, God's creative Will is itself the cause of the unrest. The God Who descends to destroy the Tower of Babel descends a second time to deliver mankind; whether in anger, or in compassion, He never leaves humanity in peace. Wherever man goes, God's creative love pursues him.

---

[1] *Ps.* lx. 1–12 (Moffat).   [2] *cf.* Jaspers, *Psych. der Weltanschauungen*, 339.
[3] *Ps.* cxxxix. 7–12 (Moffat).   [4] *Ps.* cxxxix. 13 (Moffat).

CHAPTER 93

THE DYNAMIC OF RELIGIONS. SYNCRETISM.
MISSION

1. IN Chapter 19 we discerned syncretism to be the process leading from polydemonism to polytheism. But we must now apprehend its essential nature somewhat more thoroughly:—in fact, as one form of the *dynamic of religions*. In other terms, if we wish to discover the essence of the so-called "great religions", which must now be discussed, it is imperative for us not merely to contemplate their static character, but also to consider their dynamic. A historic religion, then, is a form, an organized system. Nonetheless its characteristics are not fixed and rigid; rather they are in perpetual flux: not manufactured but growing, and in a state of incessant expansion. "Every religion, therefore, has its own previous history and is to a certain extent a 'syncretism'. Then comes the time when, from being a summation, it becomes a whole and obeys its own laws".[1]

Thus Egyptian, and similarly Greek, religion arose from a large number of local religions. In ancient Egypt this process of amalgamation had set in at a very early period, and proceeded very deliberately.[2] The priesthood of one of the capitals zealously pursued the unification of the prevailing local cults and the elucidation of the reciprocal relations between the gods. In Greece, on the other hand, this theogony was effected by the poets. Nonetheless at the culmination of Egyptian, and again of Greek, culture, there was still, for example, an Osiris religion and a Ra or Ptah religion, a religion of Apollo, and of Zeus or of Dionysus, which maintained their independence as against one another and whose incorporation into the great whole remained theoretical or poetic.[3] But as the "world" gradually became smaller, several religions came into contact, the most impressive example of this being the syncretism of the Hellenistic age, which attracted to itself the religions of the whole inhabited world and interwove and united

---

[1] Wach, *Rel. wiss.* 86.
[2] *cf.* H. Kees, *Zeitschr. für. ägypt. Sprache und Altertumskunde*, 64, 1929, 99 *f.*
[3] Chantepie, *op. cit.*, I, 75. To a certain degree, a "pantheon" is always theory or poetry; *cf.* Chap. 19 and G. Furlani, *Actes du V. Congrès*, 154. The Babylonian gods were regarded as the limbs of Nimurta.

them either into magical modes of activity, or mysteries, or philosophic speculation. It may indeed be asserted that at the close of the
imperial era there were countless religions in existence, since each
person had his private system of devotions, and many even had
several simultaneously; but it may also be said that there was only
one sole religion, since all the components, of the most varied origin,
had become unified within one single astrological-pantheistically
tinged piety, for which the name of Zeus signified a rallying-point
rather than any distinctive feature.

Every historic religion, therefore, is not one, but several; not of
course as being the sum of different forms, but in the sense that diverse
forms had approximated to its own form and had amalgamated with
this. This is true of even the great, and so-called world, religions, to a
quite specific degree. Restricting ourselves to Christianity and Islam,
for example, these are from the dynamic viewpoint syncretisms; and
thus in Christianity we find, together with the inheritance of Israel,
that of Greece and even a small bequest from Persia; and the scars on
the amalgam, especially that of the Greek and Israelite spirit, have not
yet completely healed! In Islam, similarly, Christianity, Judaism and
primitive religion met and fused together into a unique new form.[1]

In recent times, also, there exists a close parallel to the boundless
syncretism of the Roman imperial era, in the various semi-, or completely, occult tendencies which appear under the names of theosophy,
anthroposophy, Christian science or (new) *sufism*. These forms all pay
homage to syncretism, to some extent in principle, because of their
conviction that all religions, at bottom, are only one in different guise;
nevertheless they are all mixtures taken from religions and spiritual
tendencies occurring everywhere:—Oriental, Christian, modern idea-
listic, natural scientific, *etc*. Naturally these medleys often produce a
very peculiar and confused impression, which however does not at all
disturb their own adherents!

2. But at this point a more precise definition of a concept already
repeatedly encountered may be given:—the concept of *transposition*.
"Transposition", then, is the variation of the significance of any phenomenon, occurring in the dynamic of religions, while its form remains

---

[1] Shinto, the Japanese national religion, is a religion free from syncretism, and
therefore one that lacks a mission! In this instance religion has been wholly absorbed
within nationalism (*cf*. Chap. 37). R. Pettazoni, *Die Nationalreligion Japans und die
Religionspolitik des japanischen Staates, Orient und Occident*, 1932, 5.

quite unaltered. Thus the sacred word, the myth of Bethel, of the "house of God",[1] becomes "transposed" from a fetishist experience to that of a theophany, subsequently to an announcement of the nearness of God, and finally edifying consolation. Quite similarly, the killing of the ox, which was regarded in pre-Zarathustrian Parsiism as a praiseworthy release of life (for Mithra slays the animal not at all maliciously, but simply in order to render life as it were fluid), becomes "transposed" in Zarathustrianism and diabolized into Ahriman's first destructive deed.[2] In Christian worship, again, prayers of incense offering (by transposition) become an *epiclesis* of the eucharistic Lord.[3]

"Transpositions", to continue, appear at all times, but chiefly during reformations[4] and missions; and as a rule, the old possessions of religion were superseded to only a slight extent and retained in essentials with, however, an altered significance. Thus almost all Protestant religious communities retained the sacrament of communion but "transposed", with a changed meaning, and this too after the Roman Church itself had already accepted it from the ancient church and had transposed it. Israelitish prophecy, again, took over the Bedouin law of the *Decalogue* and interpreted it in a religio-ethical sense, since when we ourselves have not ceased repeatedly to transpose the Ten Commandments anew, from the Gospel down to Luther. Frequently, also, the actual character of a phenomenon is utterly lost in transposition, as in the previous example of incense prayers. But just as often we receive the impression that the essence of the phenomenon, at bottom, is retained even when its interpretation has been modified, as in the case of the Law.

3. The dynamic of religions, further, is displayed as mission. This may in the first place be completely unconscious, and merely a reciprocal influence of religions which is the outcome of local proximity, cultural interchange, *etc.* It is called mission, however, because it is a result of speaking forth, of utterance and of testimony,[5] and is accompanied by all sorts of transpositions in the life of both the influencing and the influenced religion. Frick has given an illuminating description of this effect of religions on one another.[6] Thus there occurs assimilation of religions by each other, and also substitution of a religious value with more or less changed meaning (transposition); but there likewise arises

---

[1] *Gen.* xxviii. [2] Lommel, *op. cit.*, 183.
[3] Lietzmann, *Messe und Herrenmahl*; for liturgical transpositions *cf.* Will, *op. cit.*, II, 112 *ff.* [4] Chap. 94.
[5] Chap. 58. [6] *Vgl. Rel. wiss.* 53 *ff.*

the isolation of those elements which are, as it were, to be rendered harmless. Catholicism assimilated mysticism, for example, and substituted popular religion, while at the same time it isolated asceticism within monasticism.[1] This type of mission pertains to every living religion.

But as soon as missionary expansion is understood to be the essential activity of the community, it receives a quite different character. Its influence then becomes a fully conscious propaganda of doctrine and worship, and generally of the specific characteristics of a religion. It is in this sense that Judaism has made its proselytes, but has been frustrated because it has unified the "given" community with that of salvation;[2] for in general, deliberate missionary movements presuppose the collapse of this equivalence. The great mission religions, accordingly, are the "world religions" of Buddhism, Islam and Christianity. Of these three, again, Islam is at present the typical missionary religion, because it takes the dynamic power of its faith to be wholly a matter of course: conquest, then, lies in the very essence of Islam. Consequently, it sends out no specially trained missionaries at all, every follower of the prophet being, as such, a missionary who, by his example, advocates an extremely simple worship and an equally elementary creed.[3] But also in the essence of the Christian church, *una sancta catholica*, missionary activity is inherently incorporated, although Christians themselves are realizing this afresh only very gradually. Religion, however, lives only by being active; and in Christianity this ceaseless agitation is the life movement of the Holy Spirit, on Whom no limits whatever are imposed.

H. KRAEMER, *The Christian Message in a Non-Christian World*, 1938.
R. PETTAZONI, *Sencretismo e Conversione nella Storia delle Religione* (*Bull. du Com. Int. des Sciences Hist.*, 1933).

[1] *Vgl. Rel. wiss.* 55.   [2] Chap. 32 *ff.*
[3] Chap. 62; *cf.* W. H. T. Gairdner and W. A. Eddy, "Christianity and Islam", *The Christian Life and Message in relation to non-Christian Systems, Report of the Jerusalem Meeting of the Int. Miss. Council*, I, 1928, 252 *ff.*

CHAPTER 94

THE DYNAMIC OF RELIGIONS. REVIVALS. REFORMATIONS

1. EVERY religion is perpetually *reformanda*—to be reformed—although it is always already reformed—*reformata*—also. The dynamic of life compels religion continually to change its form; while it is living it is being reformed; and it is impossible to connect the occurrence of reformations merely with certain definite conflicts, even in the case of the most important, such as (for example) those involved in the different concepts of sin.[1] Reformation, in fact, can be associated with any given condition, any controversy whatever. That of Luther undoubtedly found its life and its justification in a profounder consciousness of sin; perhaps, also, that of Mohammed; but Buddha's case was quite different, and Zarathustra's reformation too had its roots elsewhere. Provisionally, however, we may say that the reformation of any religion begins in the reformer's own experience of God, and his being a special type of religious founder.[2] Luther's penitential struggle, Buddha's experience of suffering, Moses' theophany and Mohammed's visions—all alike imply, for the religious community to which each pertains, new life which then gradually flows out into channels of new doctrine, commandments, insight, *etc.*

The essence of "being reformed", however, is particularly distinct in the historic religions; thus Buddhism is the reformation of Brahminism, but this in its turn of the ancient Vedic polydemonism; similarly, Islam the reformation of Arabian animism, Zoroastrianism of the Persian "Nature religion"; Greek religion now as the "Homeric", and again as the "Platonic", reformation of local cults;[3] Christianity, finally, is the reformation of Judaism, which itself arose from the Jahvistic reformation of Canaanite animism. And in fact every religion without exception, as it appears in its concrete form, is the reformation of a reformation: Northern Buddhism of the original, which on its part, *etc.*; protestant Christianity of the medieval, and this again of the primitive Christian form, which in its turn, *etc.* No religion, therefore, is ever completed: every religion, even the "most primitive", was

---

[1] Mensching, *Sünde*, 68.   [2] Chap. 101 f.   [3] Chap. 95.

once different and will at some time be different again. Of course these reformations are not all on quite the same level, nor do they all attain an equal profundity. The reformations which produced the "great vehicle"—that is of salvation—from Buddhism, and the medieval church out of primitive Christianity, are rather processes of change[1] whose individual stages may indeed, to some degree, be based on religious experiences, but not on such as are markedly distinguished by any original power and specific character; in part, then, they also originate by accommodation and relapse into some ante-reform phase. It must certainly not be forgotten that (for example) St. Francis' experience of God was one factor in the construction of the medieval church—and subsequently an element, too, in its dissolution. The sole certainty, then, is that living religion is in perpetual activity, and reformation is therefore not some sort of arbitrary act, but *one form of the very life of a religion*.

Still further, a reformation that fails either because it lacks the requisite energy, or because it abandons the community it is seeking to reform as utterly lost, may lead to a sect or a schism: instances are the *Shiah* in Islam, and the great schism between West and East in Christianity.[2] From such controversies it frequently results that the sect, or the schismatic church, considers itself to be genuine and true, while its opponent concedes it only the status of a sect or indeed a heresy. Protestantism, for instance, regards itself as reformed Christianity, but to Roman Catholicism it is only a heresy.[3]

In general terms, then, three types of reformation should be distinguished: (*1*) that which has arisen from various historical developments, which in their turn are derived from unnumbered minor or major religious experiences. Such a reformation would be, for example, the gradual evolution of the medieval from the ancient church; this however need not be discussed further, because it is clear and simple in itself and hardly deserves the name of reformation, although it played an equally important rôle in the same dynamic as did the Reformation proper; but it may also be regarded simply from the viewpoint of transpositions and syncretisms.[4] (*2*) A reformation springing from mass experience:— from the revitalized collective experience of God: I

---

[1] Wach (*Rel. wiss.* 162) refers to "transpositions of strain", or corrections of the structure of a religion; in this broad sense the development of Homeric religion, *e.g.*, and Augustus' reform of the cult, were "reformations" of diverse type.

[2] *cf.* O. Piper, *Sekte und Konfessionskirche, Zeitschr. für Theol. und Kirche, N. F.* 11, 1930, 258.

[3] Chap. 35 *f.*   [4] Chap. 93.

describe such a reformation as revival. (3) One that is born from some individual person's experience of God: this is reformation in the full sense.

2. By the term revival I mean that a wave of religious feeling and desire flows over a community, and draws everything along with it in the broad stream of sentiment and resolution. It may be linked with ecstatic experiences,[1] but at all events it consists of some relaxation of life's potencies, all of which are then precipitated on the religious purpose without hindrance and freed from all compulsion of regulated celebration. It may be sustained by some single personality, but it may also operate *en masse* in every respect, though it certainly always requires leaders; and while it may reform a religious society, it may also establish itself as a sect quite apart from the existing community. Such a revival was the great Dionysiac wave which, in the early history of Greece, penetrated Hellas from the North with elemental power and carried everything along with it. Like all revivals this too was contagious, as may be clearly perceived from legendary narratives of the immigration of Dionysus; some few isolated individuals offer resistance,[2] but the majority are swept away in the whirlpool of divine insanity. Thus in Orchomenos the daughters of Minyas withstood the frenzy until vine-runners suddenly twined themselves around their looms, while milk and honey dropped from the ceiling; then they too seized one of their sons, tore him in pieces and sought their salvation in the mountains with the maenads.[3] Marvellously clear in this legend is the foil of the historical event itself: the epidemic seizes all the more fiercely those who at first resisted it, and the Dionysiac revival became a popular under-current of Greek religion that maintained itself not only in various sects such as Orphism and Pythagoreanism, but had also very lasting influence on the thought and aspiration of the entire Greek people; it may therefore be asserted that though it was not a reformation in the strict sense, still it thoroughly reformed Greek religion; and without this revival neither tragedy nor Platonism would ever have arisen.

The flagellant movement of the thirteenth and fourteenth centuries was a similar revival, directed in part against the clergy and carrying all before it in the stream of penitence, while analogous to this was the

[1] Chap. 74.   [2] Euripides, *Bacchae.*
[3] G. van der Leeuw, *Goden en Menschen*, 117 f. Nilsson, *A History of Greek Religion*, 207.

Anabaptist revival, whose raptures turned towards the new Jerusalem, the kingdom of God:

> I hear the trumpet's sounding,
> Its call is heard afar,
> In Jerusalem, in Edom, in Bashan,
> The messengers call everywhere.[1]

More recent revivals also, from pietism and methodism onwards, pertain to this category, even though they usually show no pronouncedly enthusiàstic character. Nevertheless there always exists that passionate torrential surrender to the One which is necessary: in this case, to inwardness of belief, sanctification of life and the operations of the Spirit. These movements, still further, may once again become enthusiastic, as the pentecostal movement that arose from Evan Roberts's Welsh revival clearly proves to-day; while with a magnificent organization the Salvation Army hurls itself on the masses with the sole purpose of conversion.

3. As I have just observed, actual reformation arises from some one individual person's own experience of salvation. From this, new powerfulness springs into life which in part makes an end of old custom, doctrine and morals, and in general of the existing relationship between life and Power, and in part revivifies the torpid elements. Usually the second feature is stressed: the reformer comes "not to destroy, but to fulfil";[2] he wants to make the truly religious element, the very life of religion, resound once more in the vast desert calm of stagnation. This holds good of the Old Testament prophets—the Law—but that written in the heart: the sacrifice—but of a broken heart: just as it does of Jesus, of Buddha—the ideal of "true brahmins"—and of Mohammed —the appeal to Abraham.[3]

A typical reformation was that of the Egyptian "heretic king" Akhnaton.[4] Resuming primeval tendencies and endeavours, he placed in the centre the worship of the sun as that of the visible god. But in this he inevitably gave offence, on the one hand to the ancient traditional animal worship together with the anthropomorphic and theriomorphic representation of the gods in general, while on the other hand he

---

[1] Revivalist Song of the martyr Anneke Jans, in Lindeboom, *Stiefkinderen,* 211.
[2] *Matt.* v, 17.   [3] Frick, *Vgl. Rel. wiss.* 47.
[4] H. Schäfer, *Amarna in Religion und Kunst,* 1931. G. van der Leeuw, *Achnaton,* 1927.

believed that he was according the true essence of the sun-god its first proper estimation, as he had expressed this in the interpretation of his god's name. He also retained the ancient dogma of kingship,[1] filling it however with new and mystic content. It is no less typical of his reformation that, quite apart from the opposition to the old, and its fulfilment, he neglected one entire sphere of tradition:—the worship of the dead. And the same essential traits occur, more or less prominently, in all reformations. Zarathustra and Mohammed, Buddha and Jesus, Luther and Calvin: they all repeal, preserve and fulfil, or else they adopt a wholly indifferent attitude with reference to the religion they have reformed. In Jesus' own words: "Ye have heard that it was said by them of old time . . . But I say unto you . . . I am not come to destroy, but to fulfil";[2] the old is either annulled, fulfilled or set aside as quite immaterial. Luther may be similarly depicted: catholic penitential practice was abolished, while the church was affirmed in its essential nature, and worship left as it was with marked indifference.

[1] Chap. 13.   [2] *Matt.* v. 17 f.

CHAPTER 95

THE RELIGION OF STRAIN AND OF FORM

1. IN approaching the "great" forms among religions, and prepared by the consideration of their dynamic, we become increasingly aware that they can scarcely be characterized by any single term. In order to outline any adequately detailed description of these religions, therefore, nothing less than a vast number of intersecting lines would be adequate for the clear delineation of their contours. But even now, when we are concerned only with typology, we can satisfy ourselves with no single characteristic, as Hegel did. For it is undeniable that in dealing with such complicated historical structures as are the great religions, we should never analytically dissociate (at least not in phenomenology) what history itself has combined, since this has all grown up in the closest association, not merely been placed in juxtaposition. Yet at the same time we shall hardly be able to find any firm historic ground whatever without taking a cross-section which, while traversing the line that indicates the essential nature of a religion, still itself pertains to that very nature. Hence we must set to work as did the Romans when they laid out a camp, and decide on *cardo* and *decumanus*, the main road from North to South and its intersection East to West.

The *cardo* would be in the first instance strain, the *decumanus* form; and the religion of strain and of form is that of Greece. We have, in fact, long since been compelled altogether to abandon the classicist view of the Greek spirit:[1] the Greeks were not merely the people of "tranquil greatness and noble simplicity". Thus Rohde has emphasized the mystical aspect of the Greek sentiment for life, while although Nietzsche, with a brilliant anticipation of to-day's scientific achievements, has certainly modernized the discord in the Greek temperament, he nevertheless clearly perceived it. The Greeks, then, were the people of *hubris* and *sophrosyne*, of Dionysus and of Apollo, of the night of death and of bright day, of the dark stress of Eros and of clear, sharply outlined form. As Kern points out, the Dionysus of the Orphics was a god of liberation;[2] in the orgiastic cult, in the myth of the origin of sin, in mystic yearning for death, in transcendental speculation as in tragic art, Dionysus was the symbol of life ever striving beyond itself in

[1] G. van der Leeuw, *Goden en Menschen.*   [2] *Die griechischen Mysterien*, 48.

indomitable longing and seeking for deliverance, indeed for dissolution.
To Dionysus they prayed: "Men shall send hecatombs at all seasons
of the year, and shall celebrate orgies to bring about liberation from
lawless ancestors, and shall celebrate them madly. And you, deriving
strength from these, shall free whom you will from heavy toil and
endless trouble."[1] The Bacchic mystic did not sing, like the worshipper
of Apollo; once he had scaled the high peaks of ecstasy he remained
silent.[2] But the philosopher, too, knows the moment when concepts
fail him, so that he can do justice to his thought only in mystic guise.
Thus the Greeks were keenly conscious of life's farthest frontiers, and
of that beyond where actual life first begins: "who knows if this life
be not death, and death be not accounted life in the world below?" as
Euripides says.[3] In the dithyramb life becomes revealed as "deaths and
vanishings, passages out of life and new births",[4] while out of the
ecstatic experience of orgiastic worship sprang the belief in immortality.[5]

It is strain, therefore, that creates life and is the most ancient of gods,
but which also overpowers life until it ceases to breathe and finds rest
only in dissolution:

> Love resistless in fight, all yield at a glance of thine eye,
> Love who pillowed all night on a maiden's cheek dost lie,
> Over the upland fells thou roam'st, and the trackless sea,
> Love the gods captive holds. Shall mortals not yield to thee?
> Mad are thy subjects all.[6]

Eros, however, has already been discussed.[7] As a historical form he was
adopted by Plato from the yearning dreams of Dionysiac Orphism,
and fashioned into an eternal symbol. Divine strain, *Eros*, son of
poverty and wealth: this is at once the eternally striving and the
eternally vanishing, the love of the good and the beautiful, that which
man has not, the generation of an eternal life, sexual desire and the
most spiritual creation, instinct and loftiest volition. Generation,

---

[1] Kern, *Orphicorum Fragmenta*, No. 232.

> ἄνθρωποι δὲ τελήέσσας ἑκατόμβας
> πέμψουσι πάσῃσι ἐν ὥραις ἀμφιέτῃσιν
> ὄργια τ'ἐκτελέσουσι λύσιν προγόνων ἀθεμίστων
> μαιόμενοι· σὺ δὲ τοῖσιν ἔχων κράτος, οὕς κ' ἐθέλῃσθα,
> λύσεις ἔκ τε πόνων χαλεπῶν καὶ ἀπείρονος οἴστρου.

[2] Rohde, *Psyche*, II, 9; English Translation, 288.

[3] *Fr.* 639; Cornford, *Greek Religious Thought*, 155.

[4] Plutarch, *On the E at Delphi*, ix; Cornford, *ibid.*, 56.

[5] Chap. 44.

[6] Sophocles, *Antigone*, 781 *ff.* (Storr).

[7] Chap. 76.

indeed, is the very essence of the highest human capacity: "All men are bringing to the birth in their bodies and in their souls . . . procreation which must be in beauty . . . this procreation . . . is a divine thing; for conception and generation are an immortal principle in the mortal creature."[1] In the *Phaedrus Eros* leads to the turning away from body and form, the transition being here foreshadowed from the Greek spirit to Greek Christianity. But the polarity of the Greek spirit appears first of all in its proper guise in the *Symposium*: eternal strain, perpetually generating, nevertheless finds its supreme fulfilment in blissful contemplation of form.

2. For this is the other aspect of Greek religion: at one moment sober, at another rapt, but always tranquil *contemplation of form*: this is the truth of classicism and also of the famous Hegelian dictum at the transition from Egyptian to Greek religion: "The enigma is solved; the Egyptian Sphinx, according to a deeply significant and admirable myth, was slain by a Greek, and thus the enigma has been solved. This means that the content is man, free, self-knowing spirit."[2] For though Egyptian religion can scarcely be described as enigmatic, and though Oedipus' Sphinx is hardly an Egyptian, and if, still further, the "free, self-knowing spirit" could fashion itself only on free, self-conscious form, nevertheless a pedantic science should perceive that one aspect of Greek religion is quite clearly expressed here:—that is the purely human. No religion, in fact, has ever been so much a *religion of humanity* as the Greek; not even the entire oppressive weight of mysticism, pessimism and yearning for the "beyond" can stifle this pure humanity. Homer depicted the gods in beautiful human forms: but he did not deify man;[3] Homer's religion, as contrasted with Plato's— the religion of Apollo in antithesis to that of Dionysus—is perception of pure forms, contemplation of form: not dominance over the divine, and scarcely indeed the longing for this.[4] "The Greeks enjoyed an astonishingly high degree of health—their secret was to revere even disease as a god, if it only possessed *power*", as Nietzsche observed;[5]

---

[1] *Symposium*, 206; *cf.* further 186*b*.; "how great and wonderful and universal is the deity of love, whose empire extends over all things, divine as well as human" (Jowett).

[2] Hegel, *The Philosophy of Religion*, II, 122.

[3] Murray, *The Rise of the Greek Epic*, 158 *ff*. On this aspect of Greek religion, *cf.* W. F. Otto, *Der Geist der Antike und die christliche Welt*, 1923; *id. Der europäische Geist und die Weisheit des Ostens*, 1931.

[4] This formulation shows to what extent I agree with W. F. Otto's fine and weighty, but one-sided, volume; *cf.* p. 621, n. 3.   [5] *Human, All Too Human*, I, 192.

and it is just this that is specially important for us. For it appears almost as though the Homeric Greeks were deficient in that elementary necessity of every religion:—not simply to accept life, but to undertake something with it, to demand something from it, to resolve to make some use of it. The Homeric Greek was neither magician nor believer in the sense previously discussed:[1] he gazed upon the given world and adored it as divine form; thus far, again, Hegel was correct (and many after him), since if the other aspect of the Greek spirit is disregarded Greek religion was certainly a religion of the beautiful, with an essentially esthetic character. Nevertheless this religion was indeed a genuine religion, and was least of all estheticism. Reformed by poets and philosophers, it still lived among the people together with the mournful or yearning cults of the grave and the mysteries.[2] In fact, precisely this contemplation of form was "celebration" in this religion: the Greek accepted the given world just as little as any others; and he celebrated it as form. Certainly this form, for him, was neither a will which dominated him nor which he dared hope to control, neither a power that he constrained nor one that stifled himself. Otto suggests that the fear of, and the longing for, the Wholly Other were equally lacking in the Homeric Greek. In that case, however, one certainly could not understand why his *Weltanschauung* should be called a religion at all. But the Wholly Other subsists precisely in that *form* which is not fortuitous and empirical but divine, perfect and eternal, radiantly rising from the given life. And no. one has perceived and maintained this better than Otto himself.

Let us follow him, then, awhile: the Greek domain of belief is "an emanation from the wealth and profundity of existence, not from its cares and longings".[3] For the Greek spirit, therefore, it was not events and capacity that were significant, but "being. The divinities become forms of reality, wherein the manifold being of Nature finds its perfect eternal expression".[4] In form "there reposes the meaning of all being and happening. It is the true reality, the divine. Present everywhere, it is one with all the appearances of the life circle that it controls. But

---

[1] *cf.* further Chap. 82.   [2] *cf.* S. Wide, *Griechische Religion.*
[3] *Die Götter Griechenlands*, 1929[1], 371. This work, already cited, is particularly significant with regard to the psychology and phenomenology of Form; *cf.* G. van der Leeuw, *Gli dei di Omero, SM.* 7, 1931. On Greek religion, together with Rohde's *Psyche* and Harrison's *Prolegomena, cf.* especially: Wilamowitz-Möllendorf, *Die Glaube der Hellenen*, 1931-1932. O. Kern, *Die Religion der Griechen*, I, 1926. Nilsson, *History of Greek Religion.* Farnell, *Outline History of Greek Religion.* Murray, *Five Stages of Greek Religion.*   [4] *op. cit.*, 49.

as the highest essentiality and as persistent being it stands alone, high above the earthly in etherial splendour".[1] This religious sentiment, further, concerns itself little about the dead or death: the dead possess form only as life that is ended; the "form of the person who has existed is (indeed) not extinguished", but the deceased is not present as a demon.[2] Nor again does it strive for any justification whatever, neither of the world, nor of God nor man. Man should demand justice neither from the course of the world, nor from the gods superior to it; as long as "the consciousness of the divine presence" is vivid he asks absolutely nothing.[3] Obscene myths may well have a quite comprehensible origin in the syncretism of local cults,[4] but the Homeric gods do not require any such justification; their sins never offended the Olympic Greeks, simply because a god's sin is just the eternal form of an existing being, and one does not censure being for existing.[5] Human guilt, too, is indeed a fault; but it does not lead to contrition, and still less to any metaphysics of sin as, for example, in Orphism. For the gods also bring about evil deeds in man, and the passion to which these are due "has its marvellous eternal countenance among the gods, to which man may look up even out of his contrition".[6] What therefore deeply distressed the Greeks of the first, Dionysiac type—that eternal gods should allow themselves to be guilty of evil—is precisely the very ground of Homeric religious sentiment; the Euripidean Hecuba, who reproached Helen for being led astray not by the goddess but by her own concupiscence, would here be wrong, since the goddess is precisely this passion itself elevated to an eternal form.[7]

This religion of form is best displayed then—and here again we may follow Otto—in Apollo's essential and true character. His form certainly developed from various others on syncretistic lines; but in Homer's religion it became a mighty and surpassing apparition, the type of Homeric construction of form in general: embodying the ideal of proper distance, it "repulses whatever is too near, the state of being immersed in things, the trance-like glance, and equally the fusion of souls, mystic rapture and its ecstatic dream".[8] Here then there appears a sharp contrast between this religion and not merely—as Otto supposes— Judaism and Christianity as the religions of Will and Love, but also Greek mysticism and Dionysus, the god who plays almost no part at all in Homer. For Apollo is an aristocratic figure who always maintains his distance: "Are they, the perfect ones, to allow their bliss to be dis-

---

[1] 210.   [2] 182 ff.   [3] 331 f.   [4] Chap. 19.   [5] 311 ff.   [6] 225.
[7] cf. Chap. 19. Otto, op. cit., 242.   [8] 99.

turbed by any too serious a participation in man and his complaints?"[1]
Men are only men: eternal gods need not trouble too much about them;
when Poseidon challenges Apollo in battle before Ilium, the god replies:
"Shaker of Earth, as nowise sound of mind wouldest thou count me,
if I should war with thee for the sake of mortals, pitiful creatures, that
like unto leaves are now full of flaming life, eating the fruit of the field,
and now again pine away and perish."[2] And when his sister, Artemis,
chides the god for cowardice, he remains silent in his majestic self-
consciousness and self-esteem.

The religion of form, therefore, seeks no other world, but simply one
that has been given form and shape and which (in this I differ from
Otto!) precisely in thus acquiring form is then a kind of "new" world.
We stand here, in fact, at the uttermost frontier of religion: the "divine"
of the Homeric Greeks "is neither a justifying explanation, nor an
interruption and abolition of the natural course of the world; it is the
natural course of the world itself".[3] And here lies the limit already
indicated in Chapter 19: for as soon as Power thus becomes completely
identical with the world itself, no religion can live any longer; with the
"Other" it can never dispense. The salvation of Greek religion, then,
was the immortalizing and perfecting of the given form into timeless
sublimity: its weakness (deplored however by all its own "Dionysiac"
poets and philosophers!) was that it merely presupposed this sublimity
rather than strove for it. It may therefore be conceded to Otto that
Homeric religion not merely possesses esthetic value, but confronts the
Israelitish religion as an equal[4]—it may indeed even be maintained
that hardly any purer "antithesis" to Israelitish religion can anywhere
be found than just in this Greek religion. But on the other hand, we
cannot exclude the view that this polarity arises precisely from Homeric
religion having reduced the religious element to its utmost minimum.
And if it is true that it is not the striving, desiring, demanding, limitless,
uncanny and labyrinthic that is ever suggested in Homeric religion,
but form—if "the forms of being of the human appeared (to the Homeric
Greek) with such a degree of reality that he had to revere them as
gods"[5]—then, it is true, the Wholly Other may be saved in the perfection and eternity of these forms; it always hovers, nevertheless, in
danger of being entirely merged in the world itself and in humanity.
Thus this religion is sharply delimited from its own environment and
from the world of religion in general; no awful and imperious Will

[1] 165.　　　　　[2] *Iliad*, XXI, 461 (Murray).　　　　　[3] 218.
[4] 173.　　　　　　　　　　　　　　　　　　　　　　　　　　[5] 299 *f.*

asserts itself against man: no unity entices, which might dissolve all that has been separated: high and sublime stands Form, pure Form, and man may contemplate it. "In the heavenly sphere the forms stand pure and great before each other. There immaculate Artemis may gaze upon the tenderness of Aphrodite with cool wonder."[1] That is beautiful, and because it is perfect it is also sacred. But when Otto asserts that "immediate bodily presence and at the same time an eternal validity—that is the marvel of Greek creation of form",[2] then the danger is at least not at all illusory that the "immediate presence" stifles the "eternal validity". It is indeed this peril that has made the tragedians suffer, while the "Dionysiac" mystics and philosophers sought refuge from it in their hatred of the body and the world.

3. It is one of the greatest of all marvels in the history of religion that the religion of Form and that of Eros held their place in the soul of *a single* people; and this, again, not side by side but in the unity of tension and reconciliation. Eros is a beautiful *ephebos*, while Form awakens Eros by its beauty;[3] and this is a miracle, witnessing to both the affluence and the plasticity of Greek religion. For it could beget a Pheidias but also a Euripides, a Homer, but a Plato too. Ultimately, Homer's gods are no merely empirical Nature forms, but esthetically "modelled forms"; Plato's ideas too are not without form and beauty, being "in these akin to the marble statues of Pheidias".[4] And thus we can understand how *Iliad* and *Phaedrus* sprang from the genius of one and the same people.[5] To this unity of the religion of Form *and* of Eros, in conclusion, Diotima's beautiful utterance may testify, revealing as it does the ultimate vision of the Eros mystery: "He who" (in practice and knowledge) "has been instructed thus far in the things of love, and who has learned to see the beautiful in due order and succession, when he comes toward the end will suddenly perceive a nature of wondrous beauty (and this, Socrates, is the final cause of all our former toils)— a nature which in the first place is everlasting, not growing and decaying, or waxing and waning . . . And the true order of going or being led by another to the things of love, is to use the beauties of earth as steps along which he mounts upwards for the sake of that other beauty, going from one to two, and from two to all fair forms, and from fair forms to

---

[1] 309.   [2] 321.
[3] For the comprehension of the Greek spirit, *cf.* J. Geffcken, *Kantstudien* 35, 1930, 427 *ff.* G. Mehlis, *Logos* 8, 1919–1920; van der Leeuw, *Goden en Menschen, Einleitung.*
[4] Mehlis, *op. cit.*, 45.   [5] G. van der Leeuw, *Gli dei di Omero*, 19.

fair practices, and from fair practices to fair notions, until from fair notions he arrives at the notion of absolute beauty, and at last knows what the essence of beauty is . . . a beauty not after the measure of gold, and garments, and fair boys and youths . . . But what if man had eyes to see the true beauty—the divine beauty, I mean, pure and clear and unalloyed, not clogged with the pollutions of mortality, and all the colours and vanities of human life—thither looking, and holding converse with the true beauty divine and simple? Do you not see that in that communion only, beholding beauty with the eye of the mind, he will be enabled to bring forth, not images of beauty, but realities (for he has hold not of an image but of a reality), and bringing forth and nourishing true virtue to become the friend of God and be immortal, if mortal man may. Would that be an ignoble life?"[1] Here equilibrium between Form and Eros has been discovered, and the tension eschatologically relieved.

[1] *Symposium*, 210–212 (Jowett).

W. F. OTTO, *Die Götter Griechenlands*, 1929.
M. P. NILSSON, *Geschichte der griecheschen Religion*, I, 1941; II, 1950.
M. P. NILSSON, *Greek Piety*, 1948.

CHAPTER 96

THE RELIGION OF INFINITY AND OF ASCETICISM

1. THE religions of India signify the victory of longing over form. And had the Greeks not been Greeks, they too would probably have carried the desire "to escape from the cycle" onward to the unconsciousness of a *Nirvana*, and intensified care for salvation to the point of asceticism. In the light of actual historical development, however, we find that with all their contempt for the world the Greeks never recognized formlessness as the norm, while in the classical Greek world the idea of asceticism and virginity was indulged only once—by Euripides:[1] a proof both of the greatness of the keen-sighted poet and of the essential distinction between the Greek and the Hindu spirit.

If for the moment we leave Buddhism, which occupies a place of its own, out of consideration, then the religions of India appear to us as the *religion of the infinite and of asceticism*. We know quite well, of course, that the "religions of India" comprise an almost endless variety; and like Greek religion, the Indian too are erected on a primitive religion of which they have preserved very much to this day. Still further, they find their limits in *bhakti* religion, which will be discussed later. The main stream of Hindu religious sentiment, however, which has also beaten against the coasts of Europe and still powerfully influences the modern world, directs itself towards the infinite, and attempts to attain it by asceticism.

The entire world-event, then, is the "universal sacrifice" of *Purusha*, the primeval man[2] from whom everything emanated; there are certainly gods who sacrifice *Purusha*, but they are not essential; there also exists, further, an old myth of the dismembered giant, but this likewise is inessential. What is really essential is the reduction of all that happens to one single event, of all that is to one sole being: "*Purusha* is the whole Universe, what was and what shall be . . . by sacrifice the gods sacrificed the sacrifice", says a celebrated hymn in the *Rig-Veda*.[3] Fear of solitude and of possibility, concern or "care" for the world, are infinitely intensified, and possibility becomes so potent that man ceases to breathe—literally, in fact, in *Yoga* discipline; "care" extends

[1] In *Hippolytus*.   [2] Chap. 86.
[3] Lehmann-Haas, *Textbuch*, 92 *f.*; *cf.* Otto, *India's Religion of Grace*, 68.

to the very ground of the Universe, dethrones the gods themselves and
bases the world in the self, the self in the world. "In the beginning this
world was only the *ātman* in human form (*purusha*). He gazed around
and saw nothing but himself (the *ātman*). Then first he spoke the word:
'It is I'. Thence arose the word 'I'. He was afraid. Therefore does he
fear who is absolutely alone. And he mused: If there exists nothing but
myself, of whom am I actually afraid? then his fear departed", says
Yajhavalkya.[1] Thus the great equilibrium prepared a way for itself,
which carries away all care that involves celebration, and all distance
implying fear and gods, in one intense passion: the Universe is the self
and the self is the Universe, *Brahman-Ātman*. Oldenberg has acutely
depicted the development of this equilibrium,[2] which received its finest
expression in Sandilya's words: "*Brahman* is the truth: therefore it
should be revered. Man consists of will alone. Whatever is his will in
passing from this world, such shall be his will on attaining the other
world. Thus let him revere the self (*ātman*): thought is its nature,
breath its body, light its form, the ether its self—it is formed like desire,
as swift as thought: it is true in thought, true in performance: rich
in all perfumes, rich in all essences, interpenetrating all regions of the
Universe, permeating the Whole, silent and heedless. Small as a grain
of rice or barley, or millet or a millet seed, this spirit dwells within
the self, golden as smokeless flame, greater than the heavens, greater
than the ether, greater than this earth, greater than all beings. This is
the self of the breath, this is my self. To this self I shall attain by
separation from this world. Whosoever truly possesses this knowledge
has no doubts. Thus spake Sandilya. Thus it is."[3] Just as the great
edifices of Hindu worship of the gods perpetuate the same *motif* in
interminable repetition—as the great epics of Hindu literature endlessly
accumulate epithet upon epithet—so Hindu religion expands what
exists, the Universe and the self, in eternal repetition into the infinite,
wherein the two are but one.

Then all celebration ceases; but to this culmination *asceticism*[4] should
lead. Usually we distinguish between the path of action and that of
insight and knowledge; but asceticism is equally acting and insight,
insight, as it were, that has become action. The ancient brahmin ideal,
indeed, places at the close of life the existence of the *yatin*, the self-
conqueror; the *yatin* no longer sacrifices, but in rigorous asceticism
dedicates himself to contemplation: life, so to say, is prolonged into the

[1] Bertholet, *Lesebuch*, 9, 102.   [2] *Die Lehre der Upanishaden*, 55 *ff.*
[3] Oldenberg, *Lehre*, 57 *f.*   [4] Chap. 66.

infinite. Commencing as a disciple of the brahmins, the adult performs his duties of sacrifice and procreation of children; then withdrawing into the forest, he "leaves his home";[1] from the variegated, fulfilled life there has arisen the void of the infinite. Man does not simply practice asceticism: life *is* asceticism as soon as it directs itself towards its actual powerfulness. "The 'great *Text*' indicates this powerfulness in the famous *tat tvam asi*, 'that art thou', 'thou, thy true essential being, thy spirit, art one with the unity in the All: thou art the Universe.' "[2] The religio-speculative passion of the *Vedanta* is separated from the infinite, which is the real and true world, only by the deceptive veil of *Maya*: "Man should know that Nature is merely illusion and the great god the deceiver. The whole Universe is filled with elements that are only fragments of him."[3] Both world and man, therefore, must be purified, the veil removed from them by either asceticism, insight or resignation: and Hindu religion is the way of infinity. Illusion (*Maya*), *avidya* (ignorance) must cease to deprive the relationship between the "I" and the "thou" of its essential unity. The world that "appears" was brought forth by *Brahman* with *Maya*: creation is therefore an illusory act; the personal god has a merely provisional task, and is only the object of unintelligent reverence. He who penetrates to essential being knows *advaita* (non-duality): that there are not two, but one only. This "one", however, actually exists; in this respect Sankara, the greatest of the commentators on the *Vedanta*, and perhaps the greatest of all prophets of the religion of infinity, differs from Buddhism, the religion of the nought. *Brahman* is timeless, eternal being with which the self merges after it has released itself, through insight, from the nullity of the world and the *tat tvam asi*.[4] It is therefore not sufficient to characterize the religion of India as the religion of unity: for into unity is entwined the All which is infinite, whereof the human self constitutes an indistinguishable part. *Brahman* has no predicates whatever: it merely exists; to it, or from it, there is no other path at all than that of being. Man can neither seek it, nor influence it, nor even love it; he can only be it. As religion, that is as one human attitude, Brahminism is therefore a religion of infinity: its goal, its task, are alike infinite. Already the nought advances its claim, but it is rejected.

2. The religion of infinity finds its logical consequence, and also its limit, in the nought of Buddhism: another limit, however, confronts it

[1] Chap. 34.   [2] Tiele-Söderblom, *Kompendium der Religionsgeschichte*, 157.
[3] Bertholet, *op. cit.*, 9, 140.   [4] *cf.* Otto, *op. cit.*, 30 *f.*

in *bhakti* religion:—submission to the lord *Isvara*; and Otto points out, with perfect justice, that in India there was not only a Sankara, but also a Ramanuja: "In India itself there has been waged the hottest battle against this 'monistic' mysticism of an impersonal Absolute."[1] One of Sankara's followers said to Otto: "You Christians are the same as our *bhaktas*. Your relation to God is that of a child to his father (*pitri-putri-bhava*). We also approve that. Still, the true and final completion of the *ekata-bhava*, the relation of complete unity and oneness with God, lies far above and beyond it."[2] In the theistic *bhakti* religion, then, God really is "a God to inspire personal trust, love, reverence, and loyal self-surrender",[3] no mere introduction and makeshift for popular piety. His lack of duality is primarily his uniqueness; *advaita* (non-duality), nevertheless, must be assigned its full validity, since God and the world become united as soul and body.[4] It is true that this constitutes one limit of the religion of infinity; but it is by no means a bridge to the religions of Will and Form. Formlessness is certainly limited, and the passionate flight into the infinite checked; in contemplating *bhakti* religion, therefore, we are repeatedly impressed by a far-reaching agreement with Islam, but above all with Christianity:—for here is a "religion of grace", and in a certain sense a religion of love too;[5] here also contrasts can arise such as that between release by works and deliverance by *bhakti* alone: *sola fide!* The *Bhagavad-Gita*, in fact, can be read with edification by the adept of a religion of Will and faith.[6] And what ultimately and definitely makes *bhakti* religion a religion of the infinite—in spite of all these features pointing in a different direction—is in the first place its conception of life, and secondly—but not detached from this—that of the Universe.

Otto points out, still further, that the term "rebirth", which in Christianity implies a completely new creation through the Spirit, can in *bhakti* mean nothing but *samsara*, the unbroken chain of births; what in one religion is supreme grace is regarded by the other as the dark foil for this grace; while what one calls liberation is, for the other, precisely that from which man must be freed. For the one, life is something to be created wholly anew; for the other, life is lost and must finally vanish in infinity.[7] As to the Universe, again, the religion of Will and of Love regards it as a creation, as the deed of God; for the religion of infinity however, even for that which in *bhakti* is mitigated and rendered much more a religion of the heart, it is merely the sport (*lila*)

---

[1] *cf.* Otto, *op. cit.*, 17.   [2] *ibid.*, 21, 22.   [3] *ibid.*, 29.   [4] *cf. ibid.*, 32 *f.*
[5] Chap. 76.   [6] *cf.* Otto, *op. cit.*, 50.   [7] *ibid.*, 87.

of the All-one. "When I consider the chaste women of honourable families, I see in them the divine mother garbed in the raiment of the chaste lady; and when I behold the prostitutes of the town, as they sit in their open verandahs wearing the clothing of immorality and shamelessness, in them too I see the divine mother as she plays the game in a quite different way", says Ramakrishna, the last great Hindu teacher.[1] All that "appears", therefore, is only the revelation of the One, here possessing a provisional form (that of the Hindu mother-goddess) which, however, makes everything else inessential; if the Universe moves the motion can be only a game of the sole Power with itself. And thus neither God nor man finds any assigned "place" in either space or time: infinite motion draws away with it even what is most immovable and once more dissolves the most rigid forms.

H. OLDENBERG, *Die Lehre der Upanishaden und die Anfänge des Buddhismus*, 1915.
R. OTTO, *India's Religion of Grace and Christianity Compared and Contrasted*.

[1] Bertholet, *op. cit.*, 14, 83 *f*.

CHAPTER 97

THE RELIGION OF NOTHINGNESS AND
OF COMPASSION

1. IN Buddhism the way of the infinite leads to *nothingness*. For the older Buddhism, most faithfully preserved in the "little vehicle" (of salvation), *Hinayana*, is hostile to all sensuous representation: Buddhist art lived in *Mahayana*[1]; nor is this to be wondered at, since in the former every presentation of the divine is proscribed: Form disappears, and Will must be annihilated. Buddhism, then, is in the first instance the insight that this vanishing and annihilation are real; it is therefore the religion of the negative.

In this connection Frick offers an illuminating comparison between the "sacred nights" of the three great religions. In Islam the night of power, *lailat al kadr*, is the occasion on which the *Koran* was sent down. In Christianity, again, the sacred night is that of the Saviour's coming. But in Buddhism, on the holy night, Buddha received illumination on the banks of the river Neranjara—that is to say, insight into the four noble truths and the path of liberation: "Here I have cut off the briars of passion from the tree of world-being with the axe of reflection, and burnt them in the fire of knowledge; the stream of sensual desires has been dried up by the sun of knowledge; here the eye of knowledge, in its purity, was opened for me and the fabric of madness rent; all the fetters of the existence of the world have been loosed for me."[2] Failure to know and to comprehend the noble truths of suffering and its origin, of its suppression, and the way leading to this, is the cause of the "erring and wandering on this long road".[3] The extirpation of the roots of suffering, then, effects the cessation of rebirth; and since the Hindu temperament cannot conceive existence except as a cycle, it leads to nothingness. The last word of the *Tathâgata* to the monks, in fact, refers to the nullity of this cycle: "Hearken, ye monks, I say unto you: doomed to vanish are the appearances of existence (*samkara*); strive on without ceasing."[4] Then the master enters *Nirvana*, which he attains

---

[1] Mensching, *Buddh. Symbolik*, 5.
[2] *Vergl. Rel. wiss.* 68 *ff. cf.* A. Bertholet, *Buddhismus im Abendland der Gegenwart*, 1928, 29.
[3] Bertholet, 11, 17.   [4] *ibid.*, 11, 24.

by stages: the four degrees of submersion (*jhana*) bring him to the realm of "infinite space", then he attains to that of "infinite consciousness", and finally to the sphere of "non-being". But this also is too positive: imagination and perception must cease completely. At this point, according to Ananda, the master has attained perfect rest; but Anuruddha understands the matter more adequately: the road returns once more to the first stage of submersion, and then follows precisely the same course again; but now, from the fourth *jhana* Buddha reaches "complete *Nirvana*" immediately (*Parinibbana*). And the king of the gods, Sakka, provides the commentary: "Alas! appearances of existence (*samkara*) are transitory, fated to arise and to pass away. After they have come into existence they are annihilated; *their cessation is bliss.*"[1] Buddha is no god, no *gandharva* nor *yaksa*, but neither is he man: he would indeed be all these were not the "basic evils" within him extirpated. "That whereby I might again come into being as a god, as a *gandharva* living in the air, or might become a *yaksa* or a man, the basic evils namely, are annihilated within me, destroyed, eradicated. And as the beauteous lotus does not become defiled in the water, so I remain unpolluted by the world. Therefore, Oh brahmin, am I a buddha."[2]

This nothingness, certainly, has a positive significance.[3] In the *Mahayana* the nought once more appears as "immeasurableness",[4] and even as form. Always, however, everything is again denied: the "great vehicle" (of salvation) "sets out with nothing. It will halt nowhere or, again, for omniscience it will stand still in the sense of not stopping."[5] "Standing still in the sense of not stopping": the secret of mysticism cannot be more eloquently expressed: Buddhism is mysticism *par excellence*. Salvation, *Nirvana*, is neither being nor non-being; "from still profounder depths than *Brahman*, than *Purusha*, the presage of *Nirvana* meets the gaze of the pious man, who strove not to solve its riddle but to lose himself within it. The way in which thought silently turned away from this enigma may seem feeble and fainthearted to the Faustian yearning to know 'the force that binds creation's inmost energies'.[6] But how completely had Buddhism rejected such a longing! An intrinsic greatness, and indeed a unique poetry, subsist within, as man stands here before the veiled image of the Beyond, free from the desire to unveil the glory unseen by any eye, while in the depths of his

---

[1] Bertholet, 11, 25 *f*.   [2] *op. cit.*, 11, 31 *f*.
[3] *cf.* the previous discussion of mysticism, Chap. 75.
[4] Bertholet, *op. cit.*, 15, 65.   [5] *ibid.*   [6] *Faust*, Part 1, "Night."

own being, silently and blissfully, he experiences this glory itself."[1] To
these beautiful words of the sensitive specialist upon India it can only
be added that the Christian longing for deliverance is also foreign to
Buddhistic calm. For the *rex gloriae* does not rest, but is always "He
that cometh in the name of the Lord". His image does not at all resemble
the wonderful images of Buddha: in these desire is extirpated, and therewith life also; every potency, and this indeed in principle, is held at a
distance. Nor is asceticism of any assistance, except that *exercitio
spiritualis* which gradually denudes the individual in the sequences of
submersion and leads to nothingness.[2]

2. If it possesses insight, however, what is born together and also
suffers together must suffer *reciprocally*; and thus the essential meaning
of Buddhism is *compassion*.[3] Involved in the same misery, carried wholly
away into the same bliss—"be they visible or invisible, far or near,
already born or still striving for birth—may all beings whatsoever be
blessed in heart! As a mother protects her own child, her only son, even
at the cost of her own life: so man should cherish a boundless benevolence for all beings! He should cultivate a limitless spirit of love for
the whole world: above, below, on all sides, unhindered, without hate
and without enmity."[4] A *bodhisattva* need only surrender himself
completely to a single virtue, and all Buddha's virtues exist spontaneously within him; that is compassion: "Oh Lord, just as, when the
organ of life is present all the other organs act, so, Oh Lord, when the
great compassion exists all those other virtues which yield illumination
become manifest."[5] The ground of this compassion, still further, is
the essential unity of all beings involved in the cycle of births: "How
could a *bodhisattva mahasattva*, who desires to approach all beings with
his own essential being in order to help them, and who loves Buddha's
teachings, eat the flesh of any creature or living thing, the flesh of a close
relative, who has completed his existence in one birth and has been
born again in the womb of a wild animal, a cow or bird?"[6] This is
carried so far, indeed, that one brahmin disciple, who had observed his
vow of chastity for 42,000 years, broke it out of compassion for a woman
who would otherwise have died;[7] and it extends to such a degree that
the *bodhisattva*, in the guise of a hare, roasts himself at the fire for the

[1] Oldenberg, *Lehre der Upanishaden*, 333.
[2] Bertholet, *op. cit.*, 11, 17; *cf.* Friedr. Heiler, *Die buddhistische Versenkung*[2], 1922.
[3] *cf.* Willy Lütge, *Christentum und Buddhismus*, 1916, 30 *ff.*
[4] Bertholet, *op. cit.*, 11, 84.   [5] *ibid.*, 15, 35.
[6] *ibid.*, 15, 50.   [7] *ibid.*, 15, 40.

benefit of a hungry brahmin—but not until he has conscientiously shaken from his fur all the vermin so that it should not be injured![1]

Compassion, however, is not love, "even though it is a manifestation of loving understanding. Compassion is oneself to suffer in the pain of another, no matter what kind of pain this may be. Pity has no relation whatever to the Absolute, but is merely a disavowal of suffering, and is in no degree directed to the individual as an individual, but generalized. It is therefore degrading for whomever it concerns . . . and arouses . . . in the compassionate a sense of superiority, because . . . in helping he feels his own power . . . We retain the attitude for which the value-contrast between pain and pleasure is absolute. We do not love when and because we are pitiful"; and Jaspers' observations,[2] founded on Nietzsche's merciless unmasking of virtue, can be applied quite freely to Buddhism. For, as has repeatedly been observed,[3] love is always reciprocal love, and always directly related to the Absolute and to God's act, while compassion is insight into the universality of suffering. Pity is the magnanimous activity of one who knows that he can free himself: love is his act who knows that he himself is loved. Benevolence towards all living things invents neither hell nor heaven: but even in hell

Love is living when Pity is dead.[4]

3. The religion of nothingness finds its limits on the one hand in those of the infinite, and on the other in those of form and surrender. For strict Buddhism, therefore, Buddha's death is no essential loss, since the main factors, doctrine and insight, still remain. Nevertheless there have apparently been many whose sun was darkened when for them the light of salvation no longer shone from Buddha's features:—"When the Lord had finally departed to rest, many of the monks, who were not yet free from passion, wrung their hands and lamented; (others) suddenly fell to the ground and rolled to and fro (while they mourned): 'All too soon has the Lord finally gone to his rest, all too soon has the blessed one fallen completely to rest, all too soon the eye (that is, the light) of the Universe has disappeared.' But those monks who had overcome passion endured it with serious mind and keen insight (while they thought): 'all appearances of the existent are transient; how could it possibly (be otherwise) in this instance?'"[5] The

---

[1] Lüders, *Buddhistische Märchen*, No. 53.
[2] *Psychologie d. Weltanschauungen*, 128.   [3] Chap. 76.
[4] *Inferno*, Canto XX, 29.   [5] Bertholet, *op. cit.*, 11, 27.

trust of his disciples is directed, indeed, even towards the will of the departed, when Buddha Amitabha's "primeval vow" not to enter into perfect bliss until all who long for salvation have been released, transforms the "insight" and the "doctrine" into a very real act of will; for man should trust in this vow: it is a kind of deed of salvation that demands faith.[1] Here then a piety prevails which has been compared by missionaries, not without justice, with that of the Reformation, as in the case of Luther. Surrender, faith, make blessed. And Buddha's own resolve is itself a sort of sacrifice: "Out of the great abyss I must raise (all these beings), I must free them from all calamity, I must lead them out of the flood of *samsara*. I myself must take the entire mass of suffering of all beings upon myself . . . I am resolved to live countless millions of world-eras in each individual wretched form of existence. . . . Verily it is better that I alone should suffer, than that all beings should fall into situations of miserable forms of existence".[2] Nevertheless the salvation thus effected by Buddha is always blissful nothingness: "Looking for the maker of this tabernacle, I shall have to run through a course of many births, so long as I do not find him; and painful is birth again and again. But now, maker of the tabernacle, thou hast been seen; thou shalt not make up this tabernacle again. All thy rafters are broken, thy ridge-pole is sundered; the mind, approaching the Eternal, has attained to the extinction of all desires."[3]

H. Von Glasenapp, *Der Buddhismus*, 1936.
H. Oldenberg, *Buddha: His Life, His Doctrine, His Order*.

[1] *cf.* Frick, *Vergl. Rel. wiss.* 93 *f.*   [2] Bertholet, *ibid.*, 15, 34 *f.*
[3] *The Sacred Books of the East (The Dhammapada)*, X, 153, 154 (Müller).

CHAPTER 98

THE RELIGION OF WILL AND OF OBEDIENCE

1. HISTORY offers in religion, as elsewhere, only a restricted number of possibilities: the religion of Form, or of formlessness: that of Will, or of nothingness: the religion of asceticism, or of strain: of compassion or of obedience—with these the entire wealth of history appears to be practically exhausted. Just as, in the course of history, mankind turns again and again to some few symbols, so there are also but few traits wherewith the essence of Power can be depicted, and only a few attitudes that can be adopted towards it.

In the first place, then, the religion of Will and of obedience arose in Israel from dynamistic-animistic foundations; any intermediate stage of polytheism, like that of India and Greece, was absent, or almost completely so. The powerfulness therefore, which the primitive Israelite perceived in his life, always had the pronounced character of a demonic will; and as Söderblom has justly observed, the religion of Israel, at least that of Jahvistic tendency, is of the animistic type, as is also that of Islam. Jahveh was thought of as the "destroyer, sinister, dangerous and unaccountably angered, as one who rejoices in destruction, ruins unexpectedly and craftily, who punishes without mercy, demands cruelty and creates evil."[1] A mighty warrior, he annihilates his people's enemies: but he attacks his own servant, Moses, too, in order to kill him,[2] and from his friend Abraham he exacts the sacrifice of his only son. His utterance is potent: "On the third day, in the morning, there was thunder and lightning, a dense cloud on the mountain, and a loud trumpet-blast, till all the people in the camp trembled . . . and the mountain of Sinai was all wrapped in smoke, as the Eternal descended in fire upon it; the smoke rose like steam from a kiln, till the people all trembled terribly. As the trumpet-blast grew louder and louder, Moses spoke and God answered him."[3] This is the description of a volcanic eruption, but at the same time of a numinous experience, of the experience of a demonic will falling upon a people. But when his oracles fail, God's silence is even more fearful and more sinister than his speech.[4] It is terrible when he comes forth "from his place" (prob-

---

[1] P. Volz, *Das Dämonische in Jahve*, 9 (1924).   [2] *Exodus* iv. 24.
[3] *ibid.*, xix, 16, 18 *f.* (Moffat); Bertholet, 17, 39.
[4] 1 *Sam.* xiv. 37; xxviii. 6; *cf.* Volz, *op. cit.*, 13.

ably Sinai originally): "the Eternal descends, he strides on the heights
of the earth! Mountains melt away before him, valleys split asunder,
like wax before a fire, like water pouring over a fall".[1] For His will is
in the first place wrath: He is like a hot breath sweeping the desert;
and thus Israel experiences the sacredness of Power as an awful will.
It is no different in the Prophets: "the Lord of hosts; 'tis he whom you
should fear, 'tis he whom you should dread!".[2] Amos too hears Jahveh's
voice as the roaring of a lion from Zion: "the Eternal thunders loudly
from Jerusalem, then the pasture-lands are woe-begone, the ridge of
Karmel withers".[3] Jahveh is "jealous" also; he enters man's life and
ravages it in order to make it his own property: "a jealous god entered
their lives, who had assisted them with fearful power, and who now
desired their whole being and existence".[4] And with this something
colossal has been accomplished for religion.

For now the fearful desert-will becomes the God of history, the God
of *his own* people. He places the slothful people in the midst of the
world's confusion, he drives it on and desires it to execute his demonic
will, to know nothing whatever except him and his will. And actually,
however frequently the people relapsed into idolatry, however thank-
lessly and unfaithfully it acted towards its stern but loving lord, it
knew, as being unique among peoples, that its God was its sole salvation.
Volz has given a penetrating and comprehensive description of how the
experience of the powers, which Israel itself shared with all peoples,
here led to neither polytheism nor dualism, but became incorporated
within the overpowering experience of Jahveh, so that in Israel "the
one Jahveh enfolded all".[5] "Jahveh became demonic; while conversely,
since Jahveh absorbed everything demonic and was himself the
mightiest demon of all, the Israelites no longer required any demons."[6]
This, then, was the great and bold enterprise undertaken by the people
of Israel: it was bound to its own God by such potent community, the
might of the superior will which it felt to be laid upon itself was so vast,
that it was quite impossible for it to believe in any other powers whatever
except Jahveh, even if this forcible simplification of events should
involve evil power being that of God. This adventure in faith in God,
still further, was carried out by the people of Israel in all its gradations,
by the editor of the tradition who ascribed what was most sublime and
most atrocious simultaneously to Jahveh Elohim, as well as by the
Mosaic popular consciousness which appears in the *Decalogue:* "Thou

---

[1] *Micah* i. 3, 4 (Moffat); Bertholet, 17, 40.   [2] *Isaiah* viii. 13 (Moffat).
[3] *Amos* i. 2 (Moffat).   [4] Volz, *op. cit.*, 27   [5] *ibid.*, 31.   [6] *ibid.*

shalt have no other gods before me"; and again in *The Book of Job*, for which "everything is united in the one God—and therewith its God himself becomes demonic and indeed almost Satanic."[1]

Something colossal then, to repeat, has been accomplished in this little people: *faith* is born. Power now becomes believed in as Will; and this, too, even when it leads to enigmatic and dubious historic confusion, even when it appears as more demonic than the very worst demon, even, in fact, when it "forsakes" the people.

In the light of this situation, further, a characteristic parallel can be drawn with the Greeks. For neither the Old Testament Jew nor the Homeric Greek ever recognized magic. Of course magic actually appeared in the first instance just as in the other: but, in principle, it was overcome. And the reason for this was that, in Greece, man desired *nothing* from God, and God nothing from man: while in Israel *everything* was demanded from God, and by God everything from man. "In the presence of such a monstrous and frightful God, who united all the might of God and demons, magic completely disappeared: before such a God, who was not only a demon but also God, no charm could avail."[2] Thus Israel *lives* with its God, in strife and discord, in anger and contrition, in repentance and self-will, in love and faith.

A further parallel, though now certainly in the negative sense, arises with the Greeks:—among them we found the religion of Form. Here however, in the religion of Will, *Form is absent*.[3] The relationship to deity, which the vision of the Greeks perceived in the remoteness of some radiant realm of the gods, is here all too close: God is far too much a reality ever to permit His features being portrayed. On Sinai certainly, according to *Deuteronomy*, a voice "spake out of the midst of the fire:"[4] Moses heard the sound of the voice, but he "saw no similitude".[5] And so the primeval awe before the nearness of Power in the image receives, in Israel, a quite special meaning: the Will, which forces itself upon man, is so close that he sees nothing whatever, but also so "Wholly Other" that it is good to perceive nothing. For whoever sees God must die: "Thou canst not see my face; for there shall no man see me, and live", says Jahveh to Moses.[6] But the voice resounding from the awful darkness of the mount of God rings too in man's innermost heart: it is therefore all the more dreadful simply because it is so much nearer.

---

[1] Volz, *op. cit.*, 30.   [2] *ibid.*, 31.
[3] And so, almost completely, is *myth*.
[4] *Deut.* v. 20; *cf.* Bultmann, *Zeitschr. f. d. Neut. Wiss.* 29, 1930, 169 *ff.*
[5] *ibid.*, iv. 12; *cf.* Chap 65.   [6] *Exodus* xxxiii. 20; Bertholet, *op. cit.*, 17, 45.

Thus the voice speaks of wrath: but of mercy also. Certainly this is always thought of in the guise of the cessation of the wrath: "the Lord is merciful . . . neither will he keep his anger for ever";[1] but it is precisely this conditioning of Jahveh's love and grace, of his gentleness and compassion, by his wrath, that gives them their intense reality which is simultaneously "Other" and beyond, and endows them with the character of "election." The same prophet who accuses Jahveh of deluding him, and who can no longer endure God's might,[2] finds for Jahveh's love the beautiful words: "I have loved thee with an everlasting love: therefore with lovingkindness have I drawn thee."[3]

2. The voice, resounding out of the darkness, delivers the *commandment*: man's *obedience* responds to God's Will. On this subject, however, little need be added to what has already been said in Chapter 69. In the commandment likewise God is close to the people: "For this commandment which I command thee this day, it is not hidden from thee, neither is it far off. It is not in heaven, that thou shouldest say, Who shall go up for us to heaven, and bring it unto us, that we may hear it, and do it? Neither is it beyond the sea, that thou shouldest say, Who shall go over the sea for us, and bring it unto us, that we may hear it, and do it? But the word is very nigh unto thee, in thy mouth, and in thy heart, that thou mayest do it."[4]

The great watchword of Israel, therefore, is the *Shema Israel*: "Hear, O Israel: The Lord our God is one Lord: and thou shalt love the Lord thy God with all thine heart, and with all thy soul, and with all thy might. And these words, which I command thee this day, shall be in thine heart."[5] Here the voice resounds within, dominating the entire life, the culmination of this faith being *The Book of Job*.

In the commandment,[6] certainly, the religion of Will and of obedience finds its limit. For as soon as God has become law he has lost his demonic character, and with this his essential nature; and the God of many prohibitions, against which the passionate preaching of Jesus is directed, can indeed be embarrassing, but scarcely dreadful! The marvellous love of the law, obedience to the voice sounding within the heart, has become a religion of book and legalism, in which the scorching breath of the desert has sunk for ever to rest.

---

[1] *Ps.* ciii. 8, 9.   [2] *Jer.* xx. 7 *ff.*; Bertholet, *op. cit.*, 17, 78.
[3] *Jer.* xxxi. 3; Bertholet, *ibid.*, 17, 93.
[4] *Deut.* xxx. 11 *ff.*; Bertholet, *ibid.*, 17, 112.
[5] *Deut.* vi. 4 *ff.*; Bertholet, *ibid.*, 17, 112.   [6] Chap. 62.

A quite different limit to this religion, again, occurs in the modern interpretation of the convenant[1] as a correlation between man and God. For now not only man, but God also, can speak of abandonment. "Thou hast cast me forth", says Adam: and God replies:

> My son, we are so closely united
> That with thine own words thou strikest at thyself.
> Adam.   Have mercy on me!
> God.   Have mercy on me![2]

But a God whom man must himself support, and to whom he must show pity, is such a thoroughgoing development of the all-consuming Will of the Old Testament that its very essence has been developed quite out of existence.

M. BUBER, *Königtum Gottes* (*Das Kommende*, I, 1932).
J. PEDERSEN, *Israel*, I–II, 1920.
P. VOLZ, *Das Dämonische in Jahve*, 1924.

[1] Chap. 70.
[2] Franz Werfel, *Zwiegespräch an der Mauer des Paradieses*, in *Het wezen der joodsche religie*; K. H. Miskotte, 1932.

CHAPTER 99

THE RELIGION OF MAJESTY AND OF HUMILITY

1. "IN the Name of God, the Compassionate, the Merciful, say: He is God alone: God the Eternal! He begetteth not, and He is not begotten; and there is none like unto Him."[1] Here speaks the religion of majesty and of humility. Developed under powerful Jewish and Christian influences, and closely related to these two religions not merely in origin but also in its essence, Islam confronts us with the task of understanding how, nevertheless, it could become not only a "great" religion, but could acquire in this greatness a genuinely specific character. For Islam is not merely a spiritual world-power, but is also a spiritual form.

A friend who has laboured among Moslems for many years and who speaks the language (I mean of course their scientific and religious language), and can conduct a theological discussion on passages from the *Koran*, thus writes to me: "Islam is in the first, second and third place a religio-social complex, in which equal emphasis is due to each factor of this combination. . . . Its motive power is the longing to be a kingdom of God: its weakness that, quite unsuspectingly, it wishes to realize this goal from a spirit that is not reborn and remains at bottom worldly. . . . Itself historically dependent, an offshoot of Semitic prophetism, Islam is comparatively poor in thought and feeling. Nevertheless it develops a colossal power which is rooted in its faith in God, or in other words, it takes God's sovereignty in absolute seriousness."[2] For our own purposes, however, and in the light of what has already been said about the sacred community,[3] we can disregard the constitution of the kingdom of God in Islam (its peak, in the Khalifate, has in the meantime been snapped off),[4] and restrict ourselves to faith in God.

I shall begin with Nietzsche's impressive dictum: "Every religion has for its highest images an analogon in the spiritual condition of those who profess it. The God of Mohammed: the solitariness of the desert,

[1] *Koran, Sura* 112 ("Everyman" Edition); Lehmann-Haas, *Textbuch*, 350.
[2] Dr. H. Kraemer, Solo, Java; *cf.* further, W. H. T. Gairdner and W. A. Eddy, *Christianity and Islam* (*The Christian Life and Message in Relation to non-Christian Systems, Report of the Jerusalem Meeting of the Int. Miss. Council* I, 1928), 250.
[3] Chap. 32 *ff.*   [4] *cf.* R. Tschudi, *Das Chalifat*, 1926.

the distant roar of the lion, the vision of a formidable warrior. The God of the Christians: everything that men and women think of when they hear the word 'love'. The God of the Greeks: a beautiful apparition in a dream."[1] Jahveh too is a lion roaring in the desert, and a terrible warrior; and this he was long before Mohammed experienced his visions and heard Allah's voice. Nor is Islam distinguished from Judaism by the fact that Allah is a personal will, having a very definite relationship to the world,[2] and "demanding" something therefrom; for as has just been observed, we find this in the Old Testament certainly to no less a degree and with yet greater originality. And were there no more than this, Islam would indeed be nothing but an "offshoot of Semitic prophetism", a sect or, if we prefer, a reform of Judaism. But the unique feature in Islam is that (to repeat) "God's sovereignty is taken in absolute seriousness", or in Gairdner's words, that God possesses "unmitigated omnipotence", and that "man is every way surrounded by, nay, himself exists through the immediate working of Allah's will and power".[3] Islam is the "worship of unconditioned Might". "The uniqueness and living supremacy of Allah have sounded forth from every minaret through the centuries and halfway round the world."[4] In Islam, then, the concept of Power reaches its loftiest peak; just as in the Old Testament form completely disappears into the too intimate proximity of invisibility; but the burning, ardent will vivifies powerfulness and makes it the sole reality, universal Power.

We might well ask whether all this, too, was not already foreshadowed in the Old Testament; to a certain degree, indeed, it is so. For both religions, Islam and Judaism alike, are apotheoses of animism.[5] Gairdner's description of Mohammed's prophetic experience: "The Arabian prophet came to possess a fervid faith in Allah—the One God. Not only did he come to possess it; it came to possess him. He felt that he had *experienced* Allah, a living, absolutely all-powerful and irresistible being":[6] might equally well apply to that of Elijah or Jeremiah. But in Islam the distinctive and decisive factor is that enough can never be said about this omnipotence of God, while with it everything is said;[7] and this is probably what my friend meant by his "unsuspectingly". Neither of Greece nor of Brahminism, neither of Buddhism nor of Judaism, can it be maintained that they "unsuspectingly" worshipped

---

[1] *The Case of Wagner, We Philologists*, 165 (Foulis Edition).
[2] Gairdner, *op. cit.*, 239.   [3] *ibid.*   [4] *op. cit.*, 238.
[5] Chap. 9; *cf.* Frick, *Vergl. Rel. wiss.* 83.   [6] *op. cit.*, 237.
[7] On the "caprice" of this omnipotence *cf.* Mensching, *Sünde*, 90.

or assigned form to, abolished or obeyed, the Power or potencies they experienced. In all these religions, therefore, both in the founders and in the living communities, there occurred a struggle that is wholly absent from Islam. Thus the Greeks strove to assign form to Power: Islam, however, abhors all form in principle. The doctrine of *advaita* (non-duality), again, regarded the plurality of appearances as a deception, while Islam has never concerned itself with them at all; and while Buddhism ventured upon a passionate war of annihilation against life itself, Islam knows nothing whatever of this. Finally, Judaism quarrelled with its God: but Islam never produced a Job! God's mighty power is indeed "unsuspectingly" believed in by the prophet's followers and, as it were, released into life "without further ado"; which certainly implies an intense faith, but at the same time a very feeble humanity. Paradoxically, then, we might say that Islam is the *actual religion of God*. Hence the marvellous "concentration" of the Mohammedan: "wherever he may be, the Muslim has learned, during his prayers, to be alone with himself; some of the Muslims to be alone with God."[1] But hence also the complete inessentiality of revelation, in spite of prophet and "book"; "Revelation is only a formal and mechanical link between incompatibles";[2] and the whole of Islamite theology is a contest for the unity of God, always of God alone. Nothing is so keenly dreaded as is *shirk*:—the association of any other independent being whatever with God.[3]

2. Islam, to continue, is the religion of *Judgment*: "When the day that must come shall have come suddenly, none shall treat that sudden coming as a lie: Day that shall abase! Day that shall exalt!"[4] God's absolute powerfulness, His majesty, restricted by nothing whatever, as this repeatedly appears even in the profane stories of *The Arabian Nights*, implies the judgment of man. Man's own attitude, therefore, can be only that of deepest *humility*: "Praise be to God, Lord of the worlds! The compassionate, the merciful! King on the day of reckoning! Thee only do we worship, and to Thee do we cry for help. Guide Thou us on the straight path, the path of those to whom Thou hast been gracious;—with whom Thou art not angry, and who go not astray."[5] "Abu Huraira relates that the Prophet—God grant him blessing and

---

[1] Gairdner, *op. cit.*, 246.   [2] *ibid.*, 267.
[3] *cf.* I. Goldziher, *Vorlesungen über den Islam*, 1910, 111.
[4] *Koran, Sura* 56 ("Everyman" Edition); Lehmann-Haas, *op. cit.*, 348.
[5] *Sura* 1 ("Everyman" Edition); Lehmann-Haas, *ibid.*, 350.

peace!—said: a man was wasting his life; when his end approached he told his children: 'When I am dead you must burn me, grind my ashes and scatter them before the wind; for if God seized me, He would punish me as no man ever has been.' And when he was dead, so it happened. But God commanded the earth: 'Assemble together what there is in thee of him.' This was done, and accordingly he came forth. 'What made thee act thus?' God asked him. 'Fear of Thee, O Lord', he replied. Then God forgave him."[1]

The lion roars in the desert: a prophet, *the* prophet, who "represents all the prophets put together",[2] experiences his omnipotence; the book descends from eternity, and the prophet's example (*sunnah*) interprets the book. Now man knows what he has to do, and that he cannot sufficiently humble himself. Of God he knows only that He *is*, and that His Being is overpowering. This, undeniably, is very much: but on the other hand, when measured against the more sophisticated religions, it is very little.

---

[1] Lehmann-Haas, *ibid.*, 361.   [2] Gairdner, *op. cit.*, 249.

CHAPTER 100

THE RELIGION OF LOVE

1. IT has for long been the fashion in treating historical problems, especially in the sphere of religion, to set one's own religion as scrupulously as possible in the background and to create the impression that, with reference to religions, one was wholly free from prejudice. This attitude, however, was associated with the grave error of supposing that, in the spiritual realm, one may adopt any desired position or abandon it at will, as if it were possible to choose any *Weltanschauung* whatever, or to abstain provisionally from all partisanship. But gradually it is being perceived that man *exists* in the world in some quite definite way and that—with all due respect to his own *Weltanschauung*—any "unprejudiced" treatment is not merely impossible but positively fatal. For it prevents the investigator's complete personality becoming engaged in his scientific task. And even if the enquirer is not consciously a disciple of some religion or other, but is an eclectic or agnostic, or in other terms, if he is not aware of his religion (which he really has!) then too the attempt has a disastrous effect, since in his endeavour to gain a thorough understanding of religious subjects, the investigator renders his own living religious impulses inoperative; still further, this elimination is after all merely a pretence, since no one can ever release himself from his more or less definite rôle in the world. The sole possible result is an "unprejudiced"—but that is only to say unintelligent—treatment governed throughout by a religious attitude which has not been scientifically clarified, and which is therefore exempt from all criticism and discussion. For "unprejudiced" investigators are usually accustomed to beginning, without further ado, with an interpretation of religion borrowed either from some liberal Western European Christianity, or from the deism of the Enlightenment, or from the so-called monism of the natural sciences.

If then in this Chapter, as indeed in all its predecessors, I follow another course and deliberately begin our survey of religious phenomena from the Christian viewpoint, I certainly by no means advocate any dogmatic treatment which, in all religions except Christianity itself, can perceive only spurious religion and degeneration. Rather do I retain the typical phenomenological intellectual suspense (*epoche*), while at the same time I bear in mind that this is possible only in the light of one's own experience,[1] and that this can never be freed from its own religious determinateness. It would therefore be quite possible, in itself, for a buddhist to set out the phenomenology of religion, with his own as the starting point; and then he would naturally discover the culmination of religion in Buddhism. Whether he would be "right" in so doing is, however, not a matter for phenomenology itself to decide, but for theology or metaphysics. But he would be unable to proceed in any other way.

I myself regard Christianity, then, as the central form of historical religions;[2] and in general, the "comparison" of religions among themselves is possible only by thus beginning from one's own attitude to life. For religions are not wares that one can spread out on a table.[3] Surveying the realm of historic religions, therefore, from the point of view of Christianity, I consider that we perceive that the Gospel appears as the fulfilment of religion in general. But whether this "appearance" has its roots in any ultimate "reality" is again an issue which theology must decide.

The typology of Christianity needs only *one* word: *Love*.[4] This is because, in Christianity, God's activity and the reciprocal activity of man are essentially the same: the movement of Power towards the world is love, while that of the world towards God is reciprocal love; no other word is available. Mankind's love of God is the reflection of the divine love for man, or rather: "the form Christ has taken in man".[5]

2. The religion of love, still further, is *fulfilment* in the sense that it places Will at the focal point, but that it does so without disregarding

---

[1] Chap. 107, 109. The term *epoche* is a technical expression employed in current Phenomenology by Husserl and other philosophers. It implies that no judgment is expressed concerning the objective world, which is thus placed "between brackets", as it were. All phenomena, therefore, are considered solely as they are presented to the mind, without any further aspects such as their real existence, or their value, being taken into account; in this way the observer restricts himself to pure description systematically pursued, himself adopting the attitude of complete intellectual suspense, or of abstention from all judgment, regarding these controversial topics.

[2] *cf.* van der Leeuw, *Strukturpsychologie.*

[3] In this sense Comparative Religion is a fairly recent field of research; from its limited literature I select: Hegel, *The Philosophy of Religion.* Frick, *Vergl. Rel. wiss.* H. Frick, *Ghazalis Selbstbiographie,* 1919. van Gennep, *Religions Moeurs et Légendes* I, 67 *ff.* H. Groos, *Der deutsche Idealismus und das Christentum,* 1927. Lüttge, *Christentum und Buddhismus.* Mensching, *Sünde.* P. Masson Oursel, *Foi bouddhique et foi chrétienne (RHR.* 95, 1927). Otto, *West-östl. Mystik. ID., India's Religion of Grace.* M. Schlunk, *Die Weltreligionen und das Christentum,* 1923.

[4] Chap. 76.   [5] *Gal.* iv. 19.

Form, and that it is also fully aware of the limits of Will and Form in their relation to infinite Power. God: Father, Son and Holy Spirit— thus are consummated, equally, the religion of Will (Israel), of Form (Greece), and also of Infinity (India). The Father's Will is glorified as God's creative deed, whose essence is love of the world. The impetuous energy of Jahveh (and also of Allah) is experienced as an impetuous deed of love: "God so loved the world" that He gave Himself to the world in the Form of the Son.

This Form of the Son, however, is not an endowment with form like that of the Homeric Greek. Equally visible in human appearance as Apollo or Athene, His "fulfilled" form is explicitly distinguished from the Greek by becoming experienced as "given" and, in fact, given in history. With regard to "endowment with form", indeed, Christianity remains to a great extent Jewish, or again Islamite. Power, that is to say, is not perceived as a form, but the Incarnation of God in human form is believed in; essentially, then, God is Will: the world, creation: and man belongs to the world.[1] But into this world God descends and brings salvation: that is, Himself. And as opposed to nineteenth century views, we cannot emphasize too strongly the fact that in Christianity no new *Weltanschauung* of any kind, no new idea of God, has arisen.[2] The Christian *Weltanschauung*, and the Christian idea of God, are in fact purely Jewish in origin, and subsequently modified by the general concepts of Hellenistic antiquity. What is really new and unique in Christianity is, however, that the love of God has "appeared". "And it came to pass *in those days*"; so begins the Christmas Gospel. This means that God fulfils time: in time itself He sets a bound to time. The "religion of Jesus" is therefore a prophetic-Jewish religion; faith in Jesus Christ is the belief that God's Will, as Form, has become visible and actual in this world:[3] "For unto you is born *this day* a Saviour."

But the doctrine of the Holy Spirit ensures, still further, that no limitation of any kind is involved in the Will of God and in the Form of Christ, in the sense that religion itself becomes transformed into either history or esthetics. Here both creative Will and consummated form are infinitely and limitlessly powerful:

---

[1] cf. J. de Zwaan, *Paulinische Weltanschauung, Zeitschr. für syst. Theol.* 8, 578. Connelly's drama, *Green Pastures*, shows here too the primitive form of the most sublime Christian faith, especially the end of Act II.

[2] cf. R. Bultmann's admirable article: *Urchristentum und Rel. gesch.*, *Theol. Rundschau*, N. F. 4, 1932.

[3] cf. Bultmann, *Gl. u. Verst.* 144.

Come, Holy Spirit!
Fill the hearts of Thy faithful people,
Enkindle within them the fire of Thy love.
Thou Who hast gathered together,
Within the one Faith,
The peoples of all Earth's tongues.
Alleluia! Alleluia!

3. Thus all that Christianity can ever declare about God is contained in this active love: it is the very essence of God, given to man as grace. To the exile from Paradise it was said:[1]

Only add
Deeds to thy knowledge answerable; add faith·
Add virtue, patience, temperance; add love,
By name to come called Charity, the soul
Of all the rest: then wilt thou not be loth
To leave this Paradise, but shalt possess
A Paradise within thee, happier far.

All that man can either do or be, therefore, in his own attitude to Power, is contained in love: obedience, humility, holiness, hope.

The so-called "attributes" of God, too, are all comprehended within love. For these attributes are neither descriptions of God's uniqueness, nor edifying fantasies, nor even philosophic deductions, but experiences of the one love that is interpreted differently in each case. In love, again, the two demands, which we must address to religion,[2] concur in being realized. That God is ultimate is expressed by the "attributes" of omnipresence, omnisufficiency, omniscience and omnipotence; but in each of these instances alike this is only a proclamation of the love that is experienced as ultimate. But that God is "Wholly Other", that He is holy, perfectly good and perfectly just, this also is merely a proclamation of the same experience of the love that is "Wholly Other", exactly as it is ultimate; and thus in love the line ascending from man to God, and that descending from God to man, meet. The symbol of love is the Cross.

4. Reciprocal love, further, itself possesses a form: the church,[3] which displays its inseparable unity with love by being "the Body of Christ". The church's essential task, then, is to offer the sacrifice of thanksgiving,[4] which is a sacrifice of life and grants expression to reciprocal love.

---

[1] *Paradise Lost*, XII, 581 *ff*.   [2] Chap. 108.
[3] Chap. 36.   [4] Chap. 50.

But the church has always quite clearly realized that the Body of Christ is constantly being threatened:

> Far from us drive our hellish foe,
> True peace unto us bring,
> And through all perils bring us safe
> Beneath Thy sacred wing.[1]

However familiar this may be, it has nevertheless been frequently ignored in the church's history. It is forgotten that the spirit "bloweth, and thou canst not tell whence it cometh, and whither it goeth"; we forget, too, the dynamic character of love. "The Catholic type succeeds in transforming act into duration. It changes occurrence into being, and event into form. It believes that by spatializing the act it makes it eternal."[2] Against this the Protestant type of Christianity recalls to our recollection the "unconditioned menace"[3] that ever threatens man's being, and is fully aware that, within the church, the Christian occupies a frontier or "boundary situation", and that what he has he possesses merely in virtue of his status. It is true that Protestantism also ceases to be conscious of this "situation" as soon as it binds God's powerfulness to the words of the Bible, or to any immutable doctrine whatever: from being a living body the church then becomes merely a dead shell. On the other hand, if it is not to lose its essence in wholly objectless feeling, Protestant Christianity repeatedly needs the reminder addressed to it by the Roman and Orthodox Catholic churches: that God's Power in the life of the world possesses not only a ringing sound but a Form also, and that the church is not merely the period of proclamation, but is also the locus of the Incarnation, although only God's creative love can determine both the time and the place. "Surely the Lord is in this place; and I knew it not", is equally a Christian experience as is "this gate of the Lord, into which the righteous shall enter".

---

[1] *Hostem repellas longius,*
Pacemque dones protinus,
Ductore sic te praevio
Vitemus omne noxium.

[2] Frick, *Vergl. Rel. wiss.* 103 *f.*

[3] Tillich, *Rel. Verwirkl.*

B. FOUNDERS

CHAPTER 101

THE FOUNDER

1. IN Chapters 25 *ff.* the representation of Power by and in man was dealt with:—how men can become "sacred" by participating in Power and make their appearance sustaining some kind of holiness, their effectiveness being then described as that pertaining to status or "office".

Now we encounter these "sacred men" once again, but in a completely different connection: it is no longer a matter of the sacred man as a phenomenon, but of the historic bestowing of form upon religion within the respective religions, and of the question as to what part in this historical creation of form is taken by human personalities. Thus together with the historic "forms" of the various religions themselves there are the historical forms of those *founders* who, in different ways, have appeared at some turning-point of time and "established" some specific experience of Power. There are very many such "founders", quite as many as, and indeed more than, the religions themselves; I cannot deal with even all the historically known founders. But by means of a few examples I shall attempt to elucidate how religious experience assumes historic form, by considering the founder's own personality.

Of course a "founder" is not the "establisher" of a religion as he is depicted in works of reference, along with the founders of the "Gustavus Adolphus Union" and the like, or with the originators of socialism, *etc.* or, finally, any great inventors. Religions, in truth, are neither originated nor established; still, they appear as "founded". And this means that every experience of God is indubitably original, in so far as God is Himself its originator and executes nothing at second-hand. But every experience of God is also the outcome of some stimulus, and is extracted (as it were) from some predecessor; and whenever this initiating experience possesses special intensity, so that it arouses many subsequent experiences and continues to operate historically, then we speak of a "foundation of religion". This founding is, of course, not restricted merely to the "great" religions, and not even to religions in general:

every religious movement, every specific change in the course of religious life, must have some founder. Such was St. Francis, just as was Moses, and Mani equally with Zarathustra; and so, too, the "minor" figures. In the literal sense, therefore, every genuine religious experience is a *foundation*, from which some new experiences arise; but we are concerned with founding only when its historical effects are visible on a large scale. The mother, for example, may be the "founder" of her children's religion, but we begin to discuss her only when her own experience sets up historic waves. Founding, that is to say, is an eminently historical affair.

2. A founder, in the first place, is primarily a *witness*[1] to revelation: he has seen, or has heard, something; "to the numen there pertains a seer". "Without him a rainbow remains a rainbow, and heaven a blue roof of stone."[2] Then he speaks of his experience, and appears as *prophet*.[3] Founders, again, usually base a (partially) new doctrine on their own experience, some new law: in that case they are also *teachers*.[4] They must then adapt themselves to what has already been given in tradition, and can thus become *theologians*; but in any event they are always to a certain degree *reformers*.[5] Their doctrine, however, possesses power only in so far as their whole life enters into the "founding": then they are *examples*,[6] archetypes of the genuinely pious life replete with power. When, finally, they devote their entire existence to foundation, they are called *mediators*. Certainly they are all without exception mediators of revelation; nevertheless the term "mediator"[7] involves something that is more than experience and utterance, doctrine and example taken all together.

As has just been observed, then, there are infinitely many founders; and it is characteristic of any given religion that either this plurality is recognized, or else it is attempted to abolish it. In this respect, the Greeks discerned nothing whatever that prevented ceaseless creation of form; while in the case of the Jews the history of God's dealings with His people extended over the individual prophets, so that their number could be regarded as historically necessary.[8] But for Mohammedans, on the other hand, all prophetic forms ultimately resolved themselves into that of Mohammed; while for Christians all prophecies were "fulfilled" in the form of the mediator.

[1] Chap. 29.   [2] Otto. *Gefühl des Überweltlichen*, 79; *cf.* 86 *f.*   [3] Chap. 27.
[4] Chap. 28.   [5] Chap. 94, 102.   [6] Chap. 105.   [7] Chap. 106.
[8] Leo Baeck, in Miskotte, *Wezen der joodsche religie*, 95; *cf. Hebrews* i. 1 *f.*

3. Frick[1] has drawn the parallel between the three nights which are accounted sacred by the three great religions: the night of illumination of Buddha, the *lailat al-kadr* (night of power) in Islam and, in Christianity, Christmas night.[2] Strictly regarded, however, the last is not a "foundation", and I prefer, therefore, to place in parallel the actual originative experiences in these three religions and in that of Israel— or at least those which have been elevated by tradition to the level of the principal experiences.

Apart then from pre-Mosaic tradition, the foundation of the Israelitish religion is related in the story of the burning bush. I do not wish to seek too profound a meaning in the bush burning without being consumed (although theophany as a flame of fire in the desert is certainly very characteristic); but here, as later in the historically less important circumstances connected with Samuel, the essential features are God speaking and the founder listening: "God called unto him out of the midst of the bush, and said, Moses, Moses. And he said, Here am I." This is summons and obedience; and what follows is equally characteristic: "And he said, Draw not nigh hither": and Moses put off his sandals and "hid his face." "Moreover he said, I am the God of thy father, the God of Abraham, the God of Isaac, and the God of Jacob ... I am come down to deliver (Israel) out of the hand of the Egyptians."[3] Thus it is the God, who manifests His own will in history, who here declares Himself to the founder, while the foundation is the fulfilling by Moses of his God's historical commission. His own experience is then perpetuated as obedience, and as the experience of the people it must express itself as loyalty.

The *lailat al-kadr* is the night of power; that is the night on which Mohammed received his first revelation and accordingly became a founder. Here the Power is the divine authority. "Verily, we have caused It to descend on the night of Power. And who shall teach thee what the night of power is? The night of power excelleth a thousand months. Therein descend the angels and the spirit by permission of the Lord for every matter; and all is peace till the breaking of the morn."[4] It is the book that was sent down; exactly as in Judaism, the originative experience here is the divine communication, and the absolute powerfulness, which I have earlier designated as all-sufficient majesty, gives

---

[1] *Vergl. Rel. wiss.* 68 *ff. cf.* Chap. 97.

[2] Chap. 97. His comparison between the founders' parting words is also valuable; 70 *ff.*   [3] *Exodus* iii. 4 *ff.* Bertholet, *op. cit.*, 17, 34.

[4] *Sura* 97 ("Everyman" Edition); Frick, *Vergl. Rel. wiss.* 69 *f.* Lehmann-Haas, *Textbuch*, 345.

this experience its distinctive colour. The rest is instruction which becomes the written word; and everything lies in the shadow of judgment.

"One night, the old traditions narrate, the decisive turning-point came, the moment wherein was vouchsafed to the seeker (Buddha) the certainty of discovery. Sitting under the tree, since then named the Tree of Knowledge, he went through successively purer and purer stages of abstraction of consciousness, until the sense of omniscient illumination came over him."[1] Insight into the primal cause of suffering was attained in the fourfold *jhana*. "When I apprehended this, and when I beheld this, my soul was released from the evil of desire, released from the evil of earthly existence, released from the evil of error, released from the evil of ignorance. In the released awoke the knowledge of release: extinct is re-birth, finished the sacred course, duty done, no more shall I return to this world; this I knew."[2] "This moment", Oldenberg continues, "the Buddhists regard as the great turning-point in his life and in the life of the worlds of gods and men: the ascetic Gotama had become the Buddha, the awakened, the enlightened. That night which Buddha passed under the tree of knowledge, on the banks of the river Neranjara, is the sacred night of the Buddhist world."[3] The originative experience here is clearly perceptible: illuminating insight into the world's nullity. The feeling of freedom and release certainly refers to concrete knowledge; but this, in its own turn, to nullity.

Finally, the originative experience of Jesus Christ cannot be unambiguously determined, although in the tradition the baptism in Jordan, the temptation, the transfiguration and the hour of Gethsamene can all be taken into consideration. Just as in Israel there is a history concerned with God, whose founders, together with Moses, are the many prophets, so there is in the Gospel a history dealing with God which is repeatedly "founded" anew. If then we select the four experiences just cited as historically symbolic, it can be affirmed that the originative experience of Jesus, as this became effective in history, exhibits the following four leading features: the consciousness of divine sonship or, more generally, of messiahship; the certainty of a task that was assigned to Him and must be accomplished in spite of everything; the assurance of the immediate presence of God; and readiness for the sacrifice which, at its culmination in the complete deprivation of being forsaken by God, called anew in question the three preceding factors.

---

[1] *Buddha: His Life, His Doctrine, His Order,* 107.
[2] *ibid.*; *cf.* Frick, *Vergl. Rel. wiss.* 69.   [3] *ibid.,* 107, 108.

We have discovered, therefore, as the typical originative experiences when expressed in their relation to Power:—Power speaks, and is obeyed: it speaks, and gives commands: Power reveals itself to insight as nothingness: the Power pertaining to the founder demands from Him, in absolute impotence, the complete surrender of Himself.

CHAPTER 102

THE REFORMER

1. IF every religion, in accord with its essential nature, is both reformed and to be reformed,[1] then every foundation must, to a certain extent, be at the same time a reformation; and this actually is the case. No "man of God" ever erects his experience on quite new ground, but all build afresh on the ruins of previous settlements. A reformer is thus a kind of founder, and we employ the narrower designation whenever the historic emphasis falls on the transformation of what has already been given. Thus Mohammed was a reformer, as were Buddha, Zarathustra and Jesus; but I prefer to call them founders. Luther was certainly a founder; but I call him preferably a reformer. The reformer's act is indeed "rediscovery",[2] but this discovery itself is an experiencing anew; just as the founder desires not to abrogate but to fulfil, so the reformer wishes the new system, which he sets up, proved to be the genuine ancient one, and the old, which he is combatting, to be shown as being falsely understood. Adam alone therefore, the "first man", could achieve a foundation with none of the significance of a reformation; and conversely, no reformer could ever fulfil his task without "foundation".

2. From these considerations it follows that most important founders were also more or less influential reformers; Zarathustra, Buddha, Mohammed, Jesus—but also Ramanuja, St. Paul, St. Francis, Ignatius Loyola, Wesley and Pusey—were founders whose labours had reforming value.

I have here selected two examples in order to make it quite clear how this type of founder arises historically. In the first place the Egyptian king Akhnaton, who has already been dealt with,[3] was a reformer of the purest stamp. No one who has read his *Hymn to the Sun* can deny the originality of his own experience of God;[4] and its reforming quality too is plainly shown: the king reverted to an old tradition, the fifth dynasty worship of the sun, kept alive through the centuries by the Heliopolitan

---

[1] Chap. 94; *reformata* and *reformanda*. [2] Frick, *ibid.*, 48. [3] Chap. 94.
[4] *cf.* H. Schaefer, *Amarna in Religion und Kunst* (1931); van der Leeuw, *Achnaton* (1927); further: *Altorientalische Texte zum A. T.* (edited by H. Gressmann)², 1926, 15 *ff.*; Lehmann-Haas, *op. cit.*, 259 *f.*; Roeder, *Urk. zur Rel. des alten Ägypten*, 62 *ff.*; Erman, *Literatur der Ägypter*, 358 *ff.*

priesthood, and opposed the beliefs of the Theban priesthood, which he regarded as false. The manner in which, in the development of the ceremonial name of his own god, he explained the ancient divine name Ra as the designation of a god who "has returned as Aton", testifies alike to the reformatory intention of converting the new experience of the god, connected with the name Aton, into a foundation, and to the endeavour to exhibit the truth of all that was sound in the tradition.[1] He emphasized the contrast with Amon, the "hidden god" of Thebes, as intensely as possible; his own god is the visible luminary that radiates its rays of love in all directions, and he developed the service of this god with such passion, indeed, that no room was left for the other gods; they either silently perished or were drastically expunged. Despite his theological experiments with the god's name, however, the king (perhaps, to some degree, just because he was a king) evidently failed to adapt himself to the religion in which he lived and from which he had set out; he underrated the old religion, above all the religious significance of belief in the beyond, and also of Osiris worship; and he had to suffer the penalty; despite the vehemence and purity of his own originative experience, revealed as this is in almost every word that has come down to us and in almost every form created by his art, his reform scarcely outlasted his own life.[2] Akhnaton may therefore be regarded as an extreme reformer, whose figure was decisively conditioned by this attempt at reformation.

If on the other hand we turn our attention to Luther, there appears a similar subjection to an original experience of God in penitential conflicts, but also a thorough intimacy with the religion from which he began; for Luther "would not have been the reformer had he not previously been a monk".[3] We might say, in fact, that almost nothing of importance in the old religion left Luther indifferent; the intense conviction that he stood in the true church of Christ and the confident assertion of the common treasure of Christian faith, unite with the struggle against abuse and unbelief which began with the experience of foundation. The sole living feature of the old religion which, so far as I myself can see, Luther contemplated neither with hatred against its

---

[1] Chap. 84.
[2] Schaefer; van der Leeuw; *op. cit. cf.* further: Ed. Meyer, *Gottesstaat, Militär-herrschaft und Ständewesen in Ägypten (Sitz. ber. der preuss. Ak. der Wiss., phil.-hist. Kl., 1928, 28).* K. Sethe, *Amon und die acht Urgötter von Hermopolis (Abh. der preuss. Akad. der Wiss., 1929, phil.-hist. Kl. 4).*
[3] Karl Holl, *Reformation und Urchristentum (Reden und Vorträge bei der 28. General-versammlung des Evang. Bundes, 1924).*

corruption nor with fidelity to the common Christian faith, was worship, apart (that is) from the sacrificial doctrine of the mass, which he condemned as idolatry. And here Luther, with wise discretion, treated the old practices with great consideration and granted them much liberty.

In their historical importance, then, the reformations of Akhnaton and Luther are scarcely comparable. But with regard to the manner of their emergence in history, on the other hand, they are not merely characteristic instances, but are direct antitheses. For the reformatory initial experience of the one lies almost completely outside the communal, while that of the other lies almost wholly within the common experience.

CHAPTER 103

THE TEACHER

1. THE teacher has previously been discussed in Chapter 28. His historical form also is that of a founder, its peculiarity consisting in the fact that his "foundation" becomes detached, as doctrine, from the experience lying at its base. He may be priest, apostle, missionary: in any case his own experience forces him to proclamation; and this then assumes the form of an interconnected whole. The doctrine itself, again, is independent of the teacher; it goes its own way even long after he has departed and his personal activities have been forgotten. A teacher such as Buddha was, indeed, himself desired this.[1]

2. Teachers, in the strictest sense, are found in India: Buddhism is doctrine, nothing other than doctrine. And wherever insight in itself leads to salvation, the doctrine that effects this insight can continue to operate independently. Buddha, therefore, is the teacher *par excellence*; his experience solidified into a doctrine which, despite all the humanizing and deifying of the founder himself, has always remained doctrine; and Buddha's historic form is that of an instructor: the ground of suffering is desire. To him this became clear in illumination; but it can be repeated quite apart from this illumination and, indeed, from the teacher himself. Such doctrine is certainly proclamation of salvation, not however of what has occurred or happened but only of what must be achieved, of what must be attained precisely through the doctrine; and so it is, to a certain degree, with every doctrine and every teacher in India, rich in *gurus* as it is.

A wholly different type of doctrine and teacher is the Jewish-Christian: the Jew, learned in scripture, was regarded by the people as "our teacher". This doctrine also is independent of the founder who places it within history; it becomes traditional. But it refers to something that actually happened, to the living relationship of God to the people, to the covenant; it is therefore the proclamation of an event rather than instruction proper, although it is this too. In this respect, then, the teacher has a more important historical status:

> he let Moses see his purpose,
> and Israel his methods.[2]

---

[1] Chap. 28. [2] *Ps.* ciii. 7.

Doctrine thus becomes a living connection between God and man; it is indeed instruction, but above all proclamation. Similarly with the Christian teachers, of whom St. Paul may serve as the great example. He realized that he was only a late born disciple, that he himself was nothing and the word of the Cross everything; but he was equally conscious of standing in a great historical connection. Upon the *kerygma* of the original community he bestowed its historic form, and God's historical deed is the A and the Ω of his own proclamation. In other words: he himself was unimportant, but his teaching was equally so; the sole momentous factor was the redemptive history of Jesus. The teacher's own historic figure, therefore, just because it is negligible as compared with the occurrence of revelation, need not withdraw into the background so scrupulously as does that of Buddha in *Hinayana*. And in the living church it survives, like that of the Jewish teacher in the people.

CHAPTER 104

THE PHILOSOPHER AND THE THEOLOGIAN

1. IT appears quite undeniable to my own mind that the great systematists, who have influenced the religious thought of humanity, must be included among "founders". In the history of the spirit, it is true, Kierkegaard's simile of the man who builds a vast palace, and then sits down outside it, is repeatedly justified; the palace being the "system", the man the systematizer. And when we observe how the spirit's citadel again and again becomes its coffin, we can well understand Jaspers' preference for the great anti-systematizers Kierkegaard and Nietzsche. But this should not prevent us appreciating the originating influence of all system construction, since at bottom a great system springs from some primal experience, and exhibits the attempt to dominate the world from the viewpoint of this experience and to make it as it were capable of cultivation;[1] and it is not the artistic nor technical completion of systematic construction that is effective, but the power of this experience. St. Augustine, Thomas Aquinas, Luther, Calvin, obviously influenced the educated world by their logical arguments; nevertheless their actual spiritual effect sprang from the high emotional tension of their experience, and their boldness in applying it to the whole world. It is exactly the same with the great philosophers Socrates and Plato, Kant and Hegel; they all perceived something, contemplated the world from a certain definite standpoint, and had the courage to make this vision the starting point of a conquering invasion of spiritual territory.

In so doing, however, the philosophers follow the path from their own experience to the theoretical domination of the world,[2] while the theologians, on the contrary, choose the way of obedience.[3] The former look upwards from the plane of the world to that of Power; the latter down to the world level from the place of Power (the church). But of course there have frequently been philosophers who practised theological obedience and theologians who achieved philosophic dominance.

2. That philosophers pertain to the history of religion can scarcely be doubtful to anyone who regards theoretical investigation as in-

---

[1] Chap. 83.   [2] Grünbaum, *Herrschen und Lieben*, Chap. 83.   [3] Chap. 84.

separable from some commanding experience of Power. Here, however, it is not a matter of a phenomenology of philosophy, but merely of the way in which, as founder, the philosopher introduces his personal experience of Power into the historical world. Of this I have selected three examples: Hegel, to begin with, is the most philosophical of all philosophers; he lived his thought as no one else has done either before or after him. The movement of Spirit revealed itself in its majestic course; and in principle it is complete in itself. In it everything, from highest to lowest, has a place; but in it, and there alone, is the place of everything; the advance is dialectical, a monologue of Spirit; and the relationship with mysticism is obvious.[1] In this eternal movement the thinker himself participates. Here then everything is appointed, marked down and in a certain sense justified also.

Kant, again, represents the opposite type. Here too the movement of thought is contemplated; but its motion is open and unfinished. The system is thus a critique of its own authority, marked emphasis being laid on practical reason and action, and the spirit's path to absolute power leads only through this action. Not thought as such is worshipped, but something that is still purely formal: the moral law within. The human spirit is least of all the thought of God; nevertheless it is not forsaken by God. Philosophy is predominantly human and worldly, and yet a path is left open leading to the superhuman and supermundane.

Midway between these two modern philosophers stands the ancient thinker Plato. Setting forth from the interest in man and the self-criticism of Socrates, he rose to the contemplation of divine beauty. But the movement towards this vision was neither a way that had been left open, nor a dialectical necessity; it was a combat, a struggle; thus the proper place for Plato's philosophy is between heaven and earth, and its most characteristic language neither dialectic nor Socratic critical enquiry, but myth.

3. In accordance with the conception of their task, theologians follow the path of obedience; and they begin not with the world, but with revelation. They labour to serve the community: when they are Christians, the church. Between them and their own experience, therefore, there exists· an intermediate factor: the proclamation of the prophets and the apostles; in this respect they are far less "founders" than are the philosophers. Nevertheless their labour, too, is an activated experience: they have heard the call of the church, to which they now

[1] Chap. 75.

give its historic form. They may share something with prophet or apostle, and they also have much of the teacher—but their true historic task consists in systematic utterance of God's deeds; they are therefore closely linked with those teachers of the second type dealt with in the preceding chapter.

Here again I would differentiate three types: There are theologians, in the first place, whose historical task lies in elucidating the collective experience of their own community in its relation to earlier tradition, to divergent experiences, to heresy, innovation and contemporary philosophy; they thus effect the connection with what is given in tradition and with the thought of their own day. In this respect, however, it may so happen that they concede too much to what is traditionally given, and endeavour to establish it anew merely because it is given; or, again, they submit their doctrine all too readily to current thought. Their true task, nonetheless, is to avoid these two extremes and is therefore mainly that of an intermediary. Every theologian has this task; both St. Paul and St. John attempted to execute it. Certain theologians, however, represent this type more or less purely, as for example in the era of the Greek apologists of the second century who tried to bring Christianity into agreement with the prevailing popular moral philosophy; and in modern times Herder and Schleiermacher, who sought to interpret the essentials of Christianity in accordance with the spirit of the age. But the foundation laid by the second century apologists, as well as that of the theologians at the beginning of last century, still exerts its influence to-day.

The second type is represented by those theologians who seek to embrace the revelation granted to the church within one vast and finally completed system of thought. They are the Hegels of theology, but with the difference that they themselves must follow the way of obedience and are bound to revelation. Still, the system indicates its fixed place for all that is contained in revelation and also for what arises subsequently, from this as its basis, in the church's life; and since the church is the sphere wherein the indications of grace are manifested, ecclesiastical theology is the totality of the indications thus given. The precise frontier between dogma and theology is indeed difficult to determine; nevertheless the significance of the *doctor ecclesiae* for the development of dogma is willingly recognized, the great representative of this type being Thomas Aquinas.

The third type, finally, is represented by those theologians who certainly attempt to combine the construction of a system with the first kind of task, but a system that is as it were open and unfinished and in which the original experience has, and should have, a markedly disquieting influence. This type is characterized by intense emotionalism and a personal note of address: St. Paul, St. Augustine and Luther fall within this category. At the frontier of this form of theology stands the anti-systematizer Kierkegaard, who showed himself to be a genuine member of this group by setting out from the revelation preserved in dogma, and also by the fabric he himself produced from this and intentionally left unfinished in both directions:—upwards to the aspect of the eternally active and divine revealing Will, and downwards to that of living, existential thought that deals with reality; nevertheless the fabric itself must never be finally completed.

CHAPTER 105

THE EXAMPLE

1. IN our previous discussions of following after God[1] the example of the divine man came within our field of vision; and I shall now consider the way in which a foundation appears historically as an example. The personality of every founder, of course, is to a certain extent an example to his own followers. His experience in itself is the standard; but this very characteristic may become the preponderating factor in the foundation. Thus Islamite *sufis* distinguish the "saint" from the "prophet". The prophet warns, proclaiming the law in decisive terms: he is the "messenger", *rasul*;[2] and the only personal quality that need be demanded of him is faithfulness in delivering his message: he is not necessarily a saint. He "has authority over the gifts of grace and distributes these, but they have no authority over him"; the saint, on the other hand, is seized by grace and his very nature transformed, while on his own part he cannot control grace; for this reason Jesus was superior to Abu Bakr, for instance, the relationship of the former to God being twofold, that of the latter merely single: he repeated only what he had heard.[3] In this case, however, and exactly after the fashion of Islam, an important insight is exaggerated. The prophet certainly could not complete his own mission unless grace controlled him; conversely, the saint transmits the grace that has seized upon him; and Islam's striking dread of any dual relationship of any kind whatever between God and man appears in its self-expulsion by the appeal to the saint. *This*, nevertheless, has been quite accurately perceived: there are founders whose instruction is not at all the principal factor, and whose foundation can therefore be comprised in what has been manifested in them through divine grace.

2. Here then it is the life and deed of the founders themselves that are effective: they "found" a community, a communal life, a piety. When Albert Schweitzer recently gave an organ recital in a Netherlands town, many ordinary people came after the performance to the exit from the organ gallery to see him—not however to hail the artist, and still less to honour the scholar but, as someone expressed it, "to see the man

---

[1] Chap. 73.   [2] *cf.* Chap. 27.   [3] Massignon, *Al-Hallaj*, 738 *ff.*

who had done something while the others were only talking". This is precisely the power of example; we can point to some human life and say: something is happening there: in this life Power appears. St. Francis, again, was a purer type of this kind of foundation than Buddha who, though he was certainly an example to his disciples, laid chief stress on doctrine; the former's example, on the other hand, created the "Franciscan life" of poverty. Jesus also is the example for those who believe in Him, in a deeper sense, however, than as the example of one who is a founder. He too has done great deeds, but the following of this example is a mystical union with the Saviour; and St. Paul expressed this most clearly when he desired that "Christ be formed in you",[1] as did St. John in his parable of "The Vine and its Branches".[2]

[1] *Gal.* iv. 19; *cf.* Chap. 73.   [2] *John* xv.

CHAPTER 106

THE MEDIATOR

1. SINCE all "holy men" are mediators, their "representation" ensuring the relationship between Power and man, founders also are mediators. But in the truest sense he is a mediator whose whole being is mediation, and who surrenders his own life as the "means" for Power. In such cases foundation is not only an experience leading to some kind of instruction, doctrine or exemplary activity; it is identical with the founder himself: foundation and founder are one. This is most clearly perceived when we compare, for example, the salvation by the Buddha Amitabha with that by Christ. For the entrance into Buddha's Paradise is only a preparatory goal of salvation, a gateway to *Nirvana*; but Christ is Himself salvation.[1] And not merely His deed, the surrender of His life on the Cross, is effective in bringing salvation; His whole existence is the "means":—"Who for us men, and for our salvation, came down from heaven". Setting out from Judaistic Messiahism, born into the Greek-Oriental world, Jesus of Nazareth is worshipped by His followers as the mediator;[2] and what this means is most obvious in comparison with other saviours, for example with Apollonius of Tyana, who lived in the first century A.D. The life histories of both resemble each other in many respects; their busts were placed with those of Abraham and Orpheus, Alexander the Great and several emperors, all "divine" men, in the *lararium* or shrine of the emperor Alexander Severus.[3] But Apollonius is not a mediator in the truest sense, any more than was the Jewish messiah—for example, Zerubbabel. Jesus, however, is mediator because His whole essential being is a "means", a movement of man towards God and of God towards man.

2. Here, finally, we have reached the borderland of phenomenology, the region that proved to be inaccessible throughout our previous discussions of the world and the church, of guilt and faith. For Christian faith the figure of the mediator is no "phenomenon"; the phenomen-

---

[1] *cf.* Otto, *India's Religion of Grace*, Chap. I.

[2] *Hebrews* viii, 6; ix, 15; xii, 24: the mediator of the new covenant, as Moses is called the mediator of the old (*Gal.* iii, 19 f.).

[3] *cf.* Th. Hopfner, *Apollonius von Tyana und Philostratus* (*Seminarium Kondakovianum, Rec. d'Et.*, IV), Prag, 1931. *cf.* further Wendland, *Hell.-röm. Kultur*, 161.

ologist cannot perceive where and how it enters history. He observes prophet, reformer, teacher, example; but he cannot see the mediator in His historical effectiveness. It becomes apparent to him how the experience of Jesus of Nazareth has founded in history a mighty stream of faith experiences, but not how in history God gives Himself to man as mediator. He can perceive that Jesus sacrificed Himself: but he can only believe that Jesus was none other than God giving Himself. At best he can observe that the uniqueness of the mediator essentially pertains to this faith: the mediator of revelation has become revelation itself; the Word became flesh; and henceforth every revelation of God conforms to the sole revelation in Christ. "He is the head of the Body, that is, of the church, in virtue of his primacy as the first to be born from the dead—that gives him pre-eminence over all. For it was in him that the divine Fullness willed to settle without limit, and by him it willed to reconcile in his own person all on earth and in heaven alike." "It is in Christ that the entire Fullness of deity has settled bodily."[1] We can assert, further, that His mediation must concern what is deepest of all: guilt; the Saviour is the reconciler. And thus we can understand that every title of "saviour", and every representative function, belong to Him by right, from the dignity of the mediator of creation, in *The Epistle to the Colossians*, to that of the Hellenistic σωτὴρ τοῦ κόσμου, or *salvator mundi*, derived from the saviour-god and emperor;[2] from the Jewish messianic hero to the medieval champion of the joust;[3] from prophet to teacher, from reformer to example, from the merciful good shepherd to the Judge of the world at the last day. Since Christ's appearance a new comprehension of the world, of history and of man is possible:[4] "For 'there is one God' and 'one intermediary between God and men, the man Christ Jesus who gave himself as a ransom for all':—in due time this was attested."[5]

Here there lives a faith for which God, in human form, lovingly stoops over what is deepest in the world and in man, over guilt, and for which God's almighty Power assumes life in man's fragile frame. But at this point the contemplative and comprehending servant of research reverently withdraws; his own utterance yields place to that of proclamation, his service to that in the sanctuary.

---

[1] *Col.* i, 18 *ff.* ii, 9 (Moffat).   [2] *cf.* O. Weinreich, *Aegyptus*, 11, 1931, 17.
[3] Burdach, *Vorspiel*, I, 1, 245.
[4] *cf.* R. Bultmann, *Theol. Blätter* 8, 1929, 146 *f.*   [5] 1 *Tim.* ii. 5 (Moffat).

EPILEGOMENA

CHAPTER 107

PHENOMENON AND PHENOMENOLOGY[1]

1. PHENOMENOLOGY seeks the *phenomenon*, as such; the phenomenon, again, is *what "appears"*. This principle has a threefold implication: (*1*) Something exists. (*2*) This something "appears". (*3*) Precisely because it "appears" it is a "phenomenon". But "appearance" refers equally to what appears and to the person to whom it appears; the phenomenon, therefore, is neither pure object, nor *the* object, that is to say, the actual reality, whose essential being is merely concealed by the "appearing" of the appearances; with this a specific metaphysics deals. The term "phenomenon", still further, does not imply something purely subjective, not a "life" of the subject;[2] so far as is at all possible, a definite branch of psychology is concerned with this. The "phenomenon" as such, therefore, is an object related to a subject, and a subject related to an object; although this does not imply that the subject deals with or modifies the object in any way whatever, nor (conversely) that the object is somehow or other affected by the subject. The phenomenon, still further, is not produced by the subject, and still less substantiated or demonstrated by it; its entire essence is given in its "appearance", and its appearance to "someone". If (finally) this "someone" begins to discuss what "appears", then phenomenology arises.

In its relation to the "someone" to whom the phenomenon appears, accordingly, it has three levels of phenomenality: (*1*) its (relative) *concealment*; (*2*) its *gradually becoming revealed*; (*3*) its (relative) *transparency*. These levels, again, are not equivalent to, but are correlated with, the three levels of life: (*1*) *Experience*: (*2*) *Understanding*: (*3*) *Testimony*; and the last two attitudes, when systematically or scientifically employed, constitute the procedure of phenomenology.

By "experience" is implied an actually subsisting life which, with respect to its meaning, constitutes a unity.[3] Experience, therefore, is not pure "life", since in the first place it is objectively conditioned and, secondly, it is inseparably connected with its interpretation as experience. "Life" itself is incomprehensible: "What the disciple of Saïs unveils is form, not life."[4] For the "primal experience", upon which our experiences are grounded, has always passed irrevocably away by the time our attention is directed to it. My own life, for example, which I experienced while writing the few lines of the

---

[1] [In what follows a few passages of somewhat technical character are in small type.]

[2] The term "experience" (*Erlebnis*) is itself objectively oriented (we always experience something) and designates a "structure"; *cf.* Note, p. 461.

[3] Dilthey, *Gesammelte Schriften*, VII, 194.

[4] *ibid.*, 195.

preceding sentence, is just as remote from me as is the "life" associated with the lines I wrote thirty years ago in a school essay. I cannot call it back again: it is completely past. In fact, the experience of the lines of a moment ago is no nearer to me than is the experience of the Egyptian scribe who wrote his note on papyrus four thousand years ago. That he was "another" than myself makes no difference whatever, since the boy who prepared the school work thirty years ago is also, to my own contemplation, "another", and I must objectify myself in my experience of those bygone days. The immediate, therefore, is never and nowhere "given"; it must always be reconstructed;[1] and to "ourselves", that is to our most intimate life, we have no access. For our "life" is not the house wherein we reside, nor again the body, with which we can at least do something: on the contrary, confronted with this "life" we stand helpless. What appears to us as the greatest difference and the most extreme contrast possible—the difference, namely, between ourselves and the "other", our reighbour, whether close by or in distant China, of yesterday or of four thousand years ago—all that is a mere triviality when measured against the colossal *aporia*, the insoluble dilemma, in which we find ourselves as soon as we wish to approach life itself. Even when we reduce life to its appearance in history, we remain perplexed: the gate remains closed, that to yesterday just as that to olden times; and every historian knows that he may commence anywhere at all, but in any case he ends with himself; in other words, he *reconstructs*.[2] What, then, does this reconstruction imply?

It may be described, to begin with, as the sketching of an outline within the chaotic maze of so-called "reality", this outline being called *structure*. Structure is a connection which is neither merely experienced directly, nor abstracted either logically or causally, but which is *understood*. It is an organic whole which cannot be analyzed into its own constituents, but which can from these be comprehended; or in other terms, a fabric of particulars, not to be compounded by the addition of these, nor the deduction of one from the others, but again only *understood* as a whole.[3] In other words: structure is certainly experienced, but not immediately; it is indeed constructed, but not logically, causally and abstractly. Structure is reality significantly organized. But the significance, in its own turn, belongs in part to reality itself, and in part to the "someone" who attempts to understand it. It is always, therefore, both understanding and intelligibility: and this, indeed, in an unanalyzable, experienced connection. For it can never be asserted with any certainty what is my own understanding, and what is the intelligibility of that which is understood; and this is the purport of the statement that the understanding

---

[1] *cf.* E. Spranger, *Die Einheit der Psychologie, Sitzber. d. Preuss, Akad. d. Wiss.* 24, 1926, 188, 191. F. Krüger, *Ber. über den VIII. Kongress für experim. Psych.,* 33.

[2] *cf.* on a different field of research, P. Bekker, *Musikgeschichte,* 1926, 2.

[3] The so-called hermeneutic circle, to which G. Wobbermin particularly drew attention; *cf.* Wach, *Religionswissenschaft,* 49.

of a connection, or of a person or event, *dawns upon us*.[1] Thus the sphere of meaning is a third realm, subsisting above mere subjectivity and mere objectivity.[2] The entrance gate to the reality of primal experience, itself, wholly inaccessible, is *meaning*: *my* meaning and *its* meaning, which have become irrevocably one is the act of understanding.

Still further, the interconnection of meaning—structure—is experienced by understanding, first of all at some given moment; the meaning dawns upon me. But this is not the whole truth, since comprehension is never restricted to the momentary experience. It extends over several experiential unities simultaneously, as indeed it also originates from the understanding of these unities of experience. But these other experiences, which are at the same time understood in combination, and which cooperate in understanding, of course present a similarity to what has been instantaneously understood which, precisely in and through understanding itself, manifests itself as community of essential nature. The understood experience thus becomes coordinated, in and by understanding, within experience of some yet wider objective connection. *Every individual experience, therefore, is already connection*; and every connection remains always experience; this is what we mean by speaking of *types*, together with structures.[3]

The appearance, to continue, subsists as an image. It possesses backgrounds and associated planes; it is "related" to other entities that appear, either by similarity, by contrast, or by a hundred *nuances* that can arise here: conditions, peripheral or central position, competition, distance, *etc.* These relationships, however, are always *perceptible* relationships, "*structural connections*":[4] they are never factual relationships nor causal connections. They do not, of course, exclude the latter, but neither do they enunciate anything about them; they are valid only within the structural relations. Such a relation, finally, whether it concerns a person, a historical situation or a religion, is called a *type*, or an *ideal type*.[5]

"Type" in itself, however, has no reality; nor is it a photograph of reality. Like structure, it is timeless and need not actually occur in history.[6] But it possesses life, its own significance, its own law. The "soul", again, as such, never and nowhere "appears"; there is always and only some definite kind of soul which is believed in, and is in this its definiteness unique. It may even

[1] *cf.* A. A. Grünbaum, *Herrschen und Lieben*, 1925, 17. Spranger, *Lebensformen*, 6 *ff.*   [2] Spranger, *ibid.*, 436.

[3] Spranger, *Einheit der Psychologie*, 177; *cf.* Wach's observation that the close connection between the theory of types and that of hermeneutics has not yet been adequately emphasized; *Religionswissenschaft*, 149.

[4] This term was introduced by Karl Jaspers: *verständliche Beziehungen*.

[5] On the history of the idea *cf.* B. Pfister, *Die Entwicklung zum Idealtypus*, 1928.

[6] Spranger, *Lebensformen*, 115; Binswanger, *Einführung in die Probleme der allgemeinen Psychologie*, 296; van der Leeuw, *Über einige neuere Ergebnisse der psychologischen Forschung und ihre Anwendung auf die Geschichte, insonderheit die Religionsgeschichte*, SM. II, 1926, *passim*; *cf.* further P. Hofmann, *Das religiöse Erlebnis*, 1925, 8.

be said that the ideas of the soul formed by any two persons, it may be in the same cultural and religious circle, are never wholly the same. Still there is a *type* of soul, a structural relation of distinctive soul-structures. The type itself (to repeat) is timeless: nor is it real. Nevertheless it is alive and appears to us; what then are we to do in order actually to observe it?

2. We resort to phenomenology: that is to say, we must discuss whatever has "appeared" to us—in this sense the term itself is quite clear.[1] This discussion, still further, involves the following stages, which I enumerate in succession although, in practice, they arise never successively but always simultaneously, and in their mutual relations far more frequently than in series:—

A. What has become manifest, in the first place, receives a *name*. All speech consists first of all in *assigning names*: "the simple use of names constitutes a form of thinking intermediate between perceiving and imagining".[2] In giving names we separate phenomena and also associate them; in other words, we classify. We include or reject: this we call a "sacrifice" and that a "purification"; since Adam named the animals, speakers have always done this. In this assignment of names, however, we expose ourselves to the peril of becoming intoxicated, or at least satisfied, with the name—the danger which Goethe represented as "transforming observations into mere concepts, and concepts into words", and then treating these words "as if they were objects".[3] We attempt to avoid this danger by

B. The interpolation of the phenomenon into our own lives.[4] This introduction, however, is no capricious act; we can do no otherwise. "Reality" is always *my* reality, history *my* history, "the retrogressive prolongation of man now living".[5] We must, however, realize what we are doing when we commence to speak about what has appeared to us and which we are naming. Further, we must recall that everything that appears to us does not submit itself to us directly and immediately, but only as a symbol of some meaning to be interpreted by us, as something which offers itself to us for interpretation. And this interpretation is impossible unless we experience the appearance, and this, indeed, not involuntarily and semi-consciously, but intentionally and methodically. Here I cite the impressive statement of Usener who, although he knew nothing of phenomenology, was fully aware of

[1] What I myself understand by the phenomenology of religion is called by Hackmann "The General Science of Religion"; other terms for this type of research that have appeared (once more to disappear, however) are "Transcendental Psychology", "Eidology" and *Formenlehre der religiösen Vorstellungen* (Usener).

[2] McDougall, *An Outline of Psychology*, 284.

[3] *Farbenlehre* in Binswanger, *op. cit.*, 31.

[4] The expression usually employed, "Empathy" (*Einfühlung*) overstresses the feeling aspect of the process, although not without some justification.

[5] Spranger, *op. cit.* 430.

what it implies: "Only by surrendering oneself, and by submersion in these spiritual traces of vanished time[1] . . . can we train ourselves to recall their feeling; then chords within ourselves, gradually becoming sympathetic, can harmoniously vibrate and resound, and we discover in our own consciousness the strands linking together old and new."[2] This too is what Dilthey describes as the "experience of a structural connection", such experience, it is true, being more an art than a science.[3] It is in fact the primal and primitively human art of the actor which is indispensable to all arts, but to the sciences of mind also:—to sympathize keenly and closely with experience other than one's own, but also with one's own experience of yesterday, already become strange! To this sympathetic experience, of course, there are limits; but these are also set to our understanding of ourselves, it may be to an even greater degree; *homo sum, humani nil a me alienum puto*: this is no key to the deepest comprehension of the remotest experience, but is nevertheless the triumphant assertion that the essentially human always remains essentially human, and is, as such, comprehensible:—unless indeed he who comprehends has acquired too much of the professor and retained too little of the man! "When the professor is told by the barbarian that once there was nothing except a great feathered serpent, unless the learned man feels a thrill and a half temptation to wish it were true, he is no judge of such things at all."[4] Only the persistent and strenuous application of this intense sympathy, only the uninterrupted learning of his rôle, qualifies the phenomenologist to interpret appearances. In Jaspers' pertinent words: "Thus every psychologist experiences the increasing clarity of his mental life for himself; he becomes aware of what has hitherto remained unnoticed, although he never reaches the ultimate limit."[5]

C. Not only is the "ultimate limit" never attainable in the sense referred to by Jaspers: it implies, still further, the unattainability of existence. Phenomenology, therefore, is neither metaphysics, nor the comprehension of empirical reality. It observes *restraint* (the *epoché*), and its understanding of events depends on its employing "brackets".[6] Phenomenology is concerned only with "phenomena", that is with "appearance"; for it, there is nothing whatever "behind" the phenomenon. This restraint, still further, implies no mere methodological device, no cautious procedure, but the distinctive characteristic of man's whole attitude to reality. Scheler has very well expressed this situation: "to be human means to hurl a forcible 'No!' at this sort of reality. Buddha realized this when he said how magnificent it is to *contemplate* everything, and how terrible it is to *be*: Plato, too, in connecting the contemplation of ideas to a diverting of the soul from the sensuous con-

---

[1] This applies equally to the so-called "present".   [2] *Götternamen,* 1896, VII.
[3] Binswanger, *op. cit.,* 246; van der Leeuw, *op. cit.,* 14 f.
[4] Chesterton, *The Everlasting Man,* 111; cf. Hofmann, *Religiöses Erlebnis,* 4 f.
[5] K. Jaspers, *Allgemeine Psychopathologie*[3], 1923, 204.   [6] cf. Note, p. 646.

tent of objects, and to the diving at the soul into its own depths, in order to find the 'origins' of things. Husserl, also, implies nothing different than this when he links the knowledge of ideas with 'phenomenological reduction'— that is a 'crossing through' or 'bracketing' of (the accidental) coefficients of the existence of objects in the world in order to obtain their '*essentia*'."[1] This of course involves no preference of some "idealism" or other to some kind of "realism". On the contrary: it is simply maintained that man can be positive only in turning away from things, as they are given to him chaotically and formlessly, and by first assigning them form and meaning. Phenomenology, therefore, is not a method that has been reflectively elaborated, but is man's true vital activity, consisting in losing himself neither in things nor in the *ego*, neither in hovering above objects like a god nor dealing with them like an animal, but in doing what is given to neither animal nor god: standing aside and understanding what appears into view.

D. The observance of what appears implies a *clarification* of what has been observed: all that belongs to the same order must be united, while what is different in type must be separated. These distinctions, however, should certainly not be decided by appealing to causal connections in the sense that *A* arises from *B*, while *C* has its own origin uniting it to *D*—but solely and simply by employing structural relations somewhat as the landscape painter combines his groups of objects, or separates them from one another. The juxtaposition, in other words, must not become externalization, but structural association;[2] and this means that we seek the ideal typical interrelation, and then attempt to arrange this within some yet wider whole of significance, *etc*.[3]

E. All these activities, undertaken together and simultaneously, constitute genuine *understanding*: the chaotic and obstinate "reality" thus becomes a manifestation, a revelation. The empirical, ontal or metaphysical *fact* becomes a *datum*; the object, living speech; rigidity, expression.[4] "The sciences of mind are based on the relations between experience, expression and understanding":[5] I understand this to mean that the intangible experience in itself cannot be apprehended nor mastered, but that it manifests something to us, an appearance: says something, an utterance. The aim of science, therefore, is to understand this *logos*; essentially, science is hermeneutics.[6]

Now when we are concerned, as in our own case, with the domain of historical research, this would appear to be the stage at which historical scepticism threateningly intrudes into our investigations, and renders all comprehension of remote times and regions impossible to us. We might then reply that we are quite ready to acknowledge that we can *know* nothing, and that we admit, further, that perhaps we understand very little; but that, on the

---

[1] Max Scheler, *Die Stellung des Menschen im Kosmos*, 1928, 63; *cf*. Heidegger, *Sein und Zeit*, 38.   [2] Binswanger, *op. cit.*, 302; *cf*. Jaspers, *Psychopathologie*, 18, 35.

[3] Spranger, *Lebensformen*, 11.

[4] Heidegger, *op. cit.*, 37; Dilthey, *op. cit.*, VII, 71, 86.

[5] Dilthey, *ibid.*, 131.   [6] *cf*. further Binswanger, *op. cit.*, 244, 288.

other hand, to understand the Egyptian of the first dynasty is, in itself, no more difficult than to understand my nearest neighbour. Certainly the monuments of the first dynasty are intelligible only with great difficulty, but as an expression, as a human statement, they are no harder than my colleague's letters. In this respect, indeed, the historian can learn from the psychiatrist: "If we are astonished by an ancient myth or an Egyptian head, and confront it with the conviction that there is something that is intelligible in accord with our own experience, although it is infinitely remote from us and unattainable, just as we are amazed by a psycho-pathological process or an abnormal character, we have at least the possibility of a more deeply comprehending glance, and perhaps of achieving a living representation. . . ."[1]

F. But if phenomenology is to complete its own task, it imperatively requires perpetual correction by the most conscientious philological and archaeological research. It must therefore always be prepared for confrontation with material facts, although the actual manipulation of these facts themselves cannot proceed without interpretation—that is without phenomenology; and every exegesis, every translation, indeed every reading, is already hermeneutics. But this purely philological hermeneutics has a more restricted purpose than the purely phenomenological. For it is concerned in the first place with the Text, and then with the fact in the sense of what is concretely implied: of what can be translated in other words. This of course necessitates meaning, only it is a shallower and broader meaning than phenomenological understanding.[2] But as soon as the latter withdraws itself from control by philological and archaeological interpretation, it becomes pure art or empty fantasy.[3]

G. This entire and apparently complicated procedure, in conclusion, has ultimately no other goal than pure objectivity. Phenomenology aims not at things, still less at their mutual relations, and least of all at the "thing in itself". It desires to gain access to the facts themselves;[4] and for this it requires a meaning, because it cannot experience the facts just as it pleases. This meaning, however, is purely objective: all violence, either empirical, logical or metaphysical, is excluded. Phenomenology regards every event in the same way that Ranke looked on each epoch as "in an immediate and direct relation to God", so that "its value depends in no degree on whatever results from it, but on its existence as such, on its own self".[5] It holds itself quite apart from modern thought, which would teach us "to contemplate the world as unformed material, which we must first of all form, and conduct ourselves as the lords of the world".[6] It has, in fact, one sole desire: *to testify*

---

[1] Jaspers, *Psychopathologie*, 404; *cf.* Usener, *Götternamen*, 62.

[2] Spranger gives an excellent example in his comparison of the ever more deeply penetrating meanings of a biblical text; *Einheit der Psychologie*, 180 *ff.*

[3] Wach, *Religionswissenschaft*, 117; van der Leeuw, *op. cit., passim.*

[4] Heidegger, *op. cit.*, 34.   [5] L. von Ranke, *Weltgeschichte*, VIII⁴, 1921, 177.

[6] E. Brunner, *Gott und Mensch*, 1930, 40.

to what has been manifested to it.[1] This it can do only by indirect methods, by a second experience of the event, by a thorough reconstruction; and from this road it must remove many obstacles. To see face to face is denied us. But much can be observed even in a mirror; and it is possible to speak about things seen.

E. Bernheim, *Lehrbuch der historischen Methode*[5-6], 1914.

L. Binswanger, *Einführung in die Probleme der allgemeinen Psychologie*, 1922.
    Verstehen und Erklären in der Psychologie (*Zeitschr. f. d. g. Neurologie und Psychiatrie* 107, 1927).

W. Dilthey, *Gesammelte Schriften*[2], 1923 ff.

H. Hackmann, *Allgemeine Religionsgeschichte* (*Nieuw Theol. Tydschrift*, 1919).

M. Heidegger, *Sein und Zeit, Erste Hälfte*[2], 1929.

Eva Hirschmann, *Phänomenologie der Religion*, 1940.

P. Hofmann, *Allgemeinwissenschaft und Geisteswissenschaft*, 1925.

G. van der Leeuw, *Über einige neuere Ergebnisse der psychologischen Forschung und ihre Anwendung auf die Geschichte, insonderheit die Religionsgeschichte* (*SM*. II, 1926).

E. Neumann, *Ursprungsgeschichte des Bewustseins*, 1949.

B. Pfister, *Die Entwicklung zum Idealtypus*, 1928.

F. Sierksma, *Phaenomenologie der Religie en Complexe Psychologie, Een Methodologische Studie*, 1950.

E. Spranger, *Lebensformen*[5], 1925.

Anna Tumarkin, *Die Methoden der psychologischen Forschung*, 1929.

J. Wach, *Das Verstehen*, I, 1926. II, 1929. III, 1933.
    Religionswissenschaft, 1924.

[1] *cf.* W. J. Aalders, *Wetenschap als Getuigenis*, 1930.

RELIGION

1. WE can try to understand religion from a flat plain, from ourselves as the centre; and we can also understand how the essence of religion is to be grasped only from above, beginning with God. In other words: we can—in the manner already indicated—observe religion as intelligible experience; or we can concede to it the status of incomprehensible revelation. For in its "reconstruction", experience is a phenomenon. Revelation is not; but man's reply to revelation, his assertion about what has been revealed, is also a phenomenon from which, indirectly, conclusions concerning the revelation itself can be derived (*per viam negationis*).

Considered in the light of both of these methods, religion implies that man does not simply accept the life that is given to him. In life he seeks *power*; and if he does not find this, or not to an extent that satisfies him, then he attempts to draw the power, in which he believes, into his own life. He tries to elevate life, to enhance its value, to gain for it some deeper and wider meaning. In this way, however, we find ourselves on the horizontal line: religion is the extension of life to its uttermost limit. The religious man desires richer, deeper, wider life: he desires power for himself.[1] In other terms: in and about his own life man seeks something that is superior, whether he wishes merely to make use of this or to worship it.

He who does not merely accept life, then, but demands something from it—that is, power—endeavours to find some meaning in life. He arranges life into a significant whole: and thus culture arises. Over the variety of the given he throws his systematically fashioned net, on which various designs appear: a work of art, a custom, an economy. From the stone he makes himself an image, from the instinct a commandment, from the wilderness a tilled field; and thus he develops power. But he never halts; he seeks ever further for constantly deeper and wider *meaning*. When he realizes that a flower is beautiful and bears fruit, he enquires for its ampler, ultimate significance; when he knows that his wife is beautiful, that she can work and bear children, when he perceives

---

[1] Herein consists the essential unity between religion and culture. Ultimately, all culture is religious; and, on the horizontal line, all religion is culture.

that he must respect another man's wife, just as he would have his own respected, he seeks still further and asks for her final meaning. Thus he finds the secret of the flower and of woman; and so he discovers their religious significance.

The religious significance of things, therefore, is that on which no wider nor deeper meaning whatever can follow. It is the meaning of the whole: it is the last word. But this meaning is never understood, this last word is never spoken; always they remain superior, the ultimate meaning being a secret which reveals itself repeatedly, only nevertheless to remain eternally concealed. It implies an advance to the farthest boundary, where only one sole fact is understood:—that all comprehension is "beyond"; and thus the ultimate meaning is at the same moment the limit of meaning.[1]

Homo religiosus thus betakes himself to the road to omnipotence, to complete understanding, to ultimate meaning. He would fain comprehend life, in order to dominate it. As he understands soil so as to make it fruitful, as he learns how to follow animals' ways, so as to subject them to himself—so too he resolves to understand the world, in order to subjugate it to himself. Therefore he perpetually seeks new superiorities: until at last he stands at the very frontier and perceives that the ultimate superiority he will never attain, but that it reaches him in an incomprehensible and mysterious way. Thus the horizontal line of religion resembles the way of St. Christopher, who seeks his master and at last finds him too.

2. But there is also a vertical way: from below upwards, and from above downwards. This way however is not, like the former, an experience that is passed through before a frontier. It is a revelation, coming from beyond that frontier. The horizontal path, again, is an experience which certainly has an inkling or presage[2] of revelation, but which cannot attain to it. The vertical way, on the other hand, is a revelation, which never becomes completely experienced, though it participates in experience.[3] The first road is certainly not a tangible, but is all the more an intelligible, phenomenon. The second is not a phenomenon at all, and is neither attainable nor understandable; what we obtain from it phenomenologically, therefore, is merely its reflection in experience. We can never understand God's utterance by means of any purely intellectual capacity: what we can understand is only our

---

[1] Spranger, *op. cit., passim.*   [2] *Ahnung: cf.* p. 48, note 1.
[3] Chap. 67.

own answer; and in this sense, too, it is true that we have the treasure only in an earthen vessel.

Man, seeking power in life, does not reach the frontier; but he realizes that he has been removed to some foreign region. Thus he not only reaches the place from which a prospect of infinite distance is disclosed to him, but he knows too that, while he is still on the way, he is at every moment surrounded by marvellous and far-off things. He has not only a firm awareness (*Ahnung*) of the superior, but is also directly seized by it. He has not merely descried the throne of the Lord *from afar*, and fain would have sent on his heart in advance, but he realizes too that *this* place itself is dreadful, because it is a "house of God" and a "gate of heaven". Perhaps angels descend to his resting-place: perhaps demons press upon his path. But he knows quite definitely that *something meets him on the road*. It may be the angel who goes before him and will lead him safely: it may be the angel with the flashing sword who forbids him the road. But it is quite certain that something foreign has traversed the way of his own powerfulness.

And just because it is not to be found in the prolongation of man's own path, this strange element has no name whatever. Otto has suggested "the numinous", probably because this expression says nothing at all! This foreign element, again, can be approached only *per viam negationis*; and here again it is Otto who has found the correct term in his designation "the Wholly Other". For this, however, religions themselves have coined the word "holy".[1] The German term is derived from *Heil*, "powerfulness"; the Semitic and Latin, קרשׁ, *sanctus*, and the primitive expression, *tabu*, have the fundamental meaning of "separated", "set aside by itself". Taken all together, they provide the description of what occurs in all religious experience: *a strange*, "*Wholly Other*", *Power obtrudes into life*. Man's attitude to it is first of all *astonishment*,[2] and ultimately *faith*.

3. The limit of human powerfulness, in conclusion, and the commencement of the divine, together constitute the goal which has been sought and found in the religion of all time:—*salvation*. It may be the enhancing of life, improvement, beautifying, widening, deepening; but by "salvation" there may also be meant completely new life, a devaluation of all that has preceded, a new creation of the life that has been received "from elsewhere". But in any case, religion is always directed

[1] Chap. 4; *cf.* also Chap. 11, Section 1, and Otto, *The Idea of the Holy, passim.*
[2] Otto.

towards salvation, never towards life itself as it is given; and in this respect all religion, with no exception, is the religion of deliverance.[1]

P. HOFMANN, *Das religiöse Erlebnis*, 1925.
R. OTTO, *The Idea of the Holy*.

[1] Hofmann, *Das religiöse Erlebnis*, 12 *ff.*

CHAPTER 109

THE PHENOMENOLOGY OF RELIGION

1. PHENOMENOLOGY is the systematic discussion of what appears. Religion, however, is an ultimate experience that evades our observation, a revelation which in its very essence is, and remains, concealed. But how shall I deal with what is thus ever elusive and hidden? How can I pursue phenomenology when there is no phenomenon? How can I refer to "phenomenology of religion" at all?

Here there clearly exists an antinomy that is certainly essential to all religions, but also to all understanding; it is indeed precisely because it holds good for *both*, for religion and understanding alike, that our own science becomes possible. It is unquestionably quite correct to say that faith and intellectual suspense (the *epoche*)[1] do not exclude each other. It may further be urged that the Catholic Church, too, recognizes a *duplex ordo* of contemplation, on the one hand purely rational, and on the other wholly in accord with faith; while such a Catholic as Przywara also wishes to exclude every apologetic subsidiary aim from philosophy, and strenuously maintains the *epoche*.[2] But at the same time one cannot but recognize that all these reflections are the result of embarrassment. For it is at bottom utterly impossible contemplatively to confront an event which, on the one hand, is an ultimate experience, and on the other manifests itself in profound emotional agitation, in the attitude of such pure intellectual restraint. Apart from the existential attitude that is concerned with reality, we could never know anything of either religion or faith. It may certainly be advisable and useful methodically to presuppose this intellectual suspense; it is also expedient, since crude prejudice can so readily force its way into situations where only such an existential attitude would be justifiable. But, once again, how shall we comprehend the life of religion merely by contemplative observation from a distance? How indeed can we understand what, in principle, wholly eludes our understanding?

Now we have already found that not the understanding of religion alone, but *all* understanding without exception, ultimately reaches the limit where it loses its own proper name and can only be called "becoming understood". In other words: the more deeply comprehension

[1] *cf.* Note, p. 646.   *Die Problematik der Neuscholastik, Kantstudien* 33, 1928.

penetrates any event, and the better it "understands" it, the clearer it becomes to the understanding mind that the ultimate ground of understanding lies not within itself, but in some "other" by which it is comprehended from beyond the frontier. Without this absolutely valid and decisive understanding, indeed, there would be no understanding whatever. For all understanding that extends "to the ground" ceases to be understanding before it reaches the ground, and recognizes itself as a "becoming understood". In other terms: all understanding, irrespective of whatever object it refers to, is ultimately religious: all significance sooner or later leads to ultimate significance. As Spranger states this: "in so far as it always refers to the whole man, and actually finds its final completion in the totality of world conditions, all understanding has a religious factor . . . we understand each other in God."[1]

What has previously been said with reference to the horizontal line in religion can also be translated into the language of the vertical line. And that ultimately all understanding is "becoming understood" then means that, ultimately, all love is "becoming loved"; that all human love is only the response to the love that was bestowed upon us. "Herein is love, not that we loved God, but that he loved us . . . we love him, because he first loved us."[2]

Understanding, in fact, itself presupposes intellectual restraint. But this is never the attitude of the cold-blooded spectator: it is, on the contrary, the loving gaze of the lover on the beloved object. For all understanding rests upon self-surrendering love. Were that not the case, then not only all discussion of what appears in religion, but all discussion of appearance in general, would be quite impossible; since to him who does not love, nothing whatever is manifested; this is the Platonic, as well as the Christian, experience.

I shall therefore not anticipate fruitlessly, and convert phenomenology into theology. Nor do I wish to assert that the faith upon which all comprehension is grounded, and religion as itself faith, are without further ado identical. But "it is plainly insufficient to permit theology to follow on philosophy (for my purpose, read "phenomenology") purely in virtue of its content, since the fundamental problem is one of method, and concerns the claim of philosophy (again, here, phenomenology) to·justification in view of the obvious data, and also the impossibility of referring back faith, as the methodical basis of theology, to these data. In other terms: the problem becomes that of what is obviously

---

[1] *Lebensformen*, 418.   [2] 1 *John* iv. 10, 19.

evidence".[1] And I am prepared, with Przywara, to seek the intimate relationship that nevertheless exists between faith and the obvious data, in the fact that the evidence they provide is essentially a "preparedness for revelation".[2]

2. The use of the expressions: history of religion, science of religion, comparative history of religion, psychology of religion, philosophy of religion: and others similar to these, is still very loose and inexact; and this is not merely a formal defect, but is practical also.[3] It is true that the different subdivisions of the sciences concerned with religion (the expression is here employed in its widest possible sense), cannot subsist independently of each other; they require, indeed, incessant mutual assistance. But much that is essential is forfeited as soon as the limits of the investigation are lost to sight. The history of religion, the philosophy and psychology of religion, and alas! theology also, are each and all harsh mistresses, who would fain compel their servants to pass beneath the yoke which they hold ready for them; and the phenomenology of religion desires not only to distinguish itself from them, but also, if possible, to teach them to restrain themselves! I shall therefore first of all indicate what the phenomenology of religion is not, and what fails to correspond to its own essential character in the character or usage of the other disciplines.

The phenomenology of religion, then, is not the poetry of religion; and to say this is not at all superfluous, since I have myself expressly referred to the poetic character of the structural experience of ideal types. In this sense, too, we may understand Aristotle's assertion that the historian relates what has happened, while the poet recounts what might have occurred under any given circumstances; and that poetry is therefore a philosophical affair and of more serious import than history;[4] as against all bare historicism and all mere chronicle, this should always be remembered. Nor should it be forgotten that "art is just as much investigation as is science, while science is just as much the creation of form as is art".[5] But in any case there is a clear distinction between poetry and science, which forces itself into notice in the procedure of both from beginning to end: in his own work, then, the phenomenologist is bound up with the object; he cannot proceed without repeatedly confronting the chaos of the given, and without submitting again and again to correction by the facts; while although the artist certainly sets

[1] Przywara, *ibid.*, 92.   [2] *ibid.*, 95.   [3] Wach, *Religionswissenschaft*, 12.
[4] *Poetics*, Chap. 9.   [5] E. Utitz, *Ästhetik*, 1923, 18.

out from the object, he is not inseparably linked with this. In other words: the poet need know no particular language, nor study the history of the times; even the poet of the so-called historical novel need not do this. In order to interpret a myth he may completely remodel it, as for example Wagner treated the German and Celtic heroic sagas. Here the phenomenologist experiences his own limit, since his path lies always between the unformed chaos of the historical world and its structural endowment with form. All his life he oscillates hither and thither. But the poet advances.

Secondly, the phenomenology of religion is not the history of religion. History, certainly, cannot utter one word without adopting some phenomenological viewpoint; even a translation, or the editing of a Text, cannot be completed without hermeneutics. On the other hand, the phenomenologist can work only with historical material, since he must know what documents are available and what their character is, before he can undertake their interpretation. The historian and the phenomenologist, therefore, work in the closest possible association; they are indeed in the majority of cases combined in the person of a *single* investigator. Nevertheless the historian's task is essentially different from the phenomenologist's, and pursues other aims.[1] For the historian, everything is directed first of all to establishing what has actually happened; and in this he can never succeed unless he understands. But also, when he fails to understand, he must describe what he has found, even if he remains at the stage of mere cataloguing. But when the phenomenologist ceases to comprehend, he can have no more to say. He strides here and there; the historian of course does the same, but more frequently he stands still, and often he does not stir at all. If he is a poor historian, this will be due only to idleness or incapacity; but if he is a sound historian, then his halts imply a very necessary and admirable resignation.

Thirdly, the phenomenology of religion is not a psychology of religion. Modern psychology, certainly, appears in so many forms that it becomes difficult to define its limits with respect to other subjects.[2] But that phenomenology is not identical with experimental psychology should be sufficiently obvious, though it is harder to separate it from the psychology of form and structure. Nevertheless it is probably the common feature of all psychologies that they are concerned only with the psychical. The psychology of religion, accordingly, attempts to comprehend the psychical aspects of religion. In so far therefore as the

[1] Wach, *ibid.*, 56.   [2] *cf.* Spranger, *Einheit der Psychologie.*

psychical is expressed and involved in all that is religious, phenomenology and psychology have a common task. But in religion far more appears than the merely psychical: the whole man participates in it, is active within it and is affected by it. In this sphere, then, psychology would enjoy competence only if it rose to the level of the science of Spirit—of course in its philosophic sense—in general which, it must be said, is not seldom the case. But if we are to restrict psychology to its own proper object, it may be said that the phenomenologist of religion strides backwards and forwards over the whole field of religious life, but the psychologist of religion over only a part of this.[1]

Fourthly, the phenomenology of religion is not a philosophy of religion, although it may be regarded as a preparation therefor. For it is systematic, and constitutes the bridge between the special sciences concerned with the history of religion and philosophical contemplation.[2] Of course phenomenology leads to problems of a philosophic and metaphysical character, "which it is itself not empowered to submit";[3] and the philosophy of religion can never dispense with its phenomenology. Too often already has that philosophy of religion been elaborated which naïvely set out from "Christianity"—that is, from the Western European standpoint of the nineteenth century, or even from the humanistic deism of the close of the eighteenth century. But whoever wishes to philosophize about religion must know what it is concerned with; he should not presuppose this as self-evident. Nevertheless the aim of the philosopher of religion is quite different; and while he must certainly know what the religious issues are, still he has something other in view; he wishes to move what he has discovered by means of the dialectical motion of Spirit. His progress, too, is hither and thither: only not in the sense of phenomenology; rather is it immanent in the Spirit. Every philosopher, indeed, has somewhat of God within him: it is quite seemly that he should stir the world in his inner life. But the phenomenologist should not become merely frightened by the idea of any similarity to God: he must shun it as the sin against the very spirit of his science.

Finally, phenomenology of religion is not theology. For theology shares with philosophy the claim to search for truth, while phenomenology, in this respect, exercises the intellectual suspense of the *epoche*.[4]

---

[1] That psychology is concerned purely with actual, and not with historical, experiences, and that consequently a limit subsists here also, obviously cannot be admitted for one moment; without psychology we should be unable to deal with history; cf. Spranger, *Einheit der Psychologie*, 184.

[2] Wach, *Verstehen* I, 12.   [3] Wach, *Rel. wiss.* 131.   [4] cf. Note, p. 646.

But the contrast lies deeper even than this. Theology discusses not merely a horizontal line leading, it may be, to God, nor only a vertical, descending from God and ascending to Him. Theology speaks about God Himself. For phenomenology, however, God is neither subject nor object; to be either of these He would have to be a phenomenon—that is, He would have to appear. But He does not appear: at least not so that we can comprehend and speak about Him. If He does appear He does so in a totally different manner, which results not in intelligible utterance, but in proclamation; and it is with this that theology has to deal. It too has a path "hither and thither"; but the "hither" and the "thither" are not the given and its interpretation, but concealment and revelation, heaven and earth, perhaps heaven, earth and hell. Of heaven and hell, however, phenomenology knows nothing at all; it is at home on earth, although it is at the same time sustained by love of the beyond.

3. In accordance with what has been remarked in Chapter 107, the phenomenology of religion must in the first place assign names:—sacrifice, prayer, saviour, myth, *etc.* In this way it appeals to appearances. Secondly, it must interpolate these appearances within its own life and experience them systematically. And in the third place, it must withdraw to one side, and endeavour to observe what appears while adopting the attitude of intellectual suspense. Fourthly, it attempts to clarify what it has seen, and again (combining all its previous activities) try to comprehend what has appeared. Finally, it must confront chaotic "reality", and its still uninterpreted signs, and ultimately testify to what it has understood. Nevertheless all sorts of problems that may be highly interesting in themselves must thereby be excluded. Thus phenomenology knows nothing of any historical "development" of religion,[1] still less of an "origin" of religion.[2] Its perpetual task is to free itself from every non-phenomenological standpoint and to retain its own liberty, while it conserves the inestimable value of this position always anew.[3]

Kierkegaard's impressive description of the psychological observer, therefore, may serve not as a rule, and not even as an ideal, but as a permanent reproach: "just as the psychological investigator must possess a greater suppleness than a tight-rope walker, so that he can install himself within men's minds and imitate their dispositions: just as his

---

[1] Wach, *Rel. wiss.* 82.

[2] Th. de Laguna, "The Sociological Method of Durkheim", *Phil. Rev.* 29, 1920, 224. E. Troeltsch, *Gesammelte Schriften*, II, 1913, 490.

[3] Jaspers, *Allgemeine Psychopathologie*, 36.

taciturnity during periods of intimacy must be to some degree seductive and passionate, so that reserve can enjoy stealing forth, in this artificially achieved atmosphere of being quietly unnoticed, in order to feel relief, as it were in monologue: so he must have a poetic originality within his soul, so as to be able to construct totality and orderliness from what is presented by the *individuum* only in a condition of dismemberment and irregularity".[1]

G. VAN DER LEEUW, *Strukturpsychologie und Theologie* (*Zeitschrift für Theologie und Kirche*, N. F. 9, 1928).

N. SÖDERBLOM, *Natürliche Theologie und allgemeine Religionsgeschichte*, 1913.

E. SPRANGER, *Der Sinn der Voraussetzungslosigkeit in den Geisteswissenschaften* (*Sitzber. der preuss. Ak. der Wiss., phil.-hist. Kl.,* 1929, 1).

[1] *Begrebet Angest* (*The Concept of Dread*), Saml. *Vaerker*, IV², 1923, 360; *cf.* the entire fine passage.

CHAPTER 110

THE HISTORY OF PHENOMENOLOGICAL RESEARCH

1. THE history of the phenomenology of religion is brief. The history of religion is a young field of research, and its phenomenology is still in its mere childhood, having been systematically pursued only from the date of Chantepie's researches. But in the first place, no satisfactory history can ever be produced unless phenomenology is appealed to, whatever it may be called: secondly, at the most varied stages in the course of the history of religion there have arisen methodological approaches to a phenomenological mode of consideration; and these two circumstances enable us to trace the development of phenomenology to a comparatively early period. This is most readily carried out by discussing the outstanding eras in the history of religion. These are:

A. The history of religion during the age of enlightenment. The encyclopedic interest of the eighteenth century was, together with other subjects, directed to religions, which were—frequently in antithesis to the religion of revelation—interpreted as being expressions of natural religion and as forms of the innate ideas of God, immortality and virtue. There was therefore much enthusiasm for China, where all this was supposed to exist! The result was of course that the idea of toleration vaunted itself, priestly deception and thirst for power, bigotry and hypocrisy being decried, not without hinting at Christianity. In this connection the work of Meiners, the Göttingen investigator of religion, is for our purpose of outstanding importance.[1] As far as I am aware, he is the first systematic phenomenologist. Not only does he attempt a classification, an extensive allocation of names in which fetishism, worship of the dead, of stars and images, sacrifice, purifications, fasts, prayer, festivals, mourning customs, *etc.*, are discussed in an orderly manner, but his entire attitude, too, is in principle phenomenological. He wishes to discover what is essential in religion, and in doing this he does not halt at the frontier formed by the antithesis between heathen and Christian: "all religions may possess as many unique features as they please; it is nevertheless certain that each religion resembles others in many more respects than those wherein it differs from them".[2] A

---

[1] But *cf.* on a French predecessor, René Maurier, *Benjamin Constant, historien des Sociétés et des Religions*, RHR. 102, 1930.

[2] Meiners, *Allgemeine kritische Geschichte der Religionen*, I, 1.

general history of religion appears to him to be formless, and he therefore
sets forth to seek the "elements": "since a series of the histories of all
religions is either impracticable or is at least inadvisable, there remains
for the historian of religion no other course than to resolve the known
religions, especially the polytheistic, into their elements as it were, and
then observe how each essential factor of the popular religions of ancient
and modern times was, or still is, constituted".[1] He compares religions
themselves with respect to their affinities, or their contrastedness;[2] and,
primarily, he seeks a certain "harmony" that I should call structural
order, and in virtue of which definite concepts bring definite modes of
worship, *etc.*, to maturity; an "analogy or harmony . . . in virtue of
which different aspects are mutually adapted, or accord with each other.
Those peoples who recognized a certain type of god must worship them
in a certain way, and conversely. Peoples who had certain ideas about
superior beings, and about their worship, must accept a certain kind
of priest and magician", *etc.*[3] Nor are finer distinctions lacking: that a
people is poly- or monotheistic, of itself, proves nothing: if one God is
worshipped in the polytheistic way, the monotheism is not true and
genuine.[4]

B. The history of religion in the period of Romanticism is marked by
many more suggestions with respect to its phenomenological aspects.
Philosophic romanticism endeavoured to comprehend the significance
of the history of religion by regarding specific religious manifestations
as symbols of a primordial revelation. Thus Creuzer interpreted myths
and legends as "idioms of one original and general mother tongue".
For this purpose he employed a specific "mythological apperception",
which is important in that it involved a religious immersion within the
data of the history of religion.[5] In a completely different way, Hegel
sought to permit the individual religions themselves to speak the
language of reason, and thus to absorb historical diversity within the
eternal dialectic of the Spirit. Phenomenology is thus "the phenomenology of Spirit", describing the development of knowledge as it first
appears in the form of immediate spirit, which is mere sensuous
consciousness devoid of spirit, and then steadily advances toward

---

[1] Meiners, *Allgemeine kritische Geschichte der Religionen,* I, 2.   [2] *ibid.,* I, 129.
[3] II, IV.
[4] II, VI; *cf.* H. Wenzel, *Christoph Meiners als Religionshistoriker,* 1917.
[5] O. Gruppe, *Geschichte der klassischen Mythologie und Religionsgeschichte,* 1921,
126 *ff.* It is most desirable that research should be undertaken on the other depart-
ments of the history of religion in the same way as Gruppe has dealt so admirably
with classical antiquity.

Absolute Spirit.[1] Here the important feature is that what appears is not only a human mode of presentation, as for Kant, but a manifestation of Absolute Spirit, to exhibit which as Subject is the enduring task of Hegelian philosophy. The phenomenon would thus be an appearance of the eternal dialectical movement of Spirit in some definite situation; and religion then occupies the final position before that of absolute knowledge. It is the relationship of finite spirit to Absolute Spirit in the form of idea. Hegel is the first philosopher who treats history, including the history of religion, in its full seriousness: Absolute Spirit has its life in history as it is comprehended. Exceedingly fruitful for all history, and typical for all philosophy, the conclusion of the *Phenomenology* still remains: The "conservation (of spiritual forms), looked at from the side of their free existence appearing in the form of contingency, is *History*; looked at from the side of their intellectually comprehended organization, it is the *Science* of the ways in which knowledge appears ("*Phenomenology*"). Both together, or History (intellectually) comprehended, form at once the recollection and the Golgotha of Absolute Spirit, the reality, the truth, the certainty of its throne, without which it were lifeless, solitary, and alone. Only

> The chalice of this realm of spirits
> Foams forth to God His own Infinitude."[2]

The result of this merging of spirits with Spirit is that Hegel's phenomenology provides not merely a theory of knowledge and a philosophy of history, but a psychology of comprehension also.[3]

In romanticism, further, the two other extremely important names in connection with this branch of research are those of Herder and Schleiermacher. Herder was the first to understand the "voices of the peoples", and also the first for whom history became an experience and the writing of history the "art of empathy".[4] He was also the first to interpret the language of religion as poetry, and therefore as the actual mother tongue of mankind.[5] Schleiermacher, however, wished to comprehend religion solely and simply as religion, and rejected all derivation from metaphysical or moral interests; and in this way he destroyed the power of the age of enlightenment, which he also subjugated by banishing the bloodless "natural religion" into the lumber-room.

[1] Hegel, *The Phenomenology of Mind*, 85 f., 88 f.   [2] *ibid.*, 808.
[3] Fr. Brunstäd, *RGG*. "Hegel".   [4] *cf.* p. 674, note 4.
[5] *cf.* van der Leeuw, *Gli dei di Omero, SM.* 7, 1931, 2 ff.

C. The history of religion in the period of romantic philology represents, in the first place, a reaction from romanticism, since it substituted precise study of the sources for unfettered speculation. But it still continued to be romantic in its desire to comprehend religion as the expression of a universal mode of human thinking; and the conflict previously latent in Herder and Schleiermacher, between primal revelation and human predisposition, was here decided in favour of the latter. Philology and comparative philology were to be utilized to bring to light the thought of mankind when regarded in its unity. Thus comparative religion appeared on the scene, and this is still, in Anglo-Saxon countries, the name for the history of religion as such. This philological history of religion, which is connected with the names of Max Müller and Ad. Kuhn, is also romantic-symbolic in that it wishes to perceive the life of Nature symbolized in religious concepts. In the history of religion, however, this period was infinitely fruitful, owing to the discovery and exploration of yet more extensive territories; but for the phenomenological comprehension of religion, this was of less importance, since the comparative factor, which can never be more than one feature among others, was given undue prominence,[1] and thus obstructed the path to a profounder understanding.

D. The history of religion in the age of romantic positivism, although it subsists almost completely under the spell of the principle of development, remains romantic in so far as, here too, religion is taken to be the voice of humanity: in religion mankind has said something, and it has, unfortunately, spoken falsely. The primal revelation there became either an "elementary idea" (Bastian) or even the idea of humanity itself (Durkheim). During this period, undeniably, the results of research into the history of religion are incalculable: it is the culminating era in the history of religion. By this, however, phenomenology benefited comparatively little; and in the light of the conscious, or unconscious, evolutionism of that time, this is not at all strange. Yet out of its great wealth this very period produced men who sought and discovered other paths, and who to some extent prepared the way for phenomenology and, in part, actually initiated it: I refer to Hermann Usener and Albrecht Dieterich. Usener's "doctrine of religious forms", which regarded the creation of forms as the crucial feature, is phenomenologically of the utmost importance;[2] and Hackmann's *allgemeinen Religionsgeschichte* has already been mentioned. P. D. Chantepie de la Saussaye acquired the highest merit in connection with our subject in

[1] Wach, *Rel. wiss.* 181.   [2] *Vorträge und Aufsätze*², 1914, 57 *ff.*

his *Lehrbuch* of 1887, in which he first gave not merely an "Outline of the Phenomenology of Religion", but also sought to comprehend the objective apearances of religion in the light of subjective processes, and accordingly assigned a wide scope to psychology.[1] E. Lehmann followed him with an *Outline* in *RGG*[1]., which was subsequently rewritten.[2]

E. I can now be very concise. The position of phenomenology to-day is the natural outcome of previous investigations.[3] The history of religion, as influenced by psychology, produced the extremely important works of W. Wundt in Germany and of L. Lévy-Bruhl in France, which to a great extent touch upon our own subject. Attention, too, has been increasingly directed inwardly. F. Heiler has endeavoured not only to determine the direction of psychological research on the scientific aspects of religion,[4] but has given us, together with Rudolf Otto, some of its finest and most important fruits.

F. The history of religions as developed by the methodology of "Understanding", and in this regard, dealt with by W. Dilthey's school of thought, has recently enjoyed an ever freer course. Certainly this by no means implies that we to-day understand religious phenomena for the very first time, since the achievements of the nineteenth century, in this respect also, can scarcely be estimated sufficiently highly, but that we now, consciously and systematically, look upon such an understanding of the phenomena, just as they appear to us, as our goal. Among other investigators, J. Wach and myself have undertaken methodological research,[5] while a wealth, that may indeed be described as a profusion, of *Introductions to the History of Religion*, of a more or less phenomenological type, as well as of monographs, clearly shows the possibilities of fruitful labour. Nonetheless is it true that the phenomenological treatment of the greater part of the history of religion lies still in the future; but rather than cite many, I select here the great name of Nathan Söderblom. For without his acute insight and his deeply penetrating love of what "appears", we could not advance another step in our territory; and the change of direction in the history of religion, plainly set forth in the current phenomenological viewpoint, finds its symbol in this thinker's name.

---

[1] Chantepie, *op. cit.*[1] I, 48 *f.*   [2] Chantepie, *op. cit.*[4]

[3] On the history of the history of religion, and in relation to phenomenology, *cf.* my article in *RGG. Religionsgeschichte.*

[4] *Prayer*, xxiv *f.*

[5] *cf.* further, Max Scheler's "concrete phenomenology", *Vom Ewigen im Menschen*, I, 1921, 373.

2. But far more than all other spheres of knowledge, the phenomenology of religion is dynamic: as soon as it ceases to move it ceases
to operate. Its infinite need of correction pertains to its innermost being;
and so we may say of this volume, dedicated to phenomenology, what
the fairy tale tells us for its own consolation and for ours: "and so
everything has its end, and this book too. But everything that has an
end also commences anew elsewhere".

E. HARDY, *Was ist Religionswissenschaft?* (*AR.* 1, 1898).
    Zur Geschichte der Religionsforschung (*AR.* 4, 1901).
G. W. F. HEGEL, *The Phenomenology of Mind.*
E. LEHMANN, *Zur Geschichte der Religionsgeschichte* (CHANT.[4] I).
    Der Lebenslauf der Religionsgeschichte (*Actes du Ve Congrès Int. d'Hist. des
    Rel. à Lund*, 1929, 44 ff.).
C. MEINERS, *Allgemeine kritische Geschichte der Religionen*, 1806-07.
G. MENSCHING, *Geschichte der Religionswissenschaft*, 1948.
R. F. MERKEL, "Zur Geschichte der Religionsphänomenologie" (in *Deo
    Omnia Urum, Festschr*, FR. HEILIER, 1942).
R. PETTAZONI, *Svolgimento e carattere della storia delle religioni*, 1924.
H. PINARD DE LA BOULLAYE, *L'Etude comparée des religions*, 1922.
W. SCHMIDT, *Handbuch der vergleichenden Religionsgeschichte*, 1930.

APPENDIX TO THE TORCHBOOK EDITION

(NOTE: This appendix represents in condensed form the new material found in the revised German edition)

PART III

OBJECT AND SUBJECT IN THEIR RECIPROCAL OPERATION

CHAPTER 53—Service
Section 2: Movement and counter movement as constituting the "dramatic character" of service can also be seen in the Egyptian Mysteries; in the drama and conflict between the old and new gods in the Ras Shamra. (*cf.* Sethe, *Dramatische Texte*, and A. de Buck, "Egyptische Dramatischen Texten" in *Ex Oriente Lux, Meded, en Verh.*, I, 1934, 55 *ff.* See also René Dussaud, *Les Découvertes du Ras Shamra*, 1937; Joh. Friedrich, *Ras Shamra*, 1933; Th. Gaster, "An Ancient Semitic Mystery Play", in *S.M.S.R.* 10, 1934, 156 *ff.*)

As a summary we could say that service has the task of providing equilibrium between the power of man and the other powers. As soon as it is known that this equilibrium is or will be disturbed (*e.g.*, a catastrophe), we resort to extraordinary sacrifice, prayers, or the introduction of new cults, *etc.*

CHAPTER 55—Sacred Time
Section 2: Reversal in time is impossible. Yet, in most cases sacred time turns back upon itself as a time-cycle. The Pre-Asiatic peoples broke through this cycle and introduced a historical time. This history begins in Egypt and Persia, and is foremost in Israel where the acts of God are identified with the great events of national history. See H. Lommel, *Die alten Arier*, 1935, 34; J. H. Breasted in *Ancient Records of Egypt*, I, 1906, 51 *ff.*; M. P. Nilsson, "Again the Sothiac Period", in *Acta Orient.*, 19, 1941, 1 *ff.*, and O. Neugebauer, "Nochmals der Ursprung des ägyptischen Jahres" in *Acta Orient.*, 19, 1942, 138 *ff.*

CHAPTER 66—Endowment With Form in Custom
Section 2: Asceticism can replace any sacred action. In India asceti-

cism is a mystical intensification of the Vedic sacrifice, its goal is immortality which is attained through a "continuous emptiness". For a description of this point see Mircea Eliade, *Les Techniques du Yoga*, 1948, 9, 102, 117, 98, *etc.*; and P. H. Pott, *Yoga en Yantra*, 1946.

CHAPTER 72—Knowledge of God

Section 3: Next to knowledge of God stands "Wisdom". We encounter this form of knowledge above all in countries around the Eastern Mediterranean and they carry much of international significance. *cf.* W. Zimmerle, *Die Weisheit des Predigers Salamo*, 1935, 111 *ff.*, and Paul Humbert, *Recherches sur les Sources Egyptiennes de la Litterature Sapientiale*, 1929.

From a phenomenological point of view we can speak of three kinds of Wisdom: 1. Epigrammatic saying (Proverbs). The typical virtues of this kind of wisdom are inspiration, prudence, retention and contentment. *cf.* Alex Scharff, "Die Lehre für Kagemni", in *Zeitschr. f. ägypt. Spr. u. Alt.*, 77, 1941, 15 *ff.*) 2. Wisdom which is anxious about life (the first is not anxious about anything). This wisdom is pessimistic just because it views life as powerless and as nothing. The typical utterances concern the despondency of the soul with life. 3. The wisdom which has the unrest of God as its subject. The uncomparable and greatest example of this is the Book of Job.

There is an interesting tendency in all of the above for the History of Religions, namely, they tend to emphasize the moral over the cultic. In fact, there is an anti-sacramental tendency in knowledge as wisdom and this is clearly seen in F. M. Th. de Liagre Bohl's article in *Jaarbericht Ex Oriente Lux*, 8, 1942, 673 *ff.* See also P. A. Munch, "Die jüdischen Weisheitspsalmen und ihr Platz im Leben", in *Acta Orient.*, 15, 1936.

CHAPTER 79—Conversion. Rebirth

Section 4: "The Inner Life". (The following summary is taken from the revised German edition where it is under a separate chapter heading. We have placed it here as Section 4 since it follows this chapter.)

What modern man finds in the history of religions does not correspond with what he expects to find. Yet he believes that in what he finds he will hear the religious feeling speaking to him, that feeling which Benjamin Constant has put before us as the essence of religion. We shall find rituals, *etc.*, but they are only the "forms" which, through the centuries, religious feeling has taken upon itself. (*cf.* B. Constant, *De la Religion*, I, 1824, 142, also, 27, 3, 13.) The opinion of Constant is in agreement with Schleiermacher's expression of it in Germany, and it has filtered through to our own contemporary way of thinking. It is the opinion, namely, that "until now we have only considered the externals of religion; the history of religious feeling remains wholly outside our present scope. Dogmas, creeds of faith, religious exercises, *etc.*, are all forms which the inner religious feeling elects but immediately breaks." What we find, however, is something completely different. We find the cultus, magic, and all that which belongs to the equilibrium of religion. Behind this a "religious feeling" may well be hidden, but we very seldom receive even a weak sign of its existence.

We can suppose, naturally, that rituals have always accompanied feeling. The totality of the history of religions, however, speaks against the supposition that feeling is everything and the external action is only a form which contains no meaning for the essence of the phenomenon. We have already shown, in Chapter 67, that outward and inward phenomena have the same essential unity. That which is "inner" unlocks itself only through time. The phenomena which one can use as the signs which reveal the inner religious life are very rare in those religions which strive to preserve equilibrium (or balance). In any case we cannot speak about personal faith or unbelief, at least in the sense which we have given these words, in the context of these religions. In relation to the religions of equilibrium the word "faith" is an anachronism and a failure in structure.

The inner religious life begins when this equilibrium is broken. The religions which speak of this rupture, Zarathustrian, Hebraic, Islamic, and Christian, have lost the meaning of what is natural and self-understood, as well as the tolerance which distinguishes them from the primitive and near primitive religions. The above-mentioned religions are exclusive since God has stepped into human life and has consummated the essential rupture. . . . A broken world reflects a broken humanity, and when the revelation is complete it corresponds to a broken God on a cross.

For an example of what is given here see St. Augustine's *Confessions*, I, 20; XI, 3; I, 6; X, 2, 3, and VIII, 2, 4; here we read that his soul has been given to him by God, and truth has been revealed without signs or words. Augustine knows himself through knowledge of God. See also H. Frick, *Ghazalis Selbstbiographie, ein Vergleich mit Augustine Konfessionen*, 1919; also, G. van der Leeuw, "Religionsgeschichte und Personliches Religioses Leben", in *Festschrift. f. Fr. Heiler*, 1942, also in van der Leeuw, *Deus et Homo*, 1953.

PART V

FORMS

CHAPTER 100—The Religion of Love

Section 5: "The Christian Confession". (The following summary is taken from the revised German edition where it was a separate chapter.)

Here we have open for us the way to a phenomenology of Church History. Since this remains undone and though it is impossible to develop it fully in this work, we do want to indicate its main outline.

The Christian Church has two aspects; the first is authoritative in the West, the second in the East. The fundamental differentiation is not to be found, as Frick sees it, between the conflict of Catholicism and Protestantism, but in the difference between the Western and the Eastern Churches.

The spirit of the Greek Church leans toward the mysterious. It is the religion of the "implicit" Word of God, which is revealed in spiritual pictures, art and song. The advent of the mystery of God has brought about a "heaven on earth". This is the gospel of John; the transformation of the world is accomplished through the mysterious, through the reality of the advent and resurrection of the Son of God. The art of the Eastern Church is reconstructed from this gospel.

In contrast to this aspect of the Church, the spirit of the Western Church translates the mysterious, which it holds in common, into the words and practices of daily life. The Word of God is "explicit" for this religion, it reveals itself in dogmas and instruction, becoming ever more explicit in discussion and commentating, and is proclaimed in preaching. Heaven is not on earth but the earth is proclaimed and renewed as the Kingdom of God. This new order, however, is not an obvious one, faith alone permits us to see the difference between a condemned and renewed world. One must work, therefore, to spread this faith everywhere. This takes place through proclamation and strict organization, which have as their goal the restoration of the Kingdom of God. This is the Gospel of the Synoptics, above all, the gospel of Paul.

Greek Catholicism is a religion of Sacrament. Latin Catholicism is a religion of proclamation. The latter in its Roman form has reduced the Sacrament to a resource and remarkable guarantee of the Hierarchy, while in the Protestant form it has become a resource for the power of proclamation. The endless conflict over the Sacrament in the Middle Ages and in the time of the Reformation is proof that the Western Church did not understand the East. The Church of the East seldom speaks about the Sacrament, it lives it; *cf.* my *Sacramentstheologie*, 1949.

Non-Roman Catholicism is certainly alive in the West only in the Anglican Church. The Church of England is essentially Catholic and only secondarily Protestant. (See Bishop of Gloucester, *Anglican Communion*, 5.)

Protestantism can be divided into two great confessions; Lutheran and Calvinist. Both are united in their sensitivity to any final definition of faith; every form is provisional. Thus Protestantism has restrained itself from any fixation of form, be it Sacrament or discipline, church or absolution. This reservation, however, does not always allow itself to be strictly followed and it is just those Protestant confessions that stress it as most important which become the exception to it. In this way scripture, doctrine and method become the great exception to the restraining principle within Protestantism.

For further references consult Karl Adam, *Das Wesen des Katholizmus*, 1934; H. Frick, "Der katholisch-protestantische Zwiespalt als Religioses Urphanomen" (*Kairos*, 1926); F. Heiler, *Die katholische Kirche des Ostens und Westens*; H. W. Rüssel, *Gestalt eines christlichen Humanismus*, 1940; P. Tillich, "Kairos und Logos" (*Kairos*, 1926).

EPILEGOMENA

CHAPTER 110—The History of Phenomenological Research

Section 1: Benjamin Constant was certainly one of the great names in the History of Religions; he belongs to the Romantic period as well as to the Enlightenment. His great work, *De la Religion*, 1924–31, was never very popular but his two theses as found in that work have influenced generations ever since, even though they have never known the author's name. The first thesis states that "religion is a feeling" (I, 13). His second thesis, even more important, is that religious feeling is not identical with life but is the very foundation of the nature of man. To ask a man why he is religious is to ask a question concerning the very ground of his bodily structure and being (I, 3).

For a more detailed description of his work and influence see M.

Saltet, *Benjamin Constant, Historien de la Religion*, 1905; Elizabeth W. Schermerhorn, *Benjamin Constant, His Private Life and His Contribution to the Cause of Liberal Government in France, 1767–1830*, 1924; also, René Maurier, "Benjamin Constant, Historien des Sociétés et des Religions", in *RHR.*, 102, 1930.

Section 2: The many important names in the development of the phenomenological point of view should not force us into silence. Among many we can name the following: Fr. Altheim, W. Baetke, C. J. Bleeker, Martin Buber, Odo Casel, H. Frick, V. Gronbeck, Romano Guardini, K. Kerényi, H. Lommel, R. R. Marett, Rudolph Otto, Walter Otto, Maurice Leenhardt, J. Pedersen, Geo. Widengren, Mircea Eliade, and R. Callois.

The history of the development of phenomenology in the History of Religions can be indicated by the universities which provided "chairs" in the faculties for these positions. The first was authorized at Basel in 1833, and was held by Joh. G. Muller. The second was authorized in 1873 at Geneva, followed by Lausanne, Zurich, and Bern. In the Netherlands four chairs were inaugurated in 1876; among others, they were filled by P. D. Chantepie de la Saussaye, and C. P. Tiele. France came next; in 1879, the College of France, in Paris, opened a position which was given to Albert Reville. In 1884 the free University of Brussels joined the list. In 1885 the Sorbonne called into existence a department for "The Science of Religion" in the "École des Hautes Études". Finally, in 1910, a chair was authorized in Germany at the University of Berlin (O. Pfleiderer and Ed. Lehmann), this was followed by Leipzig (N. Soderblom and then Hans Haas) and Bonn (by Carl Clemen, then G. Mensching). *cf.*, H. Pinard de la Boullaye, *L'Étude Comparée des Religions*, 1922, 331 *ff.*

INDEX TO VOLUMES I AND II

The figures in italics indicate the Chapters; those in ordinary type the Sections.